A Practical Guide to AIM

A Practical Guide to AIM

Alexander Keepin
Partner, Charles Russell LLP

Published by ICSA Information & Training Ltd
16 Park Crescent
London W1B 1AH

© ICSA Information & Training Ltd, 2008

Typeset by RefineCatch Limited, Bungay, Suffolk
Printed in Great Britain by Hobbs the Printers Ltd, Totton, Hampshire

British Library Cataloguing in Publication Data
A catalogue record for this book is available from the British Library

ISBN 978–1–86072–394–0

Contents

Contents

Contents

Table of figures

Table of Figures

Legislation

The following legislation is referred to in this book:

Legislation

Financial Services and Markets Act 2000
Financial Services and Markets Act (Regulated Activities) Order 2001
Uncertificated Securities Regulations 2001
Directors' Remuneration Report Regulations 2002
Financial Services and Markets Act (Financial Promotion) Order 2005
Companies Act 2006
Fraud Act 2006
Transparency Obligations Directive (Disclosure and Transparency Rules)
    Instrument 2006
Income Tax Act 2007

Preface

The AIM market which is operated by the London Stock Exchange (formerly known as the Alternative Investment Market) has been a phenomenal success, both domestically and also internationally. This success has seen AIM evolve into what many consider to be the world's leading market for smaller and growing companies. Part of the success of AIM is its lighter approach to regulation, being as it is an exchange regulated market. This regulatory status enables the rule book for AIM companies to run to only approximately forty pages, with only ten containing the operative rules. Also, a large part of the function of deciding whether a company is suitable to join AIM is devolved from the London Stock Exchange onto the Nominated Advisers, who are the main intermediary between a company and the London Stock Exchange. As a result, a combination of guidance, experience and market practice dictates the way in which companies apply to join AIM and how AIM companies conduct themselves.

This book is targeted at company secretaries, finance directors, other directors and in-house lawyers and aims to give them an overview as to how the market operates, together with an insight into what market practice in many areas is.

Part I provides a general introduction as to the key advisers who will help guide a company through the AIM admission process. Often these will be the same firms who will continue to be involved advising the company after admission, during its life as a public company whose securities are admitted to trading on AIM.

Part II gives an overview as to how the AIM admission process works and the different routes commonly used when seeking admission to trading on AIM. This leads into Part III, which covers fundraisings. Fundraisings are often a fundamental reason why a company will seek admission of its securities to trading on AIM. The part on fundraisings also bridges the gap between the admission process and life as an AIM company, as many of the considerations in the fundraisings chapters apply not only to any initial fundraising, but also to any subsequent fundraisings.

This then sets the scene for Part IV, which deals with the continuing obligations that a company will be subject to when its securities are admitted to trading on AIM. Corporate governance, which has been the subject of many other texts, is dealt with in Part V. Part VI then concludes the book with a look at de-listing, bringing a company full circle from before the securities are admitted to trading to de-listing, either to move to the Main Market or to leave AIM.

The aim of this book is to help readers better understand what is involved in either becoming or operating as a company whose securities are admitted to trading on AIM. It also seeks to point out some of the practical considerations which the directors will need to consider, both from a personal perspective and for the benefit of shareholders as a whole. In addition to the legal and regulatory requirements, the book provides a variety of practical considerations which should answer questions commonly encountered by companies and their directors. Finally, Appendix 1 provides useful sources of information, which should allow readers to perform any further research of their own.

Alexander Keepin
Principal Author
1 March 2008

Contributors

I would like to thank the following members of the capital markets team at Charles Russell LLP for their contributions to this book:

Clive Hopewell, a partner who qualified in 1994 and became a partner in 2001. Clive has experience in relation to mergers and acquisitions and private equity work, as well as equity capital markets work on both AIM and the Main Market. Clive spent a period of two years as an adviser in the Equity Markets Group of the London Stock Exchange.

Adrian Mayer, a partner who qualified in 1998 and became a partner in 2005. Adrian has experience in relation to mergers and acquisitions including by way of public takeover and private equity work, as well as equity capital markets work on both AIM and the Main Market.

Francis Rundall, a partner who qualified in 1975 and became a partner in 1981. Francis's experience covers equity capital markets work on both AIM and the Main Market as well as mergers and acquisitions including by way of public takeover.

Simon Gilbert, Head of Corporate Finance, who qualified in 1983 and became a partner in 1989. Simon's experience includes capital markets work on AIM and the Main Market for international and domestic clients as well as public and private mergers and acquisitions

Victoria Brett, an associate who qualified at Charles Russell LLP in 1998 and who specialised in AIM, Main Market and mergers and acquisitions work before becoming a corporate professional support lawyer in 2004.

William Axtell, an associate in the Oxford office, who qualified in 2000 at a magic circle firm. William specialises in corporate finance with a particular emphasis on capital markets and mergers and acquisitions.

Mark Howard, a solicitor in the Guildford office, who qualified in 2000 at a magic circle firm. Mark's experience includes transactions with private and publicly quoted companies on AIM and the Main Market, including public takeovers, acquisitions and disposals, joint ventures, private equity investments and distressed asset sales.

Bronwen Jones, a solicitor in the Cheltenham office, who qualified in 2001 at a magic circle firm. Bronwen's experience covers general corporate matters with a particular focus on public takeovers.

Vicky Hau, a solicitor in the London office, who qualified in 2001 at a US firm. Vicky's experience includes transactions with public companies on AIM and the Main Market, including admissions, takeovers, rights issues and bond issues.

Adam Carling, a solicitor who qualified at Charles Russell LLP in 2003. Adam's experience covers admissions, fundraisings and reverse takeovers for companies listed on AIM and the Main Market. Adam also spent six months on secondment to the London office of a Nominated Adviser.

Alison Davies, a solicitor who qualified at Charles Russell LLP in 2005. Alison specialises in capital market transactions and mergers and acquisitions.

Ruth Morrow, a solicitor who qualified at Charles Russell LLP in 2006. Ruth's experience covers admissions, fundraisings and reverse takeovers for companies listed on AIM and the Main Market.

Nick Boyd, a solicitor who qualified in 2006 who works primarily on listings on AIM and the Main Market. During 2007, Nick spent six months on secondment to AIM Regulation at the London Stock Exchange.

Kelly Hutchins, a solicitor who qualified at Charles Russell LLP in 2007 and whose experience covers general corporate and commercial work including for companies listed on AIM.

Anne Marie Hodge, a solicitor who qualified in 1999. Anne Marie is a professional support lawyer and her experience covers the full ambit of general company law, mergers and acquisitions and corporate finance.

Nicola Buchanan-Clarke, a solicitor who qualified as an attorney in South Africa in 2001 and as a solicitor in 2003. Nicola advises on general corporate matters and has worked on a range of public and private company transactions, including IPOs and fundraisings on AIM.

Viv Holyoake, a company secretary, who specialises in the incorporation and administration of companies, both public and private, maintenance of corporate records and minutes.

I would also like to thank the following specialists outside the capital markets team for their contributions:

Tax Incentives and Options

Tarlochan Lall, a tax partner at Charles Russell LLP, who qualified in 1990 and who specialises in advising on business taxes and share incentive schemes. Tarl's experience covers advising public and private companies on issues in his area of expertise that affect AIM companies and those seeking admission to AIM and those moving from AIM to the Main Market.

Directors' Service Agreements

Nick Hurley, a partner in Charles Russell LLP's Employment and Pensions Service Group, who qualified in 1995 and who advises on a broad spectrum of employment law work, with particular focus on City clientele and business.

I would like to thank all contributors to *A Practical Guide to AIM* for their hard work, and, in particular, Ruth Morrow. The contributors include not only the contributors whose biographies appear above but also those responsible for researching, proof-reading, amending and collating the book. They are:

Jenny Mawer, my secretary who has worked in the Corporate and Commercial department of Charles Russell LLP for over ten years.

Joanna Allan, a trainee solicitor.

Andrew Whitby-Collins, a trainee solicitor.

Jessica Ganagasegaran, a trainee solicitor.

Christopher Birch, a trainee solicitor.

Maureen Keepin, my mother.

Susie Keepin, my wife.

CHAPTER 1

What is AIM and why seek admission to AIM?

AT A GLANCE

The AIM market of the London Stock Exchange (previously known as the Alternative Investment Market) is one of the leading international markets for smaller, growing companies, which are attracted by its access to capital and simplified regulatory environment.

OVERVIEW OF THE MARKET

1.1 AIM is one of the world's leading markets for smaller, growing companies and has been successful in attracting a large number of companies from the United Kingdom and abroad. AIM has benefited from being a part of the London Stock Exchange, which has traditionally always been one of the pre-eminent equity exchanges in the world. In fact, AIM's appeal has been such that the number of companies currently listed on AIM now outstrips the number of companies listed on the Main Market of the London Stock Exchange, albeit the Main Market focuses on larger or more developed companies.

1.2 Since its launch in 1995, AIM has had a remarkable track record, with over 2,800 companies having admitted their securities to AIM. Part of the success of AIM has been attributed to the fact that it is not sector specific but was designed and is run in a way that benefits smaller and growing companies. The companies listed on AIM come from 38 sectors and 92 sub-sectors and represent 70 countries. Such a broad market profile is one of the reasons for AIM's continued success as it provides the market with resilience.

1.3 Part of AIM's success is also attributed to its diverse shareholder base. There are currently over 1,600 companies on AIM, with a range of capitalisations and a combined market capitalisation of over £100 billion, of which £55 billion is held by institutional investors.

1.4 AIM also provides an ideal environment for young international companies wishing to use the public markets to raise their global profile and fund expansion. As a result, AIM has experienced international success with over 347 companies incorporated outside the United Kingdom listed on AIM as at 31 December 2007 and this number is continuing to rise. AIM was actually originally envisaged as a market for UK companies, but the process of internationalisation which began in 2000 has seen a striking increase in the levels of overseas interest and investment.

1.5 In addition to the growing international appeal of AIM, it has also found increasing favour with the investor community. In the past, AIM was sometimes criticised for a lack of liquidity in the securities which were listed. However, the trading volumes in AIM securities and also the value of the securities traded have risen sharply over the course of recent years. This increase in the trading of AIM securities was further bolstered in 2005 by the introduction of the FTSE AIM Index Series (which includes indices such as the FTSE AIM UK 50 Index and the FTSE AIM All-Share Index). The indices both attract additional investment, thereby enhancing liquidity further, and provide a set of benchmarks against which investors can assess AIM securities.

WHY SEEK A LISTING ON AIM?

1.6 Many of the advantages and disadvantages of having securities listed or traded on a public market are applicable to AIM. The main advantages are as follows.

Profile

1.7 As a public market, admission to AIM increases the profile of a business. Raising the profile can also increase the confidence that customers and clients have in the company, making it a more attractive business partner.

Access to capital

1.8 Once the company has its securities publicly listed or traded, it has the ability to raise finance from the investment community, whether at the time of the initial public offer or, following admission, by way of secondary fundraising.

Market for securities

1.9 Once the securities are listed or traded on a public market, current shareholders have the ability to realise their investment. Listing will also broaden the company's shareholder base by attracting new investors. This also creates an objective market value for the company.

Acquisition currency

1.10 When a company's securities are listed or traded on a public market, it makes those securities more attractive to third parties. If the company is acquisitive, this can make its securities more attractive when used as a part of the consideration when acquiring additional companies, businesses or assets.

Incentivisation of employees

1.11 Once there is a market for the securities, companies whose securities are publicly listed or traded find that share options and share ownership can be an important way to incentivise their staff.

DISADVANTAGES OF LISTING ON AIM

1.12 In addition to the advantages there are a number of additional considerations which a company should bear in mind when considering applying for a listing or trading facility for its securities, in particular in deciding whether or not it is appropriate for their particular company to continue life as a public company.

Company operations

1.13 Becoming a public company will have a considerable impact on the way in which the board of directors operates and conducts its business. This commences at the time of the initial public offer when a significant amount of management time will be taken up in producing the relevant documents needed in order to seek admission to trading on AIM.

1.14 In addition, once listed or traded, the directors will need to implement revised procedures to cover the way in which the board of directors is structured, the business is conducted, and compliance with rules and regulations, including principles of good corporate governance, is monitored. Typically, this will involve setting up specific committees, led by independent board members, to review further appointments to the board of directors, the way in which the audit is handled and the remuneration of key executives. A large amount of management time will also be required after the admission process, in fulfilling continuing obligations and, in particular, communicating with investors and potential investors and managing investor relations.

1.15 Once listed, directors are subject to additional duties and have increased accountability for key management decisions and actions. Directors also have to ensure that they run the company in the interests of all shareholders.

1.16 In addition, financial performance will need to be carefully monitored and additional checks, balances and controls put in place. Once operating, this will help the company comply with the disclosure requirements of AIM.

Costs

1.17 A further disadvantage to having securities admitted to trading on AIM is the cost to the company. Costs come from the engagement of a Nominated Adviser and broker and from the work required from the applicant company's accountants and lawyers to guide the company through the process for the admission to trading on AIM. The Nominated Adviser will usually have its own advisers, which may also add to the cost. However, despite higher initial costs, subsequent fundraisings can be conducted cost effectively.

1.18 As well as the initial costs, the additional procedures including corporate governance compliance and communication with shareholders will also lead to increased ongoing costs.

Scrutiny

1.19 As a public company with an increased profile, the company will also be subject to a greater degree of scrutiny. The scrutiny varies from the specific, such as greater review of its accounts and financial performance, to more generic scrutiny and press comment. A cornerstone of any public market is disclosure, and a company whose securities are traded or listed on a public market will be required to disclose information quickly to the market, whether this is good or bad news.

Variations in share price

1.20 Quotation on a public market brings with it uncertainty of market conditions. The share price of a listed company is susceptible to the natural volatility of external market conditions, such as general market sentiments and other factors which are outside the company's control. For AIM securities, which may often be priced in pence not pounds, a few pence movement either upwards or downwards can be very significant.

IN PRACTICE

The decision as to whether or not to list on a public market such as AIM will depend on the individual circumstances of a company and will always require a careful consideration of the advantages and disadvantages involved. AIM's remarkable success based upon its lighter regulatory environment, and its access to capital means that it will be at the top of any list of possible markets when the decision to list has been made.

CHAPTER 2

Regulation of AIM

AT A GLANCE

AIM has fought off competition from many other junior markets around the world to become one of the leading exchanges for smaller and growing companies. One of the key factors in achieving this is AIM's regulatory environment, which combines the stringency which is necessary to foster and retain investor confidence along with an element of simplicity and flexibility which benefits smaller and growing companies.

REGULATORY STATUS OF AIM

2.1   AIM is classified as an exchange regulated market. Formerly, AIM was a regulated investment exchange in line with other leading European exchanges, such as the Main Market of the London Stock Exchange, Deutsche Borse and Euronext, which meant that it was subject to all EU legislation applicable to security exchanges. However, the introduction by the *Prospectus Directive* and *Transparency Directive* of obligations on the market participants, which threatened the balance of AIM as a market with sufficiently stringent regulation to keep investor confidence without being obstructive or unduly onerous to smaller and growing companies, resulted in a change. Therefore, in October 2004, AIM was re-classified as an exchange regulated market to enable it to preserve, to a large extent, its existing admission to trading on AIM process and regulatory structure. Consequently, AIM continues to offer the flexibility that smaller and growing companies need, in tandem with a robust, and distinctive, regulatory regime that supports investor confidence and the market's development.

2.2   Instead of AIM being directly subject to EU legislation, the London Stock Exchange regulates AIM; it drafts the *AIM Rules for Companies* and monitors compliance by new market participants with the regulatory regime. In turn, the Financial Services Authority regulates all of the London Stock Exchange's activities, both relating to AIM and otherwise. The Financial Services Authority conducts an annual audit of AIM's activities to ensure that it is complying with the applicable laws for which the Financial Services Authority has responsibility, such as the *Financial Services and Markets Act 2000*.

2.3   It is worth noting that the London Stock Exchange has chosen to apply selected EU legislation as implemented by the Financial Services Authority, such as

Annexes I to III of the *Prospectus Rules,* which form the backbone to the contents requirement for an AIM admission document (which is usually required to be produced by companies seeking admission to trading on AIM). In this context, the London Stock Exchange is responsible for administering such legislation in an AIM context and can grant derogations where it feels this is appropriate. However, other legislation that is not issued by the London Stock Exchange but applicable to AIM and its market participants will be administered by the relevant body (e.g. the Financial Services Authority) and will ensure that AIM is compliant with the requirements of the *Markets in Financial Instruments Directive.*

Advantages of the London Stock Exchange setting the AIM regulatory environment

2.4   There are two main benefits to AIM being regulated by the London Stock Exchange (i.e. the regulator also being the body that operates the market). First, this enables the London Stock Exchange to be responsive to the requirements of the market. For example, the *AIM Rules for Companies* are regularly updated to keep abreast of developments in the market, such as the types of companies which are seeking admission to trading on AIM. Second, on an operational basis, AIM Regulation, the team within the London Stock Exchange that is responsible for administering the *AIM Rules for Companies,* is able to make quick and commercial decisions when interpreting and applying the *AIM Rules for Companies* because the objectives of the London Stock Exchange are closely allied to the business imperatives of AIM companies.

The regulatory regime in practice

2.5   A unique facet of AIM is that one of the key market participants, the Nominated Adviser, plays a role in regulating the market. In turn, AIM Regulation oversees the activities of the Nominated Adviser, in tandem with its other responsibilities.

2.6   The Nominated Adviser plays a dual role; its primary function is to advise a company in preparing for admission to trading on AIM and in meeting its continuing obligations after admission to trading on AIM. However, as a secondary function, the Nominated Adviser is responsible for confirming that its client companies are suitable for admission to trading on AIM. AIM Regulation is able to determine whether a Nominated Adviser is discharging its regulatory responsibilities by checking its performance against the duties set out in the *AIM Rules for Nominated Advisers.*

2.7   This system of delegated regulation works successfully because it is clear that each Nominated Adviser is largely responsible for the conduct of its AIM company clients. For example, when there is a suspected breach of the *AIM Rules for Companies* by an AIM company, AIM Regulation will investigate not only the company concerned but also its Nominated Adviser to establish why the breach has occurred and whether the Nominated Adviser has discharged its responsibilities correctly. If the breach is proven, the London Stock Exchange has the authority to sanction the Nominated Adviser to the same or to a greater extent than the AIM company. There is also a non-regulatory pressure on the Nominated Adviser to comply with its duties, otherwise it risks a loss of reputation in the marketplace. Therefore, Nominated Advisers balance their service to their clients with their obligations to the London Stock Exchange.

The role of AIM Regulation

2.8   The regulatory function of AIM Regulation is broader than simply monitoring the Nominated Advisers' delegated responsibilities. AIM Regulation also liaises with the London Stock Exchange's market monitoring team to track any AIM company stock that is trading erratically and, if necessary, asks the company's Nominated Adviser to raise this with the relevant AIM company to provide an explanation of this. In this way, the London Stock Exchange and the Nominated Adviser work together to prevent disorderly markets from developing or investors from being unfairly prejudiced by price sensitive information not being made publicly available. Further, AIM Regulation is responsible for advising Nominated Advisers and AIM companies on how to act in accordance with the *AIM Rules for Companies*, as well as providing clarification and interpretation of the *AIM Rules for Companies* to prevent breaches occurring. Where it is suspected that a breach has occurred, AIM Regulation investigates and then provides the results of its investigation to the London Stock Exchange, which will begin the appropriate disciplinary process.

2.9   AIM Regulation is able to monitor closely each Nominated Adviser because it has the authority to require information from a Nominated Adviser at any time. This authority is most commonly used as a part of an investigation, but it is also used if AIM Regulation wishes to gain a periodic update on a Nominated Adviser's level of staffing and activity, or if AIM Regulation wishes to conduct a visit to a Nominated Adviser's offices to review its client or transactional files.

IN PRACTICE

AIM has a special regulatory environment where the Nominated Adviser plays a key role in regulating the market with the London Stock Exchange, through AIM Regulation overseeing the activities of the Nominated Adviser. As a result the relationship between the company and its Nominated Adviser is important to the overall regulation of the AIM market.

AIM and tax

Investors in AIM companies receive certain tax advantages in contrast to investors in companies listed on the Main Market or other recognised stock exchanges. Those advantages fall into the following categories:

- AIM companies qualify for investment reliefs designed to encourage investment in smaller companies.
- There are other tax reliefs that can facilitate estate planning.

AIM companies, therefore, afford to investors a combination of tax breaks and a measure of liquidity. However, the principal advantage that AIM companies had over companies on the Main Market, namely the advantage under taper relief, has been withdrawn. Entrepreneurs' relief introduced from 6 April 2008 will not give AIM companies any advantage over companies on the Main Market.

TAX OVERVIEW

3.1 AIM companies are treated as unquoted companies for tax purposes even though their securities are traded on the AIM market. The same treatment was afforded to companies whose securities were traded on the former Unlisted Securities Market. The principal reason for this treatment was that despite the admission to trading on AIM, liquidity in the securities may nevertheless be restricted. For example, it was reported in the Lex column of the *Financial Times* on 19 September 2007 that in a typical month in 2007, about 40 per cent of the market's 1,789 stocks saw turnover equal to just 1 per cent or less of their market capitalisation.

3.2 The unquoted status of securities in AIM companies gives their holders access to a range of tax benefits available to private investors in unquoted securities. The most significant of these benefits was that the securities of an AIM company could be treated as business assets for capital gains tax taper relief such that following two years of ownership the tax on any gains was limited to an effective rate of 10 per cent. There was no restriction on the size of the AIM company whose investors could benefit from business asset taper relief.

3.3 The unquoted status of AIM traded securities also affords access to another valuable tax relief, namely business property relief for inheritance tax purposes.

Two years' ownership of AIM securities of a trading company makes an individual shareholder eligible for 100 per cent relief for inheritance tax purposes. The inheritance tax relief can be valuable in estate planning, whether the securities are transferred by way of gift under a will or a lifetime gift within seven years of death or transfers into trusts. There is a related capital gains tax relief for gifts which allows accrued gains to be held over and passed to the donee of a gift.

3.4   AIM securities also attract loss relief if a loss is made on their disposal. Losses can be set off against other capital gains arising in the tax year of the loss or a subsequent tax year, or against the income arising in the tax year of the loss or the previous tax year. Such losses are only available on securities that qualify for Enterprise Investment Scheme relief or were subscribed for as opposed to being purchased on AIM.

3.5   Smaller AIM companies, broadly those with gross assets of £8 million or less, are eligible for a range of reliefs designed to encourage investments in smaller companies. The principal relief is the Enterprise Investment Scheme (EIS) relief. AIM securities can be qualifying investments for Venture Capital Trusts (VCTs). EIS and VCT reliefs are designed for individuals. Corporate investors can access reliefs under a scheme known as the Corporate Venturing Scheme (CVS). EIS, VCT and CVS are the focus of Chapter 37, *Tax incentives*, which deals with tax issues arising in connection with fund raisings.

TAPER RELIEF

3.6   Taper relief was introduced in 1998. It applied to individuals and trustees but not to corporate investors. Its effect was to reduce the effective tax rate on any capital gains arising on the disposal of assets depending on the length of time those assets were held for. Assets were divided into business assets and non-business assets. Anything that was not a business asset was a non-business asset. The principal difference between the different categories of asset was that the effective rate of tax on:

- business assets fell to 10 per cent after two years of ownership; and
- non-business assets started to fall after three years of ownership by 2 per cent per annum, reducing to the lowest effective rate of 24 per cent after ten years of ownership.

3.7   However, the advantages under taper relief have been withdrawn. Entrepreneurs' relief introduced from 6 April 2008 will not give AIM companies any advantage in this respect over companies on the Main Market.

ENTREPRENEURS' RELIEF

3.8   Entrepreneurs' relief was announced following widespread outcry from the business community at the abolition of taper relief. It took effect from 6 April 2008. This outline is based on HMRC's press release of 24 January 2008, draft legislation published on 28 February 2008 and the HMRC release issued following the Budget on 12 March 2008.

3.9 Entrepreneurs' relief will be available where securities in a trading AIM company are disposed of by an individual who throughout a period of one year:

- held at least 5 per cent of the ordinary share capital and at least 5 per cent of the voting rights in the AIM company; and
- was an employee, director or other officer of the company.

3.10 Where entrepreneurs' relief is available, the first £1 million of lifetime gains will be taxed at an effective rate of 10 per cent. The balance of gains will be taxed at 18 per cent. The £1 million limit is a lifetime allowance. This means that:

- once used it is not available anymore; but
- more than one disposal giving gains within the £1 million lifetime limit can qualify. Accordingly securities sold in tranches after 1 April 2008 can qualify within the limit.

3.11 The entrepreneurs' relief must be claimed. On the basis of the draft legislation published, provided the 5 per cent ownership condition and the employment conditions are satisfied it would be available to AIM companies as well as companies on the Main Market. However, the 5 per cent shareholding requirement is considered to be too restrictive.

SECURITIES AS BUSINESS ASSETS

3.12 Under taper relief there were separate rules for securities and other assets that were treated as business assets. This chapter is only concerned with securities in AIM companies.

3.13 Securities qualified as business assets for taper relief (BTR) purposes if they were in a company:

    (a) that was unquoted (AIM companies were treated as unquoted); or
    (b) in which the investor either:
        (i) held 5 per cent or more of the voting rights in the share capital of the company; or
        (ii) was an employee of the company.

3.14 Entrepreneurs' relief will be given to "qualifying business disposals". The disposal of securities of an AIM company in respect of which the conditions in paragraph (b) of 3.13 above are satisfied will be treated as a disposal of business assets for the purposes of entrepreneurs' relief. There is no requirement as to minimum hours that have to be worked to satisfy the employment, director or other officer requirement.

3.15 For taper relief purposes the company had to be a trading company or the holding company of a trading group. However, from 6 April 2000 where a company was not a trading company or the holding company of a trading group, securities held by directors and employees could still qualify as business assets provided the individual concerned did not hold more than 10 per cent of the securities alone or jointly with persons connected with the individual. The qualifying conditions for entrepreneurs' relief also require the AIM company to be a trading company or the holding company of a trading group.

TRADING COMPANY

3.16   The trading company requirement, as adopted for taper relief, will apply for entrepreneurs' relief. The trading company requirement is also relevant to other reliefs mentioned above and outlined below. The BTR definitions of "trading company" and "trading group" also apply to the CGT hold-over relief rules outlined below. However, it should be mentioned that each set of rules could strictly have its own specific requirements, so they need to be examined closely.

3.17   In most cases, whether or not a company is trading is obvious. However, many activities commonly undertaken by companies often cast doubt on the trading status of a company.

3.18   "Trade" and "business" are expressions often used interchangeably in business parlance. Strictly there is a distinction in their respective meanings. The word business has a broader meaning. Investment activity can be a business, but for tax purposes it would not be a trade unless undertaken by a regular dealer.

3.19   In the period April 1988 to April 2002 the trading status of a company for BTR purposes rested on whether a company existed wholly for the purposes of carrying on one or more trades. From April 2002, the focus changed from the reasons for which a company existed to the actual activities of the company being used to determine the trading status of the company. Trading activities also included activities involved in preparing to start or acquire a trade or the activities leading to the acquisition of a significant interest in the share capital of a trading company or the holding company of a trading group. Preparatory work had to be followed by the actual commencement of the trade or the acquisition of the trade or securities in question.

3.20   Incidental purposes for which the company may have existed which were not capable of having any substantial effect on the extent of the company's activities were ignored. From April 2002, the test changed such that the activities of the company could not include "to a substantial extent" non-trading activities. Whether or not incidental and non-trading activities were "substantial" was in practice interpreted as being more than 20 per cent of activities. There was no single test for measuring the level of activities of a company. Although the turnover of a company provides a useful starting base, HMRC looked at actual activities undertaken by the company, with particular focus on:

- the assets of the company;
- expenses incurred by the company;
- the size of the company's staff, including directors and employees and the activities they undertook.

3.21   Surplus assets and investments held by a company could cause companies to question their trading status for BTR purposes.

TRADING GROUP

3.22   Trading group for BTR purposes meant and now for entrepreneurs' relief means a group of companies, one or more of whose members carried on trading activities and whose activities taken together did not to a substantial extent include non-trading activities. Although only one company actually needed to carry on a trading activity, the activities of the other group members could not be substantial (i.e. breach the 20 per cent test). The company was a group member if it was a 51 per cent subsidiary; that is, the parent company directly or indirectly controlled more than 50 per cent of the company's equity capital. The activities of the group were taken as a whole and treated as one activity. Intra-group activities, such as holding of investments in subsidiaries, inter-company loans, inter-company leases, etc., are disregarded.

CGT HOLD-OVER RELIEF

3.23   The securities of trading companies or holding companies of a trading group admitted to AIM also benefit from hold-over relief available to investors in unquoted trading companies. Capital gains tax can arise where there is any gift of securities or securities are transferred otherwise than at arm's length. The charge is calculated by reference to the market value of the securities on the date of disposal. The effect of hold-over relief is that the accrued gain is held over and it crystallises on the subsequent disposal of the securities by the transferee.

3.24   Hold-over relief has been restricted in recent years. Its main benefit remains for transfers between individual family members. The relief is separate from the exemption on the transfers between spouses. It is not available on transfers to companies. It may be available on transfers to trusts, but specialist advice should be taken.

3.25   The individual to whom the securities are transferred must be ordinarily resident in the United Kingdom and must remain so for a period of six years after the tax year in which the transfer is made. The relief however contained a trap on the way it interacted with taper relief. A completely new period started for the transferee unless the transfer was between spouses. The gain that was held over lost all the benefits of taper relief so the transferor's period of ownership was effectively wiped out. That trap should no longer be an issue on held-over gains crystallising after April 2008 subject to the flat rate of 18 per cent capital gains tax, but specialist advice should be taken.

3.26   The relief has to be claimed by both the transferor and the transferee. Under self assessment the period for making the claim is five years and ten months after the end of the tax year in which the transfer takes place.

INHERITANCE TAX BUSINESS PROPERTY RELIEF

3.27   The securities of companies that are trading companies or the holding company of a trading group also benefit from 100 per cent business property relief for inheritance tax purposes because again the AIM company is treated as unquoted. At least two years of ownership of the securities is required before the transfer takes place for the business property relief to kick in. The test used to determine whether a company is a trading company is different from that for BTR, i.e. there has to be over 50 per cent trading activity.

3.28 The relief dovetails with CGT hold-over relief on, for example, gifts between family members. The relief is perhaps most valuable in connection with lifetime transfers, for example into a discretionary trust or where the gift is made within seven years of death and of course where the securities form part of the estate of the shareholder on death.

SHARE LOSS RELIEF

3.29 Relief for losses arising on the disposal of EIS securities in AIM companies is mentioned in Chapter 37, *Tax incentives*. However, relief is also available on losses arising on certain disposals of AIM securities that do not qualify for EIS relief. For individuals, relief is now given under the new *Income Tax Act* introduced in 2007 and is described as "share loss relief". Share loss relief is only available on AIM securities subscribed for as opposed to those acquired in dealings on AIM.

3.30 The share loss relief allows losses to be set off against income for the tax year in which the loss arises or the previous tax year. To the extent that the loss is not used against income in the year in which the loss arises it can be carried back to the previous year. The relief must be claimed within one year of the normal deadline for filing self assessment tax returns.

3.31 Share loss relief is only available, like EIS and VCT reliefs, on securities in AIM companies with gross assets of £7 million before the securities are issued and not exceeding £8 million immediately afterwards. The gross assets test is the same as the one for EIS and VCT, which is further described in Chapter 37, *Tax incentives*. The share loss relief is only available for securities in unquoted companies, hence AIM securities qualify whereas those securities on the Main Market do not.

3.32 There are a host of conditions which attach to share loss relief, and these are broadly equivalent to those that apply to EIS and VCT reliefs. One important difference is that the trading requirement must be met for a continuous period of six years ending with the date of disposal, or for a shorter continuous period provided that prior to the commencement of the period the securities have not been excluded securities. The trading requirement is the pre-April 2002 test that existed for BTR, namely the focus is on the purpose for which the company exists. Owing to the detailed requirements for the share loss relief, expert advice should be taken upon entitlement to such relief.

IN PRACTICE

Whilst the tax reliefs may only be available to certain investors in certain (often smaller) companies, where they are available they can be a useful tool to attract interest in the AIM company's securities.

Part I
Key Team

INTRODUCTION

When looking at the obligations which a company has on its application for admission of its securities to trading on AIM and its continuing obligations when the company's securities are admitted to trading on AIM, it is important to understand who the members of the key adviser team will be and their roles.

The following is an overview of each of these key advisers and their roles.

Adviser	Role
Nominated Adviser	■ Point of contact between the company and the London Stock Exchange ■ Confirm company's suitability for AIM ■ Advise the company on compliance with the *AIM Rules for Companies*
Broker	■ Point of contact between the company and the investment community ■ Assist in raising finance
Company's lawyers (UK)	■ Advise the company on its corporate structure and its group ■ Undertake legal due diligence ■ Assist the Nominated Adviser in preparing the AIM admission document ■ Undertake verification of the AIM admission document
Company's lawyers (non-UK) (if relevant)	■ Provide a report on the company's title to any overseas assets ■ Assist on due diligence and verification ■ Advise on overseas jurisdictional issues
Reporting accountants	■ Undertake financial due diligence ■ Prepare financial information for inclusion in AIM admission document ■ Assist and report on the working capital report ■ Review the company's financial reporting systems and procedures

Adviser	Role
Nominated Adviser and broker's lawyers	■ Review AIM admission documentation ■ Draft Nominated Adviser, placing or introduction agreements
Experts	■ Produce reports on the company's material assets and liabilities for inclusion in AIM admission document (required for mining or oil and gas companies) ■ Produce opinion on complex legal issues
Public relations/investment adviser	■ Co-ordinate public announcements ■ Educate company's management in dealing with media questions
Registrar	■ Maintain company's share register
Printers	■ Print the AIM admission document ■ Print communications to shareholders following admission to trading on AIM

CHAPTER 4

Role of AIM Regulation

AT A GLANCE

AIM Regulation is responsible for ensuring that AIM companies and their Nominated Advisers comply with the regulatory regime governing AIM, and in particular the *AIM Rules for Companies*, the *AIM Rules for Nominated Advisers* and any guidance which has been issued by the London Stock Exchange.

AIM Regulation discharges its responsibilities in five ways:

- providing guidance to AIM companies and their advisers;
- real-time monitoring of AIM companies on the market;
- overseeing the activities of Nominated Advisers;
- investigating potential breaches of the AIM Rules, preparing disciplinary proceedings and enforcing sanctions where deemed necessary; and
- reviewing the effectiveness of the AIM regulatory regime and developing future policy.

INTRODUCTION

4.1 AIM Regulation consists of a combination of experienced regulators, lawyers and accountants. This wide base of skills means that the team is able to understand the technical and commercial issues which face AIM companies and their advisers.

4.2 Within the structure of the London Stock Exchange, AIM Regulation is part of the Trading Services department, the primary function of which is to operate the trading platforms of the London Stock Exchange. As Trading Services also includes the team that monitors trading on the market and the team that admits new issues of securities to the market, AIM Regulation is in close contact with the real-time market activity.

4.3 In early 2007, and in conjunction with the amendments to the *AIM Rules for Companies* and the introduction of the *AIM Rules for Nominated Advisers*, the London Stock Exchange bolstered the number of members of AIM Regulation and re-organised it into three distinct sub-teams:

- Company Regulation;
- Nominated Adviser Regulation; and
- Investigations and Enforcement.

4.4   The regulatory regime of AIM is set down by the London Stock Exchange and also by the relevant legislation, as described in Chapter 2, *Regulation of AIM*. AIM Regulation has jurisdiction over those parts of the regulatory regime set down by the London Stock Exchange, being the *AIM Rules for Companies* and the *AIM Rules for Nominated Advisers*, but has no jurisdiction over any part of the relevant legislation (such as the tax treatment of AIM securities or the *Prospectus Rules*). AIM Regulation is audited by the Financial Services Authority.

ROLES AND RESPONSIBILITIES

Providing guidance to AIM companies and their advisers

4.5   The primary operation of AIM Regulation is as a helpdesk resource that can be used by an AIM company or its advisers, although most frequently any such questions from an AIM company or its advisers are channelled through its Nominated Adviser, who will act as the primary interface with AIM Regulation. Although it deals with a wide range of enquiries, the helpdesk's primary function is to assist an AIM company if circumstances arise where either it cannot comply with an AIM Rule or it is uncertain how an AIM Rule might be applied to its situation. This is relevant either when preparing a company for admission to trading on AIM or when an AIM company needs to meet continuing obligations at any time after its admission to trading on AIM.

4.6   The *AIM Rules for Companies* are not designed to cover exhaustively every situation in which an AIM company may find itself, unlike the *Listing Rules* which apply to those companies who are admitted to trading on the London Stock Exchange's Main Market. Accordingly, many of the AIM Rules have been drafted as principles to govern an AIM company's conduct. Consequently, AIM companies are expected to comply with the spirit as well as the letter of the rules.

4.7   When assisting an AIM company to find a way in which it can comply with the *AIM Rules for Companies*, AIM Regulation pays heed to the commercial objectives of the AIM company. Therefore, it will attempt to reach a mutually acceptable course of action that complies with the relevant AIM Rule to a reasonable extent and does not adversely affect the AIM company's business.

4.8   The helpdesk's principal function falls into two parts: requests for a derogation from an AIM Rule and clarification of the AIM Rules.

Requests for derogation from an AIM Rule

4.9   When an AIM company believes that it cannot comply with an AIM Rule, it can contact AIM Regulation to request permission to derogate from the relevant rule.

4.10   Usually, an AIM company will seek derogation if its circumstances mean that it is unable to comply with a rule or if compliance with a rule would prejudice the company or its business unduly. Because the *AIM Rules for Companies* are not extensively detailed, AIM Regulation is able to take a practical approach. However, AIM Regulation will not permit derogation from a rule simply because compliance may present an obstacle to a company's commercial objectives or will create expense for the company. Instead, a derogation may be given where the company is still complying with the spirit of the relevant rule, if not the letter of it, and there is no ostensible or actual prejudice to investors or to the market or its integrity.

4.11 A formal request for derogation from an AIM Rule must be emailed by the relevant company's Nominated Adviser to AIM Regulation. Pursuant to Rule 19 of the *AIM Rules for Nominated Advisers*, AIM Regulation will not liaise with any Nominated Adviser (or any AIM company or other adviser) on a "no names" basis. AIM Regulation treats all communications between it and a Nominated Adviser as confidential.

4.12 When submitting a request for derogation, the Nominated Adviser should include as many details as they believe are required in order for AIM Regulation to make a decision. AIM Regulation will then discuss the request internally, in order to reach a consensus on the response and in order to ensure that the response is consistent with any given previously about similar issues. If necessary, AIM Regulation will discuss the request with the Nominated Adviser over the telephone.

Clarification of AIM Rules

4.13 The second area administered by the helpdesk is to clarify the *AIM Rules for Companies* and the *AIM Rules for Nominated Advisers*. This enables AIM companies and their advisers to ensure their compliance at all times and is especially important in the early stages of preparing a company for admission to trading on AIM.

4.14 Usually, the clarification requires elaboration about the guidance to the relevant rule, and sometimes an outline of standard market practice. However, as the number of companies whose securities are traded on AIM increases, there is also a greater variety of companies being admitted to AIM. As the existing *AIM Rules for Companies* were drafted principally for trading companies, it is also becoming more common for prospective issuers to require clarification about the *AIM Rules for Companies* prior to admission to trading on AIM, for non-trading companies such as funds.

Real-time monitoring of AIM companies on the market

4.15 AIM Regulation also ensures that AIM companies comply with the requirements of the *AIM Rules for Companies* by monitoring the movement of their share price on the market, in association with the London Stock Exchange's Market Monitoring team.

4.16 Most commonly, AIM Regulation will look at price movements that appear to be irregular. In this instance, AIM Regulation will first contact the Nominated Adviser and ask them to find out from the AIM company whether there is any reason for the irregular price movement. AIM Regulation will be concerned that the movement is a result of unpublished price sensitive information being leaked. If the price movement is the result of news having been leaked about an impending transaction, AIM Regulation will usually require the company to make an announcement in order to avoid a breach of Rule 11 of the *AIM Rules for Companies*.

4.17 AIM Regulation also reviews any mentions of AIM companies in the press in order to seek to capture any leaks that may cause price movement. Where price sensitive information has been leaked but the company does not yet have specific information to announce (for example, it has only just opened talks with a prospective target and an announcement may prejudice their progress), AIM Regulation will place the company on a watchlist. AIM Regulation will then monitor closely the company's price and contact the Nominated Adviser again if the leak appears to be causing it to move.

4.18 A secondary role is to co-ordinate the suspension from and restoration to trading of AIM companies. Suspension usually occurs under one of the following sets of circumstances:

- When there has been a breach of the AIM Rules whose sanction is suspension. This will last until such time as the breach has been rectified. For example, where the company has not published annual accounts within the stipulated timeframe, set out in Rule 19 of the *AIM Rules for Companies*; or
- Where trading might not be conducted in an orderly manner. For example, where there has been a leak of price sensitive information leading to some investors trading with this knowledge but which may not have caused trading to become haphazard. In this instance, restoration will occur when the company can show that the danger of disorderly trading has passed; or
- When there is a threat to the integrity and reputation of the market. For example, when it has subsequently been discovered that the disclosures made by a company on its admission to trading on AIM have been so misleading that it would not be reasonable to allow investors to continue trading in the company's stock. The company will be restored to trading on AIM only when steps have been taken to clarify or correct the relevant company information and this has been announced to the market.

Overseeing the activities of Nominated Advisers

4.19 AIM Regulation maintains the register of Nominated Advisers and has the key role of ensuring that all Nominated Advisers discharge their responsibilities adequately. The Nominated Advisers have a crucial part to play in ensuring that AIM companies are aware of their obligations under, and adhere to, the *AIM Rules for Companies*. Consequently, it is of paramount importance that the Nominated Advisers fulfil their role to the standard set down in the *AIM Rules for Nominated Advisers*. AIM Regulation conducts a three stage process to oversee compliance with this.

4.20 The first stage is the assessment of an applicant company that wishes to become a Nominated Adviser. AIM Regulation assesses the applicant and its executives against the eligibility criteria set down in the *AIM Rules for Nominated Advisers*.

4.21 If both the applicant company and its executives appear to meet the criteria on paper, AIM Regulation will then assess further their capabilities and experience by reviewing the files about their relevant transactions and interviewing the personnel involved. AIM Regulation may also canvas the opinions of other parties involved in those transactions in order to build a full picture of the applicant.

4.22 The second stage is monitoring Nominated Advisers once they have been added to the register to ensure that their eligibility is continuing. An important feature of being a Nominated Adviser is that it must meet the criteria at all times; it is not sufficient for a Nominated Adviser to be eligible only at the time of its application.

4.23 AIM Regulation monitors the continuing eligibility of Nominated Advisers by tracking the status of the qualified executives that they employ. When a corporate finance executive applies to become a qualified executive, AIM Regulation is responsible for assessing their eligibility, first through the application form and then in an interview. Similarly, when a qualified executive leaves the employment of a Nominated Adviser, it must notify AIM Regulation about their departure and which of the qualified executives remain.

4.24 In January 2007, AIM Regulation introduced the Nominated Adviser Annual Return, for completion by each of the Nominated Advisers and detailing their AIM company clients, their relevant transactions undertaken, their qualified executives employed or recently departed, their support staff and any interests in their AIM company clients. This provided AIM Regulation with a risk-based analysis of the Nominated Advisers and their ongoing eligibility. As a result, several Nominated Advisers were placed under moratorium while they took steps to meet the eligibility criteria and, consequently, a number decided that they did not wish to continue to be on the register of Nominated Advisers.

4.25 The third stage of assessing whether a Nominated Adviser remains eligible is through AIM Regulation proactively visiting the Nominated Adviser. The programme of visits began in early 2007, with the intention of visiting each of the Nominated Advisers within two years.

4.26 Each visit consists of reviewing a random selection of the Nominated Adviser's files (usually looking at one that covers the process of engaging a new client, another covering an admission to trading on AIM and a third that covers assisting an AIM company to meet its continuing obligations) and interviewing the relevant staff, being both corporate finance and compliance personnel. This combination is designed for AIM Regulation to review the proficiency of a Nominated Adviser in all areas of activity and to assess whether it has adequate procedures in place.

Investigating potential breaches of the AIM Rules, preparing disciplinary proceedings and enforcing sanctions

4.27 It is also AIM Regulation's role to investigate suspected breaches of the AIM Rules and, where necessary, to enforce the appropriate sanction against the breaching parties.

4.28   Breaches of the AIM Rules come to the attention of AIM Regulation in a number of ways; most commonly, AIM Regulation identifies them in the course of its everyday activities monitoring and advising companies on the market. However, breaches are also flagged by the Nominated Adviser to a company when it realises that its client has not complied with a relevant rule and is assisting them to rectify this. In addition, breaches can be brought to AIM Regulation's attention by a third party, such as an investor, another regulatory body or, more rarely, on an anonymous basis. In all cases, AIM Regulation respects the confidentiality of the source.

4.29   As the number and variety of companies admitted to AIM has increased rapidly over recent years, there has been a corresponding rise in the number of incidents that have needed investigating. As a result, in early 2007, AIM Regulation announced its intention to grow the Investigations and Enforcement sub-unit to cope with the growing demands.

Investigations

4.30   AIM Regulation's first step in investigating a potential breach of the *AIM Rules for Companies* is to contact the Nominated Adviser, who will usually lend assistance without hesitation because both it and the company (under Rule 22 of the *AIM Rules for Companies*) has an obligation to comply with any requests for information made by AIM Regulation and because it is in the Nominated Adviser's best interests to preserve the integrity of AIM.

4.31   The approach of AIM Regulation to an investigation is structured so that it is able to build up a picture of the events leading up to the breach from the point of view of both the Nominated Adviser and the company. Once it has sufficient information, it will then decide whether:

- the matter may merit one of the sanctions set out in Rule 42 of the *AIM Rules for Companies*; or
- a record is to be made on the London Stock Exchange's files about the company in question; or
- no further action is required.

Disciplinary proceedings

4.32   If a sanction under Rule 42 is to be considered, the procedure set out in the *Disciplinary Procedures and Appeals Handbook* will be followed as described in Chapter 41, *Disciplinary matters*. No one from AIM Regulation, as the investigating body, can sit on either the AIM Executive Panel, which acts both as a tribunal of first instance and as an appellate tribunal for breaches of the AIM Rules, or on the AIM Disciplinary Committee, which acts as a tribunal of first instance which hears and determines charges for breaches of the AIM Rules. However, AIM Regulation is responsible for passing to these bodies the material that it has uncovered in the course of its investigation. It will then step back from the proceedings and any subsequent appeal process.

4.33   If the breach is more minor, AIM Regulation will require the Nominated Adviser to ensure that the company prevents such a breach re-occurring. Usually, it will require evidence that the company has revisited its obligations under the *AIM Rules for Companies* and has put in place sufficient procedures to prevent a re-occurrence.

Enforcement

4.34 Once the disciplinary proceedings have been concluded and a sanction imposed, or where a lesser sanction has been imposed which does not require the involvement of the AIM disciplinary procedure, AIM Regulation is responsible for liaising with the company and its advisers and ensuring that the sanction is correctly administered. AIM Regulation keeps a record of any breach that a company is found to have committed.

Reviewing the effectiveness of the AIM regulatory regime and developing future policy

4.35 Because of the phenomenal growth of AIM and the increasing variety of requirements of the companies listed, the regulatory regime needs to evolve constantly. AIM Regulation's role in dealing with market participants and their concerns means that it has a unique insight into any areas of the existing regulatory regime that may require amending and where future policy may need to be developed.

4.36 In this regard, AIM Regulation has a dual role: as both a regulator and as a springboard for the development of the marketplace. The regulatory regime, although principles-based, needs to be sufficiently detailed for all of its provisions to be relevant to each market participant. Where there has been a spate of companies finding it difficult to comply with a particular rule, AIM Regulation is able to monitor whether this is a temporary anomaly or more permanent.

4.37 Likewise, AIM Regulation is well placed to assess the requirements of the market participants and develop its policy accordingly. As a commercial venture itself, AIM needs to stay ahead of rival marketplaces by developing policy that will meet the commercial needs of issuers and continue to attract new business.

4.38 At regular internal meetings, AIM Regulation reviews any issues that have frequently arisen. When an area that may need to be reviewed has been identified, a more formal assessment will be undertaken and, if there is still a requirement, the proposed amendments or areas for development will be put before the AIM Advisory Group, a committee of external advisers and senior London Stock Exchange personnel. There is sometimes also a consultation process with market participants, depending on how extensive the proposed changes are.

4.39 This process led to significant changes being made in 2007. Most significantly, the *AIM Rules for Nominated Advisers* were introduced in February. These rules codified existing best practice and have been praised by market participants for prompting a rise in the quality of service provided to AIM companies. The *AIM Rules for Companies* were amended at the same time, and further publications are expected, including guidance about listing funds and the requirement for new issuers to summarise key shareholder information so that investors can ascertain the extent of their rights when investing in companies from different countries.

IN PRACTICE

AIM Regulation has more interaction with, and a greater understanding of, market participants than any other entity at the London Stock Exchange. Consequently, it performs a unique role in safeguarding the short, medium and long-term future of AIM.

In its primary function as a regulator, AIM Regulation assists AIM companies in complying with the *AIM Rules for Companies* and ensures that Nominated Advisers comply with their obligations under the *AIM Rules for Nominated Advisers*. As part of this, it polices the marketplace to protect both investors and the reputation and integrity of AIM itself. Consequently, AIM Regulation has a strong understanding of the marketplace and its participants, which it feeds into the ongoing development of AIM.

CHAPTER 5

Role of the Nominated Adviser

AT A GLANCE

The Nominated Adviser and the role it performs for a company during the application process for admission to trading on AIM and in respect of its continuing obligations makes it the most important of the company's advisers and the key appointment that a company will make.

Under the *AIM Rules for Companies*, a company that is applying to have a class of its securities admitted to AIM must appoint a Nominated Adviser, and a company with a class of securities admitted to AIM must retain a Nominated Adviser at all times. The Nominated Adviser, which might be an investment bank, a corporate finance firm, an accountancy firm or a stockbroking firm, must be approved to act as a Nominated Adviser by the London Stock Exchange and must carry out its responsibilities in accordance with the *AIM Rules for Nominated Advisers*.

The Nominated Adviser is the most important adviser to a company, both on the route to AIM and in respect of continuing obligations. It is the Nominated Adviser that will usually vet the company, each of its directors and potential advisers for suitability and reputation issues.

The Nominated Adviser will usually be a different arm of the same finance house that acts as the company's broker and this often leads to their respective roles, which are completely different and separate, being confused. While the Nominated Adviser's client is the company and any dealings with it are private, the broker's clients are its investors and the broker will not be a party to the Nominated Adviser's confidential communications with the company. There must be a clear separation of responsibilities where the Nominated Adviser and broker come from the same finance house and an effective "Chinese wall" must be established for this purpose. The role of the broker is explained further in Chapter 6, *Role of the broker*.

INTRODUCTION

5.1 Broadly speaking, the Nominated Adviser is responsible to the London Stock Exchange for assessing a company's suitability for admission to trading on AIM, and for providing advice and guidance to the company on its continuing responsibilities following admission to trading on AIM under the *AIM Rules for*

Companies. The Nominated Adviser's responsibilities are set out in the *AIM Rules for Nominated Advisers.*

5.2   If an AIM company ceases to have a Nominated Adviser, the trading of its AIM securities will be suspended by the London Stock Exchange for a period of one month or until it appoints a new Nominated Adviser. If that company then fails to appoint a replacement Nominated Adviser, the London Stock Exchange will cancel the trading of its securities on AIM.

5.3   The Nominated Adviser's role is an important one because the London Stock Exchange does not itself assess a company's suitability for AIM. Instead, it delegates this responsibility to the Nominated Adviser, which therefore acts as a quasi-regulator and becomes the company's principal point of contact with the London Stock Exchange. Similarly, the London Stock Exchange does not vet AIM admission documents and it is also the Nominated Adviser who will review this.

CRITERIA FOR APPROVAL AS A NOMINATED ADVISER

5.4   A Nominated Adviser must be approved by the London Stock Exchange and included on the latest publication of the register maintained and kept by the London Stock Exchange. This register is available for public inspection on the London Stock Exchange's website (www.londonstockexchange.com/aim). The criteria for approval of a Nominated Adviser are set out in the *AIM Rules for Nominated Advisers* and apply in relation to ongoing eligibility. The potential Nominated Adviser must be a firm or company (i.e. not an individual), have practised in corporate finance for at least the last two years, acted on at least three "relevant transactions" during that two-year period and employ at least four "qualified executives". The London Stock Exchange may exercise discretion in applying and interpreting these criteria and may not necessarily approve a firm even if it satisfies them. The London Stock Exchange's overriding consideration will be the preservation of the reputation and integrity of AIM and these criteria are in addition to any legal or regulatory authorisation required in relation to any jurisdiction in which the company operates.

5.5   The Nominated Adviser (and its executives) must be independent from each company for which it acts and must be able to demonstrate this to the London Stock Exchange. In addition, the Nominated Adviser must not have and must take care to avoid any conflict of interest between the company and any other party and, in particular, must not act for any other party to a transaction or takeover.

5.6   It is important that the company selects its Nominated Adviser carefully. It should ensure that the Nominated Adviser has relevant experience in the sector in which it operates and understands the company's business. For some companies the choice of Nominated Adviser can be particularly important. For example, as explained in Chapter 12, *Mining, oil and gas companies*, a mining or oil and gas company will need to appoint a specialist in the sector to produce a competent person's report. For mining or oil and gas companies the choice of the competent person will be agreed in conjunction with the Nominated Adviser, who may also have appropriate contacts in this regard. It is also the Nominated Adviser that has responsibilities in relation to the preparation of the competent person's report itself.

5.7 The Nominated Adviser and the company will enter into a Nominated Adviser Agreement (also called a "Nomad Agreement"), which provides for the Nominated Adviser's terms of engagement, its continuing duties to the company under the *AIM Rules for Nominated Advisers* and its fees (which will usually comprise a fixed corporate finance fee, with retainer payable upfront, and the ability to recover all costs incurred). The Nomad Agreement will also set out the responsibilities of the company and its directors. The Nominated Adviser must notify the London Stock Exchange of its appointment by submitting a Nominated Adviser's declaration. The Nominated Adviser should also appoint a senior person within its firm's compliance or corporate finance teams to be the principal point of contact with the London Stock Exchange in relation to compliance.

ADMISSION RESPONSIBILITIES

5.8 The company's principal advisers will all play some part in carrying out a due diligence exercise on the company, which, in addition to being an information gathering exercise, should also expose any potential problems relating to the company that may have an impact on the pricing and suitability of the company's securities. This allows the company's advisers to produce a detailed document containing information on the company and its activities (including its business plan), the directors, historical financial information and other corporate information (called an "AIM admission document" (or prospectus, if required)) which will be used both for marketing purposes and to ensure compliance with the disclosure requirements in the *AIM Rules for Companies*. AIM admission documents are explained further in Chapter 10, *Admission process and AIM admission documents*.

5.9 The Nominated Adviser should agree the scope of due diligence and be satisfied that sufficient and appropriate due diligence and reporting is carried out, for example in relation to legal matters, working capital and financial systems and controls, and consider whether any commercial, specialist or technical advisers should be consulted. A thorough exercise in checking and sourcing the information put forward for inclusion in the AIM admission document will help to minimise the directors' liability in relation to its content and to raise any specific areas of concern for the Nominated Adviser. In the case of any concerns, it is the Nominated Adviser's responsibility to ensure that appropriate action is taken to resolve such matters in relation to the company's suitability for AIM. The Nominated Adviser will be required to give a declaration of suitability to AIM, which includes a statement covering, among other things, the fact that the AIM admission document has been fully and accurately verified and that it complies in all respects with the *AIM Rules for Companies*. The Nominated Adviser is required under the *AIM Rules for Nominated Advisers* to play an active role in its preparation, particularly with drafting sections relating to the business of the company and appropriate risk factors, and to ensure that any relevant public notification is made. If any derogations or interpretations are required from the *AIM Rules for Companies*, given the company's particular circumstances, it is the Nominated Adviser's responsibility to consult with AIM Regulation at the London Stock Exchange.

5.10 The Nominated Adviser should achieve a sound understanding of the company and its business. Therefore, the Nominated Adviser should ensure that it has sufficient contact with the company in order to obtain appropriate knowledge of the business and to address any jurisdictional problems. This may require using in-house specialists or enlisting the help of external experts, such as for the production of a competent person's report. The Nominated Adviser will usually undertake visits to the company's material sites and should meet the directors and key members of management. It may also be desirable for the Nominated Adviser to meet those with a key interest in the company, for example major shareholders. The Nominated Adviser will also usually appoint its own advisers, independent from the company, to assist and advise the Nominated Adviser in this process.

5.11 The Nominated Adviser and the company will discuss the composition of the company's board of directors, especially in relation to the balance of the board, its areas of expertise and the number of non-executive directors. This process will often involve the Nominated Adviser carrying out background checks and press searches on the directors. Often the Nominated Adviser will be involved in the process of identifying appropriate non-executive directors. While an AIM company is not required to comply with the *Combined Code on Corporate Governance* (the *Combined Code*), as a matter of good practice it is recommended that AIM companies should follow the core recommendations relating to corporate governance and investors will often expect this. The *Combined Code* requires, among other things, that the board of directors establishes audit, executive remuneration and nomination committees composed only of non-executive directors. A company will therefore need to appoint a sufficient number of non-executive directors for the purpose of forming these committees. The Nominated Adviser may also extend its investigations to key management personnel and consultants, particularly those who will be mentioned in the AIM admission document, and to major shareholders exerting control over the company. Further information on corporate governance is set out in Chapter 42, *Corporate governance for AIM companies*.

5.12 Where a company has had, as its main activity, a business which has not been independent and revenue earning for at least two years, key drivers behind the company (that is, "all related parties" – which includes directors of the company's group and shareholders holding 10 per cent or more of the securities – and "applicable employees") will be asked to demonstrate their commitment to the company by giving written undertakings agreeing not to dispose of their securities for a period of at least one year from the date of admission to trading on AIM, in order to comply with the *AIM Rules for Companies*. Where a company has been revenue earning for two years or more, the Nominated Adviser will still usually want this additional comfort from the company's key people, and certainly its directors, to protect new investors or the market as a whole in any event and to help to maintain an orderly market period.

5.13 The Nominated Adviser takes responsibility for co-ordinating the admission to trading on AIM process alongside the company's other advisers and will prepare and submit certain documents to the London Stock Exchange prior to the expected date of admission on behalf of the company. These include a "Ten Day Announcement", a completed AIM application form, a declaration of suitability for AIM and an electronic copy of the AIM admission document, as described further in Chapter 10, *Admission process and AIM admission documents*. The Nominated Adviser will also generally co-ordinate payment of the London Stock Exchange's fees (an admission fee) and the first year's Nominated Adviser fee.

5.14　Much of the above applies when a new Nominated Adviser is appointed by an existing AIM company. It is unlikely that the due diligence reports required for the preparation of an AIM admission document would be needed, but the company and often its directors will be required to make declarations and give warranties regarding information in relation to the company. Any actions required to be taken are likely to depend on any changes that have taken place since admission to trading on AIM or any circumstances surrounding the change in Nominated Adviser. In particular, the Nominated Adviser should achieve a sound understanding of the company and its business.

5.15　In all cases, the Nominated Adviser should ensure that the company is fully aware of its obligations under the *AIM Rules for Companies*, is aware of the practical consequences of non-compliance and has sufficient systems, procedures and controls for continuing compliance. In particular, the company should be clear as to when it should seek advice from its Nominated Adviser.

ONGOING OBLIGATIONS

5.16　A Nominated Adviser will continue to assess a company's suitability for AIM and ensure that the company understands its obligations under the *AIM Rules for Companies* on an ongoing basis. The Nominated Adviser is responsible to the London Stock Exchange for advising and guiding the company on its responsibilities under the *AIM Rules for Companies* and must be able to undertake this responsibility at all times. Where a Nominated Adviser believes that a company is no longer suitable for AIM it must contact AIM Regulation at the London Stock Exchange. A Nominated Adviser should assign at least two appropriately qualified staff (including at least one "qualified executive") to each company to which it is appointed, in order to ensure appropriate corporate finance contact and flow of information. In particular, as with preparation for admission to trading on AIM, the Nominated Adviser should play a key part in any changes to the composition of the company's board of directors.

5.17　A Nominated Adviser will be bound by, continue to observe and alert the company (where appropriate) to any changes to the *AIM Rules for Nominated Advisers* and the *AIM Rules for Companies* (including any guidance notes), any rules and procedures in supplementary documentation, AIM Notices, and any requirement, decision or direction issued by the London Stock Exchange. The Nominated Adviser must supply the London Stock Exchange with information that is correct, complete and not misleading, in appropriate form and within time limits set by the London Stock Exchange. If the information does not meet this requirement, the Nominated Adviser must notify the London Stock Exchange.

5.18   A Nominated Adviser is required to liaise with, and be available to, the London Stock Exchange on request by both the London Stock Exchange and the AIM company by which it is appointed and must, in particular, be contactable during the London Stock Exchange's market hours. If at any time the Nominated Adviser is unsure of the application or interpretation of the *AIM Rules for Nominated Advisers* or the *AIM Rules for Companies*, or in relation to the maintenance of the reputation or integrity of AIM, it must contact AIM Regulation at the London Stock Exchange at the earliest opportunity. In relation to detailed or specific matters, this contact cannot be on a "no-names" basis.

5.19   If the Nominated Adviser believes that it or the company has breached the *AIM Rules for Nominated Advisers* or the *AIM Rules for Companies*, it must notify the London Stock Exchange. Subject to the rules or requirements of any other regulatory or statutory body, all communications between the Nominated Adviser and the London Stock Exchange are confidential to the London Stock Exchange, but, unless stated otherwise by the London Stock Exchange, can be disclosed to appropriate advisers and the AIM company for which the Nominated Adviser acts.

5.20   The Nominated Adviser should review, in particular in relation to non-routine information, any relevant notifications to be released by the AIM company (without prejudice to the requirement to release information without delay) to ensure that they comply with the *AIM Rules for Companies* and any guidance, such as that relating to announcements by a mining or oil and gas company. In relation to this, the Nominated Adviser is also responsible for monitoring relevant press and trading activity in the AIM company's securities, especially at a time when there is unpublished price sensitive information. If there is substantial movement in trading activity, the Nominated Adviser should contact the company to establish whether any action is required. In addition, the Nominated Adviser will monitor all director and employee transactions in the company's securities in order to maintain an orderly market.

5.21   If a Nominated Adviser ceases to act for an AIM company, it must notify AIM Regulation at the London Stock Exchange by email as soon as possible, with reasons.

IN PRACTICE

The Nominated Adviser is the company's most important adviser in the route to AIM and in relation to its continuing obligations. Therefore it is important for the company to find a Nominated Adviser that has the relevant expertise and with which the company and its directors are likely to have a good relationship. Where a Nominated Adviser is required to consider a situation or be satisfied about a particular matter, it is expected to do so only following due and careful enquiry and exercising due skill and care, and should keep a record to evidence this. It should enlist the help of other advisers where necessary but should retain overall control of the admission to trading on AIM process and of an AIM company's continuing obligations under the *AIM Rules for Companies*.

CHAPTER 6

Role of the broker

The role of the broker is important and the broker will be one of the key advisers on the route to a company having its securities admitted to trading on AIM and in respect of its continuing obligations. Under the *AIM Rules for Companies*, a company must appoint and retain a broker at all times.

Brokers are finance houses that must also be members of the London Stock Exchange. In reality, an AIM company's principal broker will usually be a different arm of the same finance house that acts as the Nominated Adviser. If this is the case, it is necessary for effective procedures to be in place to prevent any breach of confidentiality or conflict of interest.

Before the securities are admitted to trading, the broker's role is to help the company to raise finance in the market. Following admission of the securities to trading on AIM, the broker will be the main point of contact between the company and the investment community. One of the key factors to consider when selecting a broker is that it must be capable of raising finance in the sector in which the company operates and be able to take effective soundings from the market in this regard.

INTRODUCTION

6.1   The broker is responsible for managing dealings in the company's securities. This involves preparing and undertaking marketing campaigns with the company to promote the company's securities, trading in the secondary market (i.e., the market in securities following admission to trading on AIM), and administering the collection of funds and share settlement. The broker will often also provide research on the company in the form of objective investment reports. Further information on analyst research is given in Chapter 24, *Analyst research*.

6.2   The broker will help to guide the company through the admission to trading on AIM process and during its life as a company whose securities are admitted to trading on AIM, especially in relation to any advice required surrounding new circumstances which arise when a company becomes admitted, such as decreased privacy, increased regulation, dealing with external shareholders and changes in the price of the company's securities as a result of circumstances outside its control. The flow of information between the company and the market is important and so the broker will need to keep the company informed in relation to relevant information received from or observed in the market as well as keeping investors informed about new developments, which may be positive or negative. The broker will, in particular, need to encourage interest in the company's securities where there is no market maker in the sector.

CRITERIA

6.3 The London Stock Exchange will need to be satisfied that the broker has sufficient knowledge and experience to carry out its role. As with Nominated Advisers, the London Stock Exchange maintains a register of current member firms which is available for public inspection on its website (www.londonstockexchange.com/aim). This website also contains a separate list of brokers already appointed by AIM companies. From the company's point of view, it is important to choose a broker with the placing power, appropriate level of expertise and resources required to raise the level of funding sought. In addition, the rate of the broker's commission will be a relevant factor in selecting the broker, although it is only one of the factors to be considered and there is a balance to be struck between price and the overall success of any offering of securities. The broker should have a good track record in raising finance in the company's sector and should be capable of having a good working relationship with the company.

ADMISSION RESPONSIBILITIES

6.4 Before the securities are admitted to trading, the broker's primary responsibility is to manage the fundraising process on behalf of the company. The key reasons for a company to be seeking admission to AIM will, in most cases, be to raise funds and to gain access to the capital markets. It is therefore essential that the company's broker has appropriate contacts within financial institutions who are active investors in the sector in which the company operates. It is common for fundraisings to only be targeted to such institutions (and certain other investors) since the company will then benefit from certain exemptions from regulatory restrictions in relation to its marketing documents, such as the presentation (as explained further in Paragraph 6.8) and its AIM admission document. A fundraising targeted at financial institutions is commonly known as an "institutional placing". The broker, the Nominated Adviser and the company will enter into a placing agreement which sets out the terms and conditions of the placing and governs how it will be conducted, along with detailing the broker's fees. In particular, the company, and in some cases its directors, will be required to give a broker indemnity and warranties on the company's business. Each director's liability is usually capped in the placing agreement and may be linked to a multiple of their salary. If there is not to be a fundraising, the broker, the Nominated Adviser and the company will enter into an introduction agreement containing similar warranties and indemnities to a placing agreement. Further details around institutional placings are set out in Chapter 20, *Institutional placings*.

6.5 The broker will work with the company before the securities are admitted to trading in relation to the proposed valuation of the company and the proposed pricing of the company's securities. It is important for the broker to strike an appropriate balance between rewarding the company's management and providing the market with a fair valuation of the company's securities. The broker will need to take into account how much the company is hoping to raise, the company's past performance, the market's perception of the company's management, realistic fundraising expectations given the current market climate and the sector in which the company operates (including its competitors), and the likely performance of the company's securities both immediately following their admission to trading on AIM and going forwards. It will also be important for the broker to consider the intentions of key shareholders if they are not subject to lock-in agreements since a sale by such shareholders following admission to trading on AIM could have a dramatic effect on the company's share price. Although, ultimately, the final share price of the fundraising will typically be determined by the broker and the company, the broker is expected to take into account investor feedback. Clearly, if it did not, such investors might not be willing to participate in the placing.

6.6 The broker will often have its own institutional research department, responsible for producing a report on the company (prior to admission to trading on AIM as well as on an ongoing basis). This report, which should be objective, is based both on publicly available information and on information produced by the company (in writing) or gleaned from site visits. As the report often contains predictions and forecasts as to the company's share price and business performance, it can be highly influential over the market price of the company's securities following admission to trading on AIM. For this reason, it is market practice to impose a period during which such a report should not be published. Further details on analyst research is set out in Chapter 24, *Analyst research*.

6.7 The company's securities must be freely transferable and eligible for electronic settlement with effect from admission to trading on AIM. While it is the company's lawyers who will check whether the securities are freely transferable, it is the broker (in conjunction with the company and the company's registrar) who apply for the company's securities to be traded on CREST, the electronic settlement system for UK securities. It must be noted, however, that CREST is a voluntary system and so the company must also allow shareholders to hold securities in certificated form if they wish. Further information on settlement is set out in Chapter 16, *CREST, settlement and depository interests*.

6.8 As with all the company's advisers, the broker will be involved in the preparation of the AIM admission document, particularly in relation to targeting the company's message appropriately to the audience. The marketing exercise will be driven by the broker and will involve key members of the company's management giving presentations to prospective investors. This will take up a considerable amount of management time, which should be considered in relation to the ongoing operation of the company's business. The broker will usually provide the format for the presentation, refined with the help of the company and the company's lawyers, and will ensure that the marketing message is clear and is delivered only to those audiences not prevented from participating by regulatory restrictions. The content of the presentations should, so far as is possible, be taken from the AIM admission document (which will usually be distributed at these presentations in a near-complete form, referred to as a "pathfinder") to ensure accuracy and will be communicated for maximum impact, through a series of presentations over a period of around one to two weeks, called a "roadshow". The broker is then responsible for following up with investors after the roadshow and providing feedback from the market to the company.

6.9 Towards the end of the marketing process, the broker will be responsible for co-ordinating the levels of interest, known as "book-building", and for obtaining commitment from investors in the appropriate timescale. This is usually done by way of a "placing letter" and the broker and its lawyers are responsible for co-ordinating all the associated paperwork following review by the company and its lawyers. Finally, the broker is responsible for ensuring the investors all receive their securities and that payment is received from the investors securely, which is typically done on an electronic basis through CREST, known as "delivery versus payment" (i.e. the crediting of the securities to the investors' CREST account is set up to automatically take place against a credit of the sum to be paid to the company). The broker will then pay the funds received to the company, less its commission, fees and expenses.

ONGOING RESPONSIBILITIES

6.10 An AIM company's broker is responsible for managing trading in its securities in the secondary market and will be the main point of contact between the company and the investment market. The broker may be engaged to keep the company abreast of relevant market news, including in relation to its competitors, and to advise it on current market conditions, the trading volume of its securities and their appropriate pricing. This will typically include advising the company when the market is functioning abnormally.

6.11 The broker may also help the company to raise and/or maintain its profile in the investment market to promote trading in its securities. In this regard, the broker will ensure that effective investor relations procedures are in operation, particularly in relation to communication between existing and potential shareholders and key members of management, such as presentations following the issue of the company's annual report and accounts. Under the *AIM Rules for Companies*, the broker must use its best endeavours to find matching business for the company's securities if there is no registered market maker.

6.12 The broker will also assist the company with any fundraisings it seeks to conduct once its securities have been admitted to trading on AIM.

6.13 The broker may need to discuss any potential share transactions involving directors or employees with the company in order to maintain an orderly market in the company's securities. A company will also seek to have any significant share transactions transacted through the broker so as to maintain an orderly market.

6.14 As with before the securities are admitted to trading, specialist analysts in the company's sector will produce analyst research reports on the company, usually following the publication of financial results or significant activity.

6.15 An AIM company must issue notification, without delay, of the resignation, dismissal or appointment of a broker.

IN PRACTICE

The broker must be a good fundraiser with a proven track record, particularly in the sector in which the company operates. The company's main reasons for seeking admission to trading on AIM will usually be, first, to raise finance and, second, to gain access to capital markets. It is for these reasons that the broker plays such an important role. Once its securities are admitted to trading on AIM, the broker is instrumental in the relationship between the company and the investment community.

Role of the reporting accountant

The reporting accountant has an important role, both in the route to AIM and in establishing ongoing financial reporting procedures. The reporting accountant is responsible for reviewing and reporting on historical and forecast financial information prior to admission to trading on AIM, and assisting in the resolution of problems that may arise as a result of such review. The reporting accountant provides valuable independent advice on admission to trading on AIM because it has no vested interest in the outcome.

INTRODUCTION

7.1 The reporting accountant's primary role is to perform financial due diligence on the company and to report on its historical financial information. However, in addition to this, the reporting accountant will help the company to prepare for admission to trading on AIM by advising on issues such as tax and share incentive schemes, working capital, and financial reporting procedures, and is responsible for raising potential problems early on in the preparation for admission so that they can be addressed as soon as possible. The reporting accountant will need to give adequate consideration to the funding requirements of the company, both current and future. The company's financial expectations may not be realistic and it is important that internal procedures are put in place. Preparing the company adequately at the earliest opportunity will help to save it time and money in the admission to trading on AIM process.

CRITERIA

7.2 There are no criteria under the *AIM Rules for Companies* or other regulations for the requirements which need to be fulfilled as a reporting accountant. However, the reporting accountant is expected to be a qualified UK auditor because it will often need to provide a "true and fair opinion" of the historical financial information included in the AIM admission document. A qualified auditor in the UK is normally a person who holds a practising certificate and is a "responsible person" as recognised by a professional accounting body. As it is important for the company to select a firm that is familiar with AIM, the reporting accountant for the company's admission to trading on AIM may not therefore be the company's existing auditor.

PRE-ADMISSION

7.3   One of the first considerations the reporting accountant will address is the structure of the company. It may be that the company's structure is not suitable for admission to trading on AIM and a new holding company may need to be put in place for this purpose. In addition, although the company may, in theory, be suitable for admission to trading on AIM, its structure may be too complicated. Investors are unlikely to want to be concerned about any implications this may bring and a complicated structure makes it hard to provide the necessary confidence and clarity to investors in relation to the company's future. Alternatively, the company may need to be carved out of a larger entity, so the reporting accountant will need to address separation issues.

7.4   If the company is a private company, it will need to re-register as a public company. This process will involve confirming that the company's net assets exceed its called-up share capital and undistributable reserves, and may involve auditing a balance sheet specifically produced for the purpose. It may be that the company's existing auditors perform this task, but the reporting accountant may be appointed auditor for this purpose.

7.5   In some cases, the company will not have had a proper audit and so it will be the responsibility of the reporting accountant to undertake this task. Ideally, especially due to the time it will take to audit the older financial records, the audit should be performed before the process for the application for admission to trading on AIM gets underway in order to save time and costs in the process. Also, in addition to ensuring the financial information included in the AIM admission document is recent and of good quality, this will provide a chance for any potential issues to be addressed at an early stage. For example, with forward planning it may be possible for the company to undertake advance tax planning, which could benefit both the company and its shareholders, old and new. Another area which may benefit from advance planning is the adoption of share incentive schemes for management and employees as the timing of the introduction of such schemes may affect the price and therefore the extent of the incentive.

7.6   A substantial amount of time will be taken up in the performance of financial due diligence on the company. It may also be necessary for the reporting accountant to scrutinise the company's subsidiaries. The primary purpose of this due diligence is to aid the Nominated Adviser, and highlight any issues to it, in assessing the company's suitability for AIM. The reporting accountant will investigate the company's historical financial information and performance in relation to the nature of the business, its current financial reporting procedures and its business plan, along with forecasts in relation to the company's future performance. The results of this investigation will be produced in a "long-form report" and a "working capital report".

7.7   The long-form report contains information on the company's historical financial performance. The scope of the long-form report will be pre-agreed with the company and its Nominated Adviser. It is usually a detailed report, but it may be restricted in certain circumstances, such as in cases of a short history of trading. This may be the first time an outsider has analysed the company's financial information and procedures so it may bring to light various issues which, if substantial, could delay or even prevent the admission to trading on AIM from going ahead. It is therefore important to raise these issues early. The reporting accountant will perform site visits to the company and interview various members of management and employees as well as reviewing written records. This process can take several weeks so it is usual for regular meetings to be arranged in order to update the company and its Nominated Adviser before the final report is produced. The report will not only highlight issues but will also suggest solutions for their resolution.

7.8   The working capital report is either prepared by or reported on by the reporting accountant and contains forecasts about the company's future financial performance. This information is not included in the long-form report. The directors are required, under the *AIM Rules for Companies*, to make a statement after "due and careful enquiry" that the company has sufficient working capital for at least 12 months from the date of admission to trading on AIM. It is the reporting accountant's responsibility to assure the company's directors and Nominated Adviser that such is the case. The reporting accountant will pick up any issues in its review so that it can produce a "clean" opinion. If any such issues cannot be resolved, the reporting accountant will need to address the impact on the company in its report and it may be that the company will have to seek additional funding. Again, the need for an early warning is paramount.

7.9   The reporting accountant will assist the directors in their presentation of historical financial information in the AIM admission document. It is often the case with company accounts before the securities are admitted to trading that issues such as qualified reports, changes to the company's group structure, acquisitions or disposals, and compliance with different requirements for the preparation of accounts will have to be addressed. At this point, the reporting accountant will often consult with the Nominated Adviser to deal with any issues that may arise.

7.10   The company will usually be required to disclose three financial years of historical financial information. If the company has not been trading for three financial years prior to admission to trading on AIM it may be granted an exception. This financial information must be sufficiently up to date and show comparisons to the previous financial period. It will usually be presented on a consolidated basis if the company has subsidiaries. Analysing market expectations and taking guidance from the company's Nominated Adviser will help the reporting accountant to decide whether the financial information should be even more recent than that demanded by the *AIM Rules for Companies*. The reporting accountant will usually provide a "true and fair opinion" of the historical financial information included in the AIM admission document under Schedule 2 of the *AIM Rules for Companies* and, in some cases, this may involve undertaking additional procedures to the auditors and possibly re-auditing some of the information. If there are any changes to previously published audited financial information, the reporting accountant will need to provide an explanation of the changes to the Nominated Adviser, called a "statement of adjustments".

7.11   Other information which may be presented in the AIM admission document includes pro forma financial information showing how admission to trading on AIM and any associated fundraising would or would not have affected the financial position of the company if it had happened at a certain date. A pro forma balance sheet and/or profit and loss account is the responsibility of the directors of the company, but the reporting accountant will review the information with the directors and provide a comfort letter in relation to the policies and calculations that have been applied to it. If forecast financial information is included, which is quite rare, both the reporting accountant and the Nominated Adviser will have to provide comfort on it. There is some overlap with the working capital report but the forecast financial information will provide a much more detailed view requiring a higher level of comfort. Also, since it provides shareholders with ammunition against the company if it does not meet these forecasts, it tends to be included only if the Nominated Adviser deems it absolutely necessary

7.12   In addition to the above, the reporting accountant is responsible for providing various comfort letters, such as in relation to the extraction of financial information where information has been summarised in other areas of the AIM admission document and any significant changes since the reports were produced.

ONGOING OBLIGATIONS

7.13   Following admission to trading on AIM, the company will be required to present its financial statements in a particular manner, which will be more heavily regulated than before. It is important that the presentation of the financial statements in the AIM admission document is consistent with that going forwards and it will be necessary for the company to put certain financial reporting standards and industry best practice procedures in place. The company's accounts will be subject to much greater scrutiny following admission to trading on AIM and it is the reporting accountant that will guide the company through these changes.

7.14   The Nominated Adviser will seek written confirmation from the company that it has established, and operates, reliable reporting procedures so that accurate financial information can be obtained promptly. Since it is important for a public company to be able to communicate effectively with external investors and to adhere to the rules and regulations governing it, the reporting accountant will be required to produce an opinion on this written confirmation. The procedures will be investigated when the reporting accountant carries out research for the long-form report and may result in the opinion being subject to certain conditions, which the company will need to carry out within a certain time.

IN PRACTICE

The reporting accountant will need relevant experience in the admission to trading on AIM process and a good understanding of the company's operations and its business plan. It is important for the reporting accountant to address financial issues at an early stage and to educate the company in best practice financial reporting procedures and systems. As the reporting accountant has no vested interest in the outcome of admission to trading on AIM, it can bring valuable independent advice to the process.

CHAPTER 8

Role of the other advisers

AT A GLANCE

In addition to the Nominated Adviser, the broker and the reporting accountants, there are a number of other key advisers, which include corporate lawyers, the registrar, experts, financial public relations and/or investor relations advisers and printers, and who together make up the team both for companies applying for admission of their securities to trading on AIM and those whose securities are already admitted.

INTRODUCTION

8.1 In addition to the Nominated Adviser, the broker and the reporting account-ants, there will always be at least two firms of lawyers involved in the admission to trading on AIM process and going forwards: one that acts for the company and one that acts for the Nominated Adviser and broker. If the company is an overseas company, a significant amount of the company's operations or assets are overseas, or the company is making an overseas acquisition or disposal, local lawyers will also be engaged. In addition, it may be necessary to engage legal counsel to pro-duce a formal legal opinion on a particular point of law or for a specific type of company in relation to how certain rules or regulations apply to them.

8.2 The registrar will need to be involved in matters relating to shareholder information and in distributing information to the shareholders, such as the AIM admission document. This will also involve the appointment of a specialist printing firm.

8.3 In addition to legal counsel, a technical expert may be needed and in the case of mining and oil and gas companies, a competent person's report must be pro-duced (as described in Chapter 12, *Mining, oil and gas companies*), so an expert in this field must be engaged. Companies in other sectors may also decide to appoint experts to clarify or support any information that will be included in the AIM admission document such as patent agents to report on the company's patents if these are material to its business.

8.4 The company will need to appoint a firm of financial public relations and/or investor relations advisers that will oversee any public announcements that the company will be required to make and will make suggestions as to how best to present the company and its operations, strategy, management and any corporate activity to the media and the investment community. These advisers should be specialists in the AIM market and will be responsible for the public release of announcements.

ROLE OF THE COMPANY'S LAWYERS

8.5   The company's lawyers play a key role in the admission to trading on AIM process. The company's lawyers will advise on the structure of the company, advise the directors on their responsibilities for any document and, in conjunction with the Nominated Adviser, advise on the AIM company's compliance with the *AIM Rules for Companies*. The company's lawyers will also advise on the accuracy of public information, such as that disclosed in the AIM admission document, public announcements and other documents involved in the admission process, as well as any associated fundraising and any approvals that may be required from shareholders.

8.6   A substantial part of the company's lawyers' time will be taken up performing legal due diligence on the company. This involves reviewing the company's structure, its standing and incorporation details, the company's assets (and its title to them), members of management (including board composition), material contracts and contracts of employment, and any existing or possible litigation. In addition to this, the company's lawyers will:

- negotiate the terms of any engagement letters which the company may enter into with the Nominated Adviser, the broker, the reporting accountants and any expert;
- negotiate the Nominated Adviser agreement and any placing or introduction agreement, and any other documents associated with admission of the company's securities to trading on AIM (especially regarding any warranties and indemnities to be given, which will often include the provision of advice to the company and the directors in relation thereto);
- advise on any group or corporate restructuring;
- advise on and be involved with the drafting of the AIM admission document and carry out a verification process in relation to its accuracy. The company's lawyers will also advise on its compliance with any legal or regulatory requirements and draft the section on the general corporate information about the company;
- prepare employment agreements/letters of engagement for members of the board, senior management and key employees;
- where relevant, prepare share incentive scheme documents for management and employees; and
- prepare ancillary documents such as board minutes and terms of reference for any corporate governance committees (such as the remuneration or audit committees).

8.7   It is the company's lawyers who need to provide advice so that the directors are aware of their responsibilities for the AIM admission document and as directors of an AIM company. The directors will be required to sign responsibility statements, prepared by the company's lawyers and reviewed by the Nominated Adviser's lawyers, in this regard. To help this process and to ensure that the information disclosed in the AIM admission document is accurate and not mis-leading in any way, the company's lawyers will undertake a verification process of the AIM admission document by producing "verification notes". These notes are a series of questions and answers and will take statements from the AIM admission document and will require the directors to focus on the content and provide source material to substantiate the information.

8.8 There are also various other legal obligations on the company, such as com-pliance with securities regulations in the UK (e.g. the *Prospectus Rules* published by the Financial Services Authority) along with UK legislation (in particular, the *Companies Act 2006* and the *Financial Services and Markets Act 2000*) and that of the country in which the company is incorporated if outside the UK. It is the company's lawyers who will, in conjunction with the other advisers, advise on whether a prospectus will be required and whether any documents involved in the process will need to comply with financial promotion restrictions and requirements.

8.9 The company's lawyers will, in conjunction with the Nominated Adviser, advise on the specific content requirements of the AIM admission document (as explained fully in Chapter 10, *Admission process and AIM admission documents*) along with providing guidance on any general information which should be disclosed under the *AIM Rules for Companies*. The specific requirements include statements that must be made by the directors under the *AIM Rules for Companies* in relation to working capital and their responsibility for the content of the AIM admission document. The company's lawyers will also advise the directors in relation to their responsibility for the AIM admission document.

8.10 Since the *AIM Rules for Companies* do not require a company to be incorporated in the UK, or indeed in any other specific jurisdiction, overseas com-panies can seek admission to trading on AIM. Local lawyers will need to be engaged by the company to ensure that there is no breach of any applicable law, rule or regulation in the relevant jurisdiction and, if the company is listed on another exchange, that any announcements are released simultaneously in all markets. Further information regarding overseas companies is set out in Chapter 40, *Overseas companies*.

8.11 Following admission to trading on AIM, an AIM company is subject to various continuing obligations and will need advice from its lawyers in this regard. In particular, the company's lawyers will assist the company in relation to:

- ensuring it maintains certain requirements as an AIM company, such as having freely transferable securities that are eligible for electronic settlement;
- the composition of its board of directors;
- the preparation and filing of interim and annual reports and accounts;
- its relationship with and the retention of its Nominated Adviser and broker;
- the publication of price sensitive information;
- the publication of any other information required to be disclosed;
- the operation of a share dealing code in relation to dealings in the company's securities by directors and applicable employees;
- documents to be sent to shareholders, including any new AIM admission documents that may be required; and
- any necessary shareholder approvals.

8.12 It is often the company's lawyers together with the Nominated Adviser that will be the first point of contact for the company in relation to its continuing obligations and for any corporate activity.

ROLE OF THE NOMINATED ADVISER AND BROKER'S LAWYERS

8.13 The lawyers to the Nominated Adviser and broker will also review the AIM admission document and any associated documents so that the Nominated Adviser and broker can become comfortable with the accuracy of their contents. They will also ensure that the Nominated Adviser and broker are adequately protected, both financially and in relation to their respective reputations, and will review any public announcements or investment communications to be issued by the company or the Nominated Adviser or broker. It will be the Nominated Adviser and broker's lawyers who draft and negotiate the terms of the Nominated Adviser agreement and any placing or introduction agreement with the company's lawyers.

ROLE OF THE REGISTRAR

8.14 The *AIM Rules for Companies* do not specifically provide for the appointment of a registrar in the same way as they provide for the appointment of a Nominated Adviser or broker. However, the role and function of the registrar will help provide assistance to the functions of the Nominated Adviser.

8.15 The company's registrar will be appointed primarily to deal with maintaining the share register of the company. Their terms of engagement will be set out in an agreement between the company and the registrar.

8.16 Key responsibilities of the registrar include the following:

- to maintain and keep the register of shareholders up to date;
- to prepare, approve and register transfers, including those using CREST;
- to prepare and obtain signed or sealed share certificates and distribute these to the shareholders or their brokers (as required); and
- to provide required information to the Nominated Adviser or other advisers to the company.

8.17 If the company is registered overseas there may also be other requirements, for instance if the company has to issue depository interests for the purposes of electronic settlement where its securities cannot be admitted to CREST.

8.18 As the holder of the records of the shareholder's register the registrar will be required to liaise closely with the Nominated Adviser and the company's lawyers.

8.19 As it is a requirement that, with effect from admission, the securities in the company must be freely transferable and eligible for electronic settlement, the company's securities will need to be registered and be admitted to CREST. CREST is the electronic settlement system to UK securities and it provides for individuals and institutional investors to hold and transfer securities in an uncertificated form. The registration for CREST is usually applied for by the company, its broker and registrar. As it is up to an individual shareholder whether they hold their securities in CREST, it is important for the company to still maintain the paper system of the issue and retention of share certificates for those shareholders that do not wish to use the CREST system. The registrar will also prepare a pro forma share certificate, to be approved at a board meeting of the company, so that for the certificated transfers the form of the share certificate is an approved version. Further information on settlement is set out in Chapter 16, *CREST, settlement and depository interests*.

8.20 From time to time the company will also be required to distribute information to the shareholders and the registrar should be able to provide the company with an up-to-date list of the shareholders so that any circular or similar shareholder publications can be put on a website in accordance with Rule 26 of the *AIM Rules for Companies* (Company information disclosure).

ROLE OF EXPERTS

8.21 Experts that a company may engage in connection with an application for admission of securities to trading on AIM include legal counsel, mineral experts, intellectual property or technology experts and experts in the company's main country of operation (if overseas).

8.22 The company's lawyers and Nominated Adviser will advise the company when it is appropriate to engage counsel for a particular matter. This will usually be in relation to a complex area of law or matters specific to the sector in which the company operates or to confirm that the company has any required regulatory permissions or consents which are necessary to operate its business.

8.23 As explained in Chapter 12, *Mining, oil and gas companies*, a mining or oil and gas company will need to appoint a suitably qualified individual in its specific sector to produce a competent person's report on all material assets, for example mining permits, licences and associated liabilities. The Nominated Adviser works closely with the mineral expert acting as competent person to seek to ensure that:

- the individual producing the competent person's report has the relevant and appropriate qualifications, experience and technical knowledge to produce a high-quality, independent appraisal of the assets and liabilities;
- the scope of the competent person's report is appropriate;
- the summary of the competent person's report reproduced in the AIM admission document is accurately and fairly extracted; and
- the work performed by the mineral expert acting as competent person is subjected to internal review.

8.24 Other companies may also decide to appoint an expert if it will help to clarify information to be included in the AIM admission document or otherwise released to the market. For example, if a company operates a new area of technology it may be beneficial for a patent or technology expert to review such technology and produce a report verifying or clarifying, among other things, any intellectual property, relevant licences or processes. In addition, if a company operates a significant proportion of its business overseas, experts in the relevant country's legal environment may be engaged.

ROLE OF THE FINANCIAL PUBLIC RELATIONS AND/OR INVESTOR RELATIONS ADVISER

8.25 Communication with the investment community is a key factor for any successful admission of securities to trading on AIM and in relation to maintaining the profile of the company going forwards. Not only must a company strive to achieve the best quality it can in relation to its operations and the performance of its share price, it must also communicate news effectively. The financial public relations and/or investor relations adviser will help the company to produce well thought-out and effectively directed communications.

8.26 Financial public relations and/or investor relations advisers do not have to be regulated by any of the UK's financial markets regulators and do not require prior approval before being appointed as an adviser for AIM purposes, although it is advisable to check with the Nominated Adviser before appointing a particular firm. Therefore, it can be difficult to choose the right adviser, especially if the company is from overseas and is not familiar with the market. The most important thing for a company to look for in a financial public relations and/or investor relations adviser is appropriate AIM experience, especially within the sector in which the company operates. The financial public relations and/or investor relations adviser must be familiar not only with the workings of such a company but also with how best to communicate with the investment community to ensure that the company is effectively described and stands out from its competitors. The financial public relations and/or investor relations adviser should always have the audience's perception in mind and should seek to gain its approval for any communication. To do this, it must ensure that any communication provides a thorough understanding of the company's business, strategy and management while aiming to portray such information both accurately and positively by ensuring that all communications are clear and consistent. Good financial public relations and/or investor relations advisers will have solid relationships with the media as well as with the target audience in the investment community so that any public communications can be pitched tactically and effectively. Financial public relations and/or investor relations advisers will need to have strength and depth in their expertise, especially to cope with the strategic obstacles that may present themselves in the run-up to and following admission to trading on AIM.

8.27 The growth of AIM in recent years has resulted in an extremely competitive environment and it can therefore be more important in terms of profile for an AIM company to have an effective financial public relations and/or investor relations adviser than it is for a company whose securities are admitted to trading on the Main Market of the London Stock Exchange. This will be particularly important for an overseas company seeking admission to trading on AIM due to its unfamiliarity within the investment market.

8.28 While the Nominated Adviser and company's lawyers will seek to ensure that any communications are within AIM's regulatory framework and UK law, the financial public relations and/or investor relations adviser will also need to be familiar with the regulations so that it can provide support as necessary. In relation to overseas companies, the UK financial public relations and/or investor relations adviser will co-ordinate all communications to ensure that they accurately reflect what the company is trying to achieve, that they comply with applicable regulatory requirements and that they are released at the appropriate time in all relevant markets.

8.29 In relation to admission to trading on AIM, the financial public relations and/or investor relations adviser is responsible for managing the key communication stages in the route to admission. The first task of a financial public relations and/or investor relations adviser is usually raising the company's profile, generally well in advance of expected admission to trading on AIM, using a communication strategy that will ultimately support the admission to trading. This will typically be done by reviewing existing communication materials and background information, developing or setting up the company's website, providing media training for company spokespeople (including an internal policy on communicating with the media), which often indicates guidance as to how they should respond to common questions and in relation to internal communications (especially to the company's employees at an appropriate stage), and assessing whether the company's image needs an overhaul. In short, the financial public relations and/or investor relations adviser needs to prepare the company for communication as a public company so that it is already in that mindset close to and following admission to trading on AIM.

8.30 Once the company's general profile has been raised, the next task for a financial public relations and/or investor relations adviser is preparing and releasing the company's announcement of its intention to float on AIM. This announcement is arguably the most important because it will be the company's first formal communication to the media and the wider investment community. There is no requirement to make such an announcement, but it is common practice to do so and this will also help to raise investor awareness. In addition, the financial public relations and/or investor relations adviser should prepare the company's management to answer questions from the financial media. An intense period of media scrutiny will follow so the training provided by the financial public relations and/or investor relations adviser will come into play. The financial public relations and/or investor relations adviser will also take the opportunity to investigate how other brokers have perceived the company. This is where the financial public relations and/or investor relations adviser's market relationships are important, since it can provide valuable feedback to the company in relation to market sentiment.

8.31 The next task for the financial public relations and/or investor relations adviser is in connection with the company's publication of an almost final AIM admission document, called the "pathfinder". Briefly, the pathfinder document is the final form of the AIM admission document but without certain figures which have not been finalised, for example the price of the company's securities. This document is described more fully in Chapter 20, *Institutional placings*. The financial public relations and/or investor relations adviser should prepare the company's management for questions on this document since it will be the first time the investment community has seen any potentially controversial information on the company. A good financial public relations and/or investor relations adviser will encourage management to answer such questions with a view to moving the discussion on to the purpose behind admission to trading on AIM and the company's business plan. This process will typically also involve the company undertaking a marketing roadshow (as described in Chapter 20, *Institutional placings*) and so the financial public relations and/or investor relations adviser will usually be involved in the preparations for this along with the company and its broker.

8.32 The other key task in connection with a company's application for the admission of its securities to trading on AIM surrounds communication of the publication of the AIM admission document, confirmation of the price of the company's securities, allocation of the company's securities and commencement of trading in the company's securities, which will involve dealing with how the company's securities perform following admission to trading on AIM. In particular, the financial public relations and/or investor relations adviser will need to prepare the company's management for questions in relation to any over-subscription for the company's securities if admission to trading on AIM is accompanied by a fundraising or a rise or fall in the company's securities shortly after admission, and, if such rise or fall is significant, on the inaccurate valuation of the company's securities.

8.33 Following admission to trading on AIM, the financial public relations and/or investor relations adviser's role will primarily be to maintain the company's profile and interest in its securities. This is likely to involve advising on the release of communications to the media at times when there is no legal or regulatory requirement to do so. This may also involve devising a communications calendar to catch all actual or likely relevant announcement events. The financial public relations and/or investor relations adviser should be an integral part of the ongoing advisory team to the AIM company.

8.34 In addition, the financial public relations and/or investor relations adviser may provide investor relations services. These educate the company in, among other things, communicating effectively with its shareholders, providing information on the company's performance in relation to its competitors and achieving a fair price for its securities.

ROLE OF THE PRINTERS

8.35 The printers are usually appointed once the AIM admission document has been advanced to a stage where there will not be lots of substantive amendments or additions. The printers will then typeset the AIM admission document and all further changes will then be made in manuscript by the team and then sent to the printers to be typeset, usually overnight. Once the AIM admission document is in final form the printers will arrange for its bulk printing and distribution.

IN PRACTICE

There can be many experts engaged in the AIM process and these will vary according to the particular company. However, a company should always give careful consideration to appointment of a particular person or firm and understand the role that each member of the team will perform.

Part II
Admissions to AIM

INTRODUCTION

Admission to trading on AIM usually marks the beginning of a company's life as a public company whose securities are admitted to trading on AIM. However, the build up to admission to trading on AIM usually commences at least a couple of months before admission occurs and starts with an examination of the company's suitability for admission of its securities to trading on AIM and some early preparatory steps.

A typical timetable for an admission to trading on AIM with institutional placing is as overleaf as Figure 1.

This Part looks at the admission process and, in particular, admission documents in Chapter 10, *Admission process and AIM admission documents* and "fast-track" admission in Chapter 11, *"Fast-track" admissions*.

This Part also examines how the admission process is varied for certain specific situations: for example, mining, oil and gas companies in Chapter 12, *Mining, oil and gas companies*, investing companies in Chapter 13, *Investing companies* and also admission by way of a reverse takeover in Chapter 14, *Admission to trading on AIM by reverse takeover*.

As part of the admission process the directors will have to take responsibility for the AIM admission document and the key obligations and responsibilities of directors set out in Chapter 15, *Directors' responsibilities for an AIM admission document and verification*.

Finally, the arrangements in relation to trading the company's securities when they are admitted to trading on AIM are set out in Chapter 16, *CREST, settlement and depository interests* which deals with settlement, depository interests and CREST and at Chapter 17 *Lock-ins for new businesses*, which deals with certain mandatory lock-ins.

FIGURE 1 — Typical timetable for an admission to trading on AIM with institutional placing

Preliminary Preparation

- Retain advisers:
    Nominated Adviser; broker; legal team; accountants; PR agency
- Corporate structure/Group re-organisation:
    i.   re-register company as a public company or interpose suitable holding company;
    ii. shares should be freely transferable and fully paid up;
    iii. review company's share option schemes
- Review of executive service agreements
- Accountants prepare financial report
- Legal team send out due diligence and directors' questionnaires
- Existing shareholders take tax advice with regard to their holdings and long-term planning

Week 1

- Directors reply to directors' and due diligence questionnaires
- Corporate advisers begin drafting AIM admission document
- Legal team and accountants perform due diligence exercise

Week 3

- Accountants' financial report and due diligence report circulated around team
- Settlement arrangements must be satisfactory (i.e. CREST compliant registrar appointed)

Week 5

- Commence verification process
- Nominated Adviser's lawyers prepare first draft of placing agreement

Week 7

- Board meeting to approve service agreements; pathfinder AIM admission document; verification notes and working capital report etc.
- Issue pathfinder AIM admission document if offering to institutional investors
- 10-day announcement submitted to AIM
- Company adopts corporate governance procedures and share dealing code and approves terms of reference for audit and remuneration committees

Week 8

- Marketing, roadshows and other publicity
- Finalise placing agreement, send out placing letters

Week 9

- Board meeting to confirm issue price and approve final AIM admission document and placing agreement
- Payment and clearance of subscription monies for shares
- 3-day application form submitted to AIM

Week 10

- Board meeting to approve allotment of shares to investors
- Admission to trading on AIM

CHAPTER 9

Suitability and preparation for admission

AT A GLANCE

AIM is a market designed for smaller and growing companies and so its eligibility criteria are tailored to accommodate this; even start-ups can be listed on AIM.

There are certain eligibility criteria that all companies whose securities are to be traded on AIM must meet, but generally these are to do with the securities to be listed and the requirement to retain a Nominated Adviser.

Suitability is judged by the Nominated Adviser, which takes into account a number of factors including the company, its securities, its board of directors and matters arising from due diligence.

ELIGIBILITY CRITERIA

9.1   As AIM is designed for smaller and growing companies, the eligibility criteria for companies seeking admission of a class of their securities to trading on AIM are more flexible than those of other markets, such as the Main Market of the London Stock Exchange.

9.2   There are no requirements on AIM for the applicant company to be of a certain size or to have a certain minimum market capitalisation. In addition, start-ups can also apply for admission to trading on AIM as there is no requirement for an applicant to have an established trading record or even an established management team. However, while these are not requirements for an application for admission to trading on AIM, these are factors which need to be considered by the company and its advisers, including its Nominated Adviser, when assessing whether the company is appropriate to be a company whose securities are traded on a public market.

9.3   To be admitted to trading on many markets or securities exchanges a company is required to have a minimum amount of securities held in public hands upon listing. For example, it is a requirement of the United Kingdom Listing Authority that at least 25 per cent of the securities are in public hands for a company to be admitted to the Official List of the Financial Services Authority, which is a pre-requisite for an application to admit securities to trading on the Main Market of the London Stock Exchange. For these purposes "in public hands" means that number of securities held by people other than the directors and substantial shareholders. For companies seeking admission to trading on AIM there are no such requirements, although this is one of a number of factors which a Nominated Adviser will consider when assessing an applicant's suitability to have its securities admitted to trading on AIM. Accordingly, although there is no strict requirement, a number of securities will need to be held in public hands in order to facilitate liquidity in that security, but this may be less than the strict requirement of at least 25 per cent for admission to the Official List and to trading on the Main Market of the London Stock Exchange.

9.4 Unlike many markets or securities exchanges which require the pre-vetting of an admission document, the vetting of AIM admission documents is effectively delegated by AIM to the company's Nominated Adviser and there is no formal vetting procedure. However, companies should note that if there is to be a fund-raising which involves an offer to the public, then a prospectus will be required and this prospectus will be subject to United Kingdom Listing Authority approval (see Chapter 19, *Offers to the public*). In practice, the company's Nominated Adviser will probably lead the drafting of the AIM admission document with the company's lawyers and will, in part, use this process to satisfy itself of the contents of the AIM admission document.

9.5 The principal requirements or eligibility criteria for a company planning to seek to have its securities admitted to trading on AIM are as follows:

- The company's securities must be freely transferable, free of pre-emption rights (*AIM Rules for Companies*, Rule 32).
- The company's securities must be eligible for electronic settlement (*AIM Rules for Companies*, Rule 36; further information on settlement is set out in Chapter 16, *CREST, settlement and depository interests*).
- Application must be made to list all the securities in a class (*AIM Rules for Companies*, Rule 33).
- The securities must have been unconditionally allotted (*AIM Rules for Companies*, Rule 33).
- The company must retain a Nominated Adviser at all times (*AIM Rules for Companies*, Rule 34).
- The company must also retain a broker at all times (*AIM Rules for Companies*, Rule 35).
- The company must produce an AIM admission document (*AIM Rules for Companies*, Rule 3). However, for companies applying using the "fast-track" admission procedure, the company may instead produce a supplement to its Schedule 1 announcement. Further information on the "fast-track" admission procedure is set out in Chapter 11, *"Fast-track" admissions*.
- Where the company has not been independent and revenue-earning for at least two years at the time of admission to trading on AIM, directors, certain employees and certain shareholders will be subject to lock-ins which will prevent them from disposing of those securities for a 12-month period following admission to trading on AIM except in certain, limited, circumstances. Applicants should, however, expect that, as part of the admission to trading on AIM process, the company's Nominated Adviser and/or broker may require the directors and key shareholders to be subject to lock-in arrangements to further enhance confidence in the market, regardless of whether or not the mandatory lock-in

applies. However, in circumstances where the lock-in is not mandatory, these lock-ins are usually subject to further, more widely drafted, exceptions. Further information on lock-ins is set out in Chapter 17, *Lock-ins for new businesses*. Where mandatory lock-ins are required under Rule 7 of the *AIM Rules for Companies*, these will not prevent such persons selling securities on admission to trading on AIM as part of any funding conducted on (but not after) admission to trading on AIM.

SUITABILITY

9.6   Under Rule 1 of the *AIM Rules for Companies*, it is the Nominated Adviser that is responsible to the London Stock Exchange for assessing the appropriateness of an applicant for admission to trading on AIM and for advising and guiding an AIM company and its directors on their responsibilities under the *AIM Rules for Companies*. Accordingly, provided that the eligibility criteria are met, the Nominated Adviser must confirm its view to the London Stock Exchange in its Nominated Adviser declaration, although the London Stock Exchange still retains the right not to admit securities or to impose special conditions under Rule 9 of the *AIM Rules for Companies*.

9.7   The Nominated Adviser declaration is one of the set of key documents to be submitted to the London Stock Exchange in order for the company's application for admission to trading to be considered. Although it is a simple one-page form, it carries great significance because of the statements which the Nominated Adviser will confirm by signing the form.

9.8   There are two sections of confirmations which are made by the Nominated Adviser in the declaration. The first is titled Section A and, along with a confirmation that the company has complied with all applicable rules of the *AIM Rules for Companies* and that the Nominated Adviser has complied with the *AIM Rules for Nominated Advisers*, it sets out a confirmation that the technical content of the AIM admission document that is being submitted as part of the admission process includes all the required information. For information on the content requirements of an AIM admission document, see Chapter 10, *Admission process and AIM admission documents*.

9.9   Section B of the Nominated Adviser's declaration contains a number of separate confirmations. The first of these is the most significant, stating that the Nominated Adviser is satisfied that the company and its securities are appropriate to be admitted to trading on AIM. This is a key statement and a significant portion of the general work which is performed during the admission process will be to provide the Nominated Adviser with sufficient comfort to enable them to make this statement. The different areas which the Nominated Adviser ought to have regard to in making this confirmation are set out in Schedule 3 to the *AIM Rules for Nominated Advisers*. The key elements which the Nominated Adviser will typically consider are set out in Figure 9.1.

9.10   The second confirmation statement is a confirmation that the Nominated Adviser is satisfied that the directors of the company have received advice and guidance as to their responsibilities and obligations under the *AIM Rules for*

FIGURE 9.1   Key considerations as to suitability for AIM

The key factors that a Nominated Adviser will consider when seeking to satisfy itself that the company and its securities are appropriate to be admitted to trading on AIM include the following:

The company and its securities

- The Nominated Adviser will consider the company's sector, proposition, business plan or similar, historical financial information and other corporate information, including the due diligence which has been performed.
- The Nominated Adviser will consider any issues relating to the company's country of incorporation and operation and any other issues that might affect its appropriateness.

The board and directors

- The Nominated Adviser will issue and review directors' questionnaires and review directors' CVs. It will then test the information revealed by those questionnaires and CVs, for example by conducting press searches, Companies House checks, taking-up references and, where appropriate, obtaining third party checks. For directors who are not UK-based, appropriate investigations should be undertaken.
- These investigations and considerations on the directors will then be extended, as appropriate, to key managers and consultants who are discussed in the AIM admission document.
- The Nominated Adviser will consider undertaking such investigations in relation to substantial shareholders at admission as appropriate, especially where there is uncertainty as to their identity or where they are not established institutions, in particular to enquire about the existence of persons exerting control over the company.
- The Nominated Adviser will also consider each director's suitability and experience in relation to their proposed role and consider whether each proposed director is suitable to be a director of a UK public company.
- The Nominated Adviser will consider the board of directors as a whole in relation to the company's needs, for example given its type, size, expected profile and the fact that the company will be admitted to a UK-based, English-language public market.
- The Nominated Adviser will consider, with the directors of the company, the adoption of appropriate corporate governance measures.

Due diligence

- The Nominated Adviser will need to be satisfied that appropriate working capital and financial reporting systems and controls reviews are undertaken (usually including reports or letters from the reporting accountant to the company).
- The Nominated Adviser will consider whether commercial, specialist (e.g. intellectual property) and/or technical due diligence is required and be satisfied that it is undertaken where required.

- The Nominated Adviser will agree the scope of all such due diligence and reports (including, in relation to the working capital report, assumptions and sensitivities).
- The Nominated Adviser will review and assess the above due diligence, reports and adviser comfort letters, considering any material issues, recommended actions or adverse analysis raised and be satisfied that appropriate actions have been undertaken to resolve such matters or otherwise be satisfied that such matters do not affect the appropriateness of the applicant for AIM.

AIM Rule compliance

- The Nominated Adviser will need to be satisfied that procedures within the company have been established to facilitate compliance with the *AIM Rules for Companies* (e.g. release of unpublished price sensitive information, Rule 17 notifications, regulation of close periods).
- The Nominated Adviser will need to be satisfied that the directors have been advised of their and the company's continuing responsibilities and obligations under the *AIM Rules for Companies* and that the directors are aware of when they should be consulting with or seeking the advice of the Nominated Adviser.

Companies. The Nominated Adviser will by this point have confirmed that it is satisfied with the content of the memoranda on ongoing responsibilities and obligations, which are typically provided to the directors of the company during the admission process and the Nominated Adviser will therefore have some comfort that the directors have received proper advice.

9.11 In reaching its decision as to whether or not a company is appropriate to have its securities admitted to trading on AIM, a number of preparatory steps will be carried out either at the request of, or in conjunction with, its Nominated Adviser.

The company

9.12 The company's advisers will be carrying out due diligence. Although this is basically an information gathering exercise, it is also intended to expose any commercial issues or irregularities which could have an impact on the pricing of the company's securities. The results of the due diligence will allow the company's advisers to prepare a high-quality AIM admission document for the purposes of marketing any fundraising as well as ensuring compliance with the *AIM Rules for Companies* and minimising any liability for the directors in relation to its content.

9.13 On the legal side, the company's lawyers will carry out an extensive investigation of the company's business, including its ownership of assets and property (including intellectual property and real property), its employment and pension policies, the validity of its ordinary securities, any material contracts and any current or threatened litigation. Part of this process will highlight any irregularities, such as assets not owned by the company but which are crucial to the operation of the company's business. Likewise, it should highlight any key contracts which have not been reduced to writing or which have expired, as any resultant increase in risk could reduce the investor appetite for the company's securities or reduce the price investors are willing to pay.

9.14   Further corporate restructuring may be required if, for example, there are certain assets which are currently owned by the company that will seek admission of its securities to trading on AIM but which the current shareholders wish to hold outside the AIM listed company. Conversely, there may be some assets which are fundamental to the operation of the business which are currently held outside the group of the company whose securities are to be admitted to trading on AIM which may have to be transferred to the applicant before admission.

9.15   Typically, the reporting accountants will also look at the company's financial affairs with a view to preparing a long-form report, which generally describes the history of the business over the last three completed financial periods and specifies any areas of concern regarding the applicant company and its business from a financial perspective for the Nominated Adviser. The reporting accountants will also review the company's systems and controls, particularly in relation to financial reporting.

The board of directors

9.16   The Nominated Adviser and the company will also need to consider the composition of the board of directors, especially the number of non-executive directors. As the applicant is being admitted to AIM, it is not required to comply with the *Combined Code* which covers the principles of good governance and the code of best practice. However, it is recommended that, as a matter of best practice, AIM companies should follow the same core recommendations relating to corporate governance. Among other things, the *Combined Code* requires the board of directors to establish committees of non-executive directors to deal with audit matters, executive remuneration and nominations to the board of directors. In order to establish these committees, the company should therefore seek to ensure that there is a sufficient number of non-executive directors to meet these requirements, which for AIM companies is a minimum of two non-executive directors, at least one of whom should be independent. Corporate governance and the levels of compliance expected from AIM companies is discussed in more detail in Chapter 42, *Corporate governance for AIM companies*.

9.17   Finally, whether as part of the share capital reorganisation or otherwise, it may be necessary to amend the company's current Articles of Association. In particular, from a corporate governance standpoint, investors will usually expect to see a limit on the number of directors and the remuneration to be paid to the non-executive directors. The Articles of Association should also be checked to see if there are limits on the borrowing powers of the directors as this is also often something which investors expect. It is also best practice for the company not to give an indemnity to its auditors under its Articles of Association, and again this should be checked.

The securities

9.18   Either as part of the due diligence exercise or around that time, the company's solicitors will review the company's constitutional document (i.e. its Memorandum and Articles of Association or equivalent) to ensure that the securities for which admission to trading on AIM is sought are: freely transferable with effect from admission to trading on AIM; eligible for electronic settlement; and that there are no restrictions on the transferability of the company's ordinary securities or the company's ability to offer securities to the public. In the case of a company incorporated in England and Wales the company may have to re-register as a public limited company. Where it is not possible to re-register a private company as a public limited company then it may be necessary to carry out corporate restructuring to reorganise the group so that the holding company of the group is a public limited company.

9.19   The company's share capital structure may also need to be reviewed as part of the admission to trading on AIM process, depending on the valuation which is ascribed to the company. For marketing reasons, it may be better to avoid an initial share price of, say, one pound, as psychologically investors may be unhappy when their securities fall below this price. The company, together with its advisers, will need to carefully consider the share capital structure and this may need to be re-organised prior to admission to trading on AIM. If there is more than one class of securities in existence prior to admission to trading on AIM then it may also be desirable to adopt a simplified structure, in order to give potential investors a clear understanding of the economic benefits attached to the securities which they will hold.

9.20   Additional requirements are placed on mining or oil and gas companies and investing companies (see Chapter 12, *Mining, oil and gas companies* and Chapter 13, *Investing companies* respectively).

IN PRACTICE

It is important to find a Nominated Adviser that will support the company and guide it through the AIM application process at an early stage as this is crucial to the process of admitting securities to trading on AIM. A full list of Nominated Advisers is available on the London Stock Exchange website, although it is advantageous to have a Nominated Adviser which specialises in the sector in which the applicant operates and, where the same company is appointed as Nominated Adviser and broker, that they have a track record of raising funds in that sector. Most accountants and lawyers will also be able to provide recommendations as to Nominated Advisers.

In addition, whilst some of the preparatory steps can be carried out prior to the appointment of a Nominated Adviser, the Nominated Adviser will have views on most of these matters. If they are not carried out to the Nominated Adviser's satisfaction, it may be necessary to repeat some of the steps or make further amendments. Accordingly, it is best to take most of the preparatory steps following the appointment of the Nominated Adviser to avoid unnecessary costs.

Admission process and AIM admission documents

AT A GLANCE

As a general rule, as part of the admission process most companies seeking to admit their securities to AIM must publish an AIM admission document. This detailed document sets out information necessary to give investors a full understanding of the company, its business and the securities being admitted and is prepared by the company in conjunction with its adviser team.

ADMISSION PROCESS

10.1 The *AIM Rules for Companies* sets out a timetable for the formal stages of the process of seeking admission to trading on AIM by requiring that certain announcements and forms are completed at certain prescribed times prior to the proposed date of admission. In practice, these formal stages occur towards the end of the admission process as a number of these formal stages, such as the AIM admission document and Nominated Adviser's declaration form, require the preparation of supporting reports and investigations.

10.2 The first of these formal stages is in relation to the pre-admission announcement, set out in Rule 2 of the *AIM Rules for Companies*. This requires the company to submit a range of information to the London Stock Exchange at least ten business days prior to the proposed date of admission to trading on AIM. The information should be submitted by email in the standard format of an announcement and the London Stock Exchange will then release that announcement on a regulatory information service.

10.3 The information that is required to be included in the pre-admission announcement is set out at Schedule 1 to the *AIM Rules for Companies* and comprises items such as the company's name and details of its business and various details concerning the securities to be admitted to trading on AIM. The full list of information required by Schedule 1 is set out at Figure 10.1.

10.4 Where there are any changes in the information that has been provided to the London Stock Exchange and set out in the announcement, the company is under an obligation to immediately notify the London Stock Exchange of the details of such changes. The London Stock Exchange will then determine whether it is of the opinion that the change in information represents a significant difference from that which was originally provided. Where it is significant, the London Stock

---

FIGURE 10.1   Contents of a pre-admission announcement

Pursuant to Rule 2 of the *AIM Rules for Companies*, the company must provide the London Stock Exchange with the following information:

(a) its name;

(b) its country of incorporation;

(c) its registered office address and, if different, its trading address;

(d) the website address at which the information required by Rule 26 will be available;

(e) a brief description of its business (including its main country of operation) and in the case of an investing company, details of its investing strategy; if the admission is being sought as a result of a reverse takeover under Rule 14, this should be stated;

(f) the number and type of securities in respect of which it seeks admission and the number and type of securities to be held as treasury shares, including details of any restrictions as to transfer of the securities;

(g) the capital to be raised on admission, if applicable, and its anticipated market capitalisation on admission;

(h) the percentage of AIM securities not in public hands at admission (insofar as it is aware) and details of any other exchange or trading platform on which the AIM securities (or any other securities of the company) are or will be admitted or traded as a result of an application or agreement of the applicant;

(i) the full names and functions of its directors and proposed directors (underlining the first name by which each is known or including any other name by which each is known);

(j) insofar as is known to it, the full name of any significant shareholder before and after admission, together with the percentage of each such shareholder's interest (underlining the first name by which each is known or including any other name by which each is known in the case of individuals);

(k) the names of any persons who will be disclosed in the admission document as having received fees, securities or any other benefit of a value greater than £10,000;

(l) its anticipated accounting reference date, the date to which it has prepared the main financial information in its admission document and the dates by which it must publish its first three reports as required by Rules 18 and 19 (half yearly reports and annual reports);

(m) its expected admission date;

(n) the name and address of its Nominated Adviser and broker; and

(o) details of where any admission document will be available with a statement that this will contain full details about the company and the admission of its securities.

Source: extract from *AIM Rules for Companies*, February 2007. The full *AIM Rules for Companies* is available at www.londonstockexchange.com

Exchange may delay the proposed date of admission for a further period of ten business days.

10.5   The next deadline set out by the *AIM Rules for Companies* is the submission of the application documents prescribed by Rule 5. This states that at least three business days prior to the proposed date of admission the admission fee must be paid and along with the payment the company must submit its completed application form and an electronic version of the final admission document. These documents are to be accompanied by the completed Nominated Adviser's declaration form. Further detail on the Nominated Adviser's declaration is set out in Chapter 9, *Suitability and preparation for admission.* All forms and the list of applicable fees are published on the website of the London Stock Exchange.

WHEN DOES A COMPANY NEED TO PRODUCE AN AIM ADMISSION DOCUMENT?

10.6   A company that is seeking to have a class of its securities admitted to AIM must as a general rule publish an AIM admission document. The exceptions to this general rule is if the company can benefit from the "fast-track" admission procedure because it is listed on certain overseas exchanges (see Chapter 11, *"Fast-track" admissions*). If a prospectus is required then a prospectus must be published, although this must also include the information required to be published in an AIM admission document.

10.7   If the company has had its securities traded on an AIM Designated Market (being those exchanges or markets set out in Figure 10.2) for at least 18 months

---

FIGURE 10.2   AIM Designated Markets

The AIM Designated Markets are as follows:
- Australian Stock Exchange
- Euronext
- Deutsche Börse
- Johannesburg Stock Exchange
- Nasdaq
- NYSE
- Stockholmsbörsen
- Swiss Exchange
- Toronto Stock Exchange
- United Kingdom Listing Authority Official List

The London Stock Exchange may, at any time, remove a market from its list of AIM Designated Markets where that market no longer satisfies the relevant criteria and add additional markets which do, so the London Stock Exchange's website (www.londonstockexchange.com) should be checked when considering utilising the "fast-track" exemption.

Source: extract from *AIM Designated Markets*

prior to applying to have those securities admitted to AIM then it is not required to publish an AIM admission document unless required to do so by the *Prospectus Rules* (see Chapter 11, *"Fast-track admissions"*). This "fast-track" exemption is designed to encourage overseas listed companies to join AIM by making the process more streamline and cost-effective, although in practice those benefits are not as great as the name suggests. Further information on "fast-track" admission is set out in Chapter 11, *"Fast-track" admissions.*

10.8   For further issues of securities once its securities have been admitted to trading on AIM, an AIM company will not need to publish a further AIM admission document unless: (i) it is seeking to admit a new class of securities, (ii) it is required to issue a prospectus, or (iii) it is undertaking a reverse takeover under the *AIM Rules for Companies*. Further information on reverse takeovers is set out in Chapter 14, *Admission to trading on AIM by reverse takeover.*

WHEN IS A PROSPECTUS REQUIRED?

10.9   Where an application for admission to trading on AIM is made in conjunction with an offer of a company's securities to the public, as defined in section 102B of the *Financial Services and Markets Act 2000* (FSMA), then a prospectus will be required by the FSMA unless it falls within one of the exemptions set out in the FSMA or in the *Prospectus Rules* as published by the Financial Services Authority. The exemptions include an offer made to or directed at qualified investors only and an offer made to or directed at fewer than 100 persons (other than qualified investors) per member state of the European Economic Area (EEA). Qualified investors are legal entities authorised to operate in the financial markets (e.g. investment institutions and banks), national and local governments, as well as natural persons and small and medium-sized enterprises (SMEs) that certify that they meet the required criteria. In addition, a prospectus will not be required if the total consideration of the offer is less than €2.5 million.

10.10   In practice, most companies seeking an AIM admission are likely to seek to fall within one of these exemptions to the requirement to produce a prospectus to avoid both the increased costs of preparing a prospectus and the more onerous responsibility and liability implications that the publication of a prospectus entails. Further information on offers to the public is set out in Chapter 19, *Offers to the public.*

10.11   A prospectus has to be vetted and approved by the Financial Services Authority and will be checked to the same standard and within the same timeframe as those produced for companies whose securities are admitted to the Official List and to trading on the Main Market of the London Stock Exchange. In contrast, an AIM admission document is not vetted and approved by the United Kingdom Listing Authority as this role is effectively delegated to the company's Nominated Adviser. Under the *AIM Rules for Nominated Advisers* the Nominated Adviser is required to oversee and be actively involved in the preparation of the AIM admission document, satisfying itself (in order to be able to give the required Nominated Adviser's declaration) that it has been prepared in compliance with the *AIM Rules for Companies* and with due care.

10.12 In order to meet this requirement the Nominated Adviser should usually carry out the following tasks:

■ The Nominated Adviser should oversee and be actively involved in the drafting of the sections of the AIM admission document that relate to the business of the company and the risk factors and should be satisfied that these take into account matters raised during due diligence.

■ The Nominated Adviser should be satisfied that the financial and additional information sections have been properly prepared and that appropriate verification of the AIM admission document as a whole has taken place (further information on the verification process is set out in Chapter 15, *Directors' responsibilities for an AIM admission document and verification*).

■ The Nominated Adviser should also consider whether any specialist third party reports are required (e.g. for companies in specific sectors such as mining, property or biotechnology).

■ The Nominated Adviser should ultimately be satisfied that the AIM admission document complies with the *AIM Rules for Companies*.

10.13 When a company is a mining or oil and gas company or an investing company, special rules apply to the contents of the AIM admission document, as set out in Chapter 12, *Mining, oil and gas companies* and Chapter 13, *Investing companies* respectively.

CONTENT REQUIREMENTS

10.14 If a prospectus is required in connection with the application for admission of a company's securities to trading on AIM then it will need to contain all the information required by the *Prospectus Rules*. In essence, it must contain all the information required by Annexes I to III of the *Prospectus Regulation*, which are incorporated into and set out in Appendix 3 to the *Prospectus Rules*. In addition, it will need to contain the additional specific disclosure requirements set out in Paragraphs (c) to (k) of Schedule 2 of the *AIM Rules for Companies*. As such, the content requirements for a prospectus are more onerous and detailed than those for an AIM admission document.

10.15 Where there is no requirement for a prospectus the AIM admission document must contain the information set out in specified sections only of Annexes I to III of the *Prospectus Regulation* as well as the other AIM specific requirements set out in Paragraphs (c) to (k) of Schedule 2 of the *AIM Rules for Companies*.

FORMAT

10.16 In practice, an AIM admission document will be a lengthy document and will be divided into various parts. Typically, the format will be as set out in Figure 10.3 or Figure 10.4. Both of the formats are equally acceptable, provided that they meet the disclosure and contents requirements set out in the *AIM Rules for Companies*.

10.17 *Front cover.* This sets out details of certain regulatory matters and the name of the company and gives brief details of its issued and authorised share

---

FIGURE 10.3   AIM admission document – traditional structure

- Key information
- Directors, secretary and advisers
- Definitions
- Part I – Information on the company and its business
- Part II – Risk factors
- Part III – Competent person's/expert's report
- Part IV – Financial information on the company
- Part V – Additional information about the company and its management

---

FIGURE 10.4   AIM admission document – international structure

- Risk factors
- Presentation of information
- Summary
- Part I – Information on the company and its business
- Part II – Financial information on the company
- Part III – Additional information about the company and its management
- Part IV – Competent person's/expert's report
- Definitions

---

capital. In addition, the front cover will also set out to whom the AIM admission document can be distributed within the parameters of the FSMA. This is often restricted to persons falling within article 19 (investment professionals) and article 49 (high net worth companies) of the *Financial Services and Markets Act 2000 (Financial Promotion) Order 2005* so as to avoid the need to produce a prospectus and to fall within an exemption to the financial promotion regime set out in section 21 of the FSMA. Section 21 of the FSMA prohibits financial promotion by unauthorised persons, and breach of this provision constitutes a criminal offence. However, there are various exemptions to this prohibition (including the ones mentioned above) which are often used in AIM admissions.

10.18 *Summary/key information.* This will normally include the following: the expected timetable, a summary of the main terms of the fundraising (if applicable), and details of the company's directors, secretary, registered office and advisers. Often a presentation of information section is also included dealing with how information is presented, and although this practice originates from transactions where there is a US element it is becoming increasingly common where there is no US offering.

10.19 *Part I: Information on the company and business.* This normally covers the following: history of the company, information on the business, its current trading and prospects, intended use of proceeds (if there is a fundraising), key personnel, dividend policy and corporate governance policies. It also normally details the settlement arrangements for the securities.

10.20   *Part II: Risk factors.* This section will prominently set out relevant risk factors that are material to the securities being offered in order for the investors to assess the risk associated with the company, its business and the securities. This will usually cover generic risks (e.g. investment in AIM securities and share price fluctuations) and also more specific business risks (e.g. reliance on key personnel or increased competition). It is best practice to put the company specific risk factors first followed by the more general risk factors. There should be comprehensive coverage of all relevant risk factors and the Nominated Adviser will want to make sure this is the case. Where an "international style" AIM admission document is prepared then the risk factor section is often put in the summary/key information section, although this has no bearing on its contents.

10.21   *Part III: Competent person's report or other expert's report.* Mining or oil and gas companies are required to include a competent person's report in the AIM admission document, as further described in Chapter 12, *Mining, oil and gas companies.* The Nominated Adviser may also require a technical report to be prepared by an appropriately qualified expert for other specialist companies (e.g. shipping companies, scientific research based companies, property companies and start-up companies).

10.22   *Part IV: Financial information on the company.* This will primarily consist of audited historical financial information for the last three financial years (or such shorter period that the company has been in operation). This information will either be in the form of a stand-alone report (which is then reviewed by the reporting accountants, who are required to confirm that it gives a true and fair view) or be a reproduction of the audit accounts for the last three financial periods together with the audit report in respect of each year. The general rule is that for AIM companies incorporated in the EEA the financial information must be prepared in accordance with International Accounting Standards. For non-EEA companies, certain other accounting standards are permitted (e.g. US GAAP). In some circumstances pro forma financial information is included within the AIM admission document. For example, if the admission to trading on AIM also comprises a reverse takeover then the pro forma financial information would show the enlarged group so that the financial consequences of the reverse takeover can be analysed both in terms of its effect on the balance sheet and also the profit and loss account.

10.23   *Part V: Additional information about the company and its management.* This section will set out information on items such as: the share capital of the company; the company's constitution; information on the directors (such as details of their service contracts and their interests in securities and options); any share option schemes; the company's subsidiaries; the number of employees; material contracts; any significant change since the last financial period reported on; and a statement regarding any litigation or governmental proceedings.

GENERAL DUTY OF DISCLOSURE

10.24   In addition to specific disclosures required by the *AIM Rules for Companies*, Schedule 2 to the *AIM Rules for Companies* states that the AIM admission document must also disclose any other information which the company reasonably considers necessary to enable investors to form a full understanding of:

- the assets and liabilities, financial position, profits and losses, and prospects of the company and its securities for which admission to trading on AIM is being sought;
- the rights attaching to those securities; and
- any other matter contained in the AIM admission document.

10.25 This wide general disclosure obligation is designed to ensure that the company makes a full disclosure of all information that would be material to an investor even if it is not technically caught by the specific disclosure requirements. Practically speaking, if the company is in doubt as to whether to disclose an item or not it should consult with its Nominated Adviser and lawyers and if necessary with AIM Regulation. As a general rule it is prudent to disclose where there is uncertainty as to whether to disclose a matter or not. In addition the company and its lawyers and accountants will normally be required to provide the Nominated Adviser with a comfort letter, which broadly states that they are not aware of any matter which is not disclosed in the AIM admission document and which they consider is required to be drawn to the attention of the Nominated Adviser.

SPECIFIC DISCLOSURES

10.26 Even where there is no requirement for a prospectus, the AIM admission document must contain specified parts of the information set out in Annexes I to III of the *Prospectus Rules* (which reproduce the equivalent provisions of the *Prospectus Regulation*) as well as the other AIM specific requirements set out in Paragraphs (c) to (k) of Schedule 2 of the *AIM Rules for Companies*. In practice, the company's lawyers will complete a checklist to assist the company and its directors in checking that each required disclosure item is contained in the final AIM admission document.

10.27 The parts of Annexes I to III of the *Prospectus Regulation* that must be disclosed in the AIM admission document include, among others, the following areas:

- a responsibility statement from the persons responsible for the information in the AIM admission document (see Chapter 15, *Directors' responsibilities for an AIM admission document and verification*);
- details of the company's auditors;
- disclosure of risk factors (see Paragraph 10.20);
- information on the company (including corporate legal information on the company, important events in the development of the company's business and a description of the company's principal historic, current and future investments);
- business overview (including a description of the company's operations, products or services and principal markets);
- organisational structure (description of the company's group, if applicable, and a list of significant subsidiaries);

- property, plant and equipment (description of any environmental issues that may affect the company's utilisation of its tangible fixed assets);
- trend information (details of significant trends in production, sales and inventory, and costs and selling prices and any information on known trends that are reasonably likely to have a material effect on the company's prospects for at least the current financial year);
- board practices (including details of director service contracts and a statement as to whether or not the company complies with applicable corporate governance guidelines);
- employees (including numbers of employees and details of employee share incentive schemes);
- major shareholders (details of those with holdings of 3 per cent or more for UK companies);
- related party transactions (including details of whether the related party transactions were material to the company and whether they were concluded on arm's length terms);
- financial information (including audited historical financial information covering the last three financial years, or such shorter period that the company has been in operation);
- dividend policy;
- legal proceedings;
- details of any significant change in the financial or trading position of the company's group since the end of the previous financial period;
- additional information (including details of the company's share capital and a description of the company's Memorandum and Articles of Association);
- material contracts (a summary of each material contract out of the ordinary course of business that the company or a member of its group has been a party to during the last two years or that was entered into prior to this but which contains a provision which is material);
- third party information and statements by experts (including details of any relevant expert that has a report or statement attributed to it and confirmation that third party information has been accurately reproduced in the AIM admission document);
- information on holdings (information relating to undertakings in which the company holds capital likely to have a significant effect on the company's business);
- key information (reasons for the admission to trading on AIM and fundraising, if applicable);
- information concerning the securities to be admitted (including type and class of the securities, description of rights attached to the securities, e.g. dividend and voting rights);
- selling shareholders (details of selling shareholders and any lock-up arrangements);
- expenses of the issue (details of the total net proceeds and an estimate of the total expenses of the issue); and
- dilution (details of the amount and percentage of immediate dilution resulting from the fundraising, if any).

10.28 In addition to the above sections of Annexes I to III of the *Prospectus Regulation* and the information required by the general duty of disclosure (as detailed in Paragraph 10.24), the AIM admission document must also include the following AIM specific information (as more particularly detailed in Paragraphs (c) to (j) of Schedule 2 of the *AIM Rules for Companies*):

- A statement by the directors that the company has sufficient working capital for its present requirements (i.e. the 12 months following admission to trading on AIM). The directors will prepare a working capital memorandum, which will be reviewed by the company's accountants and then be adopted by the board of directors. The reporting accountants will also prepare a working capital report, which provides assurance to the company's directors and to the Nominated Adviser on the adequacy of working capital.
- If the AIM admission document contains a profit forecast, estimate or projection (which are rarely given) then the AIM admission document must include certain statements in relation to the relevant forecast, estimate or projection having been made after due and careful enquiry and the assumptions on which they are based.
- If Rule 7 of the *AIM Rules for Companies* in relation to lock-ins for new businesses is applicable then the AIM admission document should contain a statement that the company's substantial shareholders, directors and their related parties and all applicable employees have agreed not to dispose of any interests in any securities for a period of 12 months from admission to trading on AIM. Further information on lock-ins is set out in Chapter 17, *Lock-ins for new businesses*.
- Full details of each director, including full name and age, names of all companies and partnerships which the director has been a director or partner of during the last five years, any unspent convictions in relation to indictable offences, details of any bankruptcies or individual voluntary arrangements, details of any insolvencies of the relevant companies and partnerships, details of any public criticisms of the director by relevant authorities and details of any disqualification orders.
- Details of any person who has received fees, securities or other benefits of £10,000 or more. See also Chapter 12, *Mining, oil and gas companies* for mining or oil and gas companies, for which this disclosure is extended.
- Details regarding any director (or member of a director's family) who has a related financial product referenced to the AIM securities. For example, if a director has taken out a spread bet as to the movement of the price of the AIM securities.
- If the company is an investment company, details of its investing strategy must be included, see Chapter 13, *Investing companies*.

ERRORS AND OMISSIONS

10.29 The London Stock Exchange (through AIM Regulation) may under Rules 4 and 28 of the *AIM Rules for Companies* authorise the omission of information from an AIM admission document (when it is not a prospectus) if the company's Nominated Adviser confirms that (i) the information is of minor importance only and not likely to influence assessment of the company's assets and liabilities or financial position or prospects of the company or the company's securities, or (ii) disclosure of that information would be seriously detrimental to the company and its omission would not be likely to mislead investors in relation to the facts necessary to form an informed assessment of the company or the company's securities.

10.30 If between the submission of the AIM admission document and actual admission to trading on AIM there is a material new factor, mistake or inaccuracy relating to the information in the AIM admission document then a supplementary AIM admission document must be submitted containing the full details regarding the new factor, mistake or inaccuracy.

PUBLICATION AND AVAILABILITY OF AN AIM ADMISSION DOCUMENT

10.31 The final AIM admission document is submitted to the London Stock Exchange at least three business days before the expected date of admission to trading on AIM. The AIM admission document must be in English and available publicly (free of charge) for at least one month from the admission of the company's securities to AIM. The company's most recent AIM admission document should also be available on the company's website pursuant to Rule 26 of the *AIM Rules for Companies*. Under Rule 6 of the *AIM Rules for Companies*, admission becomes effective on the publication of a dealing notice by the London Stock Exchange.

10.32 Where there is a fundraising as well as an admission to trading on AIM a draft AIM admission document, often called a "pathfinder" AIM admission document, will be used to gauge the market for the securities on offer. This should contain all the information required by the *AIM Rules for Companies* (and *Prospectus Rules* if applicable), but as the price for the securities will not have been established yet this is left blank. Further information on the marketing of securities is set out in Chapter 20, *Institutional placings*.

IN PRACTICE

For most companies seeking an admission to trading on AIM the more onerous prospectus requirements of the *Prospectus Rules* can be avoided as normally only an AIM admission document is required. Potential investors have the reassurance that the regulatory framework in essence requires disclosure in the AIM admission document of all material information about the company, its business and the securities being offered, so that they are able to make their investment decision fully informed.

CHAPTER 11

"Fast-track" admissions

AT A GLANCE

Under the *AIM Rules for Companies*, a company which already has a quotation or listing on a designated market for the securities it is seeking to admit to AIM can, provided that it satisfies the requirements for admission of securities to trading on AIM, seek admission to AIM by adopting a simplified process. This simplified process involves making a detailed announcement before the securities are admitted to trading on AIM as opposed to producing a full AIM admission document. This can make the process of seeking an admission to trading on AIM quicker and can make it more cost-effective for these companies, although a number of steps such as due diligence and verification will still need to be undertaken.

REQUIREMENTS FOR "FAST-TRACK" ADMISSION TO TRADING ON AIM

Designated markets

11.1   In addition to satisfying the standard requirements for admission to trading on AIM as set out in Chapter 9, *Suitability and preparation for admission*, an applicant whose securities have been listed or quoted on an AIM Designated Market for at least 18 months prior to the admission of those securities to trading on AIM can adopt a simplified, so called "fast-track", procedure when seeking the admission of its securities to trading on AIM. The current AIM Designated Markets are set out in Figure 11.1. Other markets may be added to this list in the future provided that they meet the London Stock Exchange's criteria to be classified as an AIM Designated Market. Similarly, if a market no longer meets the criteria then it can be removed from the list. An up-to-date list of the AIM Designated Markets can be found on the London Stock Exchange's website.

Pre-admission announcement – Schedule 1 information

11.2   As with all applicants, an applicant whose securities are already quoted or listed on an AIM Designated Market must provide the London Stock Exchange with the information set out in Schedule 1 to the *AIM Rules for Companies* at least 20 days prior to the expected admission to trading on AIM date. The information

---

FIGURE 11.1 AIM Designated Markets

The AIM Designated Markets are as follows:

- Australian Stock Exchange
- Euronext
- Deutsche Börse
- Johannesburg Stock Exchange
- Nasdaq
- NYSE
- Stockholmsbörsen
- Swiss Exchange
- Toronto Stock Exchange
- United Kingdom Listing Authority Official List

The London Stock Exchange may, at any time, remove a market from its list of AIM Designated Markets where that market no longer satisfies the relevant criteria and add additional markets which do, so the London Stock Exchange's website (www.londonstockexchange.com) should be checked when considering utilising the "fast-track" exemption.

Source: extract from *AIM Designated Markets*

that is required is set out in Figure 10.1, *Contents of a pre-admission announcement*, and is principally about the company and its country of incorporation and a description of its business and the securities to be admitted. Importantly, however, an applicant whose securities are already quoted or listed on an AIM Designated Market must, insofar as is known to it, supply the London Stock Exchange with the name of any person or persons who are interested, directly or indirectly, in 3 per cent or more of its securities, together with the percentage of each such person's interest. This may be difficult in practice where the AIM Designated Market only requires disclosure of holdings above a higher percentage (e.g. 10 per cent).

11.3   In addition, if there are any changes to the information in the announcement before the securities are admitted to trading, the applicant must notify the London Stock Exchange immediately and the London Stock Exchange may delay the date of admission to trading on AIM.

Pre-admission announcement – Supplement to Schedule 1

11.4   An applicant whose securities are already quoted or listed on an AIM Designated Market must also provide the London Stock Exchange with the information which is taken from the supplement to Schedule 1 to the *AIM Rules for Companies*. This information is to be provided at least 20 days prior to the expected date of admission to trading on AIM, and where the information is not in English it must be translated. The information which must be provided to the London Stock Exchange under the supplement to Schedule 1 is:

- the name of the AIM Designated Market upon which its securities have been traded and the date from which they have been so traded;

- confirmation, following due and careful enquiry, that it has adhered to any legal and regulatory requirements involved in having its securities traded or listed upon such market or details of any breach;
- a website address where any documents or announcements which have been made public over the last two years (in consequence of having its securities so traded or listed) are available;
- a description of any significant change in the financial or trading position of the applicant which has occurred since the end of the last financial period for which audited statements have been published;
- a statement that its directors have no reason to believe that its working capital will be insufficient for at least 12 months from the date of its admission to trading on AIM (see Paragraph 11.8);
- details of any lock-in arrangements pursuant to Rule 7 of the *AIM Rules for Companies* where the applicant's main activity is a business which has not been independent and earning revenue for at least two years (see Chapter 17, *Lock-ins for new businesses*);
- a brief description of the arrangements for settling transactions in its securities (further information on settlement is set out in Chapter 16, *CREST, settlement and depository interests*);
- a website address detailing the rights attaching to its securities;
- the information equivalent to that required from an AIM admission document which is not currently public; and
- a website address of a page containing its latest published annual report and accounts, which must have a financial year end not more than nine months prior to admission to trading on AIM. These accounts must comply with Rule 19 of the *AIM Rules for Companies*, which sets out the standards that are acceptable for reporting such financial information and the requirement as to disclosure of related party transactions. Further information is set out in Chapter 27, *Financial reporting*. Where more than nine months have elapsed since the financial year to which the latest published annual report and accounts relate, there needs to be a reference to a website address of a page containing a set of interim results for at least six months from the date of the last published annual report and accounts. The website requirements for applicants using the AIM Designated Market route are in addition to those under Rule 26 of the *AIM Rules for Companies*, which are summarised in Chapter 29, *Website disclosure*.

11.5 Where an applicant holds securities as treasury shares, then the number of these needs to be disclosed.

11.6 For an investing company, details of its investing strategy also need to be included. As to investing companies generally, see Chapter 13, *Investing companies*.

11.7 The requirement that all information to be disclosed equivalent to that required for an AIM admission document which is not public means, in practice, that a full review of the public information is required to see if the relevant information has previously been disclosed. Where it has not, the relevant information is included in the pre-admission announcement.

Working capital

11.8 It is important to note that the disclosure regarding working capital is different for applicants using the AIM Designated Market route and those which are not. The two requirements are set out in Figure 11.2.

11.9 AIM Regulation, in its guidance, has clarified that these two measures of working capital are intentionally different, the statement for applicants using the AIM Designated Market route being a lower threshold. In practice, a Nominated Adviser may well require the production of a working capital forecast and require this to be reviewed by the reporting accountants, who will be required to report their findings to the Nominated Adviser and the company. However, depending on the applicant's particular circumstances the Nominated Adviser may relax its requirements as the test for companies using the AIM Designated Market rate is less onerous than for other admissions.

FIGURE 11.2 Working capital disclosure for AIM admissions

AIM Rules for Companies working capital statement

A statement by the company's directors that in their opinion, having made due and careful enquiry, the working capital available to it and its group will be sufficient for its present requirements, that is for at least 12 months from the date of admission of its securities.

AIM Designated Markets working capital statement

A statement that its directors have no reason to believe that the working capital available to it or its group will be insufficient for at least 12 months from the date of its admission to trading on AIM.

Three-day documents

11.10 At least three business days before the expected date of admission of its securities to trading on AIM, the applicant whose securities are already quoted on an AIM Designated Market must submit an AIM application form, the AIM fee and the Nominated Adviser's declaration in the usual way. An additional requirement for companies whose securities are already traded on an AIM Designated Market is that they must also provide the London Stock Exchange with an electronic copy of its latest published annual report and accounts.

Nominated Adviser's declaration

11.11 The Nominated Adviser owes a responsibility to the London Stock Exchange. For an applicant whose securities are quoted on an AIM Designated Market the Nominated Adviser must specifically confirm in its Nominated Adviser's declaration that, to the best of its knowledge and belief, having made due and careful enquiry and considering all relevant matters under the *AIM Rules for Companies* and the *AIM Rules for Nominated Advisers*:

■ the directors of the applicant have received satisfactory advice and guidance as to the nature of their obligations to ensure compliance by the applicant with the AIM Rules;

■ in its opinion it is satisfied that the applicant and its securities are appropriate to be admitted to AIM and that the requirements of Schedule 1 and its supplement have been complied with.

11.12 Typically, the first limb of this test will be satisfied by the provision of a board memoranda by the company's solicitors who will confirm that they have given such advice as part of the *AIM Rules for Companies* Rule 39 Letter.

11.13 In addition, under the second limb of the test the Nominated Adviser is still responsible for confirming the suitablilty of the applicant and this often requires a detailed due diligence exercise to be performed. The due diligence exercise will take some time, which also needs to be factored in when considering utilising the "fast-track" admission procedure.

Fundraisings

11.14 Where it is proposed to carry out a fundraising at the same time as applying for admission to trading on AIM under the "fast-track" admission procedure then this is usually conducted by way of an institutional placing (see Chapter 20, *Institutional placings*). The benefit of applying for an admission to trading on AIM by way of the "fast-track" admission procedure is neutralised where there is an offer to the public (as opposed to an institutional placing), as the prospectus that the company would be required to prepare would contain most, if not all, disclosures required in a full AIM admission document. In addition, as a prospectus is subject to pre-vetting by the United Kingdom Listing Authority, the "fast-track" admission timetable will need to be lengthened to allow time for the United Kingdom Listing Authority's review procedure.

11.15 Where there is no fundraising at the time of admission to trading on AIM, it is not unusual for companies that apply for admission to trading on AIM by way of the "fast-track" admission to trading on AIM procedure to then raise further funds by way of a secondary issue in the same way as any other AIM company. Secondary issues are dealt with in Chapter 22, *Secondary issues*.

IN PRACTICE

In practice, the "fast-track" route to admission to trading on AIM will only be beneficial to an applicant whose securities are quoted on an AIM Designated Market which is not required to issue a prospectus in the United Kingdom (e.g. where there is not a UK public offering).

Although the "fast-track" admission procedure is designed to simplify the admission to trading on AIM procedure and make it more cost-effective, Nominated Advisers will still expect to undertake due diligence on the applicant in view of the declaration that they are required to give the London Stock Exchange that they consider the applicant to be suitable for AIM. This may lengthen the timetable for admission to trading on AIM as well as add to the cost.

Applicants should note that there is a slightly different requirement in respect of the working capital statement for a company whose securities are listed on an AIM Designated Market. The London Stock Exchange has confirmed that the difference in the wording is intentional and that this is a different (lower) standard for companies applying under the "fast-track" admission to trading on AIM procedure. However, in practice, it is likely that the Nominated Adviser will require a working capital exercise to be undertaken.

Finally, whilst the simplified admission to trading on AIM procedure is intended to make it more cost-effective to join AIM, there will still be a certain amount of fees incurred in checking that all the information that would be required to be disclosed in an AIM admission document has been already made public. In addition, it may be that Nominated Advisers and brokers may still advise potential applicants to produce an AIM admission document, for example as a marketing tool for future fundraisings in the UK.

CHAPTER 12

Mining, oil and gas companies

AT A GLANCE

In 2006 the London Stock Exchange introduced specific guidelines relating to mining and oil and gas companies which set out the minimum expectations of the London Stock Exchange for companies in the mining and oil and gas sectors which are seeking admission to trading on AIM. These guidelines place additional obligations on such companies in respect of competent person's reports, the description of their business and other disclosures in the AIM admission document and in respect of the due diligence review of their assets.

INTRODUCTION

12.1 In March 2006 the London Stock Exchange issued guidance to mining and oil and gas companies which are seeking admission to trading on AIM. These guidelines apply to mining and oil and gas companies including exploration, prospecting and production companies but not to consultancy companies or companies providing advice or similar services to such companies.

12.2 The guidance was introduced as a positive step by AIM to try to address any perception that some mining and oil and gas companies on AIM were too speculative.

12.3 The guidance sets out the minimum expectations of the London Stock Exchange in relation to companies in the mining and oil and gas sectors and both applicants and Nominated Advisers should note them when applying the *AIM Rules for Companies*. However, where application for admission to trading on AIM is sought in conjunction with a prospectus the *Prospectus Rules* and Committee of European Securities Regulators' guidelines (CESR guidelines) will take precedence over the AIM guidance.

12.4 Whilst the guidance is expressed to represent the minimum expectations of the London Stock Exchange, the London Stock Exchange expects the guidance to be followed where applicable. If it is felt by a company or its Nominated Adviser that the guidance is not applicable or appropriate to a particular company then the Nominated Adviser should consult with AIM Regulation, but an applicant should not simply disregard the guidance.

12.5 In relation to an application for admission to trading of securities on AIM, the key additional disclosures which will be required to be made by mining and oil and gas companies fall within the following categories:

- competent person's reports;
- AIM admission document disclosures; and
- material assets of the applicant.

COMPETENT PERSON'S REPORT

12.6 Mining and oil and gas companies seeking admission to trading on AIM should prepare and include in the AIM admission document a competent person's report on all material assets, licences, joint ventures or other arrangements owned by such company or proposed to be exploited or utilised by it (collectively its "assets"). In addition, the competent person's report should report on all liabilities, royalty payments, contractual agreements and minimum funding requirements relating to the company, its work programme or its assets (collectively its "liabilities").

12.7 Under the guidance, it is the Nominated Adviser's responsibility to ensure that the scope of the competent person's report is appropriate, given the nature of the assets and liabilities of the applicant.

12.8 The competent person's report should be prepared no more than six months prior to the date of the AIM admission document and should be addressed to the applicant and its Nominated Adviser. The report should either be dated the date of the AIM admission document or, whenever the report is dated prior to the date of the AIM admission document, a no material change statement should be included in the competent person's report up to the date of the AIM admission document. However, in practice, a competent person will often seek to limit the no material change statement to the information known to it or disclosed to it by the applicant. Where a competent person's report has been prepared on the assets and liabilities of the applicant within 12 months prior to the date of the AIM admission document, an explanation as to why the first-dated competent person's report was not used and its conclusions should be stated in the AIM admission document.

12.9 The competent person's report should include a summary table of assets, as set out in Appendix 1 to the *AIM Rules for Companies* (as reproduced in Figure 12.1) and a summary of reserves and resources by status, as set out in Appendix 3 to the *AIM Rules for Companies* (as reproduced in Figure 12.2), and the competent person's report should, at a minimum, cover the information set out in Appendix 2 to the *AIM Rules for Companies* (as reproduced in Figure 12.3).

12.10 In practice, it is important that the competent person includes an estimate of net present value (post-tax) at the discount rate of 10 per cent of reserves, which may take some time for the competent person to prepare. In addition, any future statements of reserves and resources should use the terms used in the glossary and definitions section of any competent person's report included in an AIM admission document and so these should be checked carefully.

12.11 The guidance also sets out the minimum requirements that a competent person should meet in order for it to be a proper person to prepare a competent

---

| **FIGURE 12.1** | Summary table of assets for mining and oil and gas companies |

Minerals and Ore

Asset[1]	Holder	Interest	Status[2]	Licence expiry date	Licence area	Comments
1. Asset A	Holder's name	50%	Exploration	16 March 2006	km²	Commencement of sampling in x months
2. Asset B	Holder's name	100%	Development	16 March 2006	km²	Drill hole and sample grades obtained to date
3. Asset C	Holder's name	30%	Production	16 March 2006	km²	Annual current production (tonnes per annum)

(1) Asset – Country and asset/project name
(2) Exploration, Development or Production only

Oil and Gas

Asset[1]	Operator	Interest	Status[2]	Licence expiry date	Licence area	Comments
1. Asset A	Operator's name	50%	Exploration	16 March 2006	km²	Commencement of exploration in x months
2. Asset B	Operator's name	100%	Development	16 March 2006	km²	Development drilling programme to commence in y months
3. Asset C	Operator's name	30%	Production	16 March 2006	km²	Current production (barrels or cubic feet per day) and estimated peak production

(1) Asset – Country, licence and block
(2) Status – Exploration, Development or Production only

Source: extract from *Guidance Note for Mining, Oil and Gas Companies*, March 2006

person's report for inclusion in an AIM admission document. These minimum requirements include having the appropriate qualifications, experience and technical knowledge to professionally and independently appraise the applicant's assets and liabilities being reported. In addition, the competent person must be independent of the applicant and its directors, senior management and advisers, must be remunerated in a way that is not linked to admission to trading on AIM or the value of the applicant, should be professionally qualified, have at least five years relevant experience and not be a sole practitioner.

12.12   Again, the London Stock Exchange has delegated responsibility for the appropriateness of the competent person preparing the competent person's report to the Nominated Adviser, and the Nominated Adviser must also subject the competent person's work to an internal review.

| FIGURE 12.2 | Summary of reserves and resources for mining and oil and gas companies |

Minerals and Ore

Category	Gross			Net attributable			Operator
	Tonnes (millions)	Grade (g/t)	Contained metal	Tonnes (millions)	Grade (g/t)	Contained metal	
Ore/Mineral reserve per asset							
Proved							
Probable							
Sub-total							
Mineral resources per asset							
Measured							
Indicated							
Inferred							
Sub-total							
Total							

Source: [name of person providing the above estimates regarded as competent]

Note: "Operator" is name of the company that operates the asset
"Gross" are 100% of the reserves and/or resources attributable to the licence whilst "Net attributable" are those attributable to the AIM company
Metal equivalent grades are not acceptable and should not be used in reporting

Oil and Gas – Reserves

(all figures in bbls or scf)	Gross			Net attributable			Operator
	Proved	Proved & probable	Proved, probable & possible	Proved	Proved & probable	Proved, probable & possible	
Oil & Liquids reserves per asset							
From production to planned for development							
Total for Oil & Liquids							
Gas reserves per asset							
From production to planned for development							
Total for Gas							

Source: [name of competent person providing the above estimates]

Note: "Operator" is name of the company that operates the asset
"Gross" are 100% of the reserves and/or resources attributable to the licence whilst "Net attributable" are those attributable to the AIM company

bbls – barrels
scf – standard cubic feet

Oil and Gas – Contingent Resources

(all figures in bbls or scf)	Gross			Net attributable			Risk factor	Operator
	Low estimate	Best estimate	High estimate	Low estimate	Best estimate	High estimate		
Oil & Liquids Contingent Resources per asset								
From development pending to development not viable								
Total for Oil & Liquids								
Gas Contingent Resources per asset								
From development pending to development not viable								
Total for Gas								

Source: [name of competent person providing the above estimates]

Note: "Risk Factor" for Contingent Resources means the estimated chance, or probability, that the volumes will be commercially extracted

"Operator" is name of the company that operates the asset

"Gross" are 100% of the reserves and/or resources attributable to the licence whilst "Net attributable" are those attributable to the AIM company

bbls – barrels
scf – standard cubic feet

Oil and Gas – Prospective Resources

(all figures in bbls or scf)	Gross			Net attributable			Risk factor	Operator
	Low estimate	Best estimate	High estimate	Low estimate	Best estimate	High estimate		
Oil & Liquids Prospective Resources per asset								
From prospect to play								
Total for Oil & Liquids								
Gas Prospective Resources per asset								
From prospect to play								
Total for Gas								

Source: [name of competent person providing the above estimates]

Note: "Risk Factor" for Prospective Resources, means the chance or probability of discovering hydrocarbons in sufficient quantity for them to be tested to the surface. This, then, is the chance or probability of the Prospective Resource maturing into a Contingent Resource

"Operator" is name of the company that operates the asset

"Gross" are 100% of the reserves and/or resources attributable to the licence whilst "Net attributable" are those attributable to the AIM company

bbls – barrels
scf – standard cubic feet

Source: extract from *Guidance Note for Mining, Oil and Gas Companies*, March 2006

12.13 This again highlights the importance of selecting a Nominated Adviser that has expertise in the sector in which the applicant operates and of the company consulting with its Nominated Adviser at an early stage.

12.14 Finally, the work of the competent person should be produced to a standard. AIM Regulation recognises the standards set out in Figure 12.4, although

---

FIGURE 12.3   Content of competent person's report (CPR)

The CPR should cover (as a minimum) the following:

Executive summary
Table of contents
Introduction

- explanation of the sources of all information on which the CPR is based (for example any site visits (including details of who undertook such visit and when), drilling results, seismic data, reservoir or well data, sample analysis, interviews with directors, details of desktop research)
- description of reserves and/or resources, where applicable detailing characteristics, type, dimensions and grade distribution, and the methods to be employed for their exploration and extraction (including Appendix 1 disclosure)

Overview of the region, location and assets

- description of the applicant's assets and liabilities, the rights in relation to them and a description of the economic conditions for the working of those licences, concessions or similar including any environmental, land access, planning and obligatory closure costs
- details of any interest (current or past) any director, CP or promoter has in any of the assets
- appropriate maps, some background on the country and location plans demonstrating the major properties comprising the assets, their workings and geographical characteristics and wells, platforms, pipelines, bore holes, sample pits, trenches and similar, to the extent they exist

Reserves and resources (separately disclosed)

- statement of reserves (if any), and where applicable resources including an estimate of volume, tonnage and grades, (in accordance with a Standard, which should be consistently applied and disclosed in line with the tables in Appendix 3), method of estimation, expected recovery and dilution factor, expected extraction and processing tonnage or volume, as appropriate, depending on whether the reserves and/or resources are of minerals or oil and/or gas. Where there are resources that have not been sufficiently appraised in order to provide the previous information, a separate statement of such resources together with any other quantified information which has been appraised in accordance with a Standard
- estimate of net present value (post tax) at a discount rate of 10% of reserves (or equivalent depending on Standard used) analysed separately and the principal assumptions (including cost assumptions, effective date, constant and or forecast prices, forex rates) on which valuation is based together with a sensitivities analysis. Additional valuations may be included within the CPR and should include an explanation of the basis of such a valuation and the method used

Other assets

- any other assets material to the applicant.
- commentary on the plant and equipment which are or will be significant to the applicant's operations, bearing in mind any forecasted rates of extraction included within the admission document

Conclusions

Qualifications and basis of opinion

- full details and qualifications of the CP (company and individual(s)) and a statement of the CP's independence

Appendices – Glossary and definitions of any terms used

Source: extract from *Guidance Note for Mining, Oil and Gas Companies*, March 2006

FIGURE 12.4	Reporting standards for competent person's report

The standard to which a competent person's report should be prepared is an internationally recognised standard that is acceptable under the following codes and/or organisations:	
For mineral resources and reserves	Canadian Institute of Mining, Metallurgy and Petroleum (CIM) Institute of Materials, Minerals and Mining (IMMM) *The Australian Code for Reporting of Exploration Results, Mineral Reserves and Ore Reserves* as published by the Joint Ore Reserves Committee of the Australian Institute of Mining and Metallurgy, Australian Institute of Geoscientists and Mineral Councils of Australia (JORC) Gosstandart of Russia (GOST), the *National Russian Standard on Mining and Minerals* published by the National Certification Body of the Russian Federation *The South African Code for Reporting of Mineral Resources and Mineral Reserves*, as published by the South African Mineral Committee under the auspices of the South African Institute of Mining and Metallurgy (SAMREC) The Society for Mining, Metallurgy and Exploration (SME)
Oil and gas resources and reserves	Canadian Institute on Mining, Metallurgy and Petroleum (CIM) The Society for Petroleum Engineers (SPE)

submissions can be made to AIM Regulation to consider other codes that may be comparable. However, the code to be used needs to be considered in conjunction with the Nominated Adviser as its view of the acceptability of the code as its view of how potential investors will view reserves and resources reported under alternative codes will be important factors.

AIM ADMISSION DOCUMENT DISCLOSURE

12.15 The "front end" of the AIM admission document typically includes the descriptive sections about the applicant, usually near the beginning of the AIM admission document, under the "Key information" or "Summary"section and/or "Part I". Any information included in these sections which is extracted from the competent person's report must not detract from the full information in the competent person's report so as not to be misleading and must provide a "balanced view of all the information contained within the rest of the AIM admission document". As part of its responsibility and engagement, the competent person should be engaged to review the AIM admission document and confirm in writing to the applicant and the Nominated Adviser that the information relating to the competent person's report is accurate, balanced, complete and not inconsistent with the competent person's report. As a practical matter, this is often addressed in the competent person's engagement letter, which should be reviewed by the company, its lawyers and also the Nominated Adviser. These obligations can either then be included in the competent person's engagement letter, by way of direct reference to the specific paragraphs of the AIM guidance, or can simply state that the competent person's report is to be prepared in accordance with the AIM guidance. Where the latter approach is adopted, the draft competent person's report needs to be monitored to ensure compliance with the provisions of the guidance.

12.16 In addition, as part of the AIM admission document disclosures, risk factors that apply to mining or oil and gas companies in general, or are sector specific, should be set out after any risk factors that are specific to the applicant.

12.17 The provisions of Rule 7 of the *AIM Rules for Companies* (lock-ins for new businesses) apply equally to mining and oil and gas companies. This means that exploration and development companies who have not been independent and earning revenue for the two years prior to the date of admission to trading on AIM have to comply with the relevant lock-in requirements for the 12 months following admission to trading on AIM. This will require the company to procure lock-ins from directors, certain employees and certain shareholders and these should be summarised in the AIM admission document.

12.18 The provisions of Schedule 2 to the *AIM Rules for Companies* (Paragraph (h)), relating to the disclosure in the AIM admission document of payments of £10,000 or more made by or on behalf of the applicant, are extended for mining and oil and gas companies to cover any payments to any government or regulatory authorities or similar bodies regarding the acquisition or maintenance of the assets of the mining or oil and gas company. In practice, it can take some time to collate this information.

12.19 In addition, the requirement to disclose material contracts in an AIM admission document is extended in the case of mining and oil and gas companies to include disclosure of all material subsisting agreements relating to the assets, irrespective of the date they were entered into or whether or not they were entered into in the ordinary course.

ASSETS

12.20 In addition to the contents of the competent person's report and AIM admission document disclosure requirements, the guidance places additional obligations on the Nominated Adviser to check the assets which the applicant owns. Accordingly, the guidance includes a list of due diligence steps to be undertaken but which most Nominated Advisers active in the sector would already have required as part of the flotation process. The guidance specifically requires that, where assets are held overseas, in addition to the standard due diligence report on the company's business and assets, a legal title opinion should be sought from reputable overseas counsel, whose details should be included in the adviser section of the AIM admission document. In addition, site visits by the Nominated Adviser are expected and strongly recommended as part of its consideration of the suitability of the applicant for admission to trading on AIM. As these costs will be unavoidable for an applicant active in these sectors, the applicant should budget for these costs which will be over and above the usual costs of the application process for applicants active in other sectors.

IN PRACTICE

The AIM guidance for mining and oil and gas companies represented a positive step by AIM to address any perception that some resource companies on AIM are too speculative.

The reality is that the guidance reflected the best practice in the market and most Nominated Advisers who are active in this sector already required similar reports and materials from their client companies. Accordingly, the guidance did not place a significant additional burden on, or increase the costs for, AIM companies and those applying for admission to trading on AIM operating in these sectors. However, companies which operate in these sectors should budget for increased costs (compared with companies active in other sectors) in preparing the competent person's report, the Nominated Adviser reviewing the competent person's report and the site visits undertaken by the Nominated Adviser. In addition, further management time will be involved in reviewing the scope and co-operating with the competent person and collating the information to satisfy the additional disclosure requirements.

Investing companies

An AIM company which, in the opinion of the London Stock Exchange, has a primary business of investing its funds in the securities of other companies or the acquisition of a particular business is designated an investing company. Special rules apply to such companies, both on application to admission of its securities to trading on AIM and on an ongoing basis.

APPLICATIONS FOR ADMISSION TO TRADING ON AIM BY INVESTING COMPANIES

Minimum fundraising

13.1 Where an applicant is a company which, in the opinion of the London Stock Exchange, has as a primary business of the investing of funds in the securities of other companies or the acquisition of a particular business it is treated as an investing company. It is a condition of the admission to trading on AIM of an investing company that it raises a minimum of £3 million in cash via an equity fundraising, on or immediately before its admission to trading on AIM (Rule 8 of the *AIM Rules for Companies*). This condition is in addition to complying with the usual requirements for an application for admission to trading on AIM (see Chapter 9, *Suitability and preparation for admission*).

AIM admission document

13.2 An investing company must include in its AIM admission document details of its investing strategy, which must, at a minimum, include the following information:

- the precise business sector(s), geographical area(s) and type of company in which it can invest;
- how long it can take before making an investment or having to return funds to shareholders;
- whether it will be an active or passive investor;
- how widely it will spread its investments; and
- what expertise its directors have in respect of evaluating its proposed

investments and how and by whom any due diligence on those investments will be effected.

"FAST-TRACK" ADMISSIONS

13.3 An investing company can still apply for admission to trading on AIM by way of the "fast-track" admission procedure provided that it raises the minimum £3 million in cash via an equity fundraising on or immediately before its admission and includes in its announcement details of its investing strategy, including the information set out in Paragraph 13.2.

SUBSEQUENT CHANGES IN STRATEGY/REVERSE TAKEOVERS

13.4 Investing companies should also note that if, following their admission to trading on AIM, they change their investment strategy then this is classified as a reverse takeover and any such change in investment strategy will be subject to shareholder approval and the other requirements of reverse takeover transactions set out in Chapter 14, *Admission to trading on AIM by reverse takeover*.

IN PRACTICE

The concept of an investing company was incorporated within the *AIM Rules for Companies* to address the perceived issue of many cash shells being listed on AIM without adequate resources. As a result, there is the minimum cash fundraising requirement and investing companies need to be specific as to what they are going to invest in, which cannot be changed without shareholder approval.

CHAPTER 14

Admission to trading on AIM by reverse takeover

The *AIM Rules for Companies* contain specific provisions dealing with acquisitions which, in view of their size, constitute reverse takeovers. This is usually the case where the purchaser (an AIM company) is smaller than the target when measured against certain prescribed indicators.

Prior to the completion of a reverse takeover, the AIM company is obliged to obtain shareholder approval. Trading in the securities of the AIM company on AIM will be cancelled on completion of a reverse takeover and the AIM company will need to re-apply for admission of its enlarged share capital to trading on AIM, as if it were a new applicant.

If the AIM company is a company to which the *City Code on Takeovers and Mergers* applies, and the consideration payable by the AIM company includes securities in the AIM company, the acquisition may require the target shareholders (who will be deemed to be acting in concert with each other) to make an offer for all the securities in the AIM company, unless an approval is sought from and granted by the Takeover Panel. In these cases, whether or not such an approval is granted, the way in which the board of directors should conduct itself will be governed by the *City Code on Takeovers and Mergers* as well as the *AIM Rules for Companies*.

WHEN IS AN ACQUISITION A REVERSE TAKEOVER?

14.1 Rule 14 of the *AIM Rules for Companies* defines a reverse takeover as an acquisition or related acquisitions in a 12-month period which for an AIM company would:

- exceed 100 per cent in any of the class tests; or
- result in a fundamental change in its business, board of directors or voting control.

In addition, any disposal by an AIM company, which, when aggregated with any other disposal or disposals over the previous 12 months, exceeds 75 per cent in any of the class tests, is deemed to be a disposal resulting in a fundamental change of business and is treated as a reverse takeover. Furthermore, in the case of an investing company, a substantial departure from its investing strategy is also treated as a reverse takeover.

14.2   Transactions completed during the 12 months prior to the date of the latest transaction should be aggregated with the latest transaction to determine whether the transaction is a reverse takeover for the purposes of Rule 14 of the *AIM Rules for Companies* where:

- they are entered into by the AIM company with the same person or persons or their families; or
- they involve the acquisition or disposal of securities or an interest in one particular business; or
- together they lead to a principal involvement in any business activity or activities which did not previously form a part of the AIM company's principal activities.

14.3   With respect to the first aggregation test referred to in Paragraph 14.2 above (whether they are entered into with the same person), it should be noted that the definition of "person" in the *AIM Rules for Companies* includes an individual, a corporation, partnership, association, trust or other entity as the context admits or requires. The definition of "family" in the *AIM Rules for Companies* includes in addition to certain family members, any trust of which the family members in question are trustees or beneficiaries and any company over which they have control of more than 20 per cent of its equity or voting rights in a general meeting.

14.4   With respect to the third aggregation test referred to in Paragraph 14.2 (a new principal business activity), the London Stock Exchange will only consider the test to be satisfied where, collectively, a class test for such business activity or activities in any 12-month period exceeds 100 per cent. While this aggregation test is more likely to apply to investing companies, it is not limited to investing companies and can also apply to operating companies.

14.5   The class tests which are used to determine whether a transaction constitutes a reverse takeover are set out in Schedule 3 to the *AIM Rules for Companies*. They involve a comparison of the target and the AIM company with respect to gross assets, profits, turnover or gross capital and a comparison of the consideration payable for the target and the market value of the securities to be issued in consideration relative to the market capitalisation of the AIM company. The class tests are set out in Figure 14.1. Definitions of the relevant terms and the sources for the relevant figures to be used in the comparisons are also set out in Schedule 3 to the *AIM Rules for Companies*.

14.6   If any of the class tests are inappropriate to the sphere of activity of the AIM company, or produce anomalous results, the London Stock Exchange may, at its discretion, disregard one or more of the class tests. Alternatively, in such cases the London Stock Exchange can substitute another test based on other relevant indicators of size, including industry specific tests, provided that the transaction is not with a related party.

APPLICATION OF THE *CITY CODE ON TAKEOVERS AND MERGERS*

14.7   In order to determine whether it has jurisdiction, the Takeover Panel usually imposes a dual test, requiring both the place of incorporation of the AIM company

FIGURE 14.1	Class tests
Gross assets test	$\dfrac{\text{Gross assets the subject of the transaction}}{\text{Gross assets of the AIM company}} \times 100$
Profits test	$\dfrac{\text{Profits attributable to the assets the subject of the transaction}}{\text{Profits of the AIM company}} \times 100$
Turnover test	$\dfrac{\text{Turnover attributable to the assets the subject of the transaction}}{\text{Turnover of the AIM company}} \times 100$
Consideration test	$\dfrac{\text{Consideration}}{\text{Aggregate market value of all the ordinary securities (excluding treasury shares) of the AIM company}} \times 100$
Gross capital test	$\dfrac{\text{Gross capital of the company or business being acquired}}{\text{Gross capital of the AIM company}} \times 100$

and the place of central management of the AIM company to be in the United Kingdom, the Channel Islands or the Isle of Man. The Takeover Panel has indicated that its discretion to depart from this dual test will rarely be exercised, so where the dual test is not met the *City Code on Takeovers and Mergers* will generally not apply to a particular company, even where there is a close connection with the United Kingdom.

14.8   If, following the application of the dual test, the *City Code on Takeovers and Mergers* is unlikely to apply to an AIM company, the Nominated Adviser will often require the company to include takeover type protections in its Articles of Association. This is to give the company's shareholders similar protections to those which would be afforded to them if the *City Code on Takeovers and Mergers* applied. However, where takeover type provisions are included in Articles of Association, they tend to be more flexible. For example, shareholders can bypass them by passing a resolution either to disapply the provisions of the Articles of Association in a particular case or to amend the Articles of Association. Both of these shareholder resolutions would typically require the resolution to be passed by 75 per cent of those shareholders attending and voting, depending on the company's country of incorporation. The company and its advisers will also need to consider whether such provisions will be binding and how they will work in practice if its securities are traded by depository interests.

NEGOTIATING A REVERSE TAKEOVER

14.9   In order to effect a reverse takeover the parties will enter into a share purchase agreement. Rule 14 of the *AIM Rules for Companies* requires the share purchase agreement to be conditional on the consent of the AIM company's shareholders (to be given in a general meeting). Such approval is sought by way of a simple majority vote (i.e. more than 50 per cent of those attending and voting being in favour of the transaction).

14.10   In addition to shareholder approval, a reverse takeover is also typically conditional on admission of the securities of the enlarged entity to trading on AIM. This is to avoid the position where the reverse takeover is completed but the enlarged entity's securities are not admitted to AIM as this would constitute a breach of the *AIM Rules for Companies*. If following the transaction it is planned that the AIM company cancels its admission to trading on AIM then specific shareholder approval should be sought for this (see Chapter 49, *Cancellation of trading on AIM*).

14.11 Reverse takeovers will often involve the issue of consideration securities in the AIM company to the target's shareholders. In such cases, negotiations will often centre on whether both the target and the AIM company should give warranties and to what extent. Another area for negotiation will be any limitation on the liability of any party giving warranties (in time and/or amount). As the AIM company will not be able to simultaneously sign the agreement and complete the acquisition (given it is required to seek shareholder approval), negotiations will also determine the passing of risk for changes to the business and its assets in the period between signing and completion. The views of the Nominated Adviser, which will be looking to protect the current investors in the AIM company, will also need to be considered.

14.12 Where the *City Code on Takeovers and Mergers* applies, care needs to be taken when negotiating any break or abort fees payable to the AIM company. Generally speaking, the payment of no more than 1 per cent of the value of the target calculated by reference to the offer price is usually acceptable. The parameters that need to be observed with respect to break or abort fees are set out in Rule 21 of the *City Code on Takeovers and Mergers*.

INSIDER DEALING AND ANNOUNCEMENTS

14.13 During the negotiations, any persons having knowledge of the proposed transaction would be an insider for the purposes of the insider dealing rules under the *Criminal Justice Act 1993* and also for market abuse under section 118 of the *Financial Services and Markets Act 2000*. Any prospective placees who are proposing to acquire securities in the AIM company by way of a private placing at the time of or as part of the acquisition would also be insiders and restricted from dealing. In this example, the inside information could relate to any or all of the knowledge that there is to be an acquisition, or that part of the placing proceeds are required in order to fund it.

14.14 Although inside information should usually be released to the market as soon as possible, the guidance to Rule 11 of the *AIM Rules for Companies* provides that an AIM company need not publicise information about impending developments or matters in the course of negotiation. Rule 11 of the *AIM Rules for Companies* further provides that an AIM company may give such information in confidence to certain recipients, including advisers and persons with whom the AIM company is negotiating, including prospective underwriters or placees. However, those recipients of information should be made aware that they may not trade in the AIM company's securities at all before that information has been made public.

14.15   The London Stock Exchange expects the negotiations leading to a reverse takeover to be kept confidential until the AIM company can notify that a binding share purchase agreement has been entered into. Typically, the notification of a binding share purchase agreement will be accompanied by the publication of the AIM admission document, which will give shareholders full information about the proposed transaction. If this is not possible, the Nominated Adviser should seek the advice of the London Stock Exchange as soon as possible as a period of suspension will be inevitable so as to ensure that all of the market is dealing based on the same knowledge. In practice, this period of suspension may be relaxed where the transaction is between two AIM companies.

14.16   The AIM company may wish to make an early announcement if it would like trading in its securities to be suspended. This might be desirable for the purposes of conducting a marketing exercise to fund the acquisition or the working capital of the enlarged group, such as a roadshow in support of a fundraising to private placees. However, the London Stock Exchange has been reluctant to suspend securities before a binding agreement has been entered into, and the AIM company and its advisers should liaise with the London Stock Exchange in the run-up to any proposed suspension and prior to any announcement.

14.17   If a breach of confidence regarding the proposed transaction occurs, or is likely to occur, and disclosure would be likely to lead to substantial movement in the price of the AIM company's securities, the AIM company must immediately issue a holding notification. A holding notification will usually be one to the effect that a transaction is under negotiation and that the AIM company expects to release the relevant information to the market shortly. Once any information has leaked into the market, the AIM company must immediately release that information. For this reason, it would be advisable for the AIM company to prepare a draft announcement and to start monitoring its share price as soon as possible after negotiations commence. Such steps will ensure that, in the event of any market rumours or significant movement in its share price, an announcement can be put out very quickly.

14.18   The *City Code on Takeovers and Mergers* also requires an announcement to be made where there is rumour or speculation or an untoward movement in the AIM company's share price, or when discussions are about to be extended to more than a very restricted number of people. An example of such a situation is when irrevocable commitments from shareholders of the AIM company in support of the transaction are being sought. Accordingly, the board of directors of the AIM company will need to approach the AIM company's shareholders very carefully, and dealings with certain shareholders (such as small companies or private individuals) may need to be cleared with the Takeover Panel in advance. Specific advice from the AIM company's legal advisers and Nominated Adviser should be obtained at the time.

14.19   The timing and content of any announcement of an acquisition is usually very important to all parties involved, including the existing Nominated Adviser and the proposed Nominated Adviser following completion, if different. Accordingly the timing and content of the acquisition should be discussed and agreed with all of them.

FIGURE 14.2   Disclosures required in the case of all reverse takeover transactions

The information required to be disclosed pursuant to Rule 14 of the *AIM Rules for Companies* is as follows:

(a) particulars of the transaction, including the name of any company or business, where relevant;
(b) a description of the business carried on by, or using, the assets which are the subject of the transaction;
(c) the profits attributable to those assets;
(d) the value of those assets;
(e) the full consideration and how it is being satisfied;
(f) the effect on the AIM company;
(g) details of any service contracts of its proposed directors;
(h) in the case of a disposal, the application of the sale proceeds;
(i) in the case of a disposal, if part of the consideration will consist of securities, whether such securities are to be sold or retained; and
(j) any other information necessary to evaluate the effect of the transaction.

Source: extract from *AIM Rules for Companies*, February 2007. The full *AIM Rules for Companies* is available at www.londonstockexchange.com

---

FIGURE 14.3   Additional disclosures required if any party to a reverse takeover transaction is related to any other party

The additional disclosures required in respect of related party transactions pursuant to Rule 13 of the *AIM Rules for Companies* are as follows:

(a) the name of the related party and the nature and extent of their interest in the transaction; and
(b) a statement that, having consulted with the Nominated Adviser and with the exception of any related party director, its directors consider, that the terms of the transaction are fair and reasonable insofar as the shareholders are concerned.

14.20   When making the announcement of a reverse takeover, Rule 14 of the *AIM Rules for Companies* requires the AIM company to disclose the information specified by Schedule 4 to the *AIM Rules for Companies* (Figure 14.2). In addition, insofar as any other party to the transaction (the target or its shareholders) is a related party (as defined in the *AIM Rules for Companies*) the additional information required by Rule 13 of the *AIM Rules for Companies* must also be disclosed (Figure 14.3). Broadly speaking, a related party is a director or a substantial shareholder of the AIM company or person related to one of them.

AIM ADMISSION DOCUMENT DISCLOSURE

14.21 On completion of a reverse takeover, trading in the securities of the AIM companies will be cancelled pursuant to Rule 14 of the *AIM Rules for Companies*. Accordingly, the enlarged AIM company must make an application for re-admission to trading on AIM of its existing securities and admission of its new securities (any consideration securities being issued to the target shareholders and any issued pursuant to any fundraising) in the same manner as any other applicant applying for admission of its securities for the first time. The applicant must therefore prepare an AIM admission document or prospectus in respect of the proposed enlarged entity, describing the new company and its business and convening the required shareholders' general meeting. The AIM admission document must be made available to the public on the AIM company's website under Rule 26 of the *AIM Rules for Companies*. Figure 14.4 shows the typical structure of an AIM admission document for a reverse takeover.

14.22 The AIM admission document disclosure requirements are set out in Schedule 2 to the *AIM Rules for Companies* and are largely based on Appendix 3

FIGURE 14.4   AIM admission document – reverse takeover typical structure

- Front cover
- Risk factors (covering both companies/businesses)
- Presentation of information
- Summary
- Part I – Information on the company and its business, including:

  - Background to and reasons for the acquisition
  - Benefits of the acquisition
  - A summary of the key terms of the acquisition
  - Brief details of the proposed board of directors of the enlarged group
  - Resolutions to be put to general meeting
  - If relevant, details of the *City Code on Takeovers and Mergers*

- Part II – Information on the AIM company and its business
- Part III – Information on the target and its business
- Part IV – Financial information on the target
- Part V – Pro forma financial information, showing the effect of the acquisition on the profit and loss account and balance sheet of the AIM company as if the transaction had occurred at the date of such balance sheet
- Part VI – Additional information about the company and its management, including enlarged group working capital and information on both the AIM company and target on litigation and significant change
- Part VII – Competent person's/expert's report on the AIM company's business
- Part VIII – Competent person's/expert's report on the target business
- Definitions
- Notice of general meeting

---

to the *Prospectus Rules* applying to companies being admitted to the Official List of the United Kingdom Listing Authority.

14.23 The front end of the AIM admission document typically includes the descriptive sections about the applicant, usually near the beginning of the AIM admission document, such as under the "Key information" section and/or "Part I". The front end should also contain a summary of the transaction. The AIM admission document will also contain a statement to the effect that, under the *AIM Rules for Companies*, the acquisition of the target constitutes a reverse takeover. As a reverse takeover, the AIM company is then obliged to obtain shareholder approval and apply for re-admission of its enlarged share capital to trading on AIM. This section should also contain brief information about the AIM company's business, as well as the target's business, and should set out the advantages of the proposed transaction. Detailed information about the business of the AIM company and the target is usually set out in separate parts. A summary of the notice of the general meeting setting out the shareholder resolutions that will be sought should be included in Part I. The notice of the general meeting will itself be set out at the end of the AIM admission document. The AIM admission document also needs to contain the information set out in Schedule 4 to the *AIM Rules for Companies* and, if the reverse takeover is also a related party transaction, Rule 13 of the *AIM Rules for Companies* (see Figure 14.3).

14.24 In some circumstances the issue of consideration securities in the AIM company to the target's shareholders will result in an obligation on the target's shareholders to make a general offer for all the securities of the AIM company, under Rule 9 of the *City Code on Takeovers and Mergers*. Where this is the case the Takeover Panel will normally waive this obligation if the issue of the consideration securities to the target's shareholders and the waiver of the operation of Rule 9 is approved by a majority of the shareholders who are independent of the transaction (a "whitewash"). For these purposes independent shareholders means shareholders who are independent of the target and the target's shareholders, who will be deemed to be acting in concert. If a whitewash of the obligation of target shareholders to make a general offer under Rule 9 of the *City Code on Takeovers and Mergers* is to be sought, the Takeover Panel should be consulted at an early stage. The Takeover Panel has discretion as to whether or not it grants the whitewash. However, the *City Code on Takeovers and Mergers* sets out some indications of where it considers that a whitewash will not be appropriate: for example if there have been "disqualifying transactions", such as when the relevant person or concert party acquires an interest in securities in the period between the posting of the circular to shareholders and the shareholders' meeting. When the Takeover Panel agrees to a whitewash, the AIM admission document and its content needs to be approved by the Takeover Panel prior to its despatch, which will impact on the timing of the transaction.

14.25 If the Panel agrees to a Rule 9 waiver, the additional disclosure requirements in the whitewash guidance note (Appendix 1 to the *City Code on Takeovers and Mergers*) will also need to be addressed in any AIM admission document. While there is some overlap between the disclosure requirements of the *AIM Rules for Companies* and Appendix 1 to the *City Code on Takeovers and Mergers*, care will need to be taken to ensure that no additional disclosure requirements of the *City Code on Takeovers and Mergers* are overlooked. For example, the *AIM Rules for Companies* require disclosure of the name of any person (excluding professional advisers and trade suppliers) who has in the past 12 months directly or indirectly received or contracted to receive fees of £10,000 or more. The *City Code on Takeovers and Mergers* requires full disclosure of any break or abort fee arrangement, but does not require the disclosure of any other fee arrangements. While disclosure of any break or abort fee is likely to be required under both the *AIM Rules for Companies* and the *City Code on Takeovers and Mergers*, this will not necessarily be the case in all circumstances. Accordingly, if a break or abort fee arrangement is not disclosable under the *AIM Rules for Companies* it should nevertheless be disclosed under the *City Code on Takeovers and Mergers*.

14.26 Furthermore, if the *City Code on Takeovers and Mergers* applies to the acquisition, and the acquisition is being made other than by way of an offer, a summary of the relevant provisions of the *City Code on Takeovers and Mergers* should be set out in reasonable detail in the AIM admission document. In addition, the details of the transaction and the steps that have been taken to obtain the necessary Rule 9 whitewash from the Takeover Panel should also be disclosed. The summary of the notice of the general meeting in Part I of the AIM admission document should include the summary of the resolution to seek approval for the requisite Rule 9 whitewash.

14.27 Under the *City Code on Takeovers and Mergers*, the AIM admission document must also contain an opinion about the transaction from an independent adviser, in accordance with Rule 3 of the *City Code on Takeovers and Mergers*. This opinion will be as to whether or not the transaction is in the best interests of the shareholders. It is usual for this Rule 3 adviser to principally deal with and advise on the *City Code on Takeovers and Mergers* aspects of the transaction. Such Rule 3 opinion will be required to be included in the AIM admission document in addition to the disclosure requirements of the *AIM Rules for Companies* and the *City Code on Takeovers and Mergers* discussed above.

14.28 If some or all of the proposed directors of the target are, or any other person is, to become directors of the enlarged AIM company, those proposed directors will need to take responsibility for all the contents of the AIM admission document. This responsibility extends to the whole of the AIM admission document relating to both the AIM company and the target, and not just the information relating to the target. It is not possible for such persons who are proposed directors to avoid liability by joining the board of directors following admission to trading on AIM. Anyone who has agreed to become a director, whether conditionally or otherwise, should be named in the AIM admission document and will be required to take responsibility for it.

TIMING

14.29 As in the case of a typical share purchase transaction, the AIM company will usually enter into heads of terms and a non-disclosure agreement with the target and carry out due diligence on the target, and a share purchase agreement will be negotiated. This process usually takes some four to eight weeks.

14.30   If the *City Code on Takeovers and Mergers* applies, and the parties are seeking a Rule 9 whitewash from the Takeover Panel (exempting the target/ target's shareholders from making a general offer for all the securities in the AIM company), the AIM admission document will need to be approved by the Takeover Panel. This approval by the Takeover Panel will then have an impact on the timing of the transaction. The procedure to be followed when seeking the Takeover Panel's approval, the disclosure requirements and the restrictions that apply are set out in the whitewash guidance note, which is at Appendix 1 to the *City Code on Takeovers and Mergers*. Checklists of the disclosure requirements must also be submitted, together with the AIM admission document, to the Takeover Panel for approval. Template checklists are available from the Takeover Panel's website.

14.31   As in the case of an initial public offering, the new enlarged AIM company will need to issue a ten-day announcement, pay an admission fee and submit an electronic version of its AIM admission document. A Nominated Adviser declaration and a company application form need to be submitted at least three business days prior to admission to trading on AIM. The applicant must also abide by all other requirements of the *AIM Rules for Companies*. It usually takes approximately three to four weeks from the publication of the AIM admission document until re-admission to trading on AIM, although this time frame can be reduced slightly if the AIM admission application documents are submitted early to AIM Regulation. AIM Regulation will usually allow admission to trading on AIM to occur on the day following shareholder approval of the transaction, provided that the application documents for admission to AIM were submitted within the required time limits.

14.32   Following the announcement that a reverse takeover has been agreed, or is in contemplation, the AIM company's securities will be suspended until the AIM admission document is published. This suspension is to avoid parts of the market dealing where they do not have all of the information on which to decide what investment activity is appropriate. Accordingly, following the publication of the AIM admission document to shareholders the suspension is lifted from the opening of the market on the following day. Once shareholder approval has been given for the reverse takeover and the acquisition completed, trading of the AIM securities of the AIM company will be cancelled. However, the new enlarged entity may apply for admission to trading on AIM in advance of the general meeting, so that the cancellation of trading of the existing AIM securities can occur simultaneously with the admission to trading on AIM of the enlarged AIM company's securities. The AIM company's existing and new securities can then be admitted to trading on AIM on the day after the general meeting.

IN PRACTICE

If the purpose of the reverse takeover is to admit the target to AIM, it would often be quicker and easier to seek a straightforward admission to trading on AIM of the target, rather than structuring the transaction as a reverse takeover. However, there may be good commercial reasons as to why the combined businesses of the two companies offers a more attractive proposition to investors, in which case a reverse takeover may be the optimum structure. However, those involved in the transaction should view it as two transactions, namely an acquisition and an application for admission to trading on AIM.

CHAPTER 15

Directors' responsibilities for an AIM admission document and verification

The directors of an AIM company will take overall responsibility for the contents of the AIM admission document, regardless of whether others take responsibility for a particular part. In accepting such responsibility the directors may be found to be liable to the persons who rely on such information, not only as a matter of civil law but they may also be held criminally liable.

The directors may be able to limit their liability in a number of ways, including by conducting a thorough verification process where each statement in the AIM admission document is checked for its accuracy and the accuracy of any implications which it may give rise to.

RESPONSIBILITY

15.1 As mentioned in Chapter 10, *Admission process and AIM admission documents*, the persons who may be responsible for the AIM admission document include each person who is a director of an applicant when the AIM admission document is published and each person who is named (with that person's authority) in the AIM admission document as a director or as having agreed to become a director, either immediately or at a future time.

15.2 In addition, any person who is stated in the AIM admission document as being responsible for any part of the AIM admission document and any person who has authorised the contents of all, or any part of, the AIM admission document will be responsible for the AIM admission document or that part (as stated). This would include the reporting accountants in relation to their accountant's report and a competent person in relation to its competent person's report. However, the directors of the company will still retain overall responsibility for the AIM admission document in its entirety.

15.3 Consistent with the directors' overall responsibility for the AIM admission document, the document must, under the *AIM Rules for Companies*, include a responsibility statement in the following form:

The directors of [the company], whose names appear on page [number], accept responsibility for the information contained in the AIM admission document.

To the best of the knowledge of the directors, who have taken all reasonable care to ensure that such is the case, the information contained in the AIM admission document is in accordance with the facts and does not omit anything likely to affect its import.

15.4 To confirm acceptance of this responsibility each director will be asked to sign a responsibility letter, which will effectively authorise the issue of the AIM admission document with the inclusion of the above statement. Copies of the AIM admission document will be lodged with the London Stock Exchange.

15.5 In view of each director's individual and collective responsibility for the AIM admission document, every director of an AIM company, whether executive or non-executive, should appreciate the importance of disclosing to the AIM company's advisers details of everything that director knows about the affairs and operations of the company. Failure to make adequate and proper disclosure may give rise to both criminal and civil liability. The potential liability of the directors for the AIM admission document is discussed in more detail in Paragraphs 15.11 to 15.37.

General duty of disclosure

15.6 The persons responsible for the AIM admission document are under a general overriding duty of disclosure. Under that general duty, the AIM admission document must contain all information which the company reasonably considers necessary to enable investors to form a full understanding of:

- the assets and liabilities, financial position, profits and losses, and prospects of the applicant and its securities for which admission to trading on AIM is being sought;
- the rights attaching to those securities; and
- any other matter contained in the AIM admission document.

15.7 Determining what information has to be included in the AIM admission document by virtue of the general duty of disclosure, regard is to be had to the nature of the securities being admitted and to the nature of the applicant. Merely flagging potential risks to investors is unlikely to discharge this responsibility. Instead, sufficient context and detail must be provided to enable investors to make an informed assessment.

15.8 In addition, it is not sufficient that each statement in the AIM admission document is factually accurate. Liability arises not only for untrue information but also for misleading information and omissions.

Specific disclosures

15.9 In addition to the general duty of disclosure referred to above, the AIM admission document must also contain the specific information prescribed by Paragraphs (a) to (j) of Schedule 2 to the *AIM Rules for Companies*, which includes:

■ A statement by the directors of the company that, in their opinion, having made due and careful enquiry, the working capital available to the company and its group will be sufficient for its present requirements, that is for at least the next 12 months after the date of admission to trading on AIM.

■ Each director must give details of:
  – full name and age, together with any previous names;
  – the names of all companies and partnerships of which the director has been a director or partner at any time in the previous five years, indicating whether or not the director is still a director or partner;
  – any unspent convictions in relation to indictable offences;
  – any bankruptcies or individual voluntary arrangements of such director;
  – any receiverships, compulsory liquidations, creditors voluntary liquidations, administrations, company voluntary arrangements or any composition or arrangement with its creditors generally, or any class of its creditors of any company where such director was a director at the time of or within the 12 months preceding such events;
  – any compulsory liquidations, administrations or partnership voluntary arrangements of any partnerships where such director was a partner at the time of or within the 12 months preceding such events;
  – receiverships of any asset of such director or of a partnership of which the director was a partner at the time of or within the 12 months preceding such events;
  – any public criticisms of such director by statutory or regulatory authorities (including recognised professional bodies), and whether such director has ever been disqualified by a court from acting as a director of a company or from acting in the management or conduct of the affairs of any company; and
  – whether such director, or member of such director's family, has a related financial product (such as a spread bet) referenced to the company's securities or the securities being admitted to AIM, together with the date and terms of the related financial product(s) and the detailed nature of the exposure.

15.10   If the AIM admission document also constitutes a prospectus, it will be necessary to comply with the specific disclosure requirements set out in Annexes I to III of the *Prospectus Rules*. These disclosures are slightly different to those highlighted in this Chapter. See Chapter 10, *Admission process and AIM admission documents*, for more details about when a prospectus is required and the content requirements for prospectuses.

LIABILITY UNDER THE *FINANCIAL SERVICES AND MARKETS ACT 2000*

15.11   Where an application for admission to trading on AIM is made in conjunction with an offer of a company's securities to the public, if the offer does not fall within one of the exemptions set out in the *Financial Services and Markets Act 2000* (FSMA) the AIM admission document will constitute a prospectus for the purpose of the FSMA and the *Prospectus Rules*. This will bring the company and its directors within the statutory provisions relating to the responsibility for prospectuses and compensation for misleading prospectuses in section 90 of the FSMA. Further information on the statutory provisions in section 90 is set out in Chapter 19, *Offers to the public.*

CIVIL LIABILITY UNDER COMMON LAW

15.12   The directors and other persons responsible for the AIM admission document need to be aware of the potential civil liabilities described below which may arise from being responsible for such a document.

Negligent misstatement

15.13   If any director is negligent in making any statement in the AIM admission document, that director may be liable in an action for damages brought by a person who has suffered loss as a result of acting on that statement, where the loss was a reasonably foreseeable consequence of the negligent misstatement. In order to establish liability, it is normally necessary for the claimant to prove that the director owed him a duty of care. It is thought that such a duty is established by virtue of the inclusion in the AIM admission document of the responsibility statement set out in Paragraph 15.3.

Deceit

15.14   Any director who permits the making of a misstatement (including a misleading omission) in the AIM admission document, knowing it is untrue or not believing it to be true or being reckless as to whether it is true or false, may be liable for damages in an action for deceit brought by a person who has suffered loss as a result of relying on that statement. Damages that may be recovered in any action for deceit are the actual damages suffered by the claimant; they are not limited to damages that were the reasonably foreseeable consequence of the misstatement (as in an action for negligent misstatement).

Rescission

15.15   A contract to purchase or acquire securities is voidable if it is induced by a material misrepresentation of fact, provided that the person acquiring the securities acts within a reasonable time of becoming aware of the misrepresentation. The contract will remain valid until rescission, but when rescinded, becomes void so that it is deemed never to have taken effect. The aggrieved party is entitled to have their name removed from the shareholders register and to be restored (by the counterparty to the contract) to the same position that they were in before the contract was made. Usually this means that their subscription money or money paid in consideration for the acquisition is refunded. The court also has jurisdiction to award damages in lieu of rescission.

Section 2 of the *Misrepresentation Act 1967*

15.16 A director may be liable for misrepresentations in the AIM admission document to anyone who acquires securities in reliance upon the misrepresentation and suffers loss, unless the director proves that they had reasonable grounds to believe, and did believe up to the time the sale of securities was concluded, that the facts represented were true. The court has power to award damages, even though the misrepresentation is innocent, and not fraudulent or negligent.

Breach of contract

15.17 If an investor can show that the misleading or untrue statement in the AIM admission document became a term of the contract for the acquisition of securities, then that investor may be able to sue for damages for breach of contract. Generally, damages will be calculated to be the difference between the actual value of the securities at the date of allotment and the price paid for them.

CRIMINAL LIABILITY

15.18 In addition to the civil liability described above, being a person responsible for an AIM admission document can also give rise to criminal liabilities.

Section 397 of the *Financial Services and Markets Act 2000*

15.19 Section 397(1) and (2) of the FSMA provides that it is an offence if a person:

(a) makes a statement, promise or forecast which that person knows to be misleading, false or deceptive in a material particular; or

(b) dishonestly conceals any material facts whether in connection with a statement, promise or forecast made by that person or otherwise; or

(c) recklessly makes (dishonestly or otherwise) a statement, promise or forecast which is misleading, false or deceptive in a material particular,

if that person does so for the purpose of inducing, or is reckless as to whether it may induce, another person (whether or not the person to whom the statement, promise or forecast is made) to enter or offer to enter into, or to refrain from entering or offering to enter into a relevant agreement, or to exercise or refrain from exercising any rights, conferred by a relevant investment (such as a share or option).

15.20 It should be noted that under section 397(1), an offence can be committed if a person makes a false or misleading statement recklessly, even though that person does not realise that it is false or misleading. However, the omission of a material fact can only involve an offence if the fact was concealed dishonestly.

15.21 Case law in respect of section 47(1) of the *Financial Services Act 1986* (the predecessor of section 397(1) of the FSMA) has established that:

- a person is reckless if, before doing an act, that person either fails to give any thought to the possibility of there being a risk of harmful consequences or, having recognised that there is such a risk that an ordinary prudent individual would not feel justified in ignoring, nevertheless goes on to do that act, disregarding the harmful consequences of the act;
- a person is dishonest if that person acts in a way which they know ordinary people consider to be dishonest, even if that person believes that they are justified in acting as they did.

15.22   Section 397(3) provides that any person who does any act or engages in any course of conduct which creates a false or misleading impression as to the market in or the price or value of any relevant investments is guilty of an offence if that person does so for the purpose of creating that impression and of thereby inducing another person to acquire, dispose of, subscribe for or underwrite those investments or to refrain from doing so or to exercise, or refrain from exercising, any rights conferred by those investments.

15.23   It should be noted that under section 380 of the FSMA, if there is a reasonable likelihood that a person will contravene section 397 (or has contravened that section and is likely to continue to do so, or do so again), the court may grant an injunction restraining the contravention or order the offender to take steps to remedy it. The court may also make a restitution order in certain circumstances.

15.24   A person guilty of an offence under section 397 of the FSMA is liable to imprisonment for up to seven years or to a fine or both. A director, manager, secretary or a similar officer of the company may also be guilty of the offence committed by the company under the FSMA if it is found to have been committed with that person's consent or connivance, or to be attributable to any neglect on that person's part (section 400 of the FSMA).

Theft Act 1968

15.25   Under section 19 of the *Theft Act 1968*, it is a criminal offence for any officer of a company to publish, with intent to deceive its members or creditors about its affairs, a written statement or account which to that person's knowledge is or may be misleading, false or deceptive in a material particular. The offence is punishable by imprisonment for up to seven years. The courts interpret the section broadly, and accordingly section 19 of the *Theft Act 1968* would cover a misleading or deceptive statement or omission in an AIM admission document.

Fraud Act 2006

15.26   Section 2 of the *Fraud Act 2006* makes it an offence dishonestly to make a false representation with the intent of making a personal gain, causing loss to another or exposing another to a risk of loss. Representations can be in relation to facts or opinions and can be expressed or implied. Section 3 of the *Fraud Act 2006* makes it an offence dishonestly to fail to disclose to another person information which that person is under a legal duty to disclose (for example under the FSMA) with the intention of making a personal gain, causing loss to another or exposing another to a risk of loss. If the *Fraud Act 2006* offences are committed by a company then, by virtue of section 12(2), if it is shown to have been committed with the consent or connivance of a director (or certain other officers) such person is also guilty of the offence. Those convicted can receive a fine, or be sentenced to imprisonment for a period of up to 10 years, or both.

CONTRACTUAL LIABILITY

15.27   The company and the directors personally may be liable in contract to its Nominated Adviser and broker for breach of warranty in the placing agreement. In addition to the warranties, the Nominated Adviser and broker will seek an indemnity from the company in respect of any liability it may incur to third parties as a result of performing the duties of Nominated Adviser and broker. A similar indemnity may be included in the engagement letters of the Nominated Adviser and broker, in respect of any liabilities they may incur as a result of performing their duties under their engagement letters.

Verification

15.28   In an attempt to minimise the risk of potential criminal or civil liability arising in respect of the issue of the AIM admission document, it is usual to undertake a detailed verification exercise and to prepare verification notes when the AIM admission document is in advanced draft form. These notes will form only part of the overall verification process; a significant amount of questioning on the basis of the statements included in the AIM admission document will take place as the document is being drafted.

15.29   Essentially, the verification notes take the form of a series of questions, answers and details of supporting information which identify and record the source of and evidence for a large number of the statements, whether of fact or opinion, contained in the AIM admission document. In particular, they are intended to ensure that any inferences an investor might reasonably draw from the statements in the AIM admission document are fully justified and that no incorrect statement is made by default.

15.30   It is acknowledged that each director cannot be expected personally to verify every detail in the AIM admission document. The idea of the verification notes is to permit a director, in appropriate cases, to rely upon the detailed work of others to check particular statements. Nevertheless, each director must be satisfied:

■ that where a director is relying upon someone else to do the detailed work to check the accuracy and completeness of a statement, it is reasonable for that director to rely on such a person in relation to the particular statement; and

■ that there are reasonable grounds for the director to believe that the person on whom that director is relying has in the event duly verified the statement.

15.31   However, directors should note that third parties are unlikely to be willing to sign the verification notes. For example, professional advisers such as lawyers and accountants will only agree to take responsibility for the verification of such matters in exceptional circumstances. Therefore, even when directors are relying on a third party to provide the verification materials, the directors retain overall responsibility for the whole of the verification exercise.

15.32 In assessing whether or not it is reasonable for a director to rely on a third party in relation to a particular statement, consideration should be given as to the quality of the source material being relied upon. It is only in circumstances where the only possible source of material is from the company that the company's own records should be used, and most statements in an AIM admission document will be verified by reference to third party materials which are produced independently of the company. Furthermore, in relation to expressions of intention or expectation, it is not unusual for any of these, which may form a key basis of a person's investment in the company, to be included in the board minutes to approve the AIM admission document (at which all of the directors will usually be present), so that the opinion of the other directors can also be canvassed.

15.33 The directors will be expected formally to approve the final version of the AIM admission document at a meeting of the board of directors to be held shortly before its publication and subsequently to confirm there have been no changes (or at least no material or significant changes since they approved the AIM admission document). In practice, the Nominated Adviser will normally expect that all the directors, illness or other unavoidable cause apart, will be available for this meeting.

15.34 In practice, the verification process will be a painstaking and time consuming exercise. However, it should be viewed as a form of insurance for directors against potential claims. The process can be made a lot smoother by each of the company and the company's lawyers nominating one person to take overall responsibility of the supply and collection of the verification materials, so that such persons become familiar with the verification materials, as this helps to avoid any duplications in requests. The verification process can also be helped by the company having its files and contracts in good order and readily accessible. Verification can also be assisted by care being taken when drafting the AIM admission document, so as to avoid the inclusion of statements which it will be difficult to substantiate with third party evidence (where possible).

Errors and omissions

15.35 If, notwithstanding the verification procedure, incorrect information is contained in, or material information is omitted from, the AIM admission document, the directors may be liable on the bases outlined above. Accordingly, the verification procedure should not be viewed as a substitute for each director reading the AIM admission document in detail and with the greatest care and each director being satisfied that the information contained in it is complete, accurate and not misleading.

15.36 If a director becomes aware, between issue of the AIM admission document and the commencement of trading in the company's securities on AIM, of any significant new matter or change affecting any matter required to be contained in the AIM admission document, that director must immediately inform the company and the Nominated Adviser with a view to all concerned considering whether it will be necessary to issue a supplementary document. For this purpose, significant means significant for the purposes of making an informed assessment of the matters set out and referred to in Paragraph 15.6.

15.37   The obligation to issue a supplementary document ceases when dealings in the securities of the company commences. However, it should be noted that liability for untrue or misleading statements in, or omission from, the AIM admission document may in certain circumstances continue even after trading has commenced in the securities. Accordingly, if a director becomes aware, at any time after submission of the AIM admission document to AIM (even after dealings have commenced), of any inaccurate or misleading statement in, or any omission from, the AIM admission document which makes, or might make, any statement in it incorrect or misleading, that director should raise the matter with the company and its professional advisers as soon as possible. In such circumstances, a public announcement may be called for.

LIMITATION OF LIABILITY

15.38   In addition to a thorough verification process, it is possible for directors to limit their potential liability by taking an indemnity from the company or taking out an insurance policy.

INDEMNITY

15.39   Under the *Companies Act 2006*, if permitted by the company's Articles of Association it may be possible for the company registered in England and Wales to give an indemnity to the director for that director's defence and judgment costs in relation to certain claims which may be brought against such a director. The extent of the indemnity for such costs and judgments are treated differently depending on whether a claim is brought by a third party or the company.

15.40   If a claim is made against a director by a third party, then pursuant to an indemnity the company may pay the director's defence costs as and when they are incurred. If the claim against the director is ultimately successful the defence costs must be repaid in respect of criminal liabilities, but not in respect of civil liabilities. In addition, the company may also indemnify a director for damages awarded against the director in civil proceedings, other than in respect of fines imposed by a regulatory body such as the Financial Services Authority.

15.41   If the claim is made against the director by the company itself then the company may still pay the director's defence costs, although these must be repaid if the company's claim against the director is successful. It is not permissible for the company either to indemnify a director against any liability which that director may have against the company, or agree to limit the director's potential liability to the company.

INSURANCE

15.42 It may also be possible for the directors to take out insurance against some of the potential liabilities arising in relation to an AIM admission document, although these cannot cover any liability arising from fraudulent, criminal or dishonest conduct or fines imposed by a regulatory body. If a company is incorporated in England and Wales then under section 233 of the *Companies Act 2006* the company may take out insurance and pay premiums on behalf of its directors, although this does not oblige it to do so. The taking out of an insurance policy should not be viewed as substitute for a full verification process. In practice, however, such insurance is difficult to obtain, and where it is obtained can be quite expensive.

NON-EXECUTIVE DIRECTORS

15.43 Under the *AIM Rules for Companies* and as a matter of English company law, there is no difference at law between an executive and a non-executive director. Accordingly, liability for an AIM admission document is shared between all of the executive directors and non-executive directors and such liability is joint and several, meaning that each director can be liable for the full amount of any loss. However, in practice this is mitigated by the fact that the director may have a statutory right of contribution against his fellow directors, although this will not prevent a shareholder from bringing a claim and a director ultimately having to settle a claim for the full amount.

15.44 While all of the directors, whether executive or non-executive, are collectively and individually responsible for the accuracy of all of the contents of the AIM admission document, it should be noted that the defences are, generally speaking, based on the state of information (i.e. actual knowledge of a particular director and whether that director has taken reasonable steps to ensure that such knowledge is accurate).

15.45 Where a non-executive director has actual knowledge of a matter then he will be liable in the same extent as any other director in possession of such knowledge. In addition, the non-executive directors have a duty of reasonable care to enquire of the other directors as to certain matters, as well as enquiring of any responsible employees. In addition, a non-executive director should satisfy himself that the verification exercise has been properly carried out; and review the draft AIM admission document to ensure that it is fair, that there is nothing in it which is incorrect according to his own awareness and that it does not omit anything which makes it misleading according to his own awareness.

IN PRACTICE

In view of the potential civil and criminal liabilities, it is essential that every director or proposed director, whether executive or non-executive, should believe, and should have reasonable grounds for believing, that:

- each item of information contained in the AIM admission document (including any negative statement deemed to be contained in the AIM admission document) is not only in accordance with the facts, but is also not misleading in its context; and
- all expressions of opinion are reasonably based and properly held; and
- the AIM admission document contains all such information as is necessary to give a true and fair view of the company's business and prospects, and nothing has been omitted which is necessary to enable investors to make an informed assessment of the company and its group.

Accordingly, every director and proposed director should carefully read the proofs of the AIM admission document and should:

- consider each statement in it;
- satisfy himself that the facts contained in it are true and not misleading, that all necessary information is included and that each statement has been the subject of sufficient verification;
- consider each forecast and each statement of opinion, belief or intention in the AIM admission document and satisfy himself that, in the case of each forecast, it is fair and reasonably based and, in the case of each statement of opinion, belief or intention, the statement is true and not misleading and the opinion, belief or intention is reasonably based; and
- generally satisfy himself that, taken as a whole, the document gives, so far as possible, a true and fair impression of the history, business and financial and trading position and prospects of the company.

CHAPTER 16

CREST, settlement and depository interests

AT A GLANCE

Rule 36 of the *AIM Rules for Companies* requires that an AIM company must ensure that appropriate settlement arrangements are put in place for the trading of its securities. Unless the London Stock Exchange agrees otherwise, the securities must be eligible for electronic settlement. The most commonly used electronic settlement system for UK securities is CREST. As part of the process leading up to flotation, the company, or its broker or registrar, will apply for the company's securities to be admitted to CREST with effect from admission to trading on AIM.

Overseas companies are subject to the same eligibility criteria as companies incorporated in England, Scotland, Wales and Northern Ireland (UK companies). However, the securities of non-UK companies are not eligible for admission to CREST, as the settlement of such securities is not a matter for the laws of England and Wales, Scotland or Northern Ireland but for the laws of the territory of incorporation. However, since AIM has become increasingly popular with overseas companies, arrangements have been put in place so that overseas securities can be held and transferred indirectly through the CREST system using depository interests.

WHAT IS CREST?

16.1 Euroclear UK & Ireland Limited ("Euroclear"), which was formerly known as CRESTCo Limited, operates CREST, which is one of the largest electronic settlement systems in the world. It is estimated by Euroclear that in terms of value, approximately 88 per cent of the UK equities market is held in CREST. CREST became operational in 1996, and since 2002 it has been part of the Euroclear group.

WHO CAN JOIN CREST?

16.2 CREST enables corporate entities and individuals to hold and transfer securities electronically in "uncertificated form" (i.e. the securities are recorded in CREST in electronic form and no certificates exist for such securities). The elimination of paper from the processing of transfers of securities makes it possible to meet the more demanding timetables of the market, so that deals can be done on markets such as AIM within a very short period of time. As well as facilitating the holding of securities in uncertificated form and providing a mechanism for the transfer of securities between CREST members, the system also enables transfers between a CREST member and an investor who holds his securities in certificated form outside of CREST.

16.3   Even though a company's securities must be eligible for electronic settlement, CREST is a voluntary system. Shareholders can decide whether they want to become members of CREST, in order to hold their securities in CREST, or whether they want to continue to hold them in certificated form. An AIM company cannot require shareholders to hold securities wholly in uncertificated form, but it is becoming increasingly uncommon for placees on an institutional placing to hold their securities in certificated form.

HOW TO JOIN CREST

16.4   There are two ways of joining CREST; either by becoming a "full" member, in which case the member himself maintains the computer equipment necessary to communicate with CREST, or by becoming a "sponsored" member, in which case the investor uses the services of another person to communicate with CREST. As most AIM companies appoint registrars and receiving agents to send and receive messages on their behalf and maintain their share registers, there is normally no need for a company itself to have the technical expertise required for a connection to the CREST computer system and they simply become a sponsored member.

HOW DOES CREST WORK?

16.5   Members of CREST are the direct legal holders of the securities which are held within CREST and their names appear on the register of members of the company. CREST is neither a custodian nor a depository, as it does not hold the UK or Irish securities itself. Instead, CREST provides a means for the owners of those securities to hold them in electronic dematerialised form.

16.6   Securities held in CREST can only be transferred through electronic instructions sent to CREST. CREST, through its central computer system, receives such electronic instructions from persons who wish to transfer securities. The central system processes these instructions and completes the transfer in its own records before generating an electronic message to the company. The message notifies the company that a transfer has been effected in the central system. All messages go via the central computer system and therefore the company and its shareholders do not communicate directly.

16.7   As well as facilitating the transfer of securities with simultaneous payment, CREST also enables certain corporate transactions, such as rights issues, reorganisations and the appointment of proxies, to be completed through electronic messaging.

LEGAL FRAMEWORK

UK law

16.8   Before the introduction of CREST, the legal position relating to the transfer of securities in England and Wales was governed by the *Companies Act 1985* and the constitutional documents of the company. The Act prohibited the transfer of securities without a proper instrument of transfer (e.g. a stock transfer form) and required the issuance of share certificates on the allotment and transfer of securities.

16.9   The law therefore needed to be changed so that title to securities could be transferred electronically. The *Uncertificated Securities Regulations 2001* (SI 2001 No 3755) (the "Regulations") create a statutory framework within which the CREST system operates. These Regulations provide for what is termed as a "relevant system", which is defined as being a computer-based system, and procedures, which enable title to units of security to be evidenced and transferred without a written instrument and which facilitate supplementary and incidental matters. Since 1995, the Regulations have been re-enacted and modified a number of times. As well as shares, the Regulations apply to securities such as stock, debentures and debenture stock, loan stock, bonds, subscription warrants, units of a collective investment scheme and depository interests, which are all eligible for CREST.

16.10   The Regulations refer to any person who wishes to run the relevant system as "the Operator", and such a person must be approved by the Financial Services Authority. Euroclear was approved as an Operator in July 1996.

16.11   The *Companies Act 2006* will further enable HM Treasury to make regulations which give the members of a company the power to adopt arrangements under which title to securities can be evidenced, or transferred, without a written instrument by the passing of an ordinary resolution.

16.12   In respect of a company's authority to recognise transfers without a proper instruction of transfer, the Regulations introduced a procedure to allow the directors of companies registered in England and Wales to resolve to do this without the need to amend the Articles of Association (see Paragraph 16.15).

Non-UK law

16.13   The Regulations only apply to securities issued by companies incorporated in England, Wales, Northern Ireland and Scotland under the relevant companies acts. They do not apply to the securities of overseas companies, although they do permit interests in foreign securities to be transferred through CREST, if such interests are constituted as securities under the laws of England, Wales, Scotland or Northern Ireland (for example, in the form of depository interests). Similar legislation to the Regulations has been introduced in the Republic of Ireland, the Isle of Man and Jersey establishing "relevant systems" in relation to each of these jurisdictions, so that it is possible for securities to be held in CREST. The States of Guernsey do not have any comparable regulations. However, under the laws of the States of Guernsey it is possible for securities to be held and transferred within CREST, subject to the inclusion of appropriate provisions in the Articles of Association.

ADMISSION OF SECURITIES TO CREST

16.14   AIM companies need to consider whether their securities are eligible for admission to CREST. Eligibility is determined by the *CREST Rules* (which are set out in a separate section at the end of the CREST Manual) and the Regulations. The two most important eligibility criteria are that a security must be fungible and must be freely transferable:

- The need for a security to be fungible means that each of the securities must be identical in all respects, including the rights attached to them. To the extent that the securities are not fungible, they must be admitted to CREST as separate participating securities with separate international stock identification numbers (ISIN).
- The company's Articles of Association must also comply with the *CREST Rules* which require securities to be freely transferable.

16.15   A company's Articles of Association will normally include provisions concerning the transfer of securities; and will refer to the need for the company to have delivered to it a properly executed stock transfer form and for the company to issue share certificates. Other provisions in the Articles of Association will also assume that the securities are held in certificated form. Regulation 10 of the Regulations facilitates the admission of securities to CREST without the need for a shareholder resolution to amend the Articles of Association. The Regulations provide that the company may resolve, through a resolution passed by its directors, that title to the securities of a class issued, or to be issued by it, may be transferred by means of a relevant system (i.e. through CREST). The effect of the directors' resolution is to disapply those provisions in the Articles of Association which are inconsistent with the Regulations. CREST has published specimen wording for such a resolution, which is usually provided to the company in the pack of standard documentation. Many AIM companies choose to pass a directors' resolution, rather than amend the Articles of Association, as this route is often quicker and administratively easier than passing a shareholders' resolution. However, if new articles are being adopted as part of a company's admission to trading on AIM process, then the equivalent provisions are usually included in the amended Articles of Association.

16.16   In addition, if there are any pre-emption rights or rights of the directors to refuse to register a transfer, other than in some very limited circumstances (e.g. a transfer to more than four persons), then the Articles of Association will need to be amended so as to comply with the *CREST Rules* and *AIM Rules for Companies*, which require that securities to be admitted are freely transferable.

ACTION TO BE TAKEN

16.17   As well as complying with the *CREST Rules* and the Regulations, the company must complete and sign a Security Application Form (SAF) for each security to be held in CREST. The SAF creates the contractual relationship between the company and Euroclear. The company's corporate broker or registrar often assists with the completion of this form (which is available from the CREST website at www.euroclear.co.uk). The SAF must be submitted to Euroclear at least two full business days prior to the enabling date for the security.

16.18   As part of the process in the lead up to an application for admission of a company's securities to AIM, the company's registrar will usually submit the SAF on behalf of the company, ten business days prior to when the securities need to be admitted to CREST. The form can be processed, if sent by fax, on the same day, but this is entirely at Euroclear's discretion. The company must indicate in the SAF if there are any conditions (e.g. admission to trading on AIM becoming effective or the approval of the relevant corporate action at a general meeting) to be fulfilled prior to CREST enabling the securities. CREST will take no action until the company has confirmed, in writing on the company's headed notepaper, that all the outstanding conditions have been satisfied; admission to trading on AIM becoming effective is usually the last of these. This confirmation is commonly referred to as the CREST enablement letter and is often pre-signed by the company and held by the corporate broker for onward transmission to Euroclear at the appropriate time.

16.19   Admission to trading on AIM nearly always takes place at 08:00 (the rare exception being limited to where there is a simultaneous initial public offer in more than one time zone, in which case AIM Regulation may vary this). Once admission to trading on AIM takes place, the corporate broker should fax the company's enablement letter to Euroclear, giving Euroclear authority to enable the security. The original should be sent to Euroclear by close of business the following day. On receipt of the fax, Euroclear will enable the security.

REGISTERS

16.20   The holders of uncertificated securities will always be recorded on a register maintained by CREST. The holders of certificated securities will be recorded on the register of members maintained by the company. The Regulations require that these two separate registers are maintained, and the two together constitute the company's register of members.

16.21   The Regulations further provide that a company must also maintain a record of entries from CREST's register of members. This record is kept up to date through CREST sending an electronic message to the company's registrar on the completion of a transfer in the CREST system. In practice, the company's record of uncertificated securities is constantly playing catch-up. The importance of this register should not be underestimated though as it, together with the register of certificated holders, will be used by the company for the purposes of sending out information to members, as well as determining entitlements to dividends.

OVERSEAS SECURITIES AND CREST

General

16.22   Overseas securities (e.g. the share capital of an Australian company) cannot be held or traded in the CREST system. To enable investors in overseas companies to settle their securities through CREST, a depository needs to be appointed to hold the relevant overseas securities on trust for the holders and to issue to the holders dematerialised depository interests, which represent the underlying overseas securities and which can be settled through CREST. This trust relationship between the depository and the shareholder is documented in a deed poll executed by the depository and is governed by English law. The depository must apply to CREST for admission of the depository interests and it is the depository who has the legal relationship with Euroclear and not the underlying overseas company. However, the overseas company has an interest in its arrangements and they are usually reviewed by the company's lawyers.

16.23   The depository interests are independent, English securities and are therefore governed by the Regulations (and any relevant CREST requirements) and are held on a register maintained by the depository. The depository interests have the same ISIN as the underlying overseas securities and are not treated as separate securities for the purposes of admission to trading on AIM. Where there is a depository interest facility for securities which are admitted to trading on AIM, the description of the security on the AIM website is usually given the suffix "(DI)" to indicate they are held in dematerialised form as depository interests. Each depository interest is usually treated as representing one share of the overseas security held, for the purposes of, for example, determining eligibility for dividend payments and voting rights. Any payments received by the depository, as holder of the underlying overseas securities, are passed on to each depository interest holder noted on the depository interest register, as the beneficial holder of the relevant overseas securities, pursuant to the terms of the declaration of trust.

16.24   Two different depository interest structures are used by AIM companies, which are described below.

CREST Depository Interests (CDIs)

16.25   CDIs are issued by a CREST depository (a Euroclear subsidiary) to CREST members through its international service. The CDIs represent an entitlement to the underlying overseas securities, which the CREST depository is holding on trust (through a CREST nominee) for the holders of the related CDIs. The CREST depository's relationship with CREST members is also established by a deed poll, which is governed by English law. The CDI facility is regarded as a settlement mechanism. This means that a trade in the underlying overseas security will be settled by a transfer of CDIs. This is why CDIs have the same ISIN as the underlying overseas securities and are not treated as separate securities for the purposes of admitting to AIM. It is important for a company to check whether any of its securities exist as CDIs before it proceeds to establish any other form of depository interest facility, as it is not uncommon for a company who has an overseas listing to have securities already settled in CREST.

Depository Interests (DIs)

16.26   DIs are very similar to CDIs except that the depository is selected by the issuer and CREST does not have any relationship with or responsibility for the DIs. Rule 9 of the *CREST Rules* requires the satisfaction of certain specific conditions for DIs of this kind, for example:

- the depository must hold the DIs on trust for the sole benefit of the holders of the DIs at all times, including all rights pertaining to the underlying securities which the DIs represent and all monies and benefits which they receive in respect of them, save for the proper expenses of the depository;
- the underlying securities to which the DIs relate and any rights, monies or benefits deriving therefrom must not be treated as the assets of the depository under the law of the respective jurisdictions of:
  - the depository's place of incorporation;
  - the company's place of incorporation;
  - the place where the registry of securities to which the DIs relate is maintained; and
  - the place of administration of the trust under which the securities are held;
- either the company's lawyers or the depository's lawyers will provide a legal opinion to Euroclear, confirming that the above conditions are satisfied, before the DIs are admitted to CREST and to do this they must get back-to-back opinions in the relevant jurisdiction(s);
- the London Stock Exchange must have agreed that the DIs are to bear the same ISIN in the CREST system as the securities which they represent;
- Euroclear must remain satisfied at all times that the use of the same ISIN continues to be appropriate;
- the DIs shall not be described as CDIs or otherwise be represented as associated in any way with Euroclear or the CREST system.

Comparisons between CDIs and DIs

16.27   The differences between CDIs and DIs are as follows:

- The company does not bear any additional cost in the establishment or ongoing operation of CDIs, as the costs are borne by the CREST members who hold the CDIs. Under a DI facility, the company usually pays a set-up fee and an annual administrative fee to the depository.
- A depository is generally able to give companies the opportunity to access the DI register online, both day and night, whereas a fee is payable to CREST for each request to view the CDI register.
- In relation to the placing of new securities in CREST, the depository is usually more efficient with the timely settlement of DIs in CREST. A depository can ensure that the DIs are credited to the relevant CREST participant at the opening of business on the effective date, enabling the Nominated Adviser/broker to

onward deliver and receive proceeds promptly. With CDIs, the credit to the relevant CREST participant will generally occur on the next business day due to time and logistical differences.

■ A depository is often more flexible in the bespoke arrangements and services that it can offer to a company in comparison with CREST. For example, a depository is often able to provide AGM services whereby it will co-ordinate the distribution and tabulation of proxies both in the UK and in the overseas jurisdiction. A depository will also assign a relationship manager to the company, both in the UK and in their overseas jurisdiction, who will work closely with the company and its investors. If required, a depository can even set up a call centre in both the UK and the foreign jurisdiction in order to field investor enquiries.

In practice, where the choice exists between using CDIs or DIs, the company's broker will have a view as to which best meets the company's needs and shareholder profile.

STANDARD DOCUMENTATION FOR A DI FACILITY

16.28   A standard documentation pack for this form of DI arrangement typically includes a depository agreement, deed poll and legal opinions.

Depository agreement

16.29   This governs the arrangements between the depository and the company and sets out the depository's fees for providing the depository services and issuing the DIs. It will also include an indemnity from the company to the depository for any loss it might suffer in performing its obligations under the agreement. It is also not unusual for the depository to seek to limit its liability to an amount which is less than the value of the deposited property. Whilst there is some scope for negotiations, particularly around the fees payable to carry out depository, this agreement is fairly standard.

Deed poll

16.30   This deed is signed by the depository and states that any overseas securities that are transferred to the depository will be held on trust for the holders of the DIs.

Legal opinions

16.31   Two legal opinions are usually required by the depository's lawyers, from the company's local lawyers in the jurisdiction where the company is incorporated. The depository will provide standard wording for these legal opinions.

16.32   The first legal opinion confirms that, if the depository were to become insolvent, the underlying overseas securities held by it would not, under local law, be available to the depository's creditors but would continue to be held for the holders of the DIs. The purpose of the second legal opinion is to give the depository comfort that the company has the power to sign the depository agreement, and that there are no restrictions in the company's Articles of Association (or other constitutional documents) which are contrary to the setting up and functioning of the DI arrangement. Both of these opinions should be requested from the company's local lawyers early on, as it can delay the admission to trading on AIM timetable if the parties are waiting to receive final signed legal opinions from overseas lawyers.

16.33   A separate legal opinion is required by the depository's lawyers from the company's UK lawyers in relation to whether stamp duty reserve tax (SDRT) is payable on the transfer of DIs. Again, this opinion is to be addressed to both Euroclear and the depository. There are certain exemptions from liability to pay SDRT on the transfers of CDIs and DIs and it is therefore important that the company obtains its own legal advice, in order to establish whether those CDIs or DIs qualify for the exemption.

16.34   An additional legal opinion may also be required by the depository's lawyers from the company's lawyers in the jurisdiction where the company maintains a branch register of its securities. This opinion also confirms that the underlying overseas securities to which the DIs relate, and any rights attaching to them, will not be treated as assets of the depository, except to the extent that the depository is allowed to sell deposited property to recover moneys that have become due to it.

16.35   The combination of these opinions enable the depository's lawyers, or the company's lawyers, to provide one complete legal opinion to CREST, although practice among the depositories varies as to whether the depository's lawyers or the company's lawyers provide this composite legal opinion.

Other documents

16.36   The pack will also include the directors' resolution and a draft operational bulletin (known as an "OPS Bulletin") which is issued by Euroclear to CREST members and which sets out the DI arrangements and whether or not SDRT is payable on the transfer of DIs.

Timetable

16.37   Figure 16.1 gives an example timetable for setting up a DI facility. This is only a guide and, as the entering into of the depository agreement and deed poll requires the board of directors' approval, it is worth liaising with Euroclear at an early stage so as to ensure that no unforeseen issues delay the admission to trading on AIM.

FIGURE 16.1 An example timetable of events for the setting up of a DI facility

T = trading in DIs

T – 17	Depository receives customer identity documents and information Any requested changes to the standard documentation to be sent to the depository's lawyers for review
T – 13	Company's lawyers to confirm to depository's lawyers that the legal opinions are in an agreed form
T – 12	Depository's lawyers submit draft opinion to Euroclear Directors' resolution passed.
T – 11	All signed documentation sent to depository: – depository agreement – certified directors' resolution – legal opinions – depository executes deed poll (date of directors' resolution is needed in order to complete the deed poll)
T – 10	Depository's lawyers provide a signed legal opinion to Euroclear OPS Bulletin is published on Euroclear's website SAF to be sent to Euroclear
T – 1	Enablement letter sent to CREST
T	Trading in DIs begins

IN PRACTICE

A company may need to set up a depository facility in order to comply with the *AIM Rules for Companies'* requirement that securities can be settled electronically. Whether a company should use the CDI or DI route will depend on a number of factors, including where the company is incorporated and whether it has any other trading facilities. The company's broker will also have a view as to whether investors will have a preference for DIs or CDIs. Whatever route is used, the process is largely mechanical but the facility may take a little time to set up.

CHAPTER 17

Lock-ins for new businesses

AT A GLANCE

A new business that has not been independent or revenue earning for at least two years at the time of the application to admit a class of its securities to trading on AIM must, pursuant to Rule 7 of the *AIM Rules for Companies*, restrict directors, substantial shareholders and certain persons connected with it from disposing of any interest in its securities for a period of one year from admission to trading on AIM.

RULE 7 OF THE *AIM RULES FOR COMPANIES*

17.1 Where the company applying for admission to trading of its securities on AIM has not been independent and revenue earning for at least two years, at the time of its application to admit such securities, the following persons must agree not to dispose of any interest in its securities for a period of one year from the admission to trading of its securities on AIM:

(a) Any person who is a director of an AIM company, or of any company which is its subsidiary or parent undertaking, or other subsidiary undertaking of its parent company.

(b) A substantial shareholder, i.e. a person who holds (directly or indirectly) 10 per cent or more of a class of security as admitted to trading on AIM or equivalent voting rights:

- the definition of a substantial shareholder excludes where such person becomes a substantial shareholder at the time of admission to trading on AIM, at a price which was more widely available, e.g. as part of an offer to the public or institutional placing;
- the definition of substantial shareholder also excludes securities held by authorised persons, being a person authorised to conduct investment business in the United Kingdom (a list of which is on the Financial Services Authority's website, www.fsa.gov.uk) and any company with securities quoted on the London Stock Exchange's markets. The exception to these exclusions is if the AIM company is an investing company. If there is any doubt as to whether a vendor is a substantial shareholder, the Nominated Adviser should contact AIM Regulation.

(c) An associate of (a) or (b) being:

(i) the family of such a person;

(ii) the trustees (acting as such) of any trust of which the individual or any of the individual's family is a beneficiary or discretionary object. The exceptions are a trust which is either an occupational pension scheme, as defined in regulation 3 of the *Financial Services and Markets Act 2000 (Regulated Activities) Order 2001*, or an employee share scheme which does not, in either case, have the effect of conferring benefits on persons all or most of whom are related parties;

(iii) any company in whose equity securities such a person, individually or taken together with his or her family, are directly or indirectly interested (or have a conditional or contingent entitlement to become interested) to the extent that they are, or could be, able to:

■ exercise or control the exercise of 30 per cent or more of the votes (excluding treasury securities) able to be cast at general meetings on all, or substantially all, matters; or

■ appoint or remove directors holding a majority of voting rights at board meetings on all, or substantially all, matters;

A similar provision applies if a director, individually or taken together with his family and any other director of that company have such an interest.

(iv) any other company which is its subsidiary undertaking, parent undertaking, or subsidiary undertaking of its parent undertaking;

(v) any company whose directors are accustomed to act in accordance with (a)'s directions or instructions;

(vi) any company in the capital of which (a), either alone or together with any other company within (iv) or (v), or both taken together, is, or would be, (on the fulfilment of a condition or the occurrence of a contingency) interested in the manner described in (iii).

(d) Any employee of the AIM company, and any employee of any parent or subsidiary of the AIM company, who together with his or her family has a holding or interest (direct or otherwise) of 0.5 per cent of the class of security to be allotted to AIM.

17.2 For these purposes a reference to a person's family includes the following persons:

■ the person's spouse or civil partner and any child, where such child is under the age of 18;

■ any trust in which such individuals are trustees or beneficiaries;

■ any company of which they have control of more than 20 per cent of its equity or voting rights in a general meeting.

17.3 It should be noted that employee share or pension schemes are excluded from the definition of trust, provided that such individuals are beneficiaries rather than trustees.

17.4 The rationale behind this restriction on disposal of interests is to enhance confidence in the market for the securities. It should be noted that the company's advisers may advise the company to extend the period of the lock-in and the lock-in arrangements to other persons to further enhance the confidence of the market, although this is not strictly required by Rule 7 of the *AIM Rules for Companies*. Any lock-ins, whether under Rule 7 or otherwise, must also be disclosed in any AIM admission document.

17.5   There are certain exceptions to Rule 7 which are set out in that rule and which are as follows:

- in the event of an intervening court order;
- the death of a party who has been subject to Rule 7 lock-in; and
- in respect of an acceptance of a takeover offer from the AIM company which is open to all shareholders.

17.6   In order to minimise the risk of parties to any such lock-in arrangements subsequently being deemed to constitute concert parties, under the *City Code of Takeovers and Mergers* it is usual for the exemptions relating to takeovers to be expanded so as to include:

- any disposal pursuant to the acceptance of a general, partial or tender offer, made by an offeror to all the shareholders of the company for the whole or part of the issued share capital of the company (other than any securities already held by the offeror or persons acting in concert with the offeror); or
- the execution of an irrevocable commitment to accept a general, partial or tender offer, made to all the shareholders of the company for the whole or part of the issued share capital of the company (other than any securities already held by the offeror or persons acting in concert with the offeror); or
- a sale to an offeror or proposed offeror who has been named in an announcement made pursuant to the *City Code on Takeovers and Mergers*.

However, it is recommended that applicants and their advisers may wish to consult with the *Takeover Panel* prior to drafting any lock-in arrangement.

ORDERLY MARKET PROVISIONS

17.7   Although not strictly required under Rule 7 of the *AIM Rules for Companies*, the Nominated Adviser or broker may also require the persons who would be subject to the *AIM Rules for Companies* Rule 7 lock-in to agree to orderly market provisions. Orderly market provisions are an undertaking by the relevant shareholder that, for a specified period after the conclusion of the lock-in period, they will only sell securities through the company's broker. This additional undertaking is often given to the company's Nominated Adviser and may be qualified for so long as that person is the company's Nominated Adviser or that the broker offers competitive terms and pricing for such disposal, excluding the timing for disposal. Whilst this is not strictly required by any AIM Rule under the *AIM Rules for Companies*, it enables the Nominated Adviser to monitor the trades in the company's securities and the disclosure of such transactions, and will also help protect the after market in the company's securities.

OTHER EXCEPTIONS TO LOCK-INS

17.8   Where a lock-in is required by the Nominated Adviser, but is not mandatory under Rule 7 of the *AIM Rules for Companies* then additional exceptions to the prohibition on dealings may also be included. It should be noted that these exceptions cannot be used if a lock-in is required under Rule 7 of the *AIM Rules for Companies*. Where such lock-ins are not mandatory, additional exceptions, which may be negotiated with a Nominated Adviser/broker, may include some or all of the following:

- A compromise, or arrangement, between the company and its creditors or any class of them, or between the company and its members or any class of them, which is agreed to by the creditors or members and sanctioned by the court under sections 895 to 901 of the *Companies Act 2006* (formerly sections 425 to 427A of the *Companies Act 1985*).
- A disposal of securities made with prior written consent of the Nominated Adviser, such consent not to be unreasonably withheld or delayed, following a representation by the board of directors that the shareholder has demonstrated to the board of directors that a sale is necessary to alleviate financial hardship.
- A disposal or agreement to dispose of securities in the company to the company, made pursuant to an offer by the company to purchase its own securities, which is made on identical terms to all holders of securities and otherwise complies with the Act and the *AIM Rules for Companies*.
- A disposal, by way of sale for cash, which is made for the purpose of funding an amount payable by that person to the Nominated Adviser or any indemnified person in respect of a claim under the placing agreement, provided that any sale is made through the Nominated Adviser.
- A renunciation of a right to subscribe for securities where such derived right is from the ordinary shares or, for the avoidance of doubt, a failure to take up such right.
- A proposed transfer to close family relatives (being the person's spouse, former spouse, parent or grandparent or child or remoter issue or brother or sister) or to trustees for such person's close family relatives or any of them. This exception is conditional upon such transferee executing an undertaking in relation to such securities in substantially similar terms to those contained in the lock-in.

IN PRACTICE

Whether a lock-in is mandatory under Rule 7 of the *AIM Rules for Companies* or not, it is likely that, as part of an admission to trading on AIM process, the Nominated Adviser and/or broker will require certain key parties (such as directors and large shareholders) to enter into lock-in arrangements. Where the company has not been independent and revenue earning for at least two years there is a requirement for such a lock-in and there is little room for discussion. However, when it is a requirement of the Nominated Adviser and/or broker the scope and duration of any lock-in can both be subject to negotiation.

Part III
Fundraisings

INTRODUCTION

One of the reasons that companies seek admission to trading on AIM is to raise capital for the development of their business. Many companies will conduct a fundraising at the time that their securities are first admitted to trading on AIM. In addition, one of the key strengths of the AIM market is the ability to raise finance once the company has been admitted to trading. The subsequent fundraisings are referred to as secondary issues and can be conducted relatively cost effectively, as in their simplest form they are conducted without any additional documentation other than a placing agreement and placing letter or announcement.

The principal documentation between the company and the broker or investment bank who will conduct the fundraising on the company's behalf is described in Chapter 18, *Contractual documentation for fundraisings*.

Chapter 19, *Offers to the public*, describes how an AIM company may make an offer to the public, although in practice this route is seldom used by AIM companies. A more common form of fundraising on AIM is via an institutional placing and Chapter 20, *Institutional placings*, looks at these. Institutional placings are not made on a pre-emptive basis, therefore they are dilutive for existing shareholders; Chapter 21, *Rights issues and open offers*, looks at the alternative routes of placings and open offers which can include a pre-emptive element. Chapter 22, *Secondary issues*, puts these rules for fundraisings into context for secondary issues.

On larger placings it is also possible that the investment bank may wish to conduct some form of stabilisation in the immediate aftermath of the placing and commence trading prior to admission. There are specific rules which govern how stabilisation and when-issued dealings can be conducted and these are examined in detail in Chapter 23, *Price stabilisation, over-allotment, greenshoes and when-issued trading*.

One aspect which may often be overlooked in connection with placings is the publicity surrounding the fundraisings and what can and cannot be said. Chapter 24, *Analyst research*, and Chapter 25, *Publicity guidelines*, deal with analyst research and publicity guidelines around the time the fundraising is conducted in the lead up to a fundraising.

CHAPTER 18

Contractual documentation for fundraisings

AT A GLANCE

Whatever form of fundraising is being conducted by the company, the mechanics of the fundraising will usually be summarised in the placing agreement, which is the contract between the company and the investment bank or broker. It is an important document for the directors as the directors may often be asked to be a party to it. Where they are a party, the directors may give undertakings as to what the company may do, but also, in a number of instances, the directors will be asked to give representations and warranties to the investment bank or broker.

The placing agreement is also important as it summarises the steps which will be taken in order to conduct the placing and ultimately remit the proceeds to the company.

PLACING AGREEMENT

18.1 The contractual relationship between the company and its investment bank or broker will be governed by a placing agreement. The placing agreement will typically comprise the following key elements:

- It will appoint the broker as agent to the company, to use its reasonable endeavours to procure subscribers for the securities to be placed.
- It will set out the mechanics for the fundraising and admission of the securities to trading on AIM and settlement of the securities, once admitted. This will include details of the steps to be carried out, the documentation required and the dates by which these steps are to be carried out.
- It will detail the remuneration payable to the broker and provide the mechanics of settlement and payment.
- It will contain comfort from the company, and often also the directors, to the broker in the form of warranties and indemnities (see Paragraphs 18.2 to 18.14).
- It may contain certain post-admission obligations and undertakings to the broker, for example to implement any recommendations made in the various due diligence reports, to consult with the broker before undertaking any corporate actions in a specified period following admission to trading on AIM, restrictions on issuing securities in a limited period following admission to trading on AIM, etc.

- It will contain termination provisions, giving the broker the right to terminate or pull the placing in the event of a major catastrophe or of a material adverse change relating to the company between the date the placing agreement is signed and the actual date of admission to trading on AIM or a material breach of warranty.

Warranties and indemnities

18.2   An important factor for the directors in connection with any fundraising is the level of comfort the broker will typically require in the placing agreement on an initial public offer as this is typically the most (if not the only) contentious aspect of the placing agreement.

18.3   Assuming the Nominated Adviser and broker are one and the same institution (as is more typical these days), the broker will perform two roles on an initial public offer, both of which expose the broker to potential liability:

- that of the agent to arrange the placing and to procure subscribers for the securities; and
- that of "gatekeeper" for AIM, in ensuring that it is satisfied the company is appropriate for admission to trading on AIM.

In addition to the due diligence which the broker will itself carry out on the company and the due diligence reports it will receive, the broker will expect the key information provided to it to be warranted, together with the contents of the AIM admission document and the key disclosure statements made in it.

18.4   When a company applies for admission of its securities to trading on AIM for the first time the broker will typically seek warranties from the directors as well as the company. Obviously, the broker will be keen to have as wide a net as possible in the event it needs to seek recourse on any third party claims. It has also become market practice in the United Kingdom for directors (and in certain cases the key founder shareholders, e.g. start-up companies) to give warranties to the broker on an initial public offer. This gives the investor some comfort that the risk of contractual claims helps to "focus the minds" of directors on the key components of the listing process which they are asked to warrant.

18.5   Whilst there will be little room for negotiation over the scope of the warranties, given they are intended to support the key disclosures in the AIM admission document, there is likely to be negotiation over the following:

- financial caps on the exposure of the directors under the warranties; typically, the company's exposure under the warranties and the indemnity (see below) will be uncapped;
- time limits after which claims cannot be made against the directors; typically, the company's exposure will only be limited by the statute of limitations; and
- (occasionally) distinguishing between the scope of warranties given by certain directors; for example, it may be considered appropriate for recently appointed non-executives to give more limited warranties and/or warrant matters subject to their knowledge.

18.6 It is impossible to generalise about the typical level of warranty cover that brokers expect from directors as each broker has its own internal policy. Also, the level of cover required is determined by the size and relative risk profile of the company and any fundraising. However, for an average sized placing in conjunction with an application for admission of a company's securities to trading on AIM for the first time, it is still relatively common for the warranty cap per director to be a multiple of salary or total remuneration. For larger placings, where the directors' potential gain may be much greater, a multiple of salary may be considered inappropriate. Instead, the broker may seek an aggregate warranty cap from all the directors which is based on a percentage of the value of the funds to be raised. How that cap is borne by the directors will be the subject of a separate discussion between them and the broker.

The indemnity

18.7 The placing agreement will almost invariably include a full form indemnity in favour of the broker. The indemnity is usually very broadly drawn, and as the indemnity is the most important protection to the broker, a company and its directors will be unlikely to be able to agree any material changes to the substance of the indemnity.

18.8 Under a typical indemnity:

- the company is required to indemnify the broker against any and all claims brought against it which relate to the placing and the work performed by the broker under the placing agreement; and
- the company agrees not to bring any claims against the broker in respect of its engagement. This second limb is sometimes referred to as the "hold harmless".

18.9 It is becoming increasingly common for brokers to include the directors as parties to the indemnity. It is therefore important to ensure that the liability caps for directors referred to in Paragraph 18.6 cover liability under the warranties as well as the indemnities.

18.10 Both limbs of the indemnity will normally be qualified to exclude certain limited scenarios, such as fraud, negligence and wilful default on the part of the brokers. In other words, the indemnity only applies to the extent that the claim brought against the broker arises other than as a result of the broker's negligence in the performance of its function as broker or as a result of some wilful wrongdoing on its part. Similarly, the hold harmless language will be qualified to allow the company to sue the broker for negligence or for some wilful wrongdoing on the part of the broker.

18.11 "Wilful default" in this context is understood to mean a deliberate and conscious neglect or default, or reckless carelessness.

18.12 There is, regularly, debate on the negligence standard. The development of indemnities in corporate finance transactions is heavily influenced by practice in the United States and those familiar with US jurisprudence will know that the concept of "gross negligence" is recognised as distinct from "negligence" in the

United States. Although there have been some judicial murmurings on the subject, "gross negligence" is not (as yet) a term of art in English law. Therefore, it is sometimes suggested that the courts will not as yet draw any distinction between gross negligence and ordinary negligence.

18.13   However, in the context of an exclusion clause within a storage services agreement, the Court of Appeal did give effect to the phrase and stated that "gross negligence" can mean a "very great negligence or a bad case of negligence and may well include an element of recklessness". The court held that the words "gross negligence" take their colour from the contrast with "wilful neglect" and refer to an act or omission not done deliberately, but which in the circumstances would be regarded by those familiar with the circumstances as a serious error, the likely consequences of the error clearly being a significant factor. Thus, in this case, the Court of Appeal was of the opinion that whether negligence is gross could be seen as a function of the nature of the error and the seriousness of the risk which results from it.

18.14   The courts are yet to draw such a distinction with regards to placing agreements, or even brokers. As recently as 2005 the English courts were of the opinion that the addition of the word "gross" added nothing to an indemnity clause in a dispute about technical advice given by a bank on fund establishment and management. However, given that it is still a grey area, brokers are likely to take the cautious view and seek to include it.

Other qualifications

18.15   In addition to negligence and wilful default, the company might wish to argue that the indemnity should be qualified so that it does not protect the broker where it has acted in breach of the placing agreement. This is unlikely to be accepted by the broker; despite best attempts, the placing agreement is rarely going to be sufficiently prescriptive to allow a clear delineation between acts which are in conformity with the placing agreement and acts which are in breach. However, there may be some scope to agree the exclusion of a material breach, especially if this does not include breaches outside the control of the broker or which were caused by a prior breach by the company, although different brokers will have their own internal policies as to whether such an exclusion is acceptable.

18.16   A company may also wish to argue that the indemnity should not be available where the broker has acted in breach of any statutory duties imposed upon it. Typically, this is listed as a breach of duties under the *Financial Services and Markets Act 2000* and the rules made under it, or their equivalents in any relevant foreign jurisdictions – the broker will argue that this is the only relevant legislation in the United Kingdom.

PLACING LETTERS

18.17   Whilst the placing agreement will provide the framework for the mechanics of the placing process, the key role of the broker is obviously to procure the subscribers for the placing securities. Once the book-building process has been concluded and the book has closed and allocations have been made by the broker among the placees, the broker will want to ensure that the placees are contractually bound to take up the securities that they have been allocated. The broker will therefore circulate placing letters to the placees. These letters will set out the number of securities to be subscribed, the price, the total subscription amount payable and relevant details to ensure their orders can be matched in CREST. Most importantly, the placees will give an irrevocable undertaking to subscribe for the securities allocated to them. In giving this commitment, the placees agree to delegate all discretions in the completion of the placing to the broker, in particular any rights to terminate the placing in the event of a force majeure event or a material adverse change or warranty breach.

18.18   The placees will also be required to give certain warranties and confirmations to the broker, including that they fall within applicable exemptions to the *Financial Services and Markets Act 2000*. If any overseas placees are to subscribe, specific placing letters may need to be drafted for them, which include wording to comply with applicable securities law, on the advice of local legal counsel. The inclusion of US placees can complicate the process significantly and it is therefore important to take US legal advice at an early stage if there is to be a US element to the placing in order to incorporate the required US wording in all the placing documents.

18.19   The placees will usually have been given a draft of the AIM admission document during the marketing roadshow. This draft is often referred to as a "pathfinder" document as it is a near final version of the AIM admission document but excludes certain fundamental information regarding the price and number of securities to be issued as these are determined during the marketing process.

18.20   Whilst it is important for investor confidence that few changes are made to the AIM admission document from its pathfinder form, there may be some changes made to this before the placing letters are sent out. In any event, by the time the placing letters are sent out, the number of securities to be issued and the price at which they will be issued will have been determined. In order to make it clear what version of the AIM admission document forms the basis of the placees' subscriptions a further draft of the AIM admission document is circulated with the placing letters. This version, often referred to as the "placing proof" or "p-proof", will be the same as the final AIM admission document save that it will not have been dated. In the placing letter, the placees will acknowledge that it is the placing proof that they are relying on as opposed to any other documents or early drafts of the AIM admission document.

CONTRACT NOTES

18.21   It is becoming increasingly common for the placing process to be sped up by using an alternative structure as opposed to placing letters. The principal reason behind this is that by the time the placing letters are prepared, have been completed with the each placee's details and the number of securities which they are willing to take as part of the placing, and been sent to the placee and returned signed, a number of days will have lapsed.

18.22 As a result, a practice has developed where, instead of a placing letter, the announcement of the placing or draft documents sent to potential placees will include terms and conditions of the placing. This will then enable the investment bank or broker to contract with the potential placee over the telephone incorporating those terms by reference.

18.23 Once the contract has been made and accepted orally, the investment bank or broker will produce a contract note summarising the terms. It should be noted that this contract note does not form part of the contract itself but is merely a record of it in writing. This method of conducting a placing allows the placing timetable to be reduced by a number of days and allows the company to close the placing earlier.

IN PRACTICE

In practice, the contractual documents which set out the terms and conditions on which the placing will be conducted are very important in the placing process. For directors personally, it also sets out the role and responsibility that they will have and their potential liability to the broker.

For these reasons, whilst a large part of the placing agreement will not be subject to extensive negotiation, the warranties, who will give them and the potential liability under the warranties form an important part of every placing.

CHAPTER 19

Offers to the public

AT A GLANCE

Under section 85(1) of the *Financial Services and Markets Act 2000* (FSMA) it is an offence to offer applicable transferable securities to the public in the United Kingdom unless an approved prospectus has been made available to the public before the offer is made. To avoid falling foul of this requirement, an AIM company contemplating a fundraising in the United Kingdom will, together with its advisers, always need to consider the following two questions. First, does the prospective fundraising constitute an offer of transferable securities to the public in the United Kingdom for the purposes of section 85(1) the FSMA? Second, if it does, can it be structured in such a way as to make use of one or more of the available exemptions, for example by restricting participation in the offer to investment professionals?

INTRODUCTION

19.1   The new statutory provisions governing offers to the public in the United Kingdom were introduced on 1 July 2005 and the relevant provisions in the FSMA follow very closely, or incorporate directly, the equivalent provisions in the *Prospectus Directive*.

19.2   The prospectus requirement introduced by section 85 of the FSMA is two-fold: an approved prospectus is required to be issued in the event of a public offer of transferable securities (section 85(1) FSMA); and also in connection with an application requesting the admission of transferable securities to trading on a regulated market (section 86(2) FSMA). The two limbs each have a series of avail-able exemptions, which are incorporated either in the FSMA itself (section 86 FSMA) or in the *Prospectus Rules* in force in the United Kingdom. As AIM is not a regulated market for these purposes (as opposed to the Main Market of the London Stock Exchange), the second of the two limbs, the admission of transfer-able securities to trading on a regulated market, is not a relevant consideration for companies seeking admission of their securities to trading on AIM.

19.3   It is worth highlighting the contrast between the prospectus obligations placed on AIM and Main Market companies. On the Main Market, an application for admission of securities to trading, irrespective of whether there is a public offer of those securities, automatically triggers the requirement to produce an approved prospectus. Accordingly, a Main Market company will be required to publish an approved prospectus on its initial admission to trading on the Main Market, and then on any subsequent issue of securities, subject to applicable exemptions. The principal exemption from the requirement to produce a prospectus is for the issue of securities representing, over a period of 12 months, less than 10 per cent of the number of securities of the same class already admitted to trading on the same regulated market. An approved prospectus for these purposes means, for a prospectus approved in the United Kingdom, approved by the United Kingdom Listing Authority or a prospectus which is passported into the United Kingdom following its approval in another EU member state.

19.4 AIM companies are not subject to the same requirements to produce a prospectus on admission to trading on AIM. Companies applying to have their securities admitted to AIM are required instead to produce an AIM admission document prior to admission to trading on AIM. Once admitted to trading on AIM, there are no documentary requirements on the issue of new securities imposed by the *AIM Rules for Companies*, beyond filing an application form (save in certain circumstances, e.g. where an issue of securities is made in consideration of an acquisition which is a reverse takeover). In essence, an AIM admission document is an abbreviated version of a prospectus, with certain substantial content requirements, such as the operating and financial review and information on capital resources, carved out. Another important distinction is that an AIM admission document is not required to go through the process of being vetted and approved by the United Kingdom Listing Authority.

19.5 For AIM companies, therefore, the requirement to publish a prospectus only arises in connection with a public offer. Publication and approval of a prospectus is perceived in the London markets as a time-consuming process, and market practice on AIM is firmly against using a prospectus as an offer document where not required to do so (unlike, for example, the Alternext market on the continent, where, although there are similar exemptions available from the requirement to publish an approved prospectus on an application to join the market, many applicant companies have still opted to do so).

19.6 For this reason, and the fact that the exemptions to section 85(1) of the FSMA have proved sufficiently wide to allow companies to utilise them in most cases where they are conducting a fundraising, few AIM companies have published approved prospectuses since the introduction of the EU prospectus regime. The most pertinent question for AIM companies in relation to section 85(1) is almost always how to structure a placing so as to fall within one or more of the applicable exemptions. First, though, a company and its advisers will need to establish whether what they are intending to do constitutes a public offer.

WHAT IS AN OFFER OF TRANSFERABLE SECURITIES TO THE PUBLIC?

19.7 The relevant definition of an offer of transferable securities to the public is provided at section 102B of the FSMA, being: "a communication to any person which presents sufficient information on:

- the transferable securities to be offered; and
- the terms on which they are offered,

to enable an investor to decide to buy or subscribe for the securities in question".

19.8 Transferable securities for these purposes does not just mean securities, albeit that for AIM companies seeking to raise money equity fundraisings will be the usual route, but includes any class of security which is negotiable on the capital market. These transferable securities include securities, bonds or other forms of securitised debt, options or warrants to acquire or sell securities, or derivatives giving rise to a cash settlement determined by reference to securities or other indicators, save for those classes of security which are expressly excluded (see Figure 19.1).

19.9 With a definition as broad as this, a public offer of securities can plainly encompass the placing of securities in an AIM company or prospective AIM company, and the documents, or other communications, through which such placings are effected. This will usually mean a placing letter or subscription agreement, or, increasingly common for secondary fundraisings of AIM listed companies, an oral contract made on a telephone call, the contents of which are then recorded in a contract note, will all be capable of falling within a public offer of securities.

19.10 The salient point for an AIM company or prospective AIM company to take from the above definition is that, unlike the regulated market trigger (section 86(2) FSMA), the public offer test draws no distinction between the type of company conducting the offering. Accordingly, it can apply to, and the same exemptions will need to be considered by, a company raising money on an initial public offering in conjunction with an admission to trading on AIM, or an already-listed AIM company carrying out a secondary fundraising, or even by a private company

---

FIGURE 19.1   What are transferable securities?

Transferable securities are defined in section 102A(3) of the FSMA as anything which is a transferable security for the purposes of the *Markets in Financial Instruments Directive*, other than money market instruments for the purposes of that directive which have a maturity of less than 12 months.

Pursuant to the *Markets in Financial Instruments Directive*, "transferable securities" means those classes of securities which are negotiable on the capital market, with the exception of instruments of payment, such as:

- securities in companies and other securities equivalent to securities in companies, partnerships or other entities, and depository receipts in respect of securities;
- bonds or other forms of securitised debt, including depository receipts in respect of such securities;
- any other securities giving the right to acquire or sell any such transferable securities or giving rise to a cash settlement determined by reference to transferable securities, currencies, interest rates or yields, commodities or other indices or measures.

---

raising money at the pre-initial public offer stage. With the latter of these examples there have been some arguments whether securities in a private company, particularly where transfer is tightly restricted, do in fact constitute transferable securities "negotiable on the capital market". However, the cautious approach, in the absence of specific guidance from the Committee of European Securities Regulators (CESR, the body that sets out the European common approaches to be adopted by securities regulators) or the Financial Services Authority on this point, is that private companies also need to pay heed to the requirements of section 85(1) of the FSMA.

19.11   Section 85(1) of the FSMA applies equally to a placing of securities by a financial intermediary on behalf of an issuer, so the relevant provisions, and exemptions, will apply in the same way to a company placing securities with investors directly, or, much more commonly for an AIM company, doing so with the assistance of a broker or investment bank.

19.12   Section 85(1) of the FSMA applies to all applicable public offers of transferable securities made in the United Kingdom, by which is meant any offer made to a person in the United Kingdom (section 102(B) FSMA). The public offer regime draws no distinction based on the home jurisdiction of the issuer, and will apply equally to UK and non-UK companies raising money from UK investors.

19.13   Schedule 11A to the FSMA lists a number of specific classes of security, such as a unit within an open ended collective investment scheme, which are excluded from the public offer regime. There is also a generic exemption which will catch any *de minimis* fundraising which raises gross proceeds that are less than the financial threshold of €2.5 million in any 12-month period. Accordingly, offers to the public of transferable securities by AIM companies where the total consideration is less than €2.5 million, aggregated over a 12-month period, are outside of the public offer regime.

OFFER TO THE PUBLIC – EXEMPTIONS

19.14   The *de minimis* €2.5 million in any 12-month period exemption is going to be of limited use for most AIM company fundraisings, for obvious reasons. In reality, most AIM companies will look to make use of one or both of the exemptions in section 86(1)(a) and (b) of the FSMA in order to avoid the requirement to produce a prospectus.

Qualified investors exemption

19.15   For a full definition of qualified investor, incorporated in section 86(7) of the FSMA, see Figure 19.2. Of the different categories of qualified investor, the most important and widely used is the first: that for Financial Services Authority-authorised entities, in other words the UK-based financial services institutions, which are authorised to carry on business by the Financial Services Authority. A list of authorised firms is accessible via the Financial Services Authority's website at: www.fsa.gov.uk/Pages/register. There is also a list of Financial Services

---

FIGURE 19.2   Definition of a qualified investor

"Qualified investor" means:

(i)   a legal entity which is authorised or regulated to operate in the financial markets or, if not so authorised or regulated, whose corporate purpose is solely to invest in securities;

(ii)   a national or regional government, central bank, or international or supranational institution such as the International Monetary Fund, the European Central Bank or similar organisation;

(iii)   a legal entity which has two or more of: (a) an average of at least 250 employees during the last financial year; (b) a total balance sheet of more than €43 million; and (c) an annual net turnover of more than €50 million; in each case as shown in its last annual or consolidated accounts;

(iv)   a person entered on the Qualified Investor Register maintained by the Financial Services Authority. Such person, if an individual, being a UK resident who has two or more of the following: (a) carried out transactions of a significant size on securities markets at an average frequency of, at least, ten per quarter over the previous four quarters; (b) a securities portfolio exceeding €0.5 million; and (c) works, or has worked for at least one year, in the financial sector in a professional position which requires knowledge of securities investment, or, if a company, being a company whose registered office is in the United Kingdom and which fails to satisfy at least two of the criteria at (iii) above; or

(v)   an investor authorised by an European Economic Area member state, other than the United Kingdom, to be considered as a qualified investor for the purposes of the *Prospectus Directive*.

Authority-authorised individuals at this location, but it is the firms, rather than individuals, that are relevant for this exemption.

19.16   If the placees on any offering are restricted to Financial Services Authority-authorised firms, then no prospectus will be required.

19.17   In its scope, this exemption covers more than just authorised firms investing in securities on their own account. Pursuant to section 86(2) of the FSMA, where an authorised firm invests in securities on behalf of its clients, but the firm is acting on a discretionary basis (i.e. the terms on which the qualified investor is engaged enable the qualified investor to make decisions concerning the acceptance of offers of transferable securities on the client's behalf, without reference to the client), then the offer of securities is treated as being made to the firm alone – there is no transparency through to the underlying clients. So, by placing securities only with institutions authorised to act on a discretionary basis on behalf of their clients, as many AIM brokers do, it is also possible to avoid the requirement to produce a prospectus.

19.18   Conversely, where a qualified investor or third party is acting on a non-discretionary basis on behalf of a client, then the offer is treated as being made to the underlying client. So, where a non-qualified investor, acting on a non-discretionary basis, invests in securities on behalf of a qualified investor, that would also be an exempt transaction. Accordingly, there will need to be a careful analysis of the persons to whom the offer is being made.

19.19   An issuer or its agents wishing to obtain a copy of the Qualified Investor Register may do so on payment of a negligible fee (currently £25 plus VAT for a copy of the Register or £150 plus VAT to receive updated copies on a monthly basis for a year). However, it is an offence to use the Qualified Investor Register for any purpose other than determining whether an investor is a qualified investor and making an offer of securities to the qualified investor, in connection with an offer of securities to the public. It should be noted that take-up by eligible investors has been minimal since the introduction of section 87R of the FSMA (also on 1 July 2005), and the Qualified Investor Register exemption is rarely used.

100 persons exemption

19.20   If the offer is made to, or directed at, fewer than 100 persons per EEA state, other than qualified investors, then again it will be exempt from the prospectus requirements.

19.21   This exemption allows AIM companies, and brokers placing securities on their behalf, to include a limited number of non-institutional placees on an offering and, as such, is clearly a useful allowance for brokers who do place securities with individuals directly as well as with institutional investors. Some brokers will not place securities with non-institutional investors, as a matter of policy, and so will be limited to the first exemption in any case. Other brokers may include individuals on a "Chair's list" of friends and family of the directors and shareholders who wish to acquire securities, although care will need to be taken in how the offer or communication to such persons are made (see Chapter 31, *Directors' responsibility*).

19.22   It should be noted in relation to the 100 persons exemption that companies will still need to have regard to the limitations imposed by section 21 of the FSMA regarding financial promotions. Section 21 of the FSMA provides that, where an invitation or inducement to engage in investment activity is communicated in the course of business, the communication must either be approved by an authorised person or only communicated to eligible categories of investor, as set out in the *Financial Services and Markets Act 2000 (Financial Promotion) Order 2005* (FPO) (as amended). There is a high degree of overlap between eligible investors under the FPO and qualified investors for institutional or corporate investors. For example, a Financial Services Authority-authorised financial institution will be both a qualified investor and an investment professional under article 19 of the FPO. However, this is not the case in respect of individual investors, for whom there are only a few, very limited exemptions available under the FPO, principally for certified high net worth individuals (article 48 FPO) (although they cannot rely on this exemption in connection with securities which are to be admitted to trading on AIM) and sophisticated investors (article 50 FPO).

Other exemptions

19.23   There are three other rarely used public offer exemptions available under section 86(1) of the FSMA, where in respect of an offer:

■ the minimum consideration is at least €50,000 per security;

■ the securities are denominated in amounts of at least €50,000; or

■ the total consideration of the offer is less than €100,000.

OTHER SCENARIOS

19.24   Aside from placings of securities, there are other situations where an AIM company may need to consider the requirements of the public offer regime, and some of these, together with additional exemptions available under the *Prospectus Rules*, are considered further below. The application of the *Prospectus Directive*, in certain situations, has been the subject of debate among regulators and market participants, and both the United Kingdom Listing Authority, in its publication *List!*, and CESR in its Q&A publication have addressed the topic.

Employee share option schemes

19.25   Share options issued to employees or executives as part of an employee remuneration scheme will not usually be assignable by the employee and, as such, CESR has expressed the view that such options, not being "negotiable instruments", are not transferable securities for the purposes of the public offer regime. Where an employee option is assignable, it will still probably not trigger the prospectus requirement on account that (again usually) there will be no consideration being provided for the option by the employee, and therefore as a free offer, by virtue of the *de minimis* €2.5 million exemption, the securities will not be applicable transferable securities.

19.26   CESR has commented that one should not be too willing to apportion hidden consideration to an option provided ostensibly for no consideration. Speculative reasoning that an employee's salary would have been higher had they not been offered participation in an option scheme will not be sufficient. Only where an option is offered directly in place of another, quantifiable, financial benefit might it be appropriate to apportion consideration to the option.

19.27   Where an employee option is both assignable and deemed not free, there may still be applicable exemptions – for example, the 100 persons for an executive scheme, or the scheme awards in any 12-month period when taken with other offers may still come within the €2.5 million exemption. There is also a specific exemption provided in the *Prospectus Rules* for options awarded to directors, former directors or employees, but this is only available where the employer has securities admitted to trading on a regulated market so would only be applicable to an AIM company where a company in its group is also listed on a regulated market in the EEA.

19.28   CESR has also commented that it does not consider the subsequent exercise of an employee option by the employee to constitute a separate offer.

Free offers

19.29 CESR has also addressed the question of "free offers", of which employee share options provided for no consideration are one example. In assessing whether "free offers" of securities trigger the requirement to publish a prospectus, CESR notes that it may be possible to rely on the *de minimis* €2.5 million exemption (see Paragraph 19.13). Similarly, where a "free offer" is made in circumstances where the recipients have no choice as to whether to accept or reject an allocation of securities, then there is no offer for the purposes of the *Prospectus Directive*. This analysis has relevance beyond the realm of employee share options. For example, where securities in an offeror company are offered to target shareholders as part of a compulsory acquisition procedure to complete a takeover, or where a takeover is effected by way of a scheme of arrangement under section 899 of the *Companies Act 2006* (formerly section 425 of the *Companies Act 1985*, which once approved by shareholder vote does not allow individual shareholders to reject the terms of the scheme), then provided that the individual shareholders are not able to reject the securities being offered – and for example to take cash instead – there is no public offer.

19.30 Finally, there is one further relevant exemption: under *Prospectus Rule* 1.2.2 securities offered or allotted or to be allotted to existing shareholders free of charge, or securities allocated to existing shareholders as a scrip dividend, are exempt from the prospectus requirement. The issuer is required, however, to make available information on the number and nature of the securities being offered, and the principal terms and reasons for the offer. This is separate from open offers and rights issues, for which a prospectus will usually be required (see Chapter 21, *Rights issues and open offers*).

Takeover or merger – equivalent document

19.31 Where transferable securities are being offered in connection with a merger or a takeover effected by an exchange offer then the requirement to publish a prospectus may be waived provided the relevant company publishes a document considered by the United Kingdom Listing Authority to be an equivalent document (*Prospectus Rule* 1.2.3 and *Prospectus Rule* 1.2.4). This will mean incorporating prospectus content into a circular or equivalent document being prepared in connection with the transaction. The United Kingdom Listing Authority has advised in *List!* that it will apply the full approval process to a document where equivalence is being claimed, and will apply only limited discretion in deciding what will be considered equivalent. As a result, the equivalence exemption will have limited substantive effect, save as follows:

- an equivalent document, unlike a prospectus, will not be subject to the requirement to issue a supplementary prospectus in the event of a significant new matter arising during the life of the document;
- not being a prospectus, an equivalent document cannot be passported into other EEA jurisdictions in the way that a prospectus can.

IN PRACTICE

AIM companies or prospective AIM companies wishing to raise money by way of a placing of securities, and wanting to avoid having to produce a prospectus in connection with the placing, will need to structure their placing so as to make use of one or more of the applicable exemptions. In most cases, this will mean placing only to Financial Services Authority-authorised entities (or another category of qualified investor) and, possibly, to a limited number of individuals or corporate entities that do not meet any of the qualified investor criteria. In all cases, but in particular when including placees that are not Financial Services Authority-authorised firms as part of a placing, issuers and their advisers will also need to take care to ensure that the placing documents satisfy the requirements of section 21 of the FSMA regarding financial promotions.

CHAPTER 20

Institutional placings

AT A GLANCE

Institutional placings are brokered offers of securities directed only at qualified investors as defined in Chapter 19, *Offers to the public*, as opposed to a general offer of those securities. Institutional placings now account for the overwhelming majority of fundraisings on AIM. As discussed in Chapter 19, *Offers to the public*, since the implementation of the *Prospectus Directive* in July 2005, companies seeking admission of their securities to trading on AIM have sought to avoid the costly and time consuming process of producing a compliant prospectus which would require approval by the United Kingdom Listing Authority.

ADVANTAGES OF AN INSTITUTIONAL PLACING

20.1   Assuming the placing is directed only at persons falling within applicable exemptions to the *Prospectus Rules*, a placing has the advantage of reducing the regulatory burden, the legal risk and consequently some of the time and costs associated with an initial public offer process.

20.2   An institutional placing also provides the company and its broker with greater certainty as to the success of the fundraising and the likely amount of funds which will ultimately be raised.

20.3   An institutional placing is a managed offer of securities and typically the company's broker will have received indications of demand for the company's securities from its institutional clients before the final offer process commences. Therefore, unless there is a dramatic fall in market demand or some unexpected event arises by the time the company publishes its AIM admission document, it will know that it has raised sufficient funds to implement its business plan, as described in the AIM admission document.

20.4   By contrast, an offer for subscription which is not limited to qualified investors will often require the publication of a compliant prospectus (unless an exemption applies) and (certainly for the smaller fundraisings) runs the risk that all the additional costs and time of the initial public offer process would be in vain. Further information on offers to the public is set out at Chapter 19, *Offers to the public*.

20.5   However, the key advantage of a successful offer of securities to the public is the opportunity to create a wide investor base. This could promote liquidity in the company's securities post admission to trading on AIM and also means the company may be less beholden to a limited number of institutions with significant shareholdings.

THE PLACING PROCESS – INSTITUTIONAL PLACING

20.6 Whilst traditionally offers of securities to the public on AIM have tended to be associated with small issuers who cannot rely on institutional demand, it is interesting to note that on the Main Market of the London Stock Exchange, the large, high-profile initial public offers tend to be structured as offers, to enable private investors as well as institutional investors to participate. As the AIM market continues to mature, some of the larger AIM floats may also consider this route.

STRUCTURE OF AN INSTITUTIONAL PLACING

20.7 North Americans often refer to institutional placings as "bought deals". This reflects the fact that the selling process on a placing happens in advance of the publication of the offer document, AIM admission document or prospectus (Figure 20.1). Assuming the institutions concerned fall within applicable exemptions to the *Prospectus Rules* and the financial promotion regime under section 21 of the *Financial Services and Markets Act 2000*, the institutions can be approached well in advance of the publication of the AIM admission document.

FIGURE 20.1 The placing process – institutional placing

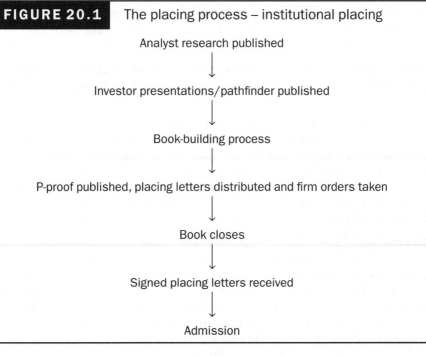

Analyst research published

↓

Investor presentations/pathfinder published

↓

Book-building process

↓

P-proof published, placing letters distributed and firm orders taken

↓

Book closes

↓

Signed placing letters received

↓

Admission

Analyst research

20.8 On the larger institutional fundraisings, the company's brokers will typically have produced or commissioned analyst research on the company, which would be made available to institutional investors around the time the initial public offer is publicly announced.

20.9 It is considered best practice to seek to ensure the analyst research report does not unduly influence the investment decision of the placees. The placees should only invest on the back of the placing proof of the AIM admission document, which will be provided to placees at the end of the marketing process. The placing proof is a copy of the AIM admission document with all the blanks from the pathfinder AIM admission document completed (other than the date of the AIM admission document). Therefore, as a rule of thumb, city best practice should be a four to six week gap between the publication of the research note and the publication of the placing proof. Further information on analyst research is set out in Chapter 24, *Analyst research*.

Investor presentations

20.10 Following publication of the research, the broker will typically organise a series of investor presentations, referred to as the roadshow. This process can be pretty arduous for management, especially those undertaking large, international fundraisings where several weeks can be spent visiting institutions in key European and North American cities.

20.11 The roadshow is management's opportunity to "sell" themselves and their company to the broker, key companies and contacts and the quality of the presentation will be one of the key factors which determine the success or otherwise of the initial public offer.

20.12 The presentation itself will normally take the form of a presentation, delivered by two or three senior executives, followed by a question and answer session.

20.13 It is crucial that the roadshow is carefully managed by the broker; on the one hand to ensure that management deliver the right message to investors and demonstrate the company to be an attractive investment proposition, on the other hand to ensure that the key information included in the investor presentation is consistent with the information in the AIM admission document. Typically, a pathfinder AIM admission document will have been prepared by the time the marketing process commences and will be provided to institutional investors during the roadshow process.

20.14 Given the importance of the presentation in influencing the investment decision of potential investors, a carefully worded disclaimer and notices will be included at the front of the presentation. It is also just as important to ensure that the presentation goes through a detailed verification process as it is for the AIM admission document. It is also important to draw up scripted answers to questions which are likely to be asked at the roadshow, in order to ensure management does not disclose information which is not included in either the presentation or the final AIM admission document.

"Book-building" and pricing

20.15 Both during and immediately following the roadshow process, the broker will be seeking indications of demand for the company's securities and the price at which investors will be prepared to subscribe. This process is often referred to as the "book-building" in that the broker is building the book of likely subscribers and is effectively allowing the market to determine the price within an indicative range set by the broker.

20.16 Once the broker has completed the book, hopefully up to and perhaps even exceeding the targeted fundraising, it will set the price on the basis of the indications of interest received and will allocate the total securities available among the investors. Brokers will be expected to have pricing and allocation policies to demonstrate appropriate management of conflicts between its corporate finance department and its sales team.

Closing

20.17 Once the placing letters have been signed and returned, the broker will sign the placing agreement, as it is only at this point that the broker has comfort that the required funds have been raised. The AIM admission document can then be published, stating the aggregate amount which *has* been raised in the placing. (Of course, if the fundraising had been an offer for subscription the amount to be raised would have to be referred to as an "up to" amount as there would be no certainty of funds raised). Assuming the institutional investors are all eligible CREST members, the details provided by each of them in their placing letters will be matched in CREST and settlement will occur automatically on admission to trading on AIM, three business days after publication of the AIM admission document.

20.18 Given the ease of process and certainty provided by an institutional placing over a classic offer of securities to the public, it is easy to see why this form of fundraising has become the norm on AIM initial public offers. Whilst an offer for subscription may give a wide investor base and possibly greater liquidity, most AIM issuers will want to ensure that their debut on the market is as smooth as possible. Therefore, saving any dramatic shifts in City practice, institutional placings are set to remain the key method of raising funds on admission to trading on AIM.

THE PLACING PROCESS – ACCELERATED BOOK-BUILD

Structure of an accelerated book-build

20.19 Where the investment bank or broker has confidence in the success of placing then they may conduct the placing by way of an accelerated book-build (Figure 20.2).

FIGURE 20.2   The placing process – accelerated book-build

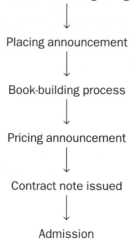

Pre-marketing
(usually carried out by the investment bank after market close on the day prior to the accelerated book-building being carried out)

↓

Placing announcement

↓

Book-building process

↓

Pricing announcement

↓

Contract note issued

↓

Admission

20.20   On the eve of the announcement of the proposed placing, and where the company is already admitted to trading on AIM, usually after market close, the investment bank or broker will conduct a limited marketing with certain of their institutions. This will be done on an insider basis. This means that the institutional investor acknowledges that it is in possession of unpublished, price sensitive information which has not been announced (the price sensitive information being that the placing will be conducted and the price at which it will be conducted). In order to avoid the potential of committing criminal offences referred to in Chapter 15, *Directors' responsibilities for an AIM admission document and verification*, the institutional investor is then unable to deal in the securities, unless and until the placing is announced or the company informs them that the placing is no longer proceeding.

20.21   Prior to the opening of the market on the morning after the initial market-ing, the company will usually make a detailed placing announcement. This placing announcement sets out a description of the placing and the reasons why the com-pany is conducting the placing. This placing announcement will usually have an appendix to it which will set out the detailed terms and conditions of the placing, including the representations and warranties to be given by the placees. These terms are often very similar to those contained in a placing letter, see Chapter 18, *Contractual documentation for fundraisings*.

20.22   Following the release of the placing announcement, the investment bank or broker will then conduct an accelerated book-building process. This book-building process will typically determine the price at which the securities are to be issued as well as the total number of securities to be issued.

20.23 Once the investment bank or broker has received sufficient indications of interest it will then hold a pricing meeting which may, to some extent, involve the company and its directors. As a result of this meeting, the price and the number of securities to be issued are determined. Following this meeting the broker's or investment banker's sales department will then telephone the potential placees to accept the offer they made in the book-building process. As part of this telephone conversation the investment bank or broker will confirm that the terms relating to the placing are those which were contained in the placing announcement released that morning. Whilst this form of offer and acceptance orally gives rise to a legally binding contract, it is market practice for this to then be recorded in writing in the form of a contract note. The contract note however is not the formal contract but a record of the oral contract.

20.24 Once all the securities have been placed in this way, the company then makes the pricing announcement which informs the market of the price at which the securities were issued and the total number of securities issued. The process for the admission of the securities placed to trading on AIM then continues in the usual way.

IN PRACTICE

In practice, the ability to access institutional money and conduct fundraisings either as part of an initial public offer or a secondary issue is one of the key motivating factors for many companies joining AIM.

Whilst at first the process may seem quite complex, it is made up of a number of relatively straightforward steps.

CHAPTER **21**

Rights issues and open offers

AT A GLANCE

Rights issues and open offers are two methods of fundraising by companies whose securities are already admitted to trading on AIM as alternatives to the more usual form of institutional placing. The key advantage of both of these forms of fundraising is that they involve a pre-emptive element and therefore the holders of securities have the option to maintain their percentage holding.

INTRODUCTION

21.1 Rights issues and open offers are both alternative means to an institutional placing by which a company raises additional capital, although in practice these tend to be more common for a company which is already admitted to trading on AIM.

21.2 As both involve the issue of securities for cash, each must be structured to comply with statutory pre-emption provisions and other authorities to allot securities, unless such pre-emption rights have been disapplied and such authorities have already been obtained.

21.3 Both of these fundraising methods also allow existing holders to invest in the additional securities, usually at a discount to the then current market price.

21.4 Whilst these fundraising methods have a number of similarities, holders who are offered securities in a rights issue have certain rights which do not apply in an open offer. These include:

■ holders may sell all or part of their right to subscribe for the securities in the rights issue in the market; and

■ to the extent that any of the holders who are offered securities in the rights issue do not take up their allocation or sell such allocation to a third party, such securities can be sold to a third party on the open market and such holders are entitled to receive (in cash) any proceeds from such sale over and above the rights issue subscription price, less costs.

RIGHTS ISSUES

21.5 A rights issue is an offer of additional securities to the existing holders, pro rata to their existing holdings, and made by sending the holders renounceable letters of allotment known as "provisional allotment letters".

21.6 The provisional allotment letters will set out the number of securities being provisionally allotted as well as the terms on which the offer may be accepted, such as the time period for acceptance, the price and the payment terms. The period for acceptance will usually last at least three weeks and it will also be open to the recipient to take up only some of the securities provisionally allotted to that holder. The length of time for which the offer is open will depend on a number of matters, including notice provisions in the Articles of Association and also whether the offer is made following the disapplication of pre-emption rights under the *Companies Act 1985* or *2006*.

21.7 Another feature of provisional allotment letters is that all or part of the right to purchase further securities at the subscription price contained in the provisional allotment letter may be traded or sold during the period up until payment is due. As payment will not normally have been made at this stage, this is normally referred to as trading "nil paid rights", although in some rights issues (usually larger issues) the right to purchase is also traded "fully paid" (i.e. after the subscription monies have been paid but before the date for submitting the relevant provisional allotment letter for registration).

21.8 The subscription price in a rights issue is usually at a discount to the market value of the securities and there is no limit to the discount which may be applied. The reason for this is that the greater the discount applied, the more likely the existing holders are to take up their entitlement and not be diluted.

21.9 Historically, the discount applied in rights issues has in practice been limited to around 10 to 20 per cent, with heavily discounted rights issues of up to around 50 per cent ("deep discounts") only being used by companies which were in severe financial difficulty. However, some companies on the Main Market have had to use deep discounts as a way of providing more liquidity in the trading of nil paid rights and such greater discounts are therefore becoming more common.

21.10 When the period for accepting the offer expires, to the extent that any of the securities offered have not been taken up, such securities may be placed by the company's broker or investment bank with third parties for the benefit of the holders who did not take up their entitlement. This means that any proceeds from such placing over and above the rights issue subscription price, less costs, are payable to such holders in cash.

21.11 Rights issues may be underwritten in return for a commission payable to the company's broker or investment bank, although underwriting is less common on AIM than it is for companies whose securities are traded on the Main Market of the London Stock Exchange. The effect of the underwriting is that if the company's broker or the investment bank is unable to place the securities which have not been taken up within a certain period of time it will be obliged to take up such securities itself. Therefore, as this is inherently risky to the company's broker or investment bank, it is common for them to sub-underwrite the issue to institutional clients of theirs, again in return for a commission. Underwriting only tends to be applicable to the smallest and largest offerings.

OPEN OFFERS

21.12 Open offers are, in their purest form, very similar to rights issues; that is, they involve a pre-emptive offer of securities to the existing holders, usually at a discount to the then market price. The key difference between a rights issue and an open offer is that rather than using provisional allotment letters, an open offer is made by way of subscription form. The effect of this is that the rights under the subscription form are personal to each holder of securities and are not therefore tradable. In addition, unlike a rights issue, if a holder does not take up the offer, it lapses and the holder will not receive any payment.

21.13 The most common form of open offers is one which is combined with an element of institutional placing. These "placings and open offers" are usually structured as a provisional "placing" to the broker or investment bank, with the existing holders having the right to "claw back" up to 100 per cent of the securities being placed. For this reason, open offers can also be referred to as "placings subject to claw back".

21.14 Although open offers can also be made through CREST, the offer is usually made by sending application forms to the existing holders, granting them the right to subscribe for the securities provisionally placed with the broker or investment bank. These application forms will usually entitle each holder to subscribe for at least their pro rata entitlement of the securities provisionally placed (the "guaranteed minimum entitlement"), but if any of the holders declines all (or part) of their guaranteed minimum entitlement, such securities can be allocated to those applying in excess of their guaranteed minimum entitlement.

21.15 Unlike the provisional allotment letters sent to holders in a rights issue, the application form sent to a holder in an open offer is not a document of title and therefore cannot be traded. There is also no sale of the securities on behalf of holders if they do not take up their entitlement because such securities will automatically be taken up by the placees procured by the broker or investment bank or, in the event that the securities have not been placed with a third party and the offer is underwritten, with the broker or placing agent itself. This means that if each holder does not take up their entitlement, not only will they be diluted, they will also not benefit from the proceeds of any placing of the relevant securities with a third party.

21.16 One benefit of the fact that there is no trading of the application forms in an open offer is that the forms can be sent out at the same time as the notice of any general meeting convened to disapply pre-emption rights, obtain authority to allot securities etc. (i.e. when the offer is still conditional). This means that the timeframe for an open offer can be significantly shorter than for a rights issue, which can therefore also have a positive impact on costs for the company.

21.17 Unlike with rights issues, companies issuing securities in an open offer and placing are considered to be subject to greater restrictions on the amount of discount they can apply to the subscription price. The reason for this practice is that companies whose securities are admitted to trading on the Main Market are bound to comply with the *Listing Rules*, which do not permit a discount of more than 10 per cent without shareholder consent. Although not bound by the *Listing Rules*,

AIM companies should bear this in mind as it represents best practice. In theory, this may make it harder to raise money, but as open offers are usually accompanied by a placing, the company can ensure that all the securities will have been subscribed for by the end of the process.

21.18   As with rights issues, where there is an element of underwriting, the underwriting institution in an open offer will want to try to limit its exposure by sub-underwriting the offer.

CONSIDERATIONS APPLICABLE TO BOTH RIGHTS ISSUES AND OPEN OFFERS

21.19   As rights issues and open offers are both offers to the public it is likely they will both require a prospectus unless the offer is for less than €2.5 million or one of the exemptions applies (see Chapter 19, *Offers to the public*, for further details).

21.20   Before undertaking a rights issue or an open offer, the directors of the company should also consider whether the company's authorised but unissued capital and their authority under section 80 of the *Companies Act 1985* are sufficient to cover the offer. In each case they should take account of pre-existing obligations to issue securities such as outstanding warrants and options.

21.21   In addition, as both rights issues and open offers involve the issue of securities for cash, both need to comply with the statutory pre-emption provisions contained in the *Companies Act 1985* if they have not already been disapplied. Therefore, as the consequences of having to comply with section 89 are disadvantageous (e.g. the period of the offer is longer and the fractional entitlements of a holder cannot be aggregated and sold but instead are rounded down) companies will nearly always seek to disapply section 89 of the *Companies Act 1985* (to the extent they have not already) as part of the process in the fundraising. Also, if section 89 is disapplied it permits the company not to have to offer securities to those of its overseas holders who may be subject to onerous securities laws (e.g. shareholders resident in the United States).

IN PRACTICE

The key advantage of both rights issues and open offers is that they involve a pre-emptive element and therefore the holders of securities have the opportunity to maintain their percentage holding. However, the use of rights issues and open offers by companies listed on AIM as a means to carry out a further fundraising has declined in recent years, with companies choosing to carry out institutional placings instead. The main reason for this is that it is usually possible to structure an institutional placing so that it is not an offer to the public and therefore avoid the requirement to produce a prospectus.

CHAPTER 22

Secondary issues

AT A GLANCE

"Secondary issue" is the term used to describe an equity fundraising by a company whose securities have already been admitted to trading on AIM. Secondary issues can be a very useful and cost-effective tool for companies whose securities are admitted to trading on AIM to raise additional funds as, in their simplest form, they require little more than a placing agreement and therefore involve the company paying limited advisers' fees, other than the commission payable to the broker.

The structure and documentation required depends, in part, on the amount being raised, the share authorities which the company has, or requires, and the method by which the broker is going to market the secondary issue.

INTRODUCTION

22.1 "Secondary issue" is a broad term which encompasses a number of concepts and methods of conducting an equity fundraising, whether by simple placing or accelerated book-building (see Chapter 20, *Institutional placings*), rights issue, open offer (see Chapter 21, *Rights issues and open offers*) or even a combination of some of these, such as a placing and open offer (see Chapter 21, *Rights issues and open offers*).

22.2 The documentation that is required in order to conduct a secondary issue will depend on the type of offer that is being made and other factors, such as the due diligence the broker requires, the approach the broker will take to marketing and also matters relating to the company's corporate structure – in particular its share authorities.

MARKETING OF A SECONDARY ISSUE

22.3 The most significant factor in determining the timetable and the structure of a secondary issue, and the documentation that will be required, is whether a secondary offer will be structured in a way that triggers the requirement to produce a prospectus. Further information on public offers is set out in Chapter 19, *Offers to the public*, but, for example, a secondary offer structured by way of rights issue or open offer can, if the company has more than 100 shareholders, trigger the requirement to publish a prospectus. Where a prospectus is required, the company will be involved in significant work in the preparation of the prospectus and will be required to include financial information and possibly technical reports. The prospectus needs to be approved by the United Kingdom Listing Authority, which can add up to a month to a timetable in addition to the time that it takes to prepare the prospectus. Further, where a prospectus is produced there are also a raft of supporting documents which are required, from directors' memoranda, accountants' reports and comfort letters to supporting letters and statements from the directors and the professional team. For this reason, many secondary issues are structured in a way which will not trigger the requirement to produce a prospectus, for example by limiting participation in the secondary issue to institutional investors. Whilst this seems an easy option – in order to avoid the requirement to produce a prospectus – the directors of a company who are proposing to make an issue on a non pre-emptive basis will need to be prepared to answer questions from shareholders as to why they are not being given the right or ability to participate in the issue, particularly where the placing is conducted at a price which is at a discount to the then current market price. Further information on the documentation and procedures for making a public offer are set out in Chapter 19, *Offers to the public*.

22.4 Where a company is also required to produce a prospectus for a secondary fundraising then, pursuant to the *AIM Rules for Companies*, the company will also need to produce an AIM admission document. In practice this is not onerous, as the relevant *AIM Rules for Companies* disclosure requirements can be included within the prospectus relatively simply.

22.5 In addition, a further AIM admission document will be required from an AIM company when it conducts a further issue of securities following admission to trading on AIM, where it is seeking admission to trading on AIM for a new class of securities, or is undertaking a reverse takeover as defined in Rule 14 of the *AIM Rules for Companies*. Further information on reverse takeovers is set out in Chapter 14, *Admission to trading on AIM by reverse takeover*.

22.6 If a prospectus or AIM admission document is not required then the documentation necessary to conduct a secondary issue will largely be dependent on whether a circular is required to be sent to shareholders, for example in support of notice of general meeting at which shareholder authorities are to be sought, and the way in which the broker will be marketing the issue.

22.7 It is not uncommon on AIM for companies to conduct further fundraisings purely on the basis of public information. In these instances the placing can be conducted in a relatively short period, with the broker simply offering its institutional clients securities on an insider basis (the inside information being that a placing is being conducted), conducting the book-building and announcing the placing and the total funds to be raised on the same day the AIM application form is submitted. Typically, this type of placing is completed three business days after the submission of the AIM application form, when the securities are admitted to trading on AIM. The securities are offered to institutional investors on an insider basis, meaning that the institutional investor acknowledges that it has unpublished, price sensitive information which has not been announced (being the price sensitive information that a placing will be conducted and the price it will be conducted at). In order to avoid civil and criminal offences, the institutional investor is then unable to deal in these securities, unless the placing is announced or the company informs them that the placing is no longer proceeding. Companies should note that institutional clients will not want to be insiders for a long period, typically more than one day, and this may influence the timing and success of the placing.

22.8 Where the broker feels it is appropriate, a mini roadshow with a presentation may be conducted on an insider basis, in place of the broker approaching its institutional clients direct. In these instances, the presentation will be reviewed and commented on by the company, its advisers and the Nominated Adviser and will be subject to some verification process. A verification process is carried out on the presentation in order to ensure the accuracy of the presentation, as placees will be relying on the information given to them as part of the presentation when making their investment decision. Again, the institutional investors will be insiders, but if the presentation includes inside information (i.e. non-published, price sensitive information) then this information must also be announced before the institutional investors can deal in the company's securities, even following the announcement of the placing. Following the marketing period at which the presentation is used, there will be placing letters sent out to potential placees, which are then signed and returned. Once all of the signed letters are received, the placing is announced and the AIM application form submitted with admission to trading on AIM occurring three business days later. Alternatively, the broker may include the terms and conditions of the placing at the end of the presentation, or in an announcement of the intention to conduct a placing, in which case placees may contract on the basis of a telephone conversation which is later summarised in a contract note, which has the effect of shortening the time before the results of the placing can be announced.

22.9 In some cases it might be that the placing is conducted on an accelerated book-build basis, where the proposed placing is announced and marketing conducted in a short period following such announcement, typically within one day. In these cases the broker will usually take orders over the telephone and then summarise the terms of the subscription in a contract note, which is then sent to the institutional investors.

22.10 The other marketing related issue which can impact significantly on the timetable for a secondary issue is in relation to due diligence. If, since the company's last AIM admission document or annual results, there has been a significant acquisition or there is another matter on which the broker feels it is appropriate to conduct some due diligence, such as the validity of a licence, then the broker may require the company's lawyers to conduct a due diligence review prior to the announcement of the secondary issue. Other factors that are considered when determining whether it is necessary, or desirable, to conduct a due diligence exercise will include the size of the offering relative to the company's market capitalisation and if the broker is new to the company. The period in which due diligence may be completed will vary significantly, depending on the jurisdictions involved and the type of information required. If due diligence is required a company should be prepared for the due diligence process to run its course; if the broker felt it necessary the broker will require a thorough exercise to be done, regardless of the time which this may take.

22.11 As a consequence, the marketing related issues will often be a key factor in the time it takes to prepare for, and conduct, a secondary fundraising. Given the broad nature of the term "secondary issue" there is no hard and fast rule as to how long this part of the process will take, although it is not uncommon to see a secondary fundraising completed in a one to two week period, even if there is some limited due diligence to be carried out, or even shorter if the placing is conducted on an accelerated book-build basis on the back of the public information.

SHARE AUTHORITIES

22.12 The marketing related issues largely impact on the first part of the timetable for the proposed secondary issue; that is, the period before the results of the fundraising can be announced. However, if share authorities are needed they can often lengthen the second part of the timetable; the time between the announcement of the results of the placing and the company receiving the proceeds. Further details on the share authorities which may be needed for a company which is registered in England and Wales are set out in Figure 22.1.

FIGURE 22.1	Authorities needed for a secondary issue by a public listed company registered in England and Wales

Authority required	Action if authority is needed
Company requires authorised share capital (Where the company is incorporated under the *Companies Act 1985*, authority will be needed. However, for companies incorporated under the *Companies Act 2006* the requirement to have an authorised share capital is repealed)	Ordinary resolution of shareholders at a general meeting to increase the authorised share capital of the company (i.e. 50 per cent of those attending and voting)
Directors authority to allot securities (Section 80 of the *Companies Act 1985* or section 551 of the *Companies Act 2006*)	Ordinary resolution of shareholders at a general meeting to authorise the directors to allot securities (i.e. 50 per cent of those attending and voting)
Disapplication of pre-emption rights (for non-pre-emptive issues) (Section 95 of the *Companies Act 1985* or section 570 to section 571 of the *Companies Act 2006*)	Special resolution of shareholders at a general meeting (i.e. 75 per cent of those attending and voting)

Note: Where shareholder authority is sought an explanatory circular should be sent to shareholders along with a notice of the general meeting.

22.13 For a company which is incorporated in England and Wales, in order for the directors to allot securities pursuant to a secondary fundraising three types of authority are needed. The first is that the company must have sufficient authorised but unissued share capital. If the company has insufficient authorised but unissued share capital then it will be required to increase its authorised share capital. To increase the authorised share capital it will require shareholders to vote in favour of a resolution increasing the capital. This resolution would be put to a general meeting of the company as an ordinary resolution and typically can be put to shareholders on 14 clear days' notice, although this can vary depending on the length of service of notice, posting requirements and other requirements set out in the company's Articles of Association. To be passed, the resolution to give the company sufficient authorised but unissued share capital requires at least 50 per cent of those attending and voting to vote in favour of the resolution.

22.14 Second, if the company is incorporated in England and Wales and it has sufficient authorised but unissued share capital then the directors also need authority to allot the securities. Typically, in line with best practice on corporate governance, the directors will often have authority to allot up to 30 per cent of the company's issued share capital at any one time but, if they do not have sufficient authority in order to complete the placing then they will need the shareholders to approve an increase in the directors' authority to allot. The directors' authority to allot securities is sought by way of an ordinary resolution at a general meeting. Again, this resolution requires at least 50 per cent of those attending and voting to vote in favour of the resolution for it to be passed and the resolution will be put to the members following 14 clear days' notice, although this can again vary depending on the length of service of notice, posting requirements and other requirements set out in the company's Articles of Association.

22.15 Finally, if the share issue is to be made on a non pre-emptive basis then the directors will need to have had the pre-emption rights attaching to the securities disapplied. It may be possible to structure an issue whereby shareholder authority to disapply pre-emption rights is not required, for example by making the offer on a pre-emptive basis such as by way of a rights issue or open offer. However, depending on the number of shareholders which the company has, by making the share issue on a pre-emptive basis it might mean that the company triggers the requirement to produce a prospectus.

22.16 Where the AIM company needs to disapply the pre-emption rights over its securities then the shareholders will need to approve this which, depending on its Articles of Association, usually requires a special resolution and the resolution may, depending on the AIM company's Articles of Association, need to be put to the members following 21 clear days' notice. A special resolution requires the approval of 75 per cent of those attending and voting at a general meeting, although this depends on the length of service of notice, posting requirements and other requirements set out in the company's Articles of Association.

22.17 If the company does not have pre-emption rights disapplied over the requisite number of securities then it should speak to its broker, as it may be possible to structure the fundraising in a way which does not require shareholder authority to be disapplied. An example of such a structure is a cash box placing, where an offshore vehicle conducts a placing and the AIM company acquires the entire issued share capital of the offshore vehicle. If the acquisition of the offshore vehicle is properly structured, it would not constitute an issue of securities for cash by the AIM company and therefore would not require pre-emption rights in the AIM company to have been disapplied. In this type of structure the offshore vehicle is usually an offshore entity which has been incorporated for the purpose and whose sole assets are cash.

22.18 If shareholder authority is needed under any of these heads, then the company will need to prepare and send to shareholders a notice of general meeting. Accompanying this notice will usually be an explanatory circular, which will set out the reasons for the placing, describe the manner in which the placing will be conducted, as well as giving shareholders certain information as to the authorities being sought. An example of the level of detail which it is best practice to give to shareholders is set out in Figure 22.2. In practice, where a circular to shareholders is being prepared, directors may also take the opportunity to update shareholders as to current trading, or to collate information which has been released in a number of regulatory announcements into one cohesive update. As part of the marketing process, potential investors may require details of the current trading of the business, which may be given to them on an insider basis prior to the announcement of the placing. Care needs to be taken in these situations as the AIM company will have an obligation to announce price sensitive information without delay. Any such circular will also be subject to verification, although it may not require all the associated comfort letters and reports that would be included in a prospectus or AIM admission document.

22.19 Where the AIM company is not incorporated in England and Wales, advice should be sought in its country of incorporation as to the authorities needed and the time that it will take to get such authority, where needed.

22.20 In practice, companies will usually have some authorised but unissued share capital, as well as authorities for the directors to allot securities and for the disapplication of pre-emption rights. These authorities will be sought on an annual basis at the companies' annual general meeting. The Association of British Insurers has guidelines as to the appropriate level of directors' authority to allot securities, which they recommend should be no more than 30 per cent of the current issued share capital. In addition, the Association of British Insurers recommends that, for the disapplication of pre-emption rights, pre-emption rights should not generally be disapplied over more than 5 per cent of a company's issued share capital in any one year and 7.5 per cent of a company's issued share capital in any rolling three-year period. However, notwithstanding that most AIM companies follow these guidelines, it is not unusual for AIM companies to seek authorities in excess of this. In particular, it is not unusual for AIM companies to seek authority to issue securities free of pre-emption rights for up to 10 per cent of the issued share capital of the company and, following discussion with the Nominated Adviser and broker, this may even be increased beyond this level provided that adequate explanation can be made to shareholders as to why such increased authorities are needed. Further information on corporate governance generally is set out in Chapter 42, *Corporate governance for AIM companies*.

FIGURE 22.2   Contents of a general meeting circular

Although there are no strict requirements as to the level of detail required in any circular calling a general meeting for an AIM company, best practice is to include the following information in respect of the following resolutions:

Authority	Detail
Increase in authorised share capital	o a statement of the proposed percentage increase in the authorised share capital of the relevant class; o the reasons for the increase.
Authority to allot securities	o statement of the maximum amount of relevant securities which the directors will have authority to allot and the percentage which that represents of the total of that class in issue; o statement by the directors of whether they have any present intention of exercising the authority and, if so, for what purpose; and o a statement as to when the authority will lapse.
Disapplying pre-emption rights	o a statement of the maximum amount of equity securities which the disapplication will cover. Where there is a general disapplication for equity securities for cash made otherwise than to existing shareholders in proportion to their existing holdings, the percentage which the amount generally disapplied represents of the total issued share capital at the latest date before publication of the circular.

PLACING AGREEMENTS

22.21   The contractual relationship between the AIM company and its broker for the secondary issue will be governed by a placing agreement.

22.22   Further information on placing agreements and the warranties and indemnities sought under them is set out in Chapter 18, *Contractual documentation for fundraisings*.

APPLICATION FOR ADMISSION TO TRADING ON AIM

22.23 Once the number of securities that are going to be issued pursuant to a secondary fundraising have been determined and an AIM admission document or prospectus (if required) has been prepared then an AIM application form is submitted by the Nominated Adviser on behalf of the company in the usual manner. Between submission of the application and the proposed date of admission to trading on AIM the company will conditionally allot the securities which are being issued pursuant to the placing conditional only upon their admission to trading and send a copy of the board minutes to the Nominated Adviser, who in turn sends them on to AIM Regulation. Admission to trading on AIM then occurs on the publication of an AIM dealing notice, which typically is three business days after the submission of the AIM application form (Figure 22.3).

FIGURE 22.3 Application procedure for secondary issues not requiring an AIM admission document

Date	Action
Admission to trading on AIM – 3 business days	Application form submitted to AIM
Any time on or before Admission to trading on AIM – 1 business day	Board of directors' resolution allotting securities to placees
Admission to trading on AIM	AIM dealing notice issued, securities admitted to trading on AIM

OTHER ISSUES

Block listings

22.24 If an AIM company is likely to be issuing securities on a regular basis it may be possible to use a block admission to trading on AIM arrangement. However, this would need to be agreed with AIM Regulation on a separate basis and is unlikely to be available for equity fundraisings as they do not fall within the class of circumstances where block listings can be used.

Close periods

22.25 Consideration also needs to be given to close periods and restrictions on deals under Rule 21 of the *AIM Rules for Companies* when planning a secondary issue. If it is expected that directors, or applicable employees, are to deal in the AIM securities as part of the secondary issue then the secondary issue to those persons cannot take place during a close period; that is, in any of the circumstances detailed in Figure 22.4.

FIGURE 22.4   What are close periods?

A close period is:

(i)   the period of two months preceding the publication of an AIM company's annual results (or, if shorter, the period from its financial year end to the time of publication) and:

  • if it reports only half-yearly, the period of two months immediately preceding the notification of its half-yearly report or, if shorter, the period from the relevant financial period end, up to and including the time of the notification; or
  • if it reports on a quarterly basis, the period of one month immediately preceding the notification of its quarterly results or, if shorter, the period from the relevant financial period end, up to and including the time of the notification;

(ii) any other period when the AIM company is in possession of unpublished price sensitive information; or

(iii) any time it has become reasonably probable that such information will be required by the *AIM Rules for Companies* to be notified.

Source: extract from *AIM Rules for Companies*, February 2007. The full *AIM Rules for Companies* is available at www.londonstockexchange.com

Related party transactions

22.26   If it is proposed that some of the securities to be placed as part of the placing will be placed with a related party, and the securities to be placed with such persons exceed 5 per cent in any of the class tests, then a notification needs to be issued. A notification of a related party transaction must include the name of the related party concerned and the nature or extent of their interests in the transaction. Most importantly, the announcement of a related party transaction must include a statement that, with the exception of any director who is involved in the transaction as a related party, its directors consider, having consulted with the Nominated Adviser, that the terms of the transaction are fair and reasonable so far as the shareholders are concerned. For the purposes of Rule 13 of the *AIM Rules for Companies*, related parties include those listed in Figure 22.5.

22.27   Where a transaction requires notification under Rule 13 of the *AIM Rules for Companies*, the details in Figure 22.6 must be included in the notification.

Announcements

22.28   Pursuant to Rule 17 of the *AIM Rules for Companies*, in addition to any other announcement that may be required the AIM company must issue a notification without delay of the reason for the application for admission to trading on AIM, or cancellation of any AIM securities. This would include an application for admission to trading on AIM of securities issued pursuant to a placing. In practice, this is usually wrapped up within the announcement that the book has closed for the placing.

FIGURE 22.5   Related parties for the purposes of Rule 13 of the *AIM Rules for Companies*

A related party is:

(a) any person who is a director of an AIM company or of any company which is its subsidiary or parent undertaking, other subsidiary undertaking of its parent company;

(b) a substantial shareholder;

(c) an associate of (a) or (b) being:

   (i) the family of such a person;

   (ii) the trustees (acting as such) of any trust of which the individual or any of the individual's family is a beneficiary or discretionary object (other than a trust which is either an occupational pension scheme as defined in regulation 3 of the *Financial Services and Markets Act 2000 (Regulated Activities) Order 2001*, or an employee share scheme which does not, in either case, have the effect of conferring benefits on persons all or most of whom are related parties);

   (iii) any company in whose equity securities such a person individually or taken together with his/her family (or if a director, individually or taken together with his/her family and any other director of that company) are directly or indirectly interested (or have a conditional or contingent entitlement to become interested) to the extent that they are or could be able:

   • to exercise or control the exercise of 30 per cent or more of the votes (excluding treasury shares) able to be cast at general meetings on all, or substantially all, matters; or

   • to appoint or remove directors holding a majority of voting rights at board meetings on all, or substantially all, matters;

   (iv) any other company which is its subsidiary undertaking, parent undertaking or subsidiary undertaking of its parent undertaking;

   (v) any company whose directors are accustomed to act in accordance with (a)'s directions or instructions;

   (vi) any company in the capital of which (a), either alone or together with any other company within (iv) or (v) or both taken together, is (or would on the fulfillment of a condition or the occurrence of a contingency be) interested in the manner described in (iii);

(d) for the purposes of Rule 13, any person who was a director of an AIM company or any of its subsidiaries, sister or parent undertakings or a substantial shareholder within the 12 months preceding the date of the transaction.

"Family" means a reference to a person's family and includes the following persons:

• his/her spouse or civil partner and any child where such child is under the age of 18;

• any trust in which such individuals are trustees or beneficiaries;

• any company of which they have control of more than 20 per cent of its equity or voting rights in a general meeting.

Note: Employee share or pension schemes are excluded from the definition of trust provided that such individuals are beneficiaries rather than trustees.

Source: extract from *AIM Rules for Companies*, February 2007. The full *AIM Rules for Companies* is available at www.londonstockexchange.com

---

FIGURE 22.6 Contents of notifications under Rule 13 of the *AIM Rules for Companies*

The details to be included in a notification under Rule 13 are:

(a) the identity of the director or significant shareholder concerned;
(b) the date on which the disclosure was made to it;
(c) the date on which the deal or relevant change to the holding was effected;
(d) the price, amount and class of the AIM securities concerned;
(e) the nature of the transaction;
(f) the nature and extent of the director's or significant shareholder's interest in the transaction;
(g) where a deal takes place when it is in any close period under Rule 21, the date upon which any previous binding commitment was notified or the date upon which the London Stock Exchange granted permission to deal in order to mitigate severe personal hardship; and
(h) where the notification concerns a related financial product, the detailed nature of the exposure.

IN PRACTICE

Secondary issues are a popular tool used by AIM companies to raise additional equity funds and can be particularly attractive as the documentation, and therefore the costs, involved in carrying out such a fundraising can be minimal.

CHAPTER 23

Price stabilisation, over-allotment, greenshoes and when-issued trading

AT A GLANCE

Price stabilisation, greenshoes and over-allotment are mechanisms used by brokers and investment banks to control the price of securities in the aftermarket of a fundraising (whether on an initial public offer or a secondary fundraising) by trading in the securities of the company, but in such a way that does not breach the Financial Services Authority regulations on market manipulation.

The company benefits because the price of the securities is not subject to normal market pressures and, if the offering is successful, the exercise of the over-allotment option allows for additional funds to be raised. The bank can use this mechanism to assist the company, and as the bank acts as principal in its dealings, the mechanisms can also provide the bank with additional revenue.

These mechanisms are only likely to be used on large fundraisings but can be used either on initial public offer or a secondary issue.

INTRODUCTION

23.1   The various mechanisms which are available to brokers and investment banks to manage the price of the company's securities during the period immediately following a fundraising are complicated, and can be used in a number of different combinations. The key to understanding how the mechanisms can be used to benefit both the company and the broker or investment bank lies in the way in which the different mechanisms interact with each other. This chapter will cover:

- over-allotment options;
- securities lending agreements;
- price stabilisation;
- greenshoe options; and
- when-issued trading.

23.2   Figure 23.1 sets out an overview of the different stages involved in an initial public offer and fundraising, which involves the use of price stabilisation and a greenshoe option, compared with an initial public offer and fundraising process without such elements.

FIGURE 23.1   The procedural differences to an initial public offer (IPO) when price stabilisation and a greenshoe option are used

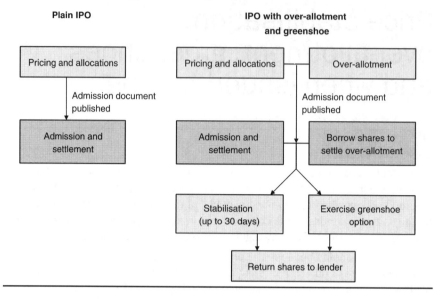

23.3 On a straightforward initial public offer, once the securities of the company have been priced by the bank and allocated to the places, the AIM admission document is published and the securities are then usually admitted to AIM three days later with settlement taking place immediately following admission to trading on AIM. The securities are then traded on AIM.

23.4 Where price stabilisation and a greenshoe option are used the process is more complicated. At the time that pricing and allocations take place, the bank will determine whether there is sufficient demand to consider over-allotment of the securities. If there is such demand, then they may consider allocating more securities to the places than are being issued by the company (or being sold by selling shareholders in the formal placing). In order to settle any securities to be sold pursuant to this over-allotment of securities, the broker or investment bank borrows securities which are already in issue from an existing shareholder. These securities are borrowed from the lender at the time that admission to trading on AIM and settlement takes place of any securities which are over-allotted; and the borrowed securities are used to settle the over-allotments with those places.

23.5 The bank then has two options as to how to return replacement securities to the lender. One option is price stabilisation, whereby the broker or investment bank may go out into the market and buy securities in the company which are then used to return the borrowed securities to the lender, putting the lender back in their original position.

23.6 The second option is to exercise a greenshoe option. This is simply a call option, granted by the company to the broker or investment bank, to subscribe for securities at the price at which the securities are placed pursuant to the placing.

The bank exercises the option, paying the subscription price, and then transfers the securities to the lender in order to satisfy the loan.

OVER-ALLOTMENT

23.7 In order for the broker or investment bank to take the initial decision to make allotments over and above the size of the agreed placing, the contractual right for them to be able to do so must previously have been set out in the document which governs the contractual relationship between the company (or the selling shareholder) and the broker, or investment bank that is acting as broker. Where different investment banks have been appointed as Nominated Adviser and broker, this is likely to be in the broker agreement or the placing agreement, rather than the Nominated Adviser agreement.

23.8 Whilst in the process of building the book for the placing, the broker or investment bank therefore has a contractual right to make over-allotments by allocating more securities to placees than are available in the agreed placing.

23.9 During the course of building the book of placees and conducting investor roadshows, the broker or investment bank will use its experience and judgement to consider whether there is sufficient appetite for the company's securities in the market for an over-allotment. The decision as to whether or not to make over-allotments will then only be finalised at the time of pricing and allocations (see Figure 23.1).

23.10 Should the broker or investment bank take the decision that an over-allotment would be appropriate, then the broker or investment bank enters into the contracts with the placees for sale of the over-allotment securities, and in so doing, the bank is acting as principal. This contrasts with the position under the agreed placing, where the broker or investment bank acts as agent for the company. By entering into these contracts as principal, the broker or investment bank puts itself in a "short position" as it has agreed to sell securities in the company to the placee despite the fact that it is not in possession of any such securities.

SECURITIES LENDING AGREEMENT

23.11 Where a broker or investment bank has over-allotted securities at the time of pricing and allocations, they need to be able to settle the over-allotment securities with the placees at the time that admission to trading on AIM takes place. In order to avoid the delay that would occur if the broker or investment bank waited until the company were able to issue and allot new securities, the broker or investment bank borrows securities, which are already issued and held by a shareholder in the company, and which will therefore be admitted to AIM once admission occurs.

23.12 The lender of the securities can be any shareholder, including a member of management if they are also a shareholder, but is most likely to be an institutional or substantial shareholder. The shareholder who has agreed to be the lender will enter into a securities lending agreement with the broker or investment bank. This agreement entitles the broker or investment bank to issue a borrowing request, or requests, for a certain number of securities (up to an amount equal to the over-allotment securities) to the lending shareholder, and the lender will then transfer that number of securities into the name of the broker or investment bank. At this point it is the broker or investment bank that is entered on the company's share register as the shareholder.

23.13 By doing this, the broker or investment bank has resolved its short position with regard to the placees, as it has acquired from the lender sufficient securities to be able to settle the contracts for the over-allotment securities with placees upon admission to trading on AIM. When admission to trading on AIM takes place, the broker or investment bank transfers those borrowed securities to the placees, who have therefore not suffered any delay by having been placed with over-allotment securities, rather than securities out of the agreed placing. From the point of view of the placees there is no distinction between securities transferred under the securities lending agreement and those issued by the company or transferred by the selling shareholder, and no difference between the over-allotted securities and those issued pursuant to the agreed placing.

23.14 However, in resolving one short position the broker or investment bank has placed itself in another, as it clearly must return securities equivalent to those that it has borrowed from the lender. The broker or investment bank has the choice between two different mechanisms which can assist them in resolving their short position and returning the securities to the lender. The two principal mechanisms for the broker or investment bank at this stage are either acquiring securities as part of its price stabilisation, or exercising a greenshoe option. There are a number of factors which will influence which mechanism the broker or investment bank chooses, but the key factor will be the performance of the company's share price in the market following admission to trading on AIM.

23.15 The securities lending agreement can be drafted either so that it requires the broker or investment bank to return securities in the company to the lender, or alternatively it can be drafted so that the broker or investment bank has the option of returning cash equivalent to the value of the securities that it has borrowed. This is a point to be negotiated between the broker or investment bank and the lending shareholder and should be reflected in the description of the placing in the AIM admission document, so as not to mislead shareholders as to who the substantial shareholders will be and the number of securities which will be in issue.

23.16 Among the other key issues to be negotiated and resolved in the drafting of the securities lending agreement are:

- the question of timing for the delivery of the securities to the broker or investment bank and re-delivery of the securities back to the lender;
- the payment of any fees or transfer taxes that are payable as a result of the loan; and
- what should happen when certain events take place during the period that the shareholder is not the registered holder of its securities. Such possible actions include the payment of dividends, the exercise of voting rights and corporate actions such as a takeover offer.

23.17 The London Stock Exchange provides a precedent securities lending agreement on its website, called the Global Lending Agreement. This precedent is for on-market trading and is a complex version of such an agreement, as it allows for the return of cash in lieu of securities and contains complicated provisions regarding corporate actions. However, a securities lending agreement is usually based on the Global Lending Agreement but with the unnecessary provisions deleted.

23.18 It should be noted that the operation of the securities lending agreement needs to be taken into consideration when the company is notifying the market of any changes to its substantial shareholders pursuant to Rule 5 of the *Disclosure Rules and Transparency Rules*, (see Chapter 38, *Disclosure Rules and Transparency Rules*, for further discussion of an AIM company's obligations under the *Disclosure Rules and Transparency Rules*) and Rule 17 of the *AIM Rules for Companies*.

23.19 The *Disclosure Rules and Transparency Rules* stipulate that the lender entering into a securities lending agreement is not treated as a disposal of securities which is notifiable to the market under the *Disclosure Rules and Transparency Rules*. However, under Rule 17 of the *AIM Rules for Companies*, where the lender is a significant shareholder (i.e. a holder of 3 per cent or more) then the transfer of the securities to the broker or investment bank pursuant to the agreement is a change in holdings, which should be notified to the market through a regulatory information service. Where the lending shareholder is also a director of the company (or members of the director's family for the purposes of Rule 17 of the *AIM Rules for Companies* – see Chapter 46, *Share dealing code*, for a further explanation of the meaning of director's family in this context) the transfer of securities under the agreement will be a notifiable dealing in the company's securities, irrespective of the size of the shareholders' shareholding.

23.20 In addition, where the securities are being transferred into the name of the broker or investment bank and where the number of securities that the broker or investment bank is receiving under the loan exceeds one of the notification thresholds under the *Disclosure Rules and Transparency Rules*, and the stock lending agreement expresses that the voting rights in relation to the loaned securities are exercisable at the discretion of the broker or investment bank, as is the case in the Global Lending Agreement, then the broker or investment bank's interest is also notifiable to the market under the *Disclosure Rules and Transparency Rules*. The transfer of the securities to the broker or investment bank will be notifiable via a regulatory information service pursuant to Rule 17 of the *AIM Rules for Companies* where the notification thresholds are breached, irrespective of how the voting rights operate under the securities lending agreement.

PRICE STABILISATION

23.21 Price stabilisation occurs following admission to trading on AIM when the company's securities are trading on AIM at a price which is lower than the issue price of the securities in the fundraising. The broker or investment bank will go out into the market and buy securities in the company, therefore increasing demand for the securities, which should prevent the continued fall of the share price. The broker or investment bank buys these securities on its own account and holds them as principal. The effect of this is that the securities that it holds fall outside of the tax indemnity and commission arrangements that will be set out in the placing or broker agreement, because those provisions only relate to the securities that are placed by the broker or investment bank acting as agent for the company.

23.22 The broker or investment bank can also theoretically stabilise the company's price, so that its share price goes down, by increasing the supply of the company's securities in the market rather than increasing demand for them but, in practice, this rarely, if ever, takes place.

23.23 By purchasing the securities on the market, the broker or investment bank has stabilised the company's share price and has also resolved its short position (in whole or in part) as the securities which it has acquired can be used to satisfy the return of securities to the lending shareholder under the securities lending agreement. In addition, this can create a profit for the broker or investment bank, because otherwise the broker or investment bank would have had to purchase the securities to repay the lender at the issue price, which would have been higher and therefore cost more. Purchasing the securities on the market when the share price has fallen following the fundraising constitutes a saving of costs (and therefore a profit) for the broker or investment bank.

23.24 In addition to this, the broker or investment bank can also go out into the market like any other buyer and purchase securities as principal, and then sell them on in a market where the company's share price has risen above the price at which the bank bought them, again creating a profit for the broker or investment bank.

23.25 Price stabilisation is the first of the mechanisms open to the bank to resolve its short position in respect of over-allotted securities in relation to the lending shareholder. The bank is more likely to choose this option in the event that the company's share price falls following admission to trading on AIM to below the placing price, as they will increase demand for the securities and therefore strengthen the price by going into the market as a buyer.

23.26 Price stabilisation in both of these different forms is ordinarily prohibited as a form of market manipulation under several pieces of legislation. Section 397(3) of the *Financial Services and Markets Act 2000* prohibits any course of conduct which creates a false or misleading impression as to the market in, or the price or value of, the securities of the company where the purpose of creating that impression is to induce others to purchase those securities. In addition, section 52 of the *Criminal Justice Act 1993* prohibits insider dealing in securities and section 118 of the *Financial Services and Markets Act 2000* creates a civil offence (where the previous two are criminal offences) by prohibiting behaviour which gives a false or misleading impression as to the supply of or demand for the securities.

23.27 However, while the mechanism of price stabilisation clearly falls within the scope of most, if not all, of these offences, if the broker or investment bank follows certain safe-harbour provisions then it can fall within an exemption and avoid committing the offences.

23.28 The safe-harbour provisions are prescribed by the *Buy-back and Stabilisation Regulations* and the essential steps comprise the following:

- Price stabilisation can only be conducted on an initial public offer or secondary issue.
- Price stabilisation can only be conducted for a limited period.
- There should be adequate disclosure of the possibility that price stabilisation may be conducted.
- Stabilisation notices should be issued at the commencement of the stabilisation period and at the end of the period.

23.29 The maximum stabilisation period in the case of an initial public offer is 30 days and the period starts from the day that trading commences. Where when-issued trading is used on an initial public offer, the start date is the date from which there is adequate public disclosure of the issue price of the securities (further information on when-issued trading are set out at the end of this chapter in Paragraphs 23.42 to 23.47). In the case of a secondary issue of securities, the stabilisation period will commence from the date of adequate public disclosure of the issue price of the securities and end a maximum of 30 days from the date when the securities are allotted. Stabilisation periods are calculated using calendar days rather than business days.

23.30 What constitutes adequate public disclosure is not defined in the *Buy-back and Stabilisation Regulations* but will include providing details on the stabilisation, if any:

- before the securities are admitted to trading;
- in announcements;
- in the AIM admission document; and
- in any announcements that are issued during the 30-day stabilisation period.

The detail to be included in the disclosure comprises the fact that stabilisation may occur and that it may be ended at any time, the rationale for the stabilisation (i.e. that it is undertaken in order to support the company's share price), the fact that there is no guarantee that stabilisation will occur, the fact that over-allotments may be made and that a greenshoe option exists and any associated conditions for their use. The stabilising manager should also be identified in the disclosure and, in the majority of cases, this will be the broker or investment bank that is acting as broker.

23.31 In addition to the notices which are issued to notify the beginning and end of the stabilisation period, the Financial Services Authority regulation also requires that, following the end of the stabilisation period, adequate public disclosure is made of:

- whether or not stabilisation took place;
- the date on which it started and the date when the latest stabilisation transaction took place; and
- the share price range within which stabilisation was conducted for each of the dates when stabilisation transactions occurred.

23.32 The reason that the Financial Services Authority permits price stabilisation to occur, even though it clearly amounts to a manipulation of the market, is that it helps to promote an orderly operation of the market, as well as reducing investor nervousness and negating the advantages of short selling. By operating price stabilisation, the broker or investment bank can reduce the amount of volatility in a company's share price, which occurs when the supply of a company's securities is increased by a new issue, and consequently increase investors' confidence in the market for those securities.

23.33   The stabilisation period can be brought to an end at any time up to the 30-day limit. Where notification has been made that the stabilisation period has commenced but the company's share price does not then fall in the market but actually rises above the issue price, then the broker or investment bank has no need to go into the market and buy securities and no stabilisation will take place as brokers and investment banks tend not to stabilise down, although this is theoretically possible.

23.34   Where a notice has been issued to commence the stabilisation period and the 30-day period is running, but the broker or investment bank is confident that it will not exercise the right to stabilise, it will issue a notice discontinuing the stabilisation period prior to the end of the 30-day maximum. It is important that the period is ended, rather than simply running to expiration, because the longer the stabilisation period is allowed to run the greater the possibility that external market factors will affect the price of the company's securities, rather than being a genuine stabilisation of the price of the company's securities. The broker or investment bank does not want to find itself in a position where it is put under pressure by the company to go out and buy securities to stabilise the price of the company's securities in a market where external factors are affecting the price of all securities, and so a broker or investment bank might terminate the stabilisation period before the 30-day period has expired.

23.35   The price stabilisation mechanism is not intended to allow a broker or investment bank to prop up a company's share price amid a falling market, but rather to allow them to help the company's securities find their own natural level in the immediate aftermarket of their admission to trading on AIM. Where the price of the company's securities finds a natural plateau level following admission to trading on AIM then price stabilisation is unlikely to be necessary. In those circumstances, the bank will use the greenshoe option mechanism rather than price stabilisation to resolve its short position resulting from the securities lending agreement.

GREENSHOE OPTIONS

23.36   Greenshoe options are so called because of the US company, the Green Shoe Company, which first used this mechanism. A greenshoe option is a call option which allows the broker or investment bank to request the company to issue additional securities to the broker or investment bank at the issue price of the agreed placing. As with the right to conduct over-allotments, the greenshoe option is likely to be contained in the placing or broker agreement. If the placing is not of new securities, then instead of subscribing for new securities it is possible that the greenshoe will be an option to purchase the securities from an existing shareholder.

23.37   The function of the greenshoe option is to protect the broker or invest-ment bank from the financial impact that the over-allotment would have on the broker or investment bank, in the event that the market price of the company's securities rises above the issue price following admission to trading on AIM. Obvi-ously, if the market price has risen, then in order to resolve its short position with respect to the lending shareholder, the broker or investment bank would be forced to buy securities at the higher market price. The greenshoe avoids this position by entitling the broker or investment bank to acquire those securities at the same price as the issue price.

23.38   The greenshoe option can either be primary in nature (i.e. the securities which the broker or investment bank will receive will be new securities issued by the company in the broker or investment bank's name) or it can be secondary (i.e. the securities are transferred to the broker or investment bank from an existing shareholder who wishes to sell securities).

23.39   If the broker or investment bank has determined that price stabilisation is inappropriate in the circumstances then its alternative mechanism is to exercise the greenshoe option and to use the securities that are issued to it pursuant to the option to satisfy the return of securities to the lending shareholder under the securities lending agreement. The exercise time of the greenshoe option is generally linked to the ending of the stabilisation period by the bank (see Figure 23.1) and it is common to see the two events notified in one announcement.

23.40   It is market practice to limit the size of greenshoe options to a maximum of 15 per cent of the agreed placing, which in practice has a knock-on effect of limiting the amount of securities that the broker or investment bank can over-allot to placees at the stage of pricing and allocation.

23.41   It is not unusual to find references to a greenshoe in the offering documen-tation where a broker or investment bank can allot an increased number of securities but that this increased number of securities will be allotted by the company. In this scenario, what is in fact taking place is not technically a green-shoe option as the company is simply applying for admission to trading on AIM for more securities as part of the fundraising. However, as with a greenshoe, this quasi-greenshoe should be disclosed in the AIM admission document.

WHEN-ISSUED TRADING

23.42   When-issued trading, also known as "conditional" or "grey-market" trad-ing, is a practice where trading in the company's securities takes place prior to admission to trading on AIM of those securities on AIM. Generally, when-issued trading only takes place on large fundraisings and can be used whether or not there are to be any over-allotments or price stabilisation.

23.43   This when-issued trading can take place for up to three days prior to admission of the securities to trading on AIM taking place, and the condition that the trading is based on is that admission will take place. Once the securities are admitted to trading then all the trades booked during the three day period are confirmed and settlement can take place. Thereafter, trading continues as normal.

Should admission to trading on AIM not take place for whatever reason, all the trades booked during the when-issued dealing period will be unwound and the money paid for securities returned to the investors.

23.44 When issued trading will only be permitted to take place where the company has been able to satisfy the London Stock Exchange: that there will be a fair and orderly market in the securities; that the security is sufficiently liquid, taking into account the size of the placing; that the security can be settled in electronic form; and that there is sufficient demand for when-issued trading in the securities.

23.45 When-issued trading is done essentially because it gives investors the ability to trade in the company's securities immediately, without waiting until admission to trading on AIM takes place. If a broker or investment bank wishes to conduct when-issued trading and the London Stock Exchange has agreed to it taking place, the formalities to be completed are straightforward and simply comprise the completion of an application form for when-issued trading, which is submitted to the London Stock Exchange.

23.46 The use of a when-issued trading period alongside price stabilisation and greenshoe option mechanisms is a complex process, which is set out in Figure 23.2.

FIGURE 23.2 The procedural differences to an initial public offer (IPO) when price stabilisation, a greenshoe option, over-allotment and when-issued trading are used

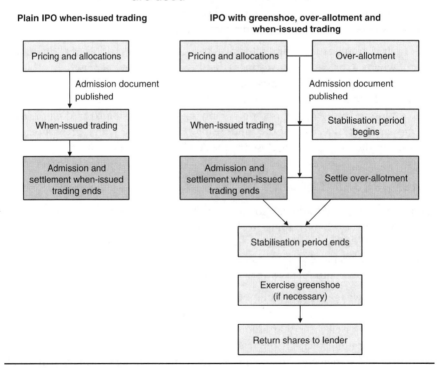

23.47 Figure 23.2 shows that when-issued trading begins up to three days prior to admission to trading on AIM taking place, and, because this is the beginning of the period when the company's securities are traded, this is also the time from which the price stabilisation period can run. It is therefore possible for the broker or investment bank to go into the market and stabilise the price of the company's securities prior to admission to trading on AIM actually taking place.

IN PRACTICE

The mechanisms of price stabilisation, over-allotments, greenshoes and when-issued trading are not often used other than on large fundraisings, but some elements or principles (e.g. the quasi-greenshoe) may be imported into other placings.

CHAPTER 24

Analyst research

AT A GLANCE

Analyst research is research written by an analyst, who is typically employed at the bank which is acting as broker on a transaction or is independent of the company (but paid for by the company), to give a view to potential investors of the company and its assets and the marketplace.

Under the *Conduct of Business Rules*, analyst research is divided into two categories: investment research and non-independent research. The two categories require different procedures to be put in place for their production and also require different warnings to be attached to them upon publication.

In the lead up to a company deciding to conduct a fundraising on AIM, whether as part of the initial public offer process or prior to a secondary fundraising, it is not unusual for analyst research on the company to be published. This published research assists potential investors in assessing the company, but it is not published by the company. It is important that procedures are in place to try to avoid the company or the bank incurring any liability for any misleading information contained in the research report. Similarly, procedures should be in place to deal with the potential conflict between the analyst and the bank, given the bank's role as broker trying to sell the maximum securities in the company through any fundraising. In practice, the extent of these procedures depends on how the research is labelled – whether "independent" or "investment research".

INTRODUCTION

24.1   Analyst research is often published in the run-up to the commencement of the marketing process for a fundraising on AIM. In order for the investment bank or broker to achieve the maximum success for such a fundraising, there must be a certain level of knowledge and understanding of the company's business in the market, and particularly among the institutional investors. This is especially important on AIM where the backing of institutional investors, rather than retail investors, is essential to a successful fundraising.

24.2   The *Conduct of Business Rules* divide analyst research into two categories: investment research and non-independent research. Analyst research will fall into the category of investment research where it recommends, or suggests, an investment strategy concerning financial instruments or the company issuing the financial instruments or offering an opinion on the present or future price of such instruments. Investment research will be presented as objective, labelled as investment research, and will be intended for distribution to the public. In addition, in order to be classified as investment research, the bank that has produced the research report will have to have in place certain appropriate systems and procedures to control conflicts of interest. The bank must also have systems and procedures with respect to the actions and permitted activities of the bank's analysts, including dealings in those securities.

24.3 Non-independent research is, in effect, research that does not meet the required standards to be classified as investment research and which is instead viewed as more of a marketing tool. Accordingly, non-independent research must:

- be clearly labelled as such;
- carry warning legends stating that it has not been prepared in accordance with legal requirements designed to promote the independence of investment research; and
- state that the bank which produced such research is not subject to any prohibition on dealing ahead of the dissemination of investment research.

In practice, most analyst research in connection with a company on AIM or going through an initial public offering on AIM will fall into the category of non-independent research, and this chapter will principally focus on that category.

24.4 Analyst research is published not only in relation to initial public offers, but also on an ongoing basis for AIM listed companies. Typically, a bank may well produce several pieces of research on a company in one year, particularly if there are significant events or acquisitions which it is important for the investment community to understand when assessing the company, its business and the market in which it competes. The intention behind analyst research is to provide shareholders or potential investors with objective information on the company which will assist them to understand the company and its business. Once written by the analyst, non-independent research will often be checked for factual accuracy by the company before being distributed to the bank's institutional clients for their consideration. With investment research, in order to preserve its independent status it is essential that no-one outside of the bank reviews the investment research prior to its distribution where it has a recommendation on target price, even for factual accuracy.

24.5 The division of the bank preparing the research report (part of the broking function) is distinct from the corporate finance division of the bank that acts as Nominated Adviser or broker to the company, which has a vested interest in the success of any fundraising because of their commission arrangements with the company. Clearly, there is then a conflict between the analyst, who must prepare the research on the company's business and its prospects as an investment, and the corporate finance division of the bank, which is trying to sell as many securities as possible to make the fundraising a success.

24.6 As the research report contains information on the company and is then distributed to investors or potential investors, there is also the important issue of which party is liable for any losses suffered by an investor as a result of any information contained in the research report being inaccurate or misleading.

24.7 This chapter considers the various types of legal liability which may attach to the bank, the company and its directors and their respective advisers as a result of the publication of a research report, principally in the case of a non-independent research report. The chapter then sets out the procedural steps which are necessary to minimise, to the extent possible, the liability attaching to those persons.

LIABILITY FOR ANALYST RESEARCH

24.8 The publication of a research report by an analyst at a bank that is connected to the company (i.e. the bank which is acting as Nominated Adviser) may lead to the risk that the company, its directors, shareholders and advisers, the bank and its analyst will incur liability as a result of the information contained in the research report. This liability can arise because there may be a perception among recipients of the research that the report has been issued on behalf of, or with the approval or authority of, those parties, and that accordingly the recipient may give extra consideration or weight to its contents.

24.9 In order to minimise the risk of an investor who has suffered a loss as a result of relying on the research report claiming against any of the company, the bank or the other associated parties, a number of preventative steps can be taken with regard to the preparation and distribution of the research report, and these are outlined in Paragraphs 24.25 to 24.51.

24.10 The liability that may attach to any of the company, its directors, shareholders and advisers, the bank or its analysts can arise from a number of sources and, depending on the source, can potentially result in either civil or criminal liability, or both. In relation to each offence it could be any one of the group of parties (the company, its directors, shareholders and advisers, the bank or its analyst) who may be found liable, and which one will largely depend on the role which each of these takes in the preparation and distribution of the research report as well as how the research is classified, whether as investment research or non-independent research.

24.11 If the analyst or the bank distributes a research report in the United Kingdom, it will be subject to potential liabilities under the *Financial Services and Markets Act 2000* (FSMA) for any false or misleading statements contained therein. For example, section 397 of the FSMA makes it a criminal offence to recklessly or knowingly make misleading, false or deceptive statements in the context of the sale or issue of securities or to engage in misleading conduct affecting securities markets. Furthermore, under the same provision of the FSMA, those parties could be subject to criminal liability for misleading, false or deceptive statements, whether about the company or the market in its securities, which are then not corrected in the AIM admission document.

24.12 The bank commits a civil offence under the market abuse regime of the FSMA (i.e. the Financial Services Authority can commence proceedings against the broker for the imposition of a penalty) if, by its research report, it creates a false or misleading impression as to the value of the company's securities.

24.13 It will also be a civil offence, under the market abuse regime of the FSMA, if the analyst or bank requires or encourages any other person to engage in an activity which, if engaged in by the analyst or bank itself, would amount to market abuse (e.g. encouraging a person to deal in securities on the basis of material information not generally available to the market).

24.14 It may also be a criminal offence under the *Criminal Justice Act 1993* for the analyst or bank to be in possession of specific or precise price sensitive information relating to listed securities which has not been made public and to encourage anyone to deal in such securities.

24.15 If the analyst intentionally or inadvertently acquires price sensitive information from the company or its advisers in the course of preparing a research report, it must take no further part in the preparation of the report if to do so would possibly mean that it is committing a criminal or civil offence.

24.16 For this reason, even if the research is labelled non-independent research, the research division of the bank will not take part in the initial public offer or preliminary steps in any fundraising, as it may inadvertently acquire price sensitive information. Accordingly, to the extent that the analyst is to be given information which could be price sensitive, it is given this information on the eve of it becoming public, for example by the release of an announcement to a regulatory information service after the market has closed. The process of giving the information to the analyst is often referred to as "bringing the analyst over the wall" – the wall in question being the Chinese wall which has been put in place to restrict the analyst's access to any information which is, or may be, price sensitive.

24.17 Civil liabilities could extend to the company, its advisers and the bank or analyst to the extent that they can be shown to have authorised, or were responsible for, inaccurate or misleading statements in the research report, should investors rely on that statement in making their investment decision. A person who acquires securities in reliance upon any misleading statement may also have rights of action against the maker of the statement, or against any person on whose behalf that statement is (or is deemed to be) made, and may also be able to avoid any contract for the subscription of securities which it is a party to.

24.18 The company, the bank or the analyst may also be liable under the *Misrepresentation Act 1967* for any misrepresentation in the research report to anyone who acquires securities in reliance upon the misrepresentation and suffers loss, unless it can be proved that the maker of the representation had reasonable grounds to believe, and did believe, that the facts represented were true. Where there has been a misrepresentation, the court has power to award damages even though the misrepresentation is innocent and not fraudulent or negligent. If an investor can show that the misleading or untrue statement in the research report became a term of the contract for the acquisition of securities, it may also be able to sue for damages for breach of contract.

RELIANCE ON RESEARCH REPORTS

24.19 One result of the potential liability is that it is important to make sure that all of the recipients of the research report acknowledge that they are not relying on the research report when making their investment decision. In most placings this is done by a specific term being included in the placing letter, the subscription agreement or the terms and conditions of the placing, that they are not relying on any information other than certain specified documents, such as an AIM admission document, on an initial public offer. Accordingly, it is important that all of the recipients of the research report receive the final AIM admission document, to give credence to the argument that they were relying on the AIM admission document when they made their investment decision, rather than the research report.

BLACKOUT PERIODS OR QUIET PERIODS

24.20 Arguably, the closer that the publication of the research report is to the publication of the company's final AIM admission document, general meeting circular or marketing documents, the more likely it is that an investor will rely on the research in making an investment decision, and so greater will be the risk that a disgruntled investor could seek to argue that the research report should be regarded as forming part of the formal offering documentation of the company. Irrespective of procedures that the bank and the analyst may follow with regard to the preparation, content and distribution of the report and the caveats that are placed upon reliance on such a report, because of the timing, the market will tend to view this form of research, whether investment research or non-independent research, as "informed" and thus place reliance on it.

24.21 It is therefore market practice to have a blackout period in the run-up to an initial public offer during which no research on the company may be published. City best practice on commencement of a blackout period on publication of research reports varies, but generally the blackout period should commence three or four weeks before publication of a pathfinder AIM admission document and four to six weeks before publication of the final AIM admission document. This is not an absolute guideline and an investment bank's or a broker's internal procedures and guidelines may permit them to adopt a shorter period, however it represents City best practice. Actual practice varies from institution to institution, but typically research will not be published later than three weeks prior to the publication of a final AIM admission document. It should be remembered that it is not just the investment bank and broker that may be liable for the content of the analyst research, and it is important that the company and its legal advisers also consider the timing of the publication of the research to ensure that there is an adequate delay between its publication and any offering.

24.22 To avoid accusations of improperly influencing the aftermarket, the blackout period normally continues for 40 days after commencement of the offering, although the bank will generally retain the discretion to alter the end date of the blackout period, unless the offering involves a US element, in which case a strict blackout period is often applied.

24.23 It is imperative that the recommendations in relation to the preparation, content and distribution of the research report are complied with by the analyst. However, despite all efforts to the contrary, the shorter the blackout period is, the more easily a disgruntled investor may claim reliance on the research report and allege that the company, its directors, the bank or their respective advisers are liable for any loss suffered by the investor relying on that report. In this regard, all disclaimers set out in the research report should be prominent and drawn to the specific attention of the recipients of the research report.

24.24 It is important to note, however, that the risk of imposition on the company and the bank of significant liabilities under English law, based on a research report published in connection with the initial public offer, cannot be wholly eliminated. What is an acceptable level of risk, when balanced with the advantages such analyst research can bring, is reflected in market practice.

PREPARATION AND CONTENT OF ANALYST RESEARCH

24.25 Whether it is investment research or non-independent research, a research report will typically be prepared by an analyst in the research department of the broker, acting independently of the corporate finance division of the bank, which acts as Nominated Adviser to the company in connection with the initial public offer. In some cases the research report may be prepared by an independent analyst not connected with the bank. This may occur either if the bank does not have a specialist analyst in the sector or if the company wants additional coverage. Even when the research is prepared by an independent analyst, it can be labelled as investment research or non-independent research, depending on its contents. The analyst should prepare the research report with the highest degree of care and steps should be taken to ensure that the report is the independent work of the analyst and that its contents are accurate and not misleading, and also that its contents are not inconsistent with the contents of the AIM admission document. In the case of a non-independent research report, these two obligations have to be balanced carefully, because the obvious way to minimise errors and inconsistencies in the research report is by having increased input from the company, the bank and their advisers. However, the more that these parties are involved, the less independent the research becomes and the greater the chance of liability for the report attaching to those parties. Typically, a company and its directors will see a copy of the non-independent research when it is in final form, to check its factual accuracy and consistency with the AIM admission document or other offering document. Any comments should be limited to this one review and to accuracy/consistency. However, in the case of investment research, such a review by the company cannot take place.

24.26 The basic requirements for the analyst are that the research report must be accurate and not misleading (whether by omission of information, inclusion of misleading information or misleading presentation of information) and any opinions expressed must be honestly held and based on reasonable grounds.

24.27 In order to prepare the research report, the analyst will look at publicly available information in relation to the company and also information which the company provides to the analyst, which can take the form of written papers, company presentations, question and answer sessions, or site visits, to allow the analyst to see the company's operations first-hand. If a company's securities are already traded on AIM, the company must ensure that none of this information is price sensitive information which has not been made public, as it might otherwise give rise to additional liabilities and even prevent the analyst from publishing the research.

24.28 The content of the research report should be clear as to what information is factual and what is the opinion of the analyst. Even though the author of the research report may have been granted limited access to the company for the purpose of preparing the non-independent research report (i.e. discussions with management, question and answer sessions and site visits), the report should be, and appear to be, an outsider's view of the company which has been produced independently of the company.

24.29 The research analyst must take great care to ensure that any opinions, estimates, forecasts or projections are fairly and reasonably based, as they inherently carry greater risks than simple reporting of facts; and it must be clear in the text that the opinions, estimates, forecasts and projections are those of the analyst alone, not of the corporate finance division of the bank, anyone responsible for the preparation of the AIM admission document, or anyone in possession of inside information regarding the company. Such estimates, forecasts and projections must also be accompanied by appropriate cautionary language indicating that the estimates, forecasts or projections are possible outcomes, which may or may not occur, setting out in full the assumptions on which they are based and stating that such assumptions may not prove to be correct and that actual results may be different. Any such estimates, forecasts or projections should be limited and the bank will have internal policies as to how far out projections may be made.

24.30 From the company perspective, it is important that even when it is non-independent research the report must not give any impression that it contains, or is based upon, information provided by the company or has in any way been approved by the company or the bank or any of their respective advisers, as this will significantly increase the risk that investors might claim that the report could be given increased importance when making the investment decision.

24.31 As part of the effort to avoid the information in the report being misleading to the reader, it should be made clear within the report if any part of the information is based on published or historic information, and this is of particular importance where such information has not been updated. The facts stated in the research report must be checked against authoritative sources, and where this is not possible a clear qualification should be included. It should also be made clear that the document does not, and does not attempt to, contain everything material which there is to be said about the company. All caveats and qualifications such as these should be set out clearly and precisely.

24.32 Non-independent research reports must not include dividend forecasts and earnings per share or dividend per share forecasts. Indeed, even the discussion of forecasts or prospects, even in the most general terms, between the company and the author of the research report should be avoided. In addition, the analyst preparing the non-independent research report should, when in contact with the company, be accompanied by a member of the advisory team involved in preparing the AIM admission document. The analyst preparing the non-independent research report must not attend any due diligence or verification meetings in connection with the float, to avoid them being given price sensitive information and to avoid compromising their independence.

24.33 All research reports should be careful not to refer to the initial public offer or fundraising itself (other than to state that the distributor of the research may be an underwriter in respect of a future offering of securities of the company). It is also common for the bank to restrict non-independent research reports so that they do not encourage any investment decision. Similarly non-independent research must not contain any investment recommendation with respect to securities in the company (e.g. avoiding the use of the words "buy", "do not buy", "subscribe", "sell" or "hold").

24.34 A non-independent research report may contain a valuation range but should not contain any reference to a target price or any pricing recommendation. In addition to a valuation range, a research report may include a discussion of valuation methodologies and companies. There must be no valuation (or valuation range) on a per share basis in non-independent research. Valuation ranges must be supported by material assumptions and a sensitivity analysis. There must be no "spot" valuation.

24.35 All research reports will contain on the front cover, or first page, disclaimers in relation to the confidential nature of the information contained in the report and the jurisdictions into which it must not be distributed due to the nature of those countries' security laws. For example, it is common to restrict such research reports from being distributed in the United States, South Africa and Japan. Similarly, the fact that the research report does not constitute an offer or invitation to subscribe for securities in the company should also be clearly stated. In addition, each page of the research report should contain (at the top or bottom) a legend stipulating the countries into which the research report may not be distributed.

24.36 It is a key feature of non-independent research under the *Conduct of Business Rules* that the report is treated as a "marketing communication". This will generally mean that it will have to be approved as a financial promotion under the FSMA. Further information on approval of financial promotions, is set out in Paragraph 24.41.

24.37 Any supplemental report must be published solely for the purpose of (i) responding to disclosure contained in the AIM admission document or other offer document which was not taken into account in connection with the preparation of the previous report, or (ii) accounting for other significant external events, which are not specific to the company. Additional disclosure should track that which is contained in the AIM admission document and should not include additional qualitative commentary.

DISTRIBUTION OF ANALYST RESEARCH

24.38 The distribution of research reports should be carefully monitored as part of the process of reducing the risk of the company, its advisers and the bank being deemed liable for false or misleading information contained in, or material omissions from, a research report, particularly in the case of non-independent research.

24.39 In addition to the imposition of the blackout period, this includes taking steps to ensure that research reports, particularly non-independent research reports, are not regarded as forming part of the formal offering documentation. All information made available to the analyst by the company that may influence an investment decision (as opposed to the analyst's own analysis) must be made available to investors in the AIM admission document or other offer document. It is also important to ensure consistency in all material respects between the non-independent research reports and the information contained in the AIM admission document.

24.40 No research in relation to the company should be distributed anywhere in the world, including the United Kingdom, during the blackout period. At no time should research reports be distributed or transmitted, directly or indirectly, by, or on behalf of, the company, the bank or their respective affiliates outside the United Kingdom – only the bank acting as broker should distribute the research report.

24.41 Under the FSMA, the distribution of research reports, particularly non-independent research reports, may be treated as a "financial promotion". Financial promotions may only be communicated in the United Kingdom if they are made by, or their contents have been approved by, a person authorised to conduct relevant permitted activities under the FSMA (an "authorised person") or if the communication falls within an applicable exemption in the *Financial Services and Markets Act 2000 (Financial Promotion) Order 2005*, for example if the promotion (i.e. the research report) is made to, and directed only at, investment professionals or high net worth entities. For more information on these categories of permitted recipients, see Figure 24.1. Irrespective of distribution arrangements, non-independent research is likely to require approval as a financial promotion in any event, due to its status as a marketing communication under the *Conduct of Business Rules*.

24.42 If research reports are distributed in the United Kingdom by an authorised person, the authorised person will have to comply with the *Conduct of Business Rules* of the Financial Services Authority, which cover such matters as the persons to whom a research report may be distributed, certain disclosures which must be included in a research report and principles to be followed in preparing the report.

24.43 The broker should therefore generally distribute research reports only within the United Kingdom to persons:

■ who are investment professionals or high net worth entities as described in Figure 24.1 or, given that the broker is authorised by the Financial Services Authority, market counterparties or intermediate customers (as defined by the *Financial Services Authority Rules*) on the broker's current research mailing list; and

■ who have addresses within the United Kingdom.

24.44 As part of its internal systems and controls, the broker will screen its list to ensure that all recipients meet these criteria. If any reasonable doubt exists regarding a recipient's status, the broker should refrain from sending the research report to that recipient. The research report should not be distributed to any person who the analyst believes will, directly or indirectly, send the report outside the United Kingdom.

FIGURE 24.1   Distribution of research reports

Distribution of the research report should be limited to institutions which fall within one of the categories of investment professionals contained in article 19(1) of the *Financial Services and Markets Act 2000 (Financial Promotion) Order 2005* or high net worth entities within article 49(1) of the Order or, given the broker is authorised by the Financial Services Authority, market counterparties or intermediate customers (as defined by the *Financial Services Authority Rules*). The principal categories are specified below:

(a) Persons who are themselves authorised by the Financial Services Authority in the United Kingdom (e.g. bankers, brokers and dealers).

(b) Exempt persons where the communication relates to a controlled activity, which is a regulated activity in relation to which such persons are exempt (this is very technical in practice and caution should be exercised before relying on it).

(c) Persons whose ordinary activities involve them in carrying on the controlled activity to which the communication relates for the purpose of the business carried on by them, or persons who it is reasonable to expect will carry on such activity for the purposes of a business carried on by them.

(d) Governments, local authorities (whether in the United Kingdom or elsewhere) or international organisations.

(e) Any person ("A") who is a director, officer or employee of a person ("B") falling within any of (a) to (d) above, where the communication is made to A in that capacity and where A's responsibilities when acting in that capacity involve him in the carrying on by B of controlled activities.

(f) Any company which has, or which is a member of the same group as an undertaking which has, a called-up share capital or net assets of not less than:

   (i) if the company has more than 20 shareholders or is a subsidiary undertaking of an undertaking which has more than 20 shareholders, £500,000;

   (ii) otherwise, £5 million.

(g) Any unincorporated associations or partnerships with net assets of not less than £5 million.

(h) The trustees of a high value trust.

(i) Any person ("A") whilst acting as director, officer or employee of a person ("B") falling within any of (f) to (h) above, where A's responsibilities when acting in that capacity involve A in the investment activity in which B has or is engaging.

(j) Persons to whom the communication may otherwise lawfully be made.

24.45   Under no circumstances should any research report be sent to the press or other media organisation, to private investors, or to members of the general public. If sent to intermediaries, the intermediaries should agree not to copy research reports to their clients.

24.46   To draw a distinction between research reports and the offering documents, research reports may not be distributed at roadshows, regardless of the blackout period. Research reports should be prepared and delivered only in physical form, and should not be submitted for inclusion in any screen-based or electronic retrieval system or posted on, or distributed through, the internet. However, research reports must not be sent out to potential investors in the same envelope or at the same time as any offering document, as this will also blur the distinction between the research and the offer document.

24.47   Research should be distributed in one mailshot only and should not be re-circulated after it is first distributed. If the broker distributes research reports, it should issue only such number of research reports as is consistent with its past practice in UK transactions. The number of research reports distributed should be controlled and a record should be kept of the person or entity to which each report is sent.

24.48   The broker should be satisfied that those individuals responsible for preparing and issuing a research report are not in possession of any information relating to specific matters concerning the company which is not, or will not, be known to the market and which, if known, would be likely materially to affect the price of the securities of the company.

24.49   The pathfinder AIM admission document and the final AIM admission document (or other offering document) itself should be sent to all those who have received a copy of the research report, thus lending weight to the argument that investors relied upon the AIM admission document rather than the research report in reaching their investment decision. To add further weight to that argument, the terms and conditions of the placing should contain an express provision to the effect that the institutional investor is making their investment decision solely on the basis of the statements and opinions contained in the final AIM admission document and no other document.

24.50   Any supplemental report (i.e. not a revised report but a separate supplemental document) taking account of any disclosures contained in the AIM admission document which were not taken into account in the original research report should be published within a short period of the date of publication of the AIM admission document or other offering document. Similarly, any other changes to otherwise reflect facts or matters not specific to the company or the securities which have occurred since the publication of the original research report should also be published within a short period of the date of the publication of the AIM admission document.

24.51   Any such supplemental report should be distributed in accordance with, and otherwise comply with, the restrictions which applied to the initial research report.

IN PRACTICE

Research is a valuable tool in heightening investor awareness in advance of an offering and is commonly used. While there are risks associated with research, these can be mitigated by carefully following practices and procedures.

On a large initial public offer, the bank or its legal advisers will produce a memorandum on the preparation of research reports to be given to their analyst, setting out the legal position and parameters within which the report can be produced and distributed. This memorandum may be produced either from its own standard form or the bank's lawyers may draft it for them. It will be tailored to each transaction and will set out a timetable stipulating the blackout period and the form of the relevant disclaimers and legends that should be placed on the research report.

CHAPTER 25

Publicity guidelines

AT A GLANCE

In order to ensure that a consistent view of a company is presented to the outside world during the period in the run-up to an initial public offer or fundraising, certain procedures should be put in place to ensure that all information which is put out into the public domain is true, accurate and consistent with the view which will be set out in the AIM admission document, offering circular or other fundraising document.

INTRODUCTION

25.1 This chapter addresses the issue of the release of information in connection with a proposed initial public offering or placing of securities in a company during the periods running up to and immediately following an initial public offer or fundraising. The chapter also discusses procedures for implementation by the company to ensure that restrictions on publicity are not breached.

25.2 The timetable in the run-up to any initial public offer or fundraising can be a drawn out process and it is important that during this period the company and its directors understand that, once the wider market is aware that the initial public offer or fundraising is being proposed, the way that further information on the company or group is presented to the outside market is crucial.

25.3 The range of information which may be subject to these restrictions is wide. It includes not only information which relates in any way to an initial public offer or fundraising, or which encourages interest in an initial public offer or fundraising, but also information which relates to the business, assets, financial position or prospects of the group if it is likely to influence a person in deciding whether or not to subscribe for, or purchase, the securities (whether or not there is an intention that it should have that effect), including statements of fact and of opinion as well as forecasts and estimates. Any marketing tool that may be used, such as press releases, employee communications, presentations and displays, information on websites, speeches and general advertising in newspapers, is capable of breaching the legal requirements and should therefore be subject to restrictions.

25.4 Information provided to the market must be accurate, verifiable, unambiguous and not misleading or untrue, and it must also be consistent with the information which subsequently will be published in the AIM admission document or fundraising circular. Care should be taken to ensure that the information also appears in the same context, and presents the same view of the company, as will the AIM admission document or fundraising circular. It is also essential that no information relating to the group that may influence a decision whether or not to invest in the securities of the company is made available publicly but is then later omitted from the AIM admission document or fundraising circular.

25.5 In addition, the laws of the jurisdictions in which the company's securities may be offered (including the United Kingdom and the United States) may, to a greater or lesser extent, restrict the circumstances in which communications concerning the company may be made during, and in the period prior to, an initial public offer or fundraising or other offering of securities.

25.6 Where information concerning the company is published in breach of publicity guidelines, and the information then transpires to be misleading, inaccurate or untrue, then it may result in the company being liable to compensate investors in relation to any misleading or untrue statements contained in such communications or other publicity.

25.7 Further, any failure by the company to comply with such securities laws and regulations, either foreign or domestic, which restrict the circumstances in which communications concerning the company may be published could constitute a criminal offence or result in civil liability being imposed on those persons responsible for publication of any such information (which may include the company's directors). Furthermore, such a failure could affect the ability of the company to enforce contracts to purchase the company's securities in the initial public offer or fundraising, and thereby potentially jeopardise the success of any such offering of securities.

25.8 In the case of the United States, a failure to comply with restrictions on communications concerning the company during the period in the run-up to and following an initial public offer or offering may cause the company to lose any exemption that it may otherwise benefit from in relation to the securities registration requirements of the US federal securities laws. Where an offering of securities is made in jurisdictions outside the United Kingdom (whether in whole or in part), local law advice should be sought in such jurisdictions.

25.9 In order to minimise, to the extent possible, the risk of information being published which is inaccurate, misleading or untrue or which is inconsistent with the information to be included in an AIM admission document or offering circular, the company's lawyers may well produce and circulate a set of guidelines which govern all publicity concerning the company during the period of the initial public offer or fundraising or other offering of securities. An understanding of, and adherence to, such publicity guidelines will help the directors and the wider working group to reduce the likelihood of such inappropriate information being published by mistake.

TIMING

25.10 The period during which the company should abide by restrictions on publicity and communications regarding the company will usually start from the beginning of the work towards the initial public offer or offering, and the publicity guidelines document will often be one of the first documents to be drafted and circulated. These restrictions will continue to apply until after completion of such initial public offer or offering; which date will be the later of the date of admission to trading on AIM and the date on which any over-allotment option is exercised. Further information on over-allotment options is set out in Chapter 23, *Price stabilisation, over-allotment, greenshoes and when-issued trading*.

25.11   Once the company is admitted to trading on AIM, the company will also become subject to continuing requirements and restrictions set out in the *AIM Rules for Companies*, details of which are summarised in Part IV, *Continuing Obligations*.

RESTRICTED INFORMATION

25.12   The publicity restrictions in relation to the company are likely to apply to a wide range of information, including where the publicity document: (i) relates to, advertises or alerts third parties to a proposed offering or solicits interest in such an offering or otherwise encourages, invites or induces, or could reasonably be expected to encourage, invite or induce, directly or indirectly, or might influence prospective investors to participate in such an offering or buy or sell securities in the company; or (ii) relates to the group's management, operations (including the company's key performance indicators), assets and liabilities, financial position or prospects, profits and losses or valuation.

25.13   Where a publicity document has any of those objectives then, whatever form it is in and by whatever means it is distributed, it is likely to be a document that should be subject to certain restrictions and checks before it is published. A non-exhaustive list of examples of the type of documents that may be caught is set out at Figure 25.1.

25.14   As a general guide, the restrictive procedures will not apply to materials issued or distributed by the group in the ordinary course of business, such as ordinary course advertising (that is, in the case of the group, the advertising of the group's products and services) or information distributed to employees, customers or suppliers in the ordinary course of their respective operations. However, care should be taken to ensure that the materials in question follow the form and timing of previously distributed information, are distributed through normal publicity channels and do not mention an initial public offer or offering.

25.15   However, where the company or the directors have any doubts concerning the status of any publicity materials, then the advisers working on the transaction should be consulted as to how to proceed.

25.16   In particular, during the period of the initial public offer or offering, the company should not publish, or allow to be published, any material which refers to the commercial success of the company or group or any part of its current or proposed business or any "corporate profile" advertising without first consulting their financial and legal advisers. Nor should the company publish forecasts, projections or predictions concerning, but not limited to, the value of the securities

---

FIGURE 25.1   Examples of publicity documents which may be subject to restrictions

The following non-exhaustive list sets out examples of publicity documents which may be subject to restrictions if they: (i) relate to, advertise or alert third parties to a proposed offering or solicit interest in such an offering or otherwise encourage, invite or induce, or could reasonably be expected to encourage, invite or induce directly or indirectly, or might influence prospective investors to participate in such an offering or buy or sell securities in the company; or (ii) relate to the group's management, operations (including the company's key performance indicators), assets and liabilities, financial position or prospects, profits and losses or valuation:

- Press releases
- Annual report and accounts, corporate reports and other related materials
- Interim reports and quarterly reports
- Brochures, fact sheets and video tapes
- Media advertising, including newspaper, TV and radio advertising
- Corporate image or brand advertising
- Any internet activities (including the website of the group)
- Speeches, press conferences, telephone conversations, roadshows, presentations and interviews (including informal conversations with journalists, analysts or other third parties)
- Investor conference calls
- Materials made available at roadshows
- Materials made available at presentations to analysts or representatives of independent research or consulting firms
- Information or material which is distributed to the public or anyone outside the offering team including among employees of the group (for example, company newsletters).

---

and the commercial success of the group including (but not limited to) revenue, income or earnings per security.

25.17   Analyst research reports which are labelled as non-independent research may also constitute restricted materials, and it is important for the company to check any non-independent research report to ensure that the views and opinions contained in the research are not attributed to the group, and that all of the material factual statements made in the research are consistent with the AIM admission document or offering circular. Further information on the production of analyst research reports is set out in Chapter 24, *Analyst research*.

PARTIES TO WHOM THE RESTRICTIONS APPLY

25.18   The restrictions outlined in this chapter will apply to all shareholders of the company, which includes all the companies included within the group and their respective shareholders, advisers, their respective subsidiaries and affiliates and each of their respective controlling persons, directors, officers and employees, the bank and Nominated Adviser and any dealer purchasers, any advertising, public relations or marketing agencies retained in connection with the initial public offer or offering, and any person acting on behalf of any of these parties. Each of these parties should ensure that all appropriate persons within their respective organisations are made aware of the restrictions which apply.

RECOMMENDED PROCEDURES

Publicity guidelines

25.19 In order to minimise, to the extent possible, the risk of materials being published which are inaccurate, misleading or untrue or which are inconsistent with the information to be included in an AIM admission document or offering circular, a set of publicity guidelines are sometimes produced.

25.20 The purpose of the publicity guidelines is to ensure that restricted materials are identified and reviewed by appropriate people within the company and its advisers, before they are released to the market. These publicity guidelines will also help ensure that price sensitive information in relation to the company is released in an appropriate way. The publicity guidelines will also help to ensure that the persons releasing communications about the company or an initial public offer/offering are restricted to those persons who are authorised to do so, as this will assist in ensuring that communications with prospective investors and the market generally are managed effectively.

25.21 It is common for a company going through a listing or fundraising process to appoint one person from within the company as an "information officer" and that person will then police the publicity guidelines. An information officer should be able to verify compliance with the publicity guidelines with respect to all communications issued to the public, from the beginning of the admission or fundraising process until the end of the restricted period, which is discussed at Paragraph 25.10.

25.22 All directors, officers or other employees of the company, their respective subsidiaries or affiliates, their shareholders and any advertising, public relations or marketing agencies retained in connection with an initial public offer or offering who, as part of their duties, will be responsible for the release of information which may constitute restricted materials should be made aware of, and comply with, the publicity guidelines. In addition, any person intending to release any information which might constitute restricted materials must, prior to its release, notify the information officer in sufficient time for a review process of the materials to be carried out.

25.23 In the process of enforcing the publicity guidelines, the information officer will work alongside, and consult with, the financial and legal advisers to the initial public offer or fundraising process in determining whether any proposed release of information does or might contain restricted materials. The information officer's role is effectively to act as a co-ordinator for the process, to ensure that no announcements slip through the net without being considered. The information officer is unlikely to be the individual who actually reviews a document in order to assess whether it contains restricted materials or who provides comments on the document, but they will co-ordinate the comments of the legal and financial advisers and pass them back to the author of the document. In this manner, all of the comments on a document are passed through one person and the procedure of agreeing the wording and form of such a document becomes easier.

25.24   One of the most likely amendments which the legal and/or financial advisers will make, if they consider the document to contain restricted materials, is the addition of a warning legend to the document. One of the most likely warnings to be applied to the document is where the document constitutes a financial promotion. In such circumstances, it will either have to state that it has been approved for release by an authorised person under section 21 of the *Financial Services and Markets Act 2000* (FSMA) (the Nominated Adviser or broker will usually be the appropriate person to make such an approval), or it will have to carry a legend stating that its circulation has been restricted in such a way that this approval is not needed.

25.25   Once the document containing restricted materials has been approved for release in a form satisfactory to all the parties involved, changes should not be made to such information either by deletion or addition.

25.26   Examples of common dos and don'ts included in publicity guidelines are:

Do:

- be cautious and objective when releasing information in the public domain (for this purpose "public domain" means any persons outside of the company and its appointed advisers, no matter how restricted it is believed that group to be);
- ensure that, to the extent that information has to be disclosed, such information is accurate, balanced, complete and not misleading, is capable of being verified as such, and is consistent with the information to be disclosed in the company's AIM admission document.

Don't:

- embark on publicity for the company which is (i) inconsistent with what the company has done in the past, (ii) could be deemed to be pre-marketing the transaction or (iii) conflicts with the company's lawyers' advice regarding the company's existing promotional materials and website;
- include any new material on the website or attend press conferences or briefings without clearing it in advance with the information officer;
- comment on any speculation about the proposed transaction; the company can state that "The board frequently evaluates its strategic objectives and continues to do so, but there is nothing to announce at this stage.";
- say anything that cannot be verified;
- say anything that the company would not wish to be disseminated more widely;
- disclose any information in relation to any unannounced policy, decision, discussion or matter (including timing and structure);
- disclose any information on current trading or prospects of the company or its subsidiaries or customers, including forecasts relating to profit, turnover, dividends and so forth;
- make any projections as to the future;

- disclose information which would amount to unpublished price sensitive information (that is information which is not already in the public domain but which would, or might be, relevant to a potential investor in assessing the company's assets and liabilities, financial position, profits and losses and/or prospects);
- distribute, publish or hand out any materials, other than existing routine material (following the company's lawyers' advice) which have not been cleared through the information officer;
- discuss matters relating to the company or its policy with any brokers, bankers or analysts, apart from the company's appointed advisers;
- offer an opinion on the merits or otherwise of an investment in the company.

Press enquiries

25.27 The publicity guidelines will also detail how the directors and other involved parties should respond to enquiries from the press or public in relation to any initial public offer or offering. Where an information officer has been appointed, they are likely to be the appropriate person to respond to any press or other enquiry, and where other parties receive such a request it should be referred immediately to the information officer who may consult with other advisers.

25.28 In order to ensure that the appropriate legal restrictions are complied with, it is important for the person who receives the initial press enquiry to establish the purpose of the enquiry, as well as the identity and location of the person making the enquiry. By way of example, due to the complexities of US securities laws it is common for enquiries from persons in the United States to be dealt with on a "no comment" basis.

25.29 The information officer should endeavour to keep the answers provided in response to the enquiry brief and confined to information which is already publicly available, and should particularly avoid making statements which could be construed as forecasts or projections. No information in relation to the financial position, current trading or future prospects or development plans of the company, which has not already been made publicly available, should be given to the person making the enquiry.

25.30 The information officer, or whichever person is responding to the enquiry in the absence of such an officer, should avoid making any comment as to the relative merits or otherwise of investing in the securities of the company or attributing any value to them. The person responding to the enquiry should also avoid making references to the anticipated proceeds of any offering that may be taking place, or to forecasts or projections regarding the performance of the company.

25.31 All press releases, public announcements and other press activity to be released or made available to the public which contains restricted materials will, generally, need to go through the approval procedures monitored by the information officer and set out in the publicity guidelines. This is particularly important in the case of a press conference, where the information officer should consult with the company's legal and financial advisers to ensure that an appropriate script or question and answer sheet is prepared. These simple steps will help ensure that restricted information is not inadvertently disclosed at a press conference.

25.32 Due to the fact that they are so widely disseminated, any press releases containing restricted materials must contain a legend stating that they should not be sent, transmitted or otherwise distributed in or into the United States, Canada, Australia or Japan or outside the United Kingdom. As previously mentioned, other legends will be required if the press announcement is a financial promotion for UK regulatory purposes. In these circumstances, it may also be necessary to restrict circulation of the press release to certain categories of investment professional as defined in the FSMA or have an authorised person (such as the Nominated Adviser or broker) approve the press release.

25.33 Marketing information, of whatever type or form, should not be released unless its content and audience (intended or otherwise), and the timing of its release, have been considered by the company's financial and legal advisers. Such consideration will help ensure that all legal and regulatory requirements are complied with and that no statements are made which may contradict other information which has been, or is proposed to be, issued by or about the company. This will remain the case whether or not the information relates to the initial public offer or offering which is being conducted at the time.

25.34 Any ongoing marketing or customer relations exercises which are being conducted by, or on behalf of, the company at the time the initial public offer or offering process is being conducted should be examined to see whether they may continue and, if so, what modifications may be appropriate in order to avoid the publication of inappropriate information.

INTERNET ACTIVITY

25.35 Internet activities are a very effective method of achieving widespread dissemination of information, due to the ease with which the general public are able to access the information. As a result, anything published via a website will require careful scrutiny, in order to ensure that the appropriate legends and warnings are attached to the communication, depending on which audience the information is intended for. It may well be the case, particularly in relation to the United States, that the website hosting the relevant information will contain a "click-through" facility, whereby any person wishing to view the information has to confirm which country they are from and, depending on their response, there will be different disclaimers and legends appended to the information, or access may be restricted. By using such a facility the company can ensure that appropriate procedures are in place to limit access to the restricted information by persons in certain jurisdictions.

25.36 In addition, where an information officer has been appointed, they should take precautions in relation to any internet activities, including the following:

■ establishing a "watch" procedure, to be monitored by the information officer, to co-ordinate any internet-related activities of the company's investor relations, finance, legal and other relevant offices;

- engaging in a summary review of any product-oriented or service-oriented communications of the company on the internet and also of internet communications in the nature of "institutional" advertising, to eliminate hyperbole and to establish consistency with normal advertising policy;
- immediately inspecting any information that has been posted which concerns the company on a site maintained by another entity (e.g., by a stock exchange or a business association) to ensure that such information does not contain any information which should be restricted;
- eliminating information on the company's website which conflicts with information that is (or may be) included in the AIM admission document;
- eliminating out-of-date and "stale" information on the company's website;
- examining other internet-transmitted communications, to identify and to consider retention or temporary deletion of items such as information relating to the offer/initial public offer, business forecast information, projections of financial information and analysis of business trends or uncertainties.

25.37 It is prudent not to communicate to third parties any information which may be restricted by email, unless procedures are in place to ensure that each recipient is not located in a jurisdiction, such as the United States, where specific legends and disclaimers would be required in order to comply with local securities laws.

Verification

25.38 It is important that all materials relating to the company, and not just restricted information, which are to be released should be accurate, complete and clear and not misleading. In particular, both the facts and opinions (and facts on which opinions are based) should be capable of verification. Where an item of information cannot be satisfactorily verified it should be amended or deleted. Supporting documentary evidence of the verification should be obtained and kept on record.

25.39 Generally speaking, predictions, forecasts and other forward looking statements should be avoided, as these are often difficult to substantiate. Where clear implications would reasonably be drawn from certain statements contained in the information, then the implied information, as well as the explicit information, should be verified.

IN PRACTICE

Around the time of an initial public offering or fundraising, care needs to be taken that communications with third parties are consistent with the company's public information and information to be released in connection with fundraising.

A suitable person at the company should be given overall responsibility for checking all such information. This will help protect the company and its directors against claims that a person relied on any such statements or material when making their investment decisions.

Part IV
Continuing Obligations

INTRODUCTION

For so long as the company's securities are traded on AIM the company must comply with the continuing obligations set out in the *AIM Rules for Companies*. These contain specific requirements in relation to the company's continuing eligibility (see Chapter 26, *Continuing eligibility requirements*), the company's financial reporting (see Chapter 27, *Financial reporting*), the circumstances in which announcements must be made and an analysis of what constitutes price sensitive information (see Chapter 28, *Announcements including price sensitive information*), the contents of its website (see Chapter 29, *Website disclosure*) and further issues of securities (see Chapter 30, *Further issues of securities*). In addition, the *AIM Rules for Companies* set out requirements in respect of directors' responsibility for the company's compliance with the *AIM Rules for Companies* (see Chapter 31, *Directors' responsibility*), and provisions affecting directors' dealings (see Chapter 32, *Directors' dealings*). Market practice for directors' service agreements is also considered (see Chapter 33, *Directors' service agreements*).

This part also considers several other areas which affect a company whose securities are admitted to trading on AIM, including acquisitions and disposals (see Chapter 34, *Acquisitions and disposals*), AIM companies and takeovers (see Chapter 35, *Takeovers*), options and share incentives (see Chapter 36, *Options and share incentives*), tax incentives (see Chapter 37, *Tax incentives*) and the *Disclosure Rules and Transparency Rules* and AIM (see Chapter 38, *Disclosure Rules and Transparency Rules*).

In addition, there are certain continuing obligations which relate to specific companies, such as mining and oil and gas companies (see Chapter 39, *Mining, oil and gas companies*) and overseas companies (see Chapter 40, *Overseas companies*).

Finally, this part considers disciplinary matters and proceedings where there are found to be breaches of the *AIM Rules for Companies* (see Chapter 41, *Disciplinary matters*).

CHAPTER 26

Continuing eligibility requirements

AT A GLANCE

The *AIM Rules for Companies* contain a number of important provisions, which must be complied with on a continuing basis, relating to the company, its securities and the retention of certain advisers. These are often referred to as the "continuing eligibility requirements".

INTRODUCTION

26.1 The key continuing eligibility requirements for AIM companies relate to the: transferability of securities; securities to be admitted; settlement; broker; Nominated Adviser; fees; and contact information.

TRANSFERABILITY OF SECURITIES

26.2 An AIM company must ensure that any of its securities which are admitted to trading on AIM are freely transferable (*AIM Rules for Companies*, Rule 32). There are specific exceptions in limited circumstances, namely where:

- the law of particular jurisdiction imposes restrictions on transferability; or
- the company is seeking to limit the number of shareholders domiciled in a particular jurisdiction to ensure that it does not become subject to the law of that jurisdiction.

26.3 The transferability of securities is, generally speaking, one of the fundamental principles of trading securities on any public market and so exceptions to this Rule are particularly limited. The first limb of the exception is aimed at accommodating overseas companies whose local law may impose a restriction on transferability. A common example of this is in respect of the laws of the state of Jersey where certain anti money laundering provisions need to be complied with before a transfer of a security can be registered. The second limb of the exception is aimed at assisting UK and overseas companies from becoming subject to the laws of an overseas territory as a consequence of their securities being freely transferable, which may be unduly burdensome to the company or expensive for the company to comply with.

SECURITIES TO BE ADMITTED

26.4 Under Rule 33 of the *AIM Rules for Companies*, only securities which have been unconditionally allotted can be admitted to trading and all securities of a class must be admitted to trading. This Rule is designed to make sure that all shareholders are treated equally and that none of the securities have any conditions or provisions attached to them which may disadvantage certain shareholders. For example, if a share had been issued partly paid it could expose the holder to a call to pay up the remainder of the nominal value and any premium on it, but there would be no way of a potential shareholder differentiating that share from one which has been fully paid.

26.5 In practice, to avoid any timing issues, AIM securities are issued subject to one condition, that being their admission to trading on AIM.

26.6 When making further issues of securities, confirmation of the allotment of the securities subject only to the condition of admission to trading on AIM must be made no later than 16:30 on the business day prior to the intended date of admission to trading on AIM, unless otherwise agreed with AIM Regulation. Where there is to be a change in the number of AIM securities admitted to trading or the AIM company is considering a corporate action or dividend which will require it to issue further new shares then the company, through its Nominated Adviser, should discuss this with AIM Regulation or the Stock Situation Analysis Team at the London Stock Exchange.

SETTLEMENT

26.7 An AIM company must ensure that appropriate arrangements are in place for the settlement of its securities pursuant to Rule 36 of the *AIM Rules for Companies*. In particular, AIM securities must continue to be eligible for electronic settlement unless AIM Regulation agrees otherwise. Further information on settlement arrangements is set out in Chapter 16, *CREST, settlement and depository interests*.

26.8 Despite retaining the flexibility to agree that AIM securities need not be eligible for electronic settlement, the London Stock Exchange stated in its guidance that it will only grant derogations from this requirement in the most exceptional circumstances. An example of such exceptional circumstances would be where none of the current electronic settlement systems can cope with the AIM company securities or where its local law prohibits such settlement.

BROKER

26.9 Pursuant to Rule 35 of the *AIM Rules for Companies*, an AIM company must retain a broker at all times. This is a requirement as the broker will carry out certain important functions for the AIM company. For example, the broker will use its best endeavours to find matching business if there is no registered market maker in the AIM company's securities.

26.10 Any member of the London Stock Exchange may act as broker to an AIM company (subject to any authorisation required to be granted by any other regulator). The website of the London Stock Exchange contains a list of current member firms together with a separate list of brokers who have already been appointed by AIM companies.

26.11   Further information on the roles performed by the broker is set out in Chapter 6, *Role of the broker*.

NOMINATED ADVISER

26.12   Similar to the requirement to retain a broker, under Rule 1 of the *AIM Rules for Companies* an AIM company must retain a Nominated Adviser.

26.13   All Nominated Advisers must be approved by the London Stock Exchange and there is a list of the approved Nominated Advisers available on the London Stock Exchange website.

26.14   In contrast to the broker, an AIM company can only retain the services of one Nominated Adviser at any one time. Importantly, where an AIM company needs to notify the loss of its Nominated Adviser it should first liaise with AIM Regulation, who will require the trading in the companies securities to be suspended. This suspension will take effect from the notification of the loss of the Nominated Adviser. When a new Nominated Adviser is appointed the new Nominated Adviser is required to submit a new Nominated Advisers' declaration pursuant to the *AIM Rules for Nominated Advisers*.

26.15   Further information on the role of the Nominated Adviser is set out in Chapter 5, *Role of the Nominated Adviser*.

FEES

26.16   An AIM company must pay the AIM fees prescribed from time to time by the London Stock Exchange pursuant to Rule 37 of the *AIM Rules for Companies*. Details of the current fees are available from the London Stock Exchange website. Failure to pay the fees when required may result in a precautionary suspension (see Chapter 41, *Disciplinary matters*).

CONTACT INFORMATION

26.17   Pursuant to Rule 38 of the *AIM Rules for Companies*, contact details for the company, including an email address, must be provided on admission to trading to AIM. Where there are any changes to the contact details then these must be notified to AIM Regulation without delay.

IN PRACTICE

The key continuing eligibility requirements relate to the smooth operation of the market, and in particular to the transferability and settlement of transfers in the AIM company securities. The other key continuing eligibility requirement is the retention of key advisers, being the Nominated Adviser and broker, which is fundamental to the smooth operation of the market given its regulatory structure.

Financial reporting

The *AIM Rules for Companies* contain obligations relating to the reporting of financial matters on a regular, ongoing basis. Although the *AIM Rules for Companies* does not lay down a required format for an AIM company's annual report, investors will generally expect that it will meet the standards laid down for companies admitted to trading on the Main Market for listed securities. AIM companies are also required to report financial information in respect of each six-month period.

INTRODUCTION

27.1   The key elements which make up an AIM company's financial reporting are its annual accounts and its half-yearly reports. In addition, in some cases the preparation of quarterly reports may give rise to additional obligations.

ANNUAL ACCOUNTS

27.2   Pursuant to Rule 19 of the *AIM Rules for Companies*, an AIM company must publish annual audited accounts. The annual accounts must be sent to the holders of its AIM securities without delay and, in any event, no later than six months after the end of the financial period to which they relate.

27.3   Where an AIM company wishes to change its accounting reference date its Nominated Adviser should contact AIM Regulation in advance to discuss the revised reporting timetable that will result from such a change.

27.4   The standards to which the annual report and accounts need to be produced vary depending on whether the AIM company is incorporated in a European Economic Area (EEA) country or not.

27.5   An AIM company which is incorporated in an EEA country and is a parent company must prepare and present its annual accounts in accordance with international accounting standards. If the company is not a parent company, it may elect to present such financial information in accordance with international accounting standards or in accordance with the accounting and company legislation and regulations that are applicable to the company in its country of incorporation. However, the London Stock Exchange encourages all companies to use international accounting standards both on admission to trading on AIM and in the preparation of all financial information after admission. Accordingly, in practice most AIM companies adopt international accounting standards when reporting their financial information.

27.6 As at the date of publication, EEA countries are those countries which comprise the European Union member states, together with Norway, Iceland and Lichtenstein and, for the purposes of the *AIM Rules for Companies*, includes the Channel Islands and Isle of Man.

27.7 In relation to an AIM company incorporated in a non-EEA country, it must prepare and present its annual accounts in accordance with one of the following standards:

- international accounting standards;
- US generally accepted accounting principles;
- Canadian generally accepted accounting principles;
- Australian international financial reporting standards (as issued by the Australian Accounting Standards Board); or
- Japanese generally accepted accounting principles.

27.8 AIM companies incorporated outside the EEA should, however, note that Rule 30 of the *AIM Rules for Companies* requires annual accounts to be in English regardless of what standard they are prepared to.

27.9 Once an AIM company, wherever incorporated, has started reporting using a particular standard, a different standard should only be used with the prior approval of AIM Regulation.

27.10 The annual accounts which are prepared by an AIM company must contain certain information regarding any transactions with related parties where the transaction exceeds 0.25 per cent in any of the class tests. This requirement applies whether or not the transaction with the related party has previously been disclosed under the *AIM Rules for Companies*. In particular, the annual report and accounts must specify the identity of the related party and the consideration for the transaction. Further information on the class tests is set out in Chapter 34, *Acquisitions and disposals*.

27.11 Once the annual report and accounts have been prepared, they must be made available to shareholders on the company's website pursuant to Rule 26 of the *AIM Rules for Companies* and must be notified to a Regulatory Information Service. Further information on the requirements of Rule 26 is set out in Chapter 29, *Website disclosure*.

27.12 It should be noted that the London Stock Exchange will suspend AIM companies which are late in publishing their annual accounts.

COMBINED CODE

27.13 Although not directly applicable to AIM companies, the key principles set out in the *Combined Code* in relation to the financial information and the audit process are used by many AIM companies as a guide, particularly as many AIM companies make a statement on their admission to trading on AIM that they intend to comply with the *Combined Code* as far as is reasonable given the size of the company and its stage of development.

27.14   The key principles set out in the *Combined Code* include that the board of directors:

- presents a balanced and understandable assessment of the company's position and prospects;
- maintains a sound system of internal controls to safeguard shareholders' investments and the company's assets;
- establishes formal and transparent arrangements for considering how it should apply the financial reporting and internal control principles and for maintaining an appropriate relationship with the company's auditors;
- should establish an audit committee of at least two non-executive directors (in the case of smaller companies) with written terms of reference which deal clearly with authority and duties of the committee and that the board of directors should satisfy itself that at least one member of the audit committee has recent and relevant experience. The terms of reference of the audit committee, including its role and the authority delegated to it by the board of directors, should be made available on request and should be included on the AIM company's website. A separate section of the annual report should describe the work of the committee in discharging its responsibilities. Further information on audit committees is set out in Chapter 44, *Audit committee.*

27.15   The *Combined Code* also sets out that the audit committee should:

- review the arrangements by which staff of the company may, in confidence, raise concerns about possible improprieties in matters of financial reporting or other matters;
- monitor and review the effectiveness of the internal audit activities, where applicable;
- have primary responsibility for making a recommendation on the appointment, reappointment and removal of external auditors.

27.16   If the auditor provides a non-audit service, the annual report should explain to shareholders how the auditor's objectivity and independence are safeguarded.

27.17   Whilst the *Combined Code* is not directly binding on AIM companies, it represents best practice and most AIM companies will, either voluntarily or at the instigation of their Nominated Adviser, follow these provisions where applicable to the company given the size of the company and its stage of development. For example, smaller AIM companies may not have an internal audit function.

27.18   The AIM company should make a disclosure statement in two parts in its annual report and accounts as to its compliance with the *Combined Code*. In the first part of the statement the company is required to report on how it applied the principles set out in the *Combined Code*, providing an explanation which enables shareholders to evaluate how the principles of the *Combined Code* have been applied. In the second part of the statement the company is required to confirm whether or not it has complied throughout the accounting period with the *Combined Code*. A company that has not complied with the provisions of the

Combined Code should specify the provisions with which it has not complied and the reasons for such non-compliance. The company should also include in its annual report and accounts a report by the board of directors to the shareholders of the company on the company's policies on executive directors' remuneration, giving prescribed details relating to directors' remuneration, share options, incentive schemes and service contracts. Further information on directors' remuneration is set out in Chapter 43, *Remuneration committee*.

HALF-YEARLY REPORTS

27.19 Pursuant to Rule 18 of the *AIM Rules for Companies*, an AIM company must prepare a half-yearly report in respect of the six-month period from the end of the financial period for which financial information has been disclosed in its AIM admission document and for at least every subsequent six-month period thereafter. However, the requirements for half-yearly reporting do not apply in the final period of six months preceding the accounting reference date, for which an AIM company is required to produce annual audited accounts. The half-yearly report does not have to be audited. However, where it has been audited a statement to the effect that it has been audited must be included in the report. Most, if not all, AIM companies nevertheless have their half-yearly report reviewed by their auditors, although this is a lower standard of review than a formal audit.

27.20 Unlike for annual report and accounts, the *AIM Rules for Companies* sets out, in detail, the contents requirements for half-yearly reports. The minimum which should be included in a half-yearly report is:

- a balance sheet;
- an income statement; and
- a cash flow statement.

27.21 In respect of each of these items to be included, the half-yearly report must contain comparative figures for the corresponding period in the preceding financial year. Additionally, the half-yearly report must be presented and prepared in a form consistent with that which will be adopted in the company's annual accounts, having regard to the accounting standards applicable to such accounts.

27.22 All half-yearly reports must be notified to a Regulatory Information Service without delay and, in any event, no later than three months after the end of the relevant period.

27.23 The consequences of a failure to comply with the notification deadlines are severe and the London Stock Exchange will suspend a company which is late in publishing its half-yearly report.

27.24 Where an AIM company has been recently admitted to trading on AIM and the financial information which has been disclosed in the AIM admission document is that of the main trading subsidiary, this may be used for determining when the first six-month period begins. If there is any uncertainty as to what period should be covered by the half-yearly report then a company's Nominated Adviser should contact AIM Regulation.

27.25   Half-yearly information must be put on the AIM company's website pursuant to Rule 26 of the *AIM Rules for Companies*. Further information on the requirements of Rule 26 is set out in Chapter 29, *Website disclosure*.

QUARTERLY REPORTING

27.26   There is no requirement under the *AIM Rules for Companies* for an AIM company to report on a quarterly basis. However, it should be noted that where the AIM company prepares such quarterly information then, notwithstanding any other provision of the *AIM Rules for Companies*, it should be made available to shareholders where it contains a new development in relation to the performance of the business or a change in its financial condition pursuant to Rule 11 of the *AIM Rules for Companies*. In addition, notwithstanding any other provision of the *AIM Rules for Companies*, if information is disclosed about the AIM company to another market on which its securities are admitted then it must also disclose it to a Regulatory Information Service. For example, if a company has its securities admitted to trading on AIM and they are also listed on the Toronto Stock Exchange, any quarterly reports prepared by the company under the rules of the Toronto Stock Exchange should also be disclosed to a Regulatory Information Service.

27.27   Where an AIM company does report on a quarterly basis, the quarterly report should also be put on the company's website pursuant to Rule 26 of the *AIM Rules for Companies*. Further information on the requirements of Rule 26 is set out in Chapter 29, *Website disclosure*.

IN PRACTICE

The annual report and half-yearly report represent two of the most fundamental disclosures made by an AIM company each year.

Given the work involved in preparing such audited financial information under local law, the requirement to follow the standards set out in the *AIM Rules for Companies* should not be unduly burdensome.

For companies which were private companies before their admission to trading on AIM, it is particularly important to note the more strict time deadlines for the preparation and announcement of financial information and the penalties for not complying with these requirements.

CHAPTER 28

Announcements including price sensitive information

AT A GLANCE

One of the key aspects of both the *AIM Rules for Companies* and the principles of good corporate governance is disclosure. Full and timely disclosure encourages investors' trust and confidence.

In addition to the disclosure of financial results, which are covered in Chapter 27, *Financial reporting*, and the need to include certain information on its website, which is covered in Chapter 29, *Website disclosure*, an AIM Company is subject to continuing obligations to disclose various matters to the market under the *AIM Rules for Companies*. In certain cases the requirement is clear, for example when a new director is appointed. Other times the situation is less clear, for example the requirement to notify any new developments which are not public knowledge concerning a change in the financial condition of the company which, if made public, would be likely to lead to a substantial movement in the price of its AIM securities.

It should be noted that the provisions of the FSMA relating to market abuse apply to AIM companies and failure to disclose price sensitive information as well as being a breach of the *AIM Rules for Companies* can also constitute market abuse, for which the penalties are severe.

INTRODUCTION

28.1 AIM companies need to be aware of the requirements to make announcements which are set out primarily in Rules 11, 17 and 18 of the *AIM Rules for Companies*.

28.2 The requirement in Rule 11 is to notify, without delay, a Regulatory Information Service of any new developments which are not public knowledge concerning a change in the financial condition of the company which, if made public, would be likely to lead to a substantial movement in the price of its AIM securities. It can be difficult to assess whether an announcement is required by Rule 11, but such decision should be taken by the company after consultation with its advisers.

28.3 In addition, Rule 10 requires an AIM company to take reasonable care to ensure that any information notified to a Regulatory Information Service for distribution to the public is not misleading, false or deceptive and does not omit anything likely to affect the import of such information. The company must also ensure that the information is not published elsewhere before it is so notified. Rule 10 of the *AIM Rules for Companies* also requires that an AIM company retain the services of a Regulatory Information Service provider to ensure information can be announced as and when required. A list of such providers can be found on the website of the London Stock Exchange.

NOTIFICATION OF PRICE SENSITIVE INFORMATION

AIM Rules for Companies

28.4 The most significant of the *AIM Rules for Companies* relating to announcements is Rule 11, but it can be difficult to assess whether an announcement is required by this Rule. Rule 11 imposes a general duty to notify, without delay, a Regulatory Information Service of any new developments, which are not public knowledge, concerning a change in any of:

- the financial condition of the company;
- the company's sphere of activity;
- the performance of the company's business; or
- the company's expectation of its performance;

which if made public would be likely to lead to a substantial movement in the price of its AIM securities.

28.5 The assessment as to whether the information would lead to a substantial movement in the price of its AIM securities is best made following a discussion between the company, its Nominated Adviser and Broker and, if necessary, its legal advisers. It should be noted that the requirements of Rule 11 are in addition to any requirements regarding notification contained elsewhere in the *AIM Rules for Companies*. The London Stock Exchange may, in exceptional cases, grant a dispensation from the obligation to disclose information where such disclosure might prejudice the company's legitimate interests.

28.6 The directors will have to decide whether the information is significant enough to require immediate notification in accordance with this general obligation. Generally, information about impending developments or matters in the course of negotiation need not be notified. Whether or not it is decided that a notification is required, the information must be kept strictly confidential unless and until a notification is made. If the necessary degree of confidentiality cannot be maintained, or if that confidentiality has or may have been breached, a warning announcement should be made to the effect that the AIM company expects shortly to release information. If the information has been made or becomes public, the AIM company must ensure that a notification of such information is made as soon as possible. As a general principle, a company should monitor its share price carefully, particularly in a period when it is negotiating a transaction or raising finance, and prepare a holding announcement in case it is needed.

28.7 Information required to be notified must not be given to a third party beforehand except in very limited circumstances, such as to the company's advisers or to persons with whom the company is negotiating a transaction, representatives of its employees or trade unions acting on their behalf, the Bank of England, the Competition Commission, any government department or other statutory or regulatory body. The AIM company must be satisfied that the recipients of such information are aware that they must keep the information confidential and not trade in the securities before the information has been notified to a Regulatory Information Service. Accordingly, in practice, except in relation to the Bank of England, the Competition Commission and any government department or other statutory or regulatory body, the AIM company will require the person to whom such information is disclosed to enter into a confidentiality or non-disclosure agreement. In all cases, whether a confidentiality agreement or non-disclosure agreement is used, the recipient's attention should be drawn to its obligations not to trade in the securities. Ideally the recipient should, where possible, acknowledge this in writing.

28.8   The London Stock Exchange has shown itself particularly concerned to end the practice that had developed of disclosing price sensitive information to selected professionals, such as investment analysts, without making a formal trading statement via a Regulatory Information Service. This practice was previously justified as a means of allowing a share price to adjust gradually to unexpected information, but it is no longer acceptable.

28.9   The *AIM Rules for Companies* contain little guidance on what constitutes price sensitive information. It used to be possible to rely on the *Guidance on the Dissemination of Price Sensitive Information* published by the Financial Services Authority for listed companies, but this guidance was withdrawn when the *Disclosure Rules* (now the *Disclosure Rules and Transparency Rules* or "DTRs") (part of the *Financial Services Authority Handbook*) came into force on 1 July 2005. Some of the obligations set out in the DTRs, including those in relation to inside information, do not apply to AIM companies because AIM is not a regulated market for the purposes of EU law. However, the DTRs do contain some guidance on what constitutes inside information and when an announcement is required and, in practice, they still provide a useful source of guidance in this respect.

28.10   It is impossible to give general guidance on what constitutes price sensitive information, other than to say the more specific the information the greater the risk that it will be price sensitive. Price sensitive information cannot be defined mechanically by price movements of a certain percentage. In any case of doubt, directors of an AIM company should make use of their advisers to assist them in determining whether information is potentially price sensitive.

28.11   Particular caution regarding the disclosure of price sensitive information must be taken at general meetings of shareholders. Where it is proposed to announce at any meeting of shareholders information which might affect the company's share price, arrangements must be made for earlier, or at the very least simultaneous, notification of that information to a Regulatory Information Service.

Financial Services and Markets Act 2000

28.12   It should be noted that, notwithstanding any requirements in the *AIM Rules for Companies* to announce information which may lead to a substantial movement in the price of its AIM securities, the provisions of the *Financial Services and Markets Act 2000* (FSMA) relating to market abuse apply to AIM companies. Accordingly, the failure to disclose price sensitive information can constitute market abuse. Further information on what constitutes market abuse is set out in Chapter 32, *Directors' dealings.*

28.13   In addition, section 397(1) of the FSMA provides, in summary, that any person who knowingly or recklessly makes a statement, promise or forecast which is untrue, misleading or deceptive, or who dishonestly conceals material facts about the company, is guilty of an offence if such action is taken with the intention of inducing, or is reckless as to whether it will induce, others to trade or refrain from trading in the company's securities. A person may be taken to be acting "dishonestly" for these purposes by deliberately or recklessly not complying with market practice or market regulation. Accordingly, deliberate or reckless failure to comply with the disclosure obligations of the *AIM Rules for Companies* might constitute evidence of dishonest concealment of material facts under section 397.

28.14   It is also an offence to do any act or engage in any course of conduct which creates a false or misleading impression as to the market in, or the price or value of, any investments and is intended to induce others to trade (or refrain from trading) in the company's securities.

28.15   The penalty in each case is an unlimited fine or imprisonment for a maximum of seven years or both.

NOTIFICATION OF MAJOR INTERESTS IN SECURITIES

Disclosure Rules and Transparency Rules sourcebook

28.16   AIM companies and their shareholders need to comply with the rules set out in Chapter 5 of the DTRs.

28.17   DTR5 sets out the circumstances in which a person who holds voting rights attaching to the securities of an AIM company must notify the company of that holding. In DTR5 a distinction is drawn between UK and non-UK companies. Non-UK companies on AIM are not required to comply with DTR5 but must comply with Rule 17 of the *AIM Rules for Companies* discussed below.

28.18   For UK incorporated companies, a person must notify the company of the percentage of its voting rights it holds as shareholder if the percentage of those voting rights reaches, exceeds or falls below 3 per cent, and each 1 per cent threshold thereafter up to 100 per cent of the voting rights attaching to the company's ordinary share capital. Certain holdings of financial instruments in respect of securities in the company to which voting rights are attached are also notifiable. There are certain exemptions, including for voting rights held by market makers (if it holds less than 10 per cent of the total voting rights) provided such market maker is authorised and does not intervene in the management of the relevant company.

28.19   All disclosable interests must be notified by the relevant person to the company within two trading days. The company must then make a notification of the information received (by way of a Regulatory Information Service) "without delay". In practice, it is important to note that although the DTRs state that the company must make the notification by no later than the end of the third trading day following receipt of the information, AIM companies are subject to Rule 17, which provides that the notification must be made "without delay". In addition, AIM companies are required to notify the information to a Regulatory Information Service rather than the general obligation to make the information "public" as set out in the DTRs.

28.20   If the AIM company acquires, or disposes of, its own securities, it must disclose to a Regulatory Information Service the percentage of voting rights attributable to those securities within four trading days of the acquisition or disposal, where such percentage reaches, exceeds or falls below the thresholds of 5 per cent or 10 per cent of the voting rights attached to the company's securities.

28.21   In order for voteholders to calculate whether their holding has triggered an announcement obligation as referred to in Paragraph 28.18, UK AIM companies are obliged to announce to a Regulatory Information Service at the end of each calendar month during which an increase or decrease in the AIM company's issued share capital has occurred the total number of voting rights and capital in respect of each class of share issued and the total number of voting rights attaching to any of its securities held in treasury.

28.22   Where the AIM company is UK incorporated, if voteholders do not comply with their disclosure obligations, the Financial Services Authority is able to order that the information be disclosed to it or even to suspend trading in the securities.

28.23   A more detailed discussion of the requirements of AIM companies under the DTRs is set out in Chapter 38, *Disclosure Rules and Transparency Rules*.

NOTIFICATION OF OTHER MATTERS

AIM Rules

28.24   In addition to the general disclosure obligations in relation to information which may lead to a significant movement in the price of the AIM securities, an AIM company is obliged by Rule 17 of the *AIM Rules for Companies* to make a notification to a Regulatory Information Service without delay of certain specific matters including:

- dealings in securities by directors (further information on this is set out in Chapter 32, *Directors' dealings*);
- holdings of significant shareholders (i.e. those with a holding of 3 per cent or more or any movement through a whole percentage point above 3 per cent) (see Paragraph 28.18 and Chapter 38, *Disclosure Rules and Transparency Rules*);
- the resignation, dismissal or appointment of any director (and any changes to the details declared relating to unspent convictions or bankruptcies of such director);
- any change in its accounting reference date (which, as noted in Chapter 27, *Financial reporting*, should only be made with the prior approval of AIM Regulation);

- any change in its registered office address;
- any change in its legal name;
- any material change between its actual trading performance or financial condition and any profit forecast, estimate or projection included in the AIM admission document or otherwise made public on its behalf;
- acquisitions and disposals of business or assets (depending on the size) (for further information see Chapter 34, *Acquisitions and disposals*);
- any decisions to pay or make any dividend or other distribution on AIM securities or to withhold any dividend or interest payment on AIM securities, giving details of the exact net amount payable per share, the payment date and the record date (where applicable);
- the reason for the application for admission to trading on AIM or cancellation from trading on AIM of any AIM securities;
- the occurrence and number of securities taken into and out of treasury;
- any resignation, dismissal or appointment of its Nominated Adviser and/or Broker (see Chapter 26, *Continuing eligibility requirements*);
- any change in the website address at which the information required by Rule 26 is available (see Chapter 29, *Website disclosure*, regarding the website content requirements); and
- the admission to trading (or cancellation from trading) of the AIM securities on any other exchange or trading platform, including details of the exchange or trading platform.

28.25 As will be evident, complying with the requirements of Rule 17 should not cause too much difficulty for an AIM company. If the AIM company is required to make any notification in relation to the information referred to above, the company should immediately contact its Nominated Adviser and Broker and they will then make the necessary arrangements for the notification. The company must also forward to the London Stock Exchange by email copies of all announcements and three copies of all circulars, notices, reports or other documents at the same time as they are issued to shareholders. In addition, if the AIM company changes its legal name, a copy of the change of name certificate should also be sent to the London Stock Exchange and they will require this prior to amending the company's name on the screen.

28.26 As Rule 1 of the *AIM Rules for Companies* requires that all AIM companies have a Nominated Adviser, the AIM company should liaise with AIM Regulation prior to making a notification that the Nominated Adviser has resigned or has been dismissed as, if no replacement Nominated Adviser has been appointed, the London Stock Exchange will suspend trading in the AIM securities at the same time as the notification is made.

28.27 Rule 17 of the *AIM Rules for Companies* requires that an AIM company makes a notification of any changes to the holding of a significant shareholder (above 3 per cent) which increase or decrease such holding through any single percentage. Such notification must include: the identity of the significant shareholder concerned; the date on which the disclosure was made to the AIM company; the date on which the change was effected; the price, amount and class of

AIM securities concerned; and the nature and extent of the shareholder's interest in the transaction.

28.28 For UK companies, compliance with the DTRs will usually mean the company is complying with the significant shareholder disclosure obligations in Rule 17 except that an AIM company must, in order to comply with Rule 17, make a notification to a Regulatory Information Service "without delay" notwithstanding the time limits for disclosure set out in the DTRs.

28.29 All AIM Companies are required to use reasonable endeavours to comply with Rule 17 notwithstanding that the local law applicable to some AIM companies does not contain provisions that are similar to the DTRs. The guidance to the *AIM Rules for Companies* advises an AIM company to include provisions in its constitution requiring significant shareholders to notify the AIM company of any changes to their shareholding as per the levels set out in the DTRs (although this may be of limited use where there is a depository which holds all or substantially all the securities of a class). Such AIM companies are also advised to disclose the fact that statutory disclosures of significant shareholdings is different and may not always ensure compliance with the requirements of Rule 17. In practice this has not been adopted by all AIM companies, but any proposed deviation from best practice should be discussed by the AIM company and its Nominated Adviser.

28.30 The London Stock Exchange has indicated that it appreciates that it may not be reasonably practicable for an overseas company to change or amend its constitutional documents to account for Rule 17. However, in any event, overseas companies are recommended to include reference to the company's obligation pursuant to this rule in the investor relations section of their website, encouraging shareholders to notify the company of any relevant changes to their shareholding, so that the company will be able to comply with this aspect of Rule 17.

28.31 The guidance to the *AIM Rules for Companies* also recommends that the company makes appropriate disclosure of the fact that the statutory disclosure regime in the company's country of incorporation for significant shareholders is different to that required by the DTRs and may not always ensure compliance with the requirements of Rule 17. Again, such disclosure would be appropriately made on the investor relations section of the company's website.

28.32 AIM companies should also be aware that under Rules 24 and 25 of the *AIM Rules for Companies* and the guidance to the *AIM Rules for Companies*, an AIM company must inform the London Stock Exchange "in advance" (meaning by no later than 09:00 on the business day before any proposed notification) of the timetable (or an amendment of such timetable) for any proposed action affecting the rights of the existing shareholders. For example, this would include the timetable for a proposed open offer. It would also include a timetable for the payment of dividends but this does not need to be disclosed to the London Stock Exchange in advance provided the notification to a Regulatory Information Service includes details of the net amount and the record and payment dates and it does not require the AIM company to issue securities. The London Stock Exchange can request amendments to any such timetables for the purpose of maintaining orderly markets.

28.33 Under Rule 20 of the *AIM Rules for Companies*, an AIM company must also notify the distribution of any document to shareholders to a Regulatory Information Service and send an electronic copy of the document to the London Stock Exchange.

IN PRACTICE

One of the key aspects of the *AIM Rules for Companies* is full and timely disclosure of information to the market.

The requirements of the *AIM Rules for Companies* should not be unduly difficult to comply with, but it is important for an AIM company to make sure that it has procedures in place to identify the information which it is required to disclose.

Most of the questions in this area relate to what information is price sensitive, and in this regard the AIM company and its directors should have procedures in place to identify potentially price sensitive information and discuss any potential announcement with its Nominated Adviser.

CHAPTER 29

Website disclosure

AT A GLANCE

The *AIM Rules for Companies* require that all AIM companies set up and maintain a website disclosing certain fundamental details regarding the company and its directors and from which investors and potential investors should be able to obtain certain fundamental information on the AIM company

---

WEBSITE

29.1 A further aspect of notification to shareholders and potential shareholders is the requirement in the *AIM Rules for Companies* to set up and maintain a website with certain key information. This requirement was introduced from August 2007.

29.2 Rule 26 of the *AIM Rules for Companies* requires that the website from which the information is available must be the company's website, although it may be hosted externally. The information on such website must be kept up to date and it should be made clear on the website when the information was last updated. The information should be easily accessible from one part of the website and there should be a statement that the information is included for the purposes of Rule 26. Most AIM companies do this by having a section of their website in the investors' area labelled "Rule 26".

29.3 The information that must be included on the website (and available free of charge) is:

- a description of the business of the AIM company;
- the names of the company's directors and brief biographical details (in similar detail to the information included in an AIM admission document);
- a description of the responsibilities of the members of the board of directors and details of any committees that such directors sit on;
- the country of incorporation and main country of operation of the company (i.e. the geographic location from which the AIM company derives (or intends to derive) the largest proportion of its revenues or where the largest proportion of its assets are (or will be) located, as is most appropriate depending on the business);
- where the AIM company is not incorporated in the UK, a statement that the rights of shareholders may be different to the rights of shareholders in a UK incorporated company;

- the current constitutional documents of the company (e.g. its Articles of Association);
- details of any other exchanges or trading platforms on which the company has applied or agreed to have any of its securities admitted or traded (and which securities this relates to);
- whether there remain securities in issue (noting any held as treasury shares) and, so far as it is aware, the percentage of AIM securities not in public hands, together with the identity and percentage holdings of significant shareholders (which should be updated at least every six months);
- details of any restrictions on the transfer of the company's AIM securities (i.e. jurisdictional exemptions or restrictions that an AIM company is seeking to make use of and that may operate by virtue of non-UK securities laws);
- the company's most recent annual report (as sent to shareholders) and all half-yearly, quarterly or similar reports published since the last annual report;
- copies of all notifications that the company has made in the last 12 months;
- the company's most recent AIM admission document, together with any circulars or similar documents sent to shareholders within the previous 12 months; and
- details of the company's Nominated Adviser and other key advisers (as would be listed in an AIM admission document).

29.4 In practice, companies may decide to provide more than the minimum stated in Rule 26 to enable investors or potential investors to form a clearer view of the company. For example, in the management information section the company may decide to include further information regarding directors' shareholdings and dealings, information regarding the senior management team and possibly photographs of the directors and senior management team. In addition to the announcements required to be included, the company may decide to include prior year archives and news clippings referring to the company. In relation to share information, the company may decide to include a chart showing the share price over the last year.

29.5 An AIM company should take legal advice on how to make available any AIM admission document (and other circular or prospectus) so that the company does not infringe any securities laws that may be applicable. This may be done by putting either protections on the relevant web page so that recipients in certain countries cannot view the information on that web page or a disclaimer on that section of the website. However, it is important that measures taken to restrict access to the AIM admission document do not make it unnecessarily difficult for those who are allowed to view the document.

29.6 In addition to the *AIM Rules for Companies*, there are also company law requirements relating to corporate websites. All UK companies must display certain key information on their website, including the registered number, registered office address and full company name.

29.7 AIM companies should consider pitching the contents of their website to the relevant audience through the content, wording and style. The use of audio or video webcasts may also be appropriate. Companies often find it helpful to monitor use of their website, and there are various programmes that can be installed to analyse the data to see which parts of the site audiences are visiting.

QCA AIM WEBSITE GUIDE – RULE 26

29.8 With an AIM company's website being a primary source of information for investors researching a company, it is beneficial for companies to consider including more information than the minimum required. The Quoted Companies Alliance (QCA) has published guidance on compliance with Rule 26 of the *AIM Rules for Companies* which suggests including the following additional information as a matter of best practice:

- the company's strategy, history, structure and organisation, information about its products or services, and a company fact sheet;
- terms of reference for board committees, directors' shareholdings and dealings, senior management information and photographs, and broader governance information;
- prior year news archives (including a search facility), news clippings and email alerts for news;
- prior year documents archives, presentations, case studies and white papers, and a five-year results summary;
- share price display and chart; and
- company contact details, including named contacts for investors and the media.

IN PRACTICE

The best practical solution for accessibility to information for investors and other audiences seems to be to provide a single page within the website listing each disclosure point. It is important to note that any redirection of a user to other areas of a website or to a document included on the website should be to a specific location for that information and users should not have to enter search criteria in order to locate information.

It is also important to ensure that the company's website is clear and simple, and is the definitive source of information on the company and its position within the sector. To help encourage website traffic, the company should use a recognisable website address, undertake active promotion of the existence of the website (including promotion to leading search engines) and maintain an active programme to notify the company's intended audience of any change in the website address.

CHAPTER 30

Further issues of securities

AT A GLANCE

Where an AIM company issues further securities of the class of securities which have already been admitted to trading on AIM, that AIM company is obliged to make an application for admission to trading on AIM for the further securities; Rule 33 of the *AIM Rules for Companies* also requires that all securities of the same class should be admitted to trading on AIM.

In most cases, the admission to trading on AIM of further issues of securities takes place by a simple process of submission of an application form three days prior to the date when an AIM company wishes the newly issued securities to be admitted. Where an AIM company anticipates that it will be issuing further securities of the same class on a regular basis, the *AIM Rules for Companies* permits the use of a block admission to cover all such securities, irrespective of whether or not they have yet been issued.

INTRODUCTION

30.1   Once a company has been admitted to AIM and its securities are trading successfully, it may be the case that the company wishes to issue further securities in the same class as those already admitted to trading. The *AIM Rules for Companies* provide a straightforward process for admitting such further issues of securities to trading on AIM.

FURTHER ISSUES

30.2   Where an AIM company has issued further securities in the same class of securities as those already admitted to trading on AIM, Rule 29 of the *AIM Rules for Companies* allows the new securities to be admitted by way of submission of an application form at least three business days prior to the date on which the AIM company wishes the new securities to be admitted to AIM. In such circumstances, an AIM company is in fact obliged to make such an application for admission under Rule 33 of the *AIM Rules for Companies*, which requires that all securities of the same class should be admitted to trading on AIM.

30.3   Along with the AIM application form, the AIM company will also usually submit a copy of the AIM company's board minutes which allotted the securities that are the subject of the application, or alternatively a confirmation from the AIM company's Nominated Adviser that the securities have been allotted. Such proof of allotment is required in order to satisfy the requirements of Rule 33 of the *AIM Rules for Companies* which specifies that all securities admitted to trading on AIM must be unconditionally allotted. The definition of allotted includes provisionally allotted securities where such provisional allotments are unconditional. For example, nil paid rights must be allotted without condition even where further action will be required to be taken by the holders of the provisional allotments in order to transform them into another class of securities, such as fully paid securities. The only condition which securities may be allotted subject to is their admission to trading on AIM.

30.4   Rule 27 of the *AIM Rules for Companies* specifies that in certain circumstances, a further issue of securities will require the production of a further AIM admission document. A further AIM admission document will be required whenever an AIM company is seeking admission for a new class of securities or whenever an AIM company undertakes a reverse takeover pursuant to Rule 14 of the *AIM Rules for Companies*. (Further information on reverse takeovers is set out in Chapter 14, *Admission to trading on AIM by reverse takeover*). The other circumstance where a further AIM admission document is required is when an AIM company is required to produce a prospectus pursuant to the *Prospectus Rules* as a result of the further issue of securities. This will only be the case where the further issue of securities constitutes an offer to the public – as defined in section 102B of the *Financial Services and Markets Act 2000* (FSMA) – and does not fall within one of the exemptions set out in the FSMA or in the *Prospectus Rules*. Further information on what constitutes an offer to the public is set out in Chapter 19, *Offers to the public*.

30.5   Following submission of the necessary documents three days prior to admission to trading on AIM, the London Stock Exchange will on the date of admission to trading on AIM release a dealing notice through a regulatory information service which effectively admits the additional securities to trading on AIM.

BLOCK ADMISSIONS

30.6   Where an AIM company intends to issue further securities of a class already admitted to trading on AIM on a regular basis, the London Stock Exchange may permit the admission to trading on AIM of such securities by way of a block admission arrangement. The application form for a block admission will have to specify the number of securities in question even though they are not yet issued.

30.7   Block admissions can be used in the following circumstances:

- employee share schemes;
- personal equity plans;
- dividend reinvestment plans;
- ordinary shares arising from the exercise of warrants; and
- ordinary shares arising from a class of convertible securities.

30.8 In order to use a block admission in any other circumstances, the AIM company's Nominated Adviser should consult with AIM Regulation. A block admission can not be used where the number of securities to be issued under the scheme covered by the block admission exceeds 20 per cent of the existing class of an AIM security. Once the number of securities to be issued exceeds this threshold, the AIM company must make a separate application.

30.9 Where an AIM company has filed an application for a block admission, the company is then obliged to notify once every six months by way of an announcement through a Regulatory Information Service the information which is set out at Schedule 6 to the *AIM Rules for Companies*. The information required to be set out in the announcement is:

- the name of the AIM company;
- the name of the share scheme or circumstance which is the subject of the block admission;
- the period of return (i.e. the dates the six-monthly information contained in the announcement relates to);
- the numbers and class of securities not yet issued under the scheme;
- the number of securities which have been issued under the scheme during that period;
- the balance of the securities under the scheme which have not yet been issued during that period;
- the number and class of those securities which were originally admitted on the date of their admission to trading on AIM; and
- a contact name and telephone number.

IN PRACTICE

Applications for further issues of securities to be admitted to trading on AIM are relatively straightforward unless they are to be issued pursuant to an offer to the public, are a new class of security or are to be issued pursuant to a reverse takeover.

CHAPTER 31

Directors' responsibility

AT A GLANCE

The directors of a company with its securities listed on AIM must ensure that the company complies with both the *AIM Rules for Companies* and the relevant provisions of the law of the company's country of incorporation and any country in which it operates or carries out activities. For companies incorporated in England and Wales, the directors need to be aware of and ensure that they, and the company, comply with various statutes, including the *Companies Act 2006*.

INTRODUCTION

31.1 The purpose of this chapter is to provide an overview of the continuing obligations and responsibilities of the directors once a company's securities have been admitted to trading on AIM.

31.2 Any company whose securities have been admitted to trading on AIM (wherever it is incorporated) must comply with the *AIM Rules for Companies*. If an AIM company's directors fail to comply with the continuing obligations in the *AIM Rules for Companies*, the company may be fined or censured by the London Stock Exchange. Further details of disciplinary actions which may be brought against an AIM company are set out in Chapter 41, *Disciplinary matters*.

31.3 In addition to any requirement in the *AIM Rules for Companies*, all directors will also have responsibilities set out under the laws of the country of incorporation. All directors of companies incorporated in England and Wales have specific duties by virtue of their position and an outline of the most important of these duties is set out in Paragraphs 31.36 to 31.65. In addition, public companies incorporated in England and Wales are also subject to many more legal controls and restrictions than private companies for the protection of a wider number of shareholders who may have little control over its daily management. These relate principally to the allotment and issue of securities, maintenance of capital and transactions with directors.

31.4 In addition, all AIM companies and prospective AIM companies (wherever they are incorporated) must be aware that documents they issue in the United Kingdom during the course of their business are governed by the *Financial Services and Markets Act 2000* (FSMA), certain details of which are set out below.

AIM RULES FOR COMPANIES

31.5 Every AIM company must ensure that its directors accept responsibility, collectively and individually, for the company's compliance with the *AIM Rules for Companies*. Failure to comply with any of the continuing obligations of the *AIM Rules for Companies* may result in the London Stock Exchange fining the company, censuring the company, publishing the fact that the company has been fined or censured for failing to comply with the *AIM Rules for Companies* or, in certain circumstances, cancelling the trading of the company's securities on AIM. The London Stock Exchange can also suspend trading in the company's securities where it considers that an AIM company has failed to comply with the *AIM Rules for Companies*.

31.6 The directors of an AIM company should ensure that they are familiar with the provisions contained in the *AIM Rules for Companies* and that all employees of the company and, where relevant, those of any subsidiary undertakings are provided with a copy. The London Stock Exchange may, from time to time, alter its requirements and the company and the directors will be expected to comply with the revised requirements.

Announcements

31.7 One of the principal objectives of the continuing obligations set out in the *AIM Rules for Companies* is to maintain an orderly market in the securities admitted to trading on AIM, which requires that all users of the market have simultaneous access to the same information. This is achieved by the immediate release of information which might reasonably be expected to have a material effect on market activity in, and prices of, the company's AIM securities. Chapter 28, *Announcements including price sensitive information*, covers the obligations to make announcements.

31.8 Many of the documents issued by an AIM company during the course of its business are governed by the FSMA; see Paragraphs 31.17 to 31.21 for more details.

Acquisitions and disposals

31.9 The *AIM Rules for Companies* set down certain guidelines relating to the company's responsibilities in relation to acquisitions and disposals (which are not of a revenue nature in the ordinary course of business) and transactions to raise finance (which do not involve a change in the fixed assets of the company and its subsidiaries). See Chapter 34, *Acquisitions and disposals*, for details.

31.10 The *City Code on Takeovers and Mergers* governs on a statutory basis conduct of any takeover offer for all the companies which have registered offices in the United Kingdom, the Channel Islands or the Isle of Man, if any of their securities are admitted to trading on a regulated market in the UK (which includes the London Stock Exchange's Main Market but not AIM) or any stock exchange in the Channel Islands or the Isle of Man. The *City Code on Takeovers* *and Mergers* also applies to all offers for other companies not falling into those mentioned above, being public and certain private companies which have their registered offices in the United Kingdom, the Channel Islands or the Isle of Man, and which are considered to have their place of central management and control in one of those territories. This will cover a great many UK AIM listed companies. The *City Code on Takeovers and Mergers* contains both general principles of conduct to be observed in takeovers and also a series of more detailed rules designed to cover specific aspects and forms of takeover, including disclosure of and limitations on market purchases and other dealings by an offeror company in a target company's securities. See Chapter 35, *Takeovers*, for further details.

Transactions with related parties

31.11 The directors should be aware that the *AIM Rules for Companies* set out specific requirements for any transactions between the company and certain parties that are connected with the company. See Chapter 34, *Acquisitions and disposals*, for details.

Dealings in securities

31.12 The directors should always bear in mind the *AIM Rules for Companies* relating to dealings by them in the company's securities, which are described in further detail in Chapter 32, *Directors' dealings*.

CORPORATE GOVERNANCE

31.13 In addition to the *AIM Rules for Companies*, directors of AIM companies should be aware of the principles and detailed provisions of the *Combined Code on Corporate Governance*. The *Combined Code* is a code of desirable corporate governance practices and procedures for public companies trading on markets in the United Kingdom.

31.14 AIM companies should seek to comply with these rules so far as practicable, in view of the size and stage of development of the company. See Chapter 42, *Corporate governance for AIM companies*, for further details on these provisions.

31.15 The board of directors should establish committees of non-executive directors to deal with audit matters, executive remuneration and nominations to the board of directors. These are explained in further detail in Chapter 43, *Remuneration committee*, Chapter 44, *Audit committee*, and Chapter 45, *Nomination committee*.

FINANCIAL SERVICES AND MARKETS ACT 2000

31.16 Directors of public companies must take care to ensure that they, as well as the company, do not breach the FSMA.

Financial promotions

31.17   The directors of a public company must ensure that the company complies with the FSMA in respect of any announcements or other documents released by the company. The company must not, in the course of business, "communicate" (whether in writing or verbally) an invitation or inducement to engage in "investment activity", such as buying, or entering into an agreement to buy, securities in a company. This does not apply if the person is an authorised person or the content of the communication is approved by an authorised person, for example the Nominated Adviser or the broker.

31.18   In its guidance note on the interpretation of section 21 of the FSMA, the Financial Services Authority considers an "inducement" to be "a form of communication which, in itself, does not amount to an invitation but which is a step in a chain which leads, whether directly or indirectly, to a person engaging in investment activity".

31.19   The directors should note that most documents a company issues (e.g. placing documents, press announcements and annual accounts) will be a "communication" and the wording in section 21 of the FSMA is wide enough to include communications by email and internet sites, telephone calls and conversations.

31.20   Care will need to be taken to ensure that, unless the communication has been approved by an authorised person or an exemption applies, it does not contain any invitation or inducement to engage in an investment activity. In particular, the company's solicitors and/or Nominated Adviser and Broker should be contacted prior to despatch of any documents or a director making a speech or presentation. The directors should be particularly careful when dealing with the media or with analysts not to infringe the rules on financial promotion.

31.21   It should be noted that if a communication is made outside the United Kingdom, it will still be within the scope of section 21 of the FSMA if it is capable of having an effect in the United Kingdom.

Market abuse

31.22   The directors must also ensure that their behaviour does not constitute "market abuse". Section 118 of the FSMA sets out this civil offence which supplements the offences of "insider dealing" under the *Criminal Justice Act 1993* and "market manipulation/misleading statements" offences under the FSMA. There are seven types of behaviour which can constitute market abuse, which are set out in Figure 31.1. These are wide ranging and include tipping off others.

31.23   The offence of market abuse applies in relation to certain "qualifying investments", which include securities traded on AIM and where a request has been made to trade on AIM.

31.24   It should be noted that sections 118(4) relating to insider dealing and 118(8) relating to distortion are under review by HM Treasury.

31.25   It should be noted that encouraging someone else to engage in market abuse is also an offence. The offence applies to any person (corporate as well as individuals). It can catch behaviour outside the United Kingdom, it is purely effect

---

FIGURE 31.1   The seven types of behaviour which can constitute market abuse

- Insider dealing: dealing or attempting to deal in a qualifying investment or a related investment on the basis of inside information, subject to certain defences (section 118(2), FSMA).
- Tipping off: disclosing inside information relating to a qualifying investment or a related investment otherwise than in the proper course of the exercise of one's employment, profession or duties (section 118(3), FSMA).
- Misuse of information: behaviour (not falling within either of the above categories) relating to a qualifying investment or a relevant product which is based on information which is not generally available to those using the market, but would be regarded as relevant information and which is likely to be regarded by a regular user as a failure on the part of the person concerned to observe the standard of behaviour reasonably expected of that person, taking into account their position in relation to the market (section 118(4), FSMA). The "regular user" is a hypothetical reasonable person who regularly deals on the market and in the investments of the kind in question (section 130A(3), FSMA).
- Misleading transactions or orders: affecting transactions or orders to trade which gives, or is likely to give, a false or misleading impression as to the supply of, or demand for, or as to the price of, one or more qualifying investments, or secure the price of one or more such investments at an abnormal or artificial level (section 118(5) FSMA).
- Deception: affecting transactions or orders to trade which employ fictitious devices or any other form of deception or contrivance (section 118(6) FSMA).
- Dissemination of misleading information: dissemination of information by any means which gives, or is likely to give, a false or misleading impression in relation to the qualifying investment by a person who knew or could reasonably be expected to have known, that the information was false or misleading (section 118(7) FSMA).
- Distortion: behaviour (not falling within any of the three preceding categories) relating to a qualifying investment which is likely to give a regular user of the market a false or misleading impression as to the supply of, demand for, or price or value of qualifying investments, or would be, or would be likely to be regarded to be by a regular user of the market, as behaviour that would distort, or would be likely to distort the market in such an investment. The behaviour is likely to be regarded by a regular user of the market as a failure on the part of the person concerned to observe the standard of behaviour reasonably expected of that person, taking into account their position in relation to the market (section 118(8) FSMA).

---

based (i.e. no intention is required) and no transaction is required. Furthermore, in some circumstances "behaviour" includes inaction.

31.26 An insider, for the purpose of the market abuse regime, includes any person who has inside information as a result of being a director of an AIM company or as a result of having access to the information through the exercise of employment, profession or duties.

31.27 The Financial Services Authority has powers to impose an unlimited fine or make a public statement that a person has engaged in market abuse and to apply to court for an injunction restraining the market abuse or requiring a person to take steps to remedy the abuse. In addition, it has wide investigatory powers.

31.28 The Financial Services Authority has produced a *Code of Market Conduct* which sets out its opinion on behaviour it considers is/is not market abuse and the factors it will take into account when determining the question.

Market manipulation and misleading statements

31.29 Section 397 of the FSMA creates a criminal offence where a person makes a statement, promise or forecast which he knows to be misleading, false or deceptive or dishonestly conceals any material facts, or recklessly makes (dishonestly or otherwise) a statement, promise or forecast which is misleading, false or deceptive for the purpose of inducing (or being reckless as to whether it may induce) a person to buy or sell securities or exercise any rights relating to securities. For further information on the offence of making misleading statements, see Chapter 15, *Directors' responsibilities for an AIM admission document and verification.*

31.30 Section 397(3) of the FSMA also provides that a person will be guilty of a criminal offence if he does any act or engages in any course of conduct which creates a false or misleading impression as to the market in, or value of, any securities if it is done for the purpose of creating that impression and of thereby inducing the acquisition or disposal of such securities or the exercise of any rights relating to such securities. Under section 397(5), there is a defence to any action brought under this provision if the person can show:

- that he reasonably believed that his act or conduct would not create an impression that was false or misleading as to the matters mentioned in section 397(3);
- that he acted or engaged in the conduct (i) for the purpose of stabilising the price of investments; and (ii) in conformity with price stabilising rules; or
- that he acted or engaged in the conduct in conformity with control of information rules.

For further information on compliance with the rules on price stabilisation see Chapter 23, *Stabilisation, over-allotment, greenshoes and when-issued trading.*

31.31 A person guilty of an offence under section 397 is liable to a maximum of seven years imprisonment and/or to a fine.

CRIMINAL JUSTICE ACT 1993

31.32 Directors and employees, like all other individuals, are prohibited from insider dealing by Part V of the *Criminal Justice Act 1993*. Under this Act, subject to a range of defences, it is a criminal offence for an individual who has information as an insider to:

- deal on a regulated market (which in these circumstances includes AIM) or through a professional intermediary, in shares whose price would be significantly affected if such information were made public;
- encourage another to do so;
- disclose such information otherwise than in the proper performance of the functions of an office, employment or profession.

31.33 It should be noted that the director or employee concerned can commit an offence under this legislation even if that director or employee does not deal in the company's securities for themselves. In fact, the offence of encouragement can be committed even though the individual in question is acting in the proper performance of the functions of his office or employment.

31.34 For the offence of disclosure, the prosecution does not have to prove that the individual insider knew or had reasonable cause to believe that the recipient of the information would deal in the securities. However, it would be a defence for the insider to show that he did not expect anyone to deal as a result of his disclosure.

31.35 A director or employee may be guilty of insider dealing in relation to the securities of a separate company (i.e. not the company for which they are employed/appointed) if they obtain information which they know is unpublished price sensitive information in relation to that separate company because of their position as a director or employee at their own company or because they had access to the information by virtue of their employment or office. In addition, a director or employee who communicates information which is unpublished price sensitive information in relation to the company's securities to selected share-holders or analysts is also likely to commit an offence. In relation to this last point, where unpublished price sensitive information is to be communicated to third parties the directors will almost inevitably, in any event, be obliged to announce it via the a Regulatory Information Service under the *AIM Rules for Companies*.

COMPANY LAW

31.36 All directors of companies incorporated in England and Wales have specific duties by virtue of their position, and an outline of the most important of these duties is set out below. In addition, public companies are also subject to many more legal controls and restrictions than a private company for the protection of a wider number of shareholders who may have little control over the company's daily management. These relate principally to the allotment and issue of securities, maintenance of capital and transactions between a company and its directors. Where an AIM company is incorporated in any other jurisdiction it will, of course, be subject to applicable local companies legislation in the jurisdiction in which it is incorporated.

31.37 For companies incorporated in England and Wales, the company law is changing as a result of the implementation of the *Companies Act 2006*. Certain sections of the Act came into force in 2007 and in April 2008 and further provisions will come into force throughout 2008 and 2009.

DUTIES OF DIRECTORS OF COMPANIES REGISTERED IN ENGLAND AND WALES

31.38 From 1 October 2007, the *Companies Act 2006* introduced a statutory statement of directors' duties that replaced many existing common law and equitable rules. The stated aim was to make the law clearer for directors.

31.39 The UK Government has stated that the new statutory expression of the duties is essentially the same as the existing duties established by case law, but one of the new sections has provoked much debate. Section 172 states that a director must exercise his duties in a way that he considers, in good faith, would be most likely to promote the "success of the company for the benefit of its members as a whole". This statement is not defined but the UK Government has stated that "success" will usually mean long-term increase in value. In exercising this duty, the statute states that the directors must have regard to (among other matters) the following six factors:

- the likely consequences of the decision in the long term;
- the interests of the company's employees;
- the need to foster the company's business relationships with suppliers, customers and others;
- the impact of the company's operations on the community and the environment;
- the deliverability of the company maintaining a reputation for high standards of business conduct; and
- the need to act fairly as between members of the company.

31.40 In addition, if the company is nearing insolvency there is a duty to consider the interests of the creditors of the company. This list is not exhaustive and directors must also bear in mind the statutory duty to exercise reasonable care, skill and diligence. A director must exercise the care, skill and diligence which would be exercised by a reasonably diligent person with both the general knowledge, skill and experience that might reasonably be expected of a person carrying out the functions of that director in relation to the company and the general knowledge, skill and experience that the director actually has.

31.41 In practice, in a well run company, the directors will consider the factors set out in section 172 and other factors when exercising their judgement. The Association of General Counsel and Company Secretaries of the FTSE 100 (GC 100), which is a body established to provide a forum for business focused input on legislative reform common to UK limited companies, is of the view that directors should only specifically record in the board minutes consideration of any of the above factors where the particular circumstances make it necessary or relevant.

31.42 The *Companies Act 2006* also includes a duty to avoid conflicts of interest, not to accept benefits from third parties and to declare an interest in a proposed transaction or arrangement with the company, but these sections of the *Companies Act 2006* are due to come into force on 1 October 2008. There are, however, provisions of the common law which cover these areas and which directors should bear in mind. For example, the common law fiduciary duties to act in good faith in what the director considers are the best interests of the company, to exercise powers for a proper purpose and not put himself in a position where there is an actual or potential conflict of interest between the director's duty to the company and his personal interests. This also extends to not misusing company property and keeping all information received by the director by virtue of his office which is confidential.

Breach of duties

31.43   A breach of the common law duties or the statutory duties by a director enables the company to take action against the director and sue the director for its loss. Alternatively, in some cases a general meeting of the company can, by ordinary resolution, ratify actions of a director in contravention of his duties.

TRANSACTIONS WITH DIRECTORS

31.44   In addition to the restrictions on related party transactions under the *AIM Rules for Companies* (see Chapter 34, *Acquisitions and disposals*), local law in the company's country of incorporation may place further restrictions on any transactions with directors. Paragraphs 31.45 to 31.48 give some of the restrictions placed on directors of companies registered in England and Wales.

Loans

31.45   Subject to certain exceptions, public companies are not able to make loans or give guarantees to directors, including indirect arrangements, such as assignments of loans or back to back loan transactions which result in a director obtaining a loan or guarantee. There are also additional restrictions prohibiting "quasi-loans" and "credit transactions"; and the provisions apply not only to transactions entered into with or for a director but also with or for a wide circle of persons connected with that director. Pursuant to the *Companies Act 2006*, such loans can be given provided shareholder approval is obtained.

Interests in contracts

31.46   The *Companies Act 2006* requires a director to disclose the nature of his interest in a contract or proposed contract with the company at the first board of directors meeting at which this contract is to be discussed. This provision provides the minimum level of protection for shareholders and cannot be disapplied by the Articles of Association.

Acquisitions by and disposals to directors

31.47   The *Companies Act 2006* requires a director (or a person connected with a director) who wishes to acquire from the company (or its holding company), or transfer to the company (or its holding company), non-cash assets with a value (i) exceeding 10 per cent of the company's asset value and more than £5,000 or (ii) in excess of £100,000, to have that contract or arrangement approved by ordinary resolution of the company (or in some circumstances its holding company). It is now possible to enter into the agreement provided it is conditional on shareholder approval being obtained. If the director or connected person is a director of the company's holding company or a person connected with such a director, the arrangement must also have been approved by a resolution of the members of the holding company or be conditional on such approval being obtained. A director who contravenes this provision can be compelled to make restitution to the company or, if this is no longer possible, pay damages.

Miscellaneous

31.48   There are other restrictions which apply to directors, whether of a public company or not, including the prohibition on "golden parachutes" and other compensation payments and the entry into service contracts of more than two years' duration in each case without shareholder approval.

INSOLVENCY OF COMPANIES REGISTERED IN ENGLAND AND WALES

General

31.49   The *Insolvency Act 1986* makes various kinds of misconduct by officers in relation to companies which become insolvent a criminal offence carrying potential sentences of imprisonment and/or a fine. The offences include dishonest misconduct by officers of the company during the 12 months immediately preceding the commencement of the winding-up, and effecting transactions to defraud creditors within five years prior to the commencement of the winding-up. Directors and officers who are guilty of misfeasance are liable to make restitution to the company. The two most significant provisions, however, deal with fraudulent and wrongful trading respectively.

Fraudulent trading

31.50   The *Insolvency Act 1986* imposes civil liability on a director who is shown to have knowingly carried on the company's business with the intention of defrauding creditors of the company or of any other person, or for any fraudulent purpose. Fraudulent trading is a criminal offence punishable by imprisonment and/or fine.

Wrongful trading

31.51   The *Insolvency Act 1986* imposes civil liability on a director of a company which becomes insolvent, where the director knew or ought to have concluded that there was no reasonable prospect that the company would avoid going into insolvent liquidation. The facts which a director ought to have known or ascertained, the conclusions he ought to have reached and the steps he ought to have taken are deemed to be those which would be known or ascertained, or reached or taken, by a reasonably diligent person having both (i) the general knowledge, skill and experience reasonably expected of a person carrying out the same functions as the director and (ii) the general knowledge, skill and experience of the particular director in question. The test is therefore an objective one supplemented by subjectivity if the particular director has any relevant expertise.

31.52 Liability can only be avoided if the director can satisfy the court that he took every step to minimise the potential loss to the creditors. To minimise their personal risk of liability, each director should therefore keep himself fully informed as to the company's cash and trading position and take a realistic view of the company's future prospects.

Transactions at an undervalue

31.53 Once the company is, or may be, insolvent, the interests of its creditors become the directors' main concern. In addition to the offences already described, statutory rules under the *Insolvency Act 1986* permit certain transactions to be overturned where they may have the effect of disadvantaging the company's creditors.

31.54 In certain circumstances a liquidator or administrator can apply to court for an order to set aside transactions made by the company at the time it became insolvent. In some cases a transaction will be vulnerable if entered into as long ago as two years before the company actually went into liquidation.

31.55 A transaction at an undervalue may occur when the company confers a benefit, without obtaining adequate consideration, at a time when it is unable to pay its debts. If the transaction is between the company and a connected person, such as a director, the onus is on that person to prove that the company was not insolvent at the time. The court has power to reverse such a transaction if it took place within two years prior to the company going into liquidation or administration.

31.56 It is a defence to show that the transaction was made in good faith for the carrying on of the business and in the reasonable belief that the company would benefit.

Preferences

31.57 Preferences are transactions which improve the position of a particular creditor of the company on liquidation. The court can set these transactions aside if the company was "influenced by a desire" to bring about the improvement. Preferences are voidable if made at a time when the company was insolvent and in the six months prior to liquidation. This period is extended to two years if the preference is in favour of a connected person. In that case, there is a presumption that the company was insolvent and influenced by a desire to improve the connected person's position in the event of a liquidation.

ADDITIONAL LEGAL REQUIREMENTS

31.58 There are additional requirements with which directors of a public company must ensure compliance. Specific legal advice should be sought in case of doubt.

Statutory pre-emption rights

31.59 No company incorporated in England and Wales may allot "equity securities" for cash unless it has first offered them on a pre-emptive basis to shareholders (unless shareholders authorise otherwise by a 75 per cent majority). Equity securities are, broadly, all securities and rights to subscribe for or convert into securities except those giving a right to participate to a limited extent only on a distribution of profits or assets (e.g. preference securities, but not convertible preference securities). Unlike a private company, a public company cannot exclude altogether the relevant provisions of the statute, although it may disapply them upon authorisation by shareholders. Such authority must be limited in time to the directors' authority to allot securities and therefore may only be for a maximum duration of five years, requiring renewal by special resolution when the authority expires.

31.60 The Pre-Emption Group has issued a Statement of Principles (which is supported by the Association of British Insurers and Investment Management Association) with which all AIM companies (wherever incorporated) are encouraged to comply. This states that a disapplication of pre-emption rights should be limited to 5 per cent of the issued ordinary share capital as shown by the latest published annual accounts and a cumulative limit which is currently 7.5 per cent of issued ordinary share capital in any three-year period.

Payment for securities

31.61 There are certain more onerous statutory provisions concerning the payment for securities allotted by public companies incorporated in England and Wales. These are as follows:

- securities may not be allotted unless at least 25 per cent of the nominal value and the whole of any premium has been paid up;
- an undertaking to do work or perform services cannot be accepted as consideration for the allotment of securities; and
- upon the allotment of securities as fully or partly paid in exchange for a non-cash consideration, any undertaking which forms part of that consideration (such as an undertaking to transfer assets to the company) must be performed within five years of the allotment. Further, a prior expert's valuation and report on the consideration given will normally be required.

Reduction in net assets

31.62 Where the net assets of a public company incorporated in England and Wales are reduced to 50 per cent or less of its called-up share capital, the directors must convene a general meeting to consider how to deal with the situation within 28 days of the date upon which any one of them becomes aware of the fact. Failure to call such a meeting may render each of the directors liable to a fine.

Distribution of profits

31.63 In addition to the requirement imposed on all companies incorporated in England and Wales, whether public or private, that no distribution may be made except out of profits available for that purpose, a public company may only make a distribution if the amount of its net assets is not less than the aggregate of its called-up share capital and undistributable reserves and such net asset value is not reduced upon the distribution being made. The interim accounts prepared for a proposed distribution by a public company must be "properly prepared" (which is defined in the company legislation) and a copy delivered to the Registrar of Companies.

Purchase of own securities

31.64 There is a general rule prohibiting a company incorporated in England and Wales (whether public or otherwise) from acquiring its own securities. On and off market purchases are permissible if carried out in accordance with the strict requirements of the company legislation, which include obtaining shareholder consent, although in all cases such purchases by public companies can only be made out of distributable profits or the proceeds of a fresh issue for the purpose. A company whose securities are traded on AIM may purchase securities into treasury (i.e. the securities purchased remain in issue in the name of the company itself and are available for sale for cash by the company or for transfer for the purposes of an employee securities scheme). Subject to certain exemptions, every purported act of a company in contravention of these provisions may render a company liable to a fine. Every director of the company who is in default is also liable to a fine or imprisonment. Furthermore, any such acquisition is void.

Financial assistance for acquisition of securities

31.65 The ability of a company incorporated in England and Wales, whether public or private, to give assistance for the acquisition of securities in itself or its holding company is generally prohibited by the *Companies Act 1985*, although the prohibition for private companies will be abolished when the relevant provisions of the *Companies Act 2006* come into force.

IN PRACTICE

Once a company has its securities admitted to trading on AIM, the directors will be subject to the requirements of the *AIM Rules for Companies* as well as any legislation applicable to them in the country in which the company is incorporated. In addition, certain parts of the UK legislation may also apply to them.

An important part of the AIM admission process will be the company's legal advisers advising the directors of these increased responsibilities and liabilities.

Directors' dealings

Once a company has had its securities admitted to trading on AIM, restrictions are placed on the directors as to the manner in which they deal in those securities, both under the *AIM Rules for Companies* and as a matter of general law. In addition, as a matter of good corporate governance, a company will normally introduce a share dealing code, which further restricts the ability of certain key directors and employee shareholders in the way in which they deal in the company's securities.

Furthermore, when a company has not been independent or revenue earning for a period of two years prior to its admission to trading on AIM its directors, their families, related trusts and related companies and substantial shareholders will be prohibited from disposing of any interest in the securities for a period of one year from the admission of those securities to AIM.

INTRODUCTION

32.1   In addition to any obligation placed on them under Rule 7 of the *AIM Rules for Companies* for new businesses, once the company's securities are admitted to trading on AIM the directors and their related persons will be restricted in the manner in which they can deal in securities in the company. These restrictions on the directors are imposed by various rules and regulations, including Rule 21 of the *AIM Rules for Companies*, the *Criminal Justice Act 1993* and the *Financial Services and Markets Act 2000* (FSMA).

RULE 21 OF THE *AIM RULES FOR COMPANIES*

32.2   Rule 21 of the *AIM Rules for Companies* requires that a company must ensure that its directors and applicable employees do not deal in any of its securities which are admitted to trading on AIM during a close period. For this purpose, applicable employees are the employee and their family who have a holding or interest directly or indirectly in 0.5 per cent or more of a class of AIM security. The definition of family is very wide and encompasses certain trusts and companies. For a full definition of family, see Figure 32.1.

FIGURE 32.1   Definition of family

A reference to a person's family includes the following persons:

- his or her spouse or civil partner and any child where such child is under the age of 18;
- any trust in which such individuals are trustees or beneficiaries;
- any company of which they have control of more than 20 per cent of its equity or voting rights in a general meeting.

It should be noted that employee share or pension schemes are excluded from the definition of trust provided that such individuals are beneficiaries rather than trustees.

32.3   The purpose of Rule 21 of the *AIM Rules for Companies* is to ensure that, even if not prohibited by the insider dealing legislation from dealing, the directors of the company, certain employees and persons connected with them do not abuse or place themselves under suspicion of abusing price sensitive information that they may have or thought to possess. This is especially the case in the period leading up to an announcement.

32.4   In summary, this AIM Rule prohibits dealings (except in exceptional circumstances) during the following periods:

- the one-month period immediately preceding the announcement of the company's quarter-year results (if it publishes financial information on a quarterly basis);
- the two-month period immediately preceding the announcement of the company's half-year results; and
- the two-month period immediately preceding the preliminary announcement of the company's annual results.

In each of these periods, a director can be presumed to be in possession of inside information. The AIM Rule also prohibits dealings when a director is in possession of unpublished, price sensitive information outside of these periods.

32.5   In order to police such dealings and to assist in discharging the director's responsibility to ensure the AIM company's compliance with the *AIM Rules for Companies*, it is best practice that the company adopts an internal dealing code for directors and senior executives, which should formally be approved by the board of directors. The directors of the company should then ensure that they are familiar with the provisions contained in the *AIM Rules for Companies* and the company's share dealing code and that all employees of the company, and where relevant any subsidiary undertakings, are provided with a copy. The terms of a share dealing code are considered in more detail in Chapter 46, *Share dealing code*.

CRIMINAL JUSTICE ACT 1993 – PART V

32.6   In addition to the restrictions on dealings in the company's securities imposed on directors and employees under Rule 21 of the *AIM Rules for*

Companies, directors and employees, like other individuals, are prohibited from insider dealing by Part V of the *Criminal Justice Act 1993*. Under the Act, subject to a range of defences, it is a criminal offence for an individual who has information as an insider to:

- deal on a regulated market or through a professional intermediary in securities whose price would be significantly affected if such information were made public;
- encourage another to do so;
- disclose such information otherwise than in the proper performance in the functions of an office, employment or profession.

32.7   In respect of the insider dealing regime under the *Criminal Justice Act 1993*, it should be noted that AIM is a regulated market and the director or employee concerned can commit an offence even if he doesn't deal in the company's securities himself. The offences under the Act are widely drafted and the offence of encouragement can be committed even though the individual in question is acting in the proper performance of the functions of his office or employment.

32.8   For the offence of disclosure, the prosecution does not have to prove that the insider knew or had reasonable cause to believe that the recipient of the information would deal. However, it would not be an offence for the insider to show that he did not expect anyone to deal as a result of his disclosure.

32.9   In particular, it is worth noting that a director or employee may be guilty of insider dealing in relation to the securities of another company, if he has obtained information which he knows is unpublished price sensitive information in relation to that other company because he is a director or employee of the company whose securities are admitted to trading on AIM or because he has access to the information by virtue of his employment.

32.10   It is also an offence for the director or employee to communicate information which is unpublished price sensitive information related to companies whose securities are admitted to trading on AIM, to selected shareholders or analysts. For further information in relation to the release of information to analysts, see Chapter 24, *Analyst research*. Directors should also bear in mind that where unpublished price sensitive information is to be communicated to third parties, the directors will almost inevitably be obliged to announce the information via the company's Regulatory Information Service under Rule 17 of the *AIM Rules for Companies*.

FINANCIAL SERVICES AND MARKETS ACT 2000

32.11   The FSMA introduced a civil offence regime relating to market abuse which supplements the existing offences of insider dealing and market manipulation/statements offences under the Act. The offence, which can also apply to securities traded upon AIM, applies inter alia:

- where there is behaviour (including anything said or done or written or not), including misuse of non-public information, misleading the market or distorting the market; and

■ the behaviour falls below the standard or behaviour that a regular user of the relevant market would reasonably expect of a person in the same position as the person who is committing the offence in relation to that market.

32.12 Encouraging someone else to engage in market abuse is also an offence and the offence applies to any person (i.e a legal person such as a corporation or limited liability partnership as well as individuals). Not only does the offence of market abuse catch behaviour inside the United Kingdom, but it can also catch behaviour outside the United Kingdom. The market abuse regime is quite widely drafted and is effect based (i.e. no intention is required and it is not necessary for a transaction to be completed for an offence to be committed).

32.13 If a director or other person is found guilty of market abuse then the Financial Services Authority has powers to impose an unlimited fine or make a public statement about the market abuse and to apply for court orders to remedy incidences of market abuse. The *Financial Services Authority Code of Market Conduct* also sets out the Financial Services Authority's opinion on behaviour it considers is/is not market abuse and the facts it will take into account when determining the question.

RULE 17 OF THE *AIM RULES FOR COMPANIES*

32.14 In addition to the restrictions placed under Rule 21 of the *AIM Rules for Companies*, the *Criminal Justice Act 1993* and the FSMA impose additional obligations on an AIM company in respect of the notification of certain transactions and dealings. These include any deals by directors, and where there has been such a deal then a notification must be made in the prescribed form set out in Figure 32.2.

FIGURE 32.2 Form of notification of dealings by directors

Pursuant to Rule 17 of the *AIM Rules for Companies*, an AIM company must make notification of the following:

- the identity of the director or significant shareholder concerned;
- the date on which the disclosure was made to it;
- the date on which the deal or relevant change to the holding was effected;
- the price, amount and class of the AIM securities concerned;
- the nature of the transaction;
- the nature and extent of the director's or significant shareholder's interest in the transaction;
- where a deal takes place when it is in any close period under Rule 21, the date upon which any previous binding commitment was notified or the date upon which the London Stock Exchange granted permission to deal in order to mitigate severe personal hardship; and
- where the notification concerns a related financial product, the detailed nature of the exposure.

Source: extract from *AIM Rules for Companies*, February 2007. The full *AIM Rules for Companies* is available at www.londonstockexchange.com

32.15   In addition, where any significant shareholder who holds 3 per cent or more of any class of AIM security deals then there must be notification of this. Such notification must include the information set out in Figure 32.2 in so far as the AIM company has such information. Further information regarding significant shareholder disclosures for AIM companies is set out in Chapter 38 *Disclosure Rules and Transparency Rules*.

IN PRACTICE

A company's lawyers will advise the directors regarding the restrictions that will be placed on them and certain key shareholders as part of the AIM admission process. However, directors and their families and connected persons, trusts and companies must take care before any form of dealing in the AIM company's securities is undertaken. Where appropriate, the directors should take specific advice from the company's Nominated Adviser or lawyers and not just rely on the terms of the company's share dealing code as a dealing which may fall outside the code may still constitute an offence under insider dealing or market abuse legislation. As all such transactions are also required to be notified to AIM by a Regulatory Information Service, notwithstanding any provision of the company's share dealing code or other restriction, a director should notify the Nominated Adviser of such dealings in advance so that the effect that it may have on the market can be considered.

CHAPTER 33

Directors' service agreements

AT A GLANCE

When admitting a company's securities to trading on AIM it is common practice to review the terms of the company's contractual arrangements with executive and non-executive directors and, where appropriate, require the directors to enter into new service agreements or letters of appointment. This chapter considers the key terms relevant to a director's service agreement and the corporate governance and legal factors that must be borne in mind when drafting such agreements.

INTRODUCTION

33.1　In any transaction involving a proposed admission of a company's securities to trading on AIM it will be necessary to review the existing terms of the service agreements between the company and its directors. The term "service agreement" in company law now embraces contracts of service, contracts for services and letters of appointment to the office of director, and it is important to ensure that appropriate documentation is in place regulating the relationship between the company and its officers. In particular, for a company registered in England and Wales it is crucial to ensure that any documentation does not offend the legal requirements set out in the *Companies Act 2006*. Additionally, whilst there is no formal corporate governance regime applicable to AIM companies, regard must be paid to the relevant aspects of the London Stock Exchange's *AIM Rules for Companies* and the voluntary guidelines published by the National Association of Pensions Funds (NAPF). The *NAPF Guidelines* encourage observance with the principles espoused by the *Combined Code on Corporate Governance* ("the *Combined Code*"), which are applicable to all public listed companies quoted on the London Stock Exchange.

33.2　Often the existing directors will be asked to enter into new service agreements, particularly where there may be deficiencies or concerns expressed over the efficacy of some of the terms of the existing documentation, which may be acceptable for a private company but fall short of the standards expected of public companies. The following guidance sets out the key aspects and terms to consider when preparing fresh service agreements for both executive and non-executive directors (although the latter will focus on letters of appointment rather than more complex contracts for services/consultancy agreements).

DIRECTORS' SERVICE AGREEMENTS (CONTRACTS OF SERVICE)

33.3 All executive directors should have a service agreement that sets out the principal terms of the director's employment with the company. Often the service agreement will need to be read in conjunction with other documents, such as a staff handbook, and any scheme rules that may, for example, be applicable to a bonus, pension or an interest in share options.

33.4 When drafting a service agreement careful consideration should be given to the key elements of the agreement, namely the term of employment, the director's duties, remuneration provisions, termination arrangements and post-termination covenants that restrict the director from competing with the company and harming its legitimate business interests after the employment has ended. Each area is dealt with in more detail below.

Term

33.5 The term of a service agreement will usually be either indefinite subject to notice or for a fixed period (or a hybrid of the two). The arrangements that are agreed between the company and its directors will largely be driven by striking a balance between providing flexibility and security of tenure. Typically, if the term is expressed to be indefinite and subject to notice, the notice period applicable will be between six and twelve months' duration. If a fixed term is preferred this will usually be for a period of twelve to eighteen months. Restrictions on the length of a fixed period are imposed by the *Companies Act 2006*, which requires shareholders' consent to be sought for any fixed period of two years or more. Additionally, the *Combined Code* generally discourages the use of a fixed term (or notice period) that exceeds a year.

Directors' duties

33.6 Whilst a director's duties are prescribed by the *Companies Act 2006* (and by common law) and cannot be contracted out of, a service agreement should state expressly the duties that are required of the director. Typically, such duties will include obligations to:

- follow the reasonable and lawful instructions of the board of directors of the company;
- promote, develop and protect the interests of the company;
- abide by all statutory, fiduciary and common law duties;
- where required, share responsibilities with other executives appointed by the board of directors of the company; and
- keep the board of directors properly informed regarding the affairs of the company.

Remuneration provisions

33.7 A director's remuneration package will normally include such items as basic salary (with provision for a salary review, usually not more than once a year), bonus, pension and insurance based benefits, and will often entail provision for interests in long term incentive plans and share options.

33.8 Following the principles of corporate governance, a director's remuneration should be approved by the company's remuneration committee (see Chapter 43, *Remuneration committee*). In recent years there has been increased focus on ensuring that remuneration packages are proportionate and tied in with the performance of the company and that they do not reward directors for failure. For this reason, a large proportion of a director's remuneration is usually delivered through discretionary bonus, share options and long term incentive plans, which incentivise the director to ensure the company performs well for the benefit of the shareholders and themselves.

33.9 Provisions dealing with salary should make it clear that salary is inclusive of any director's fees paid. The service agreement should also make it clear that increases in salary are not guaranteed. Normally, the agreement will specify that the salary of the director will be subject to review annually by the remuneration committee and, whilst the salary will not decrease, there is no right to an automatic increase.

33.10 Bonus provisions are often drafted in discretionary and non-contractual terms, although the legal distinction between contractual and non-contractual bonuses is often blurred and care needs to be taken in the drafting, to ensure that the bonus terms are genuinely discretionary and do not confer a contractual right on the director.

33.11 Bonus provisions should stipulate how and when the bonus is paid, including details as to the criteria against which the director's eligibility for the bonus is to be assessed.

33.12 Normally, bonus provisions will include restrictions on the director's access to a bonus, by stipulating that if the director's employment has ceased or notice of termination has been served before the bonus payment date, the director will not be entitled to receive a bonus. Whilst such clauses can have harsh consequences, for example where the director has worked most of the year over which the bonus is assessed but is given notice immediately before the bonus payment date, the courts seem prepared to uphold such provisions and these should be incorporated when drafting.

Pensions, share options and long term incentive plans, and insurance based benefits

33.13 Usually, if an employer operates an occupational pension scheme the service agreement will provide that a director will be eligible to join, provided the director meets the relevant requirements (normally service-linked). In the past, many directors received top-up pensions in excess of the (then) Inland Revenue approved limits. Since "A day", on 6 April 2006, the approval regime has been replaced with a lifetime allowance, which caps the value of pension benefits (that attract advantageous tax treatment), and an annual allowance that limits the contributions or benefit accrual in a tax year. Accordingly, top-up schemes have become much less attractive for highly paid directors, who may have already reached these limits, as the top-up amounts will be effectively taxed at 55 per cent.

33.14 Partly driven by the more restricted pension regime and the influence of corporate governance, high earning executive directors increasingly are remunerated through share option schemes or long term incentive plans (see Chapter 36, *Options and share incentives*, for details about options and share incentives). It is generally regarded as poor practice to include details of any share option or long term incentive plan schemes in a service agreement, other than perhaps to make mention of the director's participation in these schemes in a conditional manner and with reference to the appropriate scheme rules. This is to avoid the share options or long term incentive plans from forming part of the employment agreement and therefore allowing a director to include these elements as a head of loss should there be a claim of wrongful dismissal.

33.15 In any event it is good practice to include a clause known as a "Micklefield" clause in the appropriate scheme (or service agreement), which will stipulate that the director is not entitled to claim for any loss arising out of the lapse of share options or long term incentive plans on termination of employment or loss of office.

33.16 A director's service agreement will often provide for a number of insurance based benefits, such as medical health, disability/permanent health cover and life assurance, for the benefit of the director (and often their spouse and family).

33.17 Case law has provided that a company may be subject to a number of implied duties with regard to the application and termination of such benefits. By way of example, it will be implied into the employment contract that if the director is benefiting from disability/permanent health insurance, the company should not terminate the employment without good cause if to do so would disentitle the director from continuing to receive the benefits of the insurance. Accordingly, consideration should be given as to the inclusion of express provisions that will allow the company to terminate employment in such circumstances, even if this may result in a loss of benefit to the director.

Termination of a director's employment

33.18 Corporate governance encourages companies to think ahead when considering the terms that will apply to a director should the employer wish to part company with any of its officers.

33.19 When drafting a service agreement it is common to include provisions that give the company flexibility on termination, such as the use of a payment in lieu of notice (PILON) clause or garden leave provisions. Consideration should also be given to the use of a liquidated damages clause, in appropriate circumstances. Provisions should also be included that allow the company to terminate without notice in certain circumstances, that will not necessarily be restricted to situations involving gross misconduct.

33.20 Inclusion of a PILON clause in a service agreement is relatively orthodox practice. A properly drafted clause will allow a company to terminate the employment summarily by making a payment in lieu of the notice period. This may be attractive for a variety of reasons, such as to remove a director who has resigned from an environment where the director will continue to have access to sensitive confidential information. PILON clauses are also commonly incorporated to preserve the enforceability of restrictive covenants. Once a PILON clause is exercised the director's employment comes to an end immediately. Often a PILON clause will specify that only basic salary will be paid in lieu of notice. A PILON clause may, more uncommonly, provide for payments by instalments over the period that would have been the notice period and require the director to give credit for any sums earned in mitigation over this period. One notable disadvantage of including a PILON clause is that any sums paid pursuant to it will be subject to tax and national insurance contributions. For this reason, they are often unpopular with senior employees and directors, who would prefer to take advantage of the tax exemption applicable to genuine compulsory termination payments (currently capped at £30,000). This tax exemption may apply to a non-contractual payment in lieu of notice, which HMRC is normally prepared to treat as a technical breach of the contract falling within the ambit of the exemption.

33.21 Garden leave provisions should always be included expressly in a service agreement as the courts are very reluctant to imply such terms. As opposed to a PILON clause, a garden leave clause allows the employment to continue after one of the parties has served notice. A garden leave clause usually entitles the company to require the director not to attend work and to suspend the director from carrying out any duties, provided they continue to receive their normal remuneration during the notice period. A well drafted clause will stipulate the terms applicable to the director while serving garden leave, which may include restrictions on contacting clients and suppliers of the company, requiring the director to resign from office and allowing the company to announce that the director has been given notice or has resigned (as the case may be).

33.22 The service agreement should always expressly state the reasons for which the company may terminate the director's employment summarily without notice or a payment in lieu of notice clause. Typical provisions for summary termination would include situations where:

- the director has committed an act of gross misconduct or serious breach of contract;
- the director becomes incapable of holding office by reason of ill health, bankruptcy or disqualification;
- the director is convicted of a serious criminal offence or does anything that brings the company into serious disrepute;
- the director has failed to meet specified mandatory performance targets; and
- the director has committed a breach of the *AIM Rules for Companies*.

33.23 Whilst at common law a clearly expressed reason for summary termination will be capable of being relied on to avoid wrongful dismissal claims, the company should always seek legal advice in case the termination of employment offends any statutory employment protections available to the director (e.g. unfair dismissal or a claim under one of the discrimination strands, such as sex or race discrimination).

33.24 Liquidated damages clauses operate, so as to compensate the outgoing employee by the payment of a fixed monetary sum, where the company has dismissed the employee in breach of contract. These provisions have formed part of the focus and scrutiny of corporate governance, which has sought to limit the inclusion of "golden parachute" provisions in directors' service agreements. Now, by virtue of the fact that long notice or fixed term periods are becoming less common, liquidated damages clauses are similarly less used and have become unfashionable.

33.25 If drafting a liquidated damages clause, care needs to be taken to ensure that any specified payment terms represent a genuine pre-estimate of loss arising from termination to avoid the provision being struck down as a penalty. Consideration therefore needs to be given to such issues as the director's ability to mitigate any loss when drafting such provisions.

33.26 Liquidated damages provisions may also require shareholder approval, unless the clause does no more than articulate a payment of damages made in good faith in discharge of an existing legal obligation.

Post-termination restrictive covenants

33.27 In addition to the inclusion of an express confidentiality provision, consideration should be given to the inclusion of post-termination restrictive covenants in the service agreement.

33.28 Typically, these post-termination restrictions will take the form of restraints on the ex-director from:

- competing with the company by obtaining work with a competitor in a similar capacity as that carried out by the director for the company for a limited period (usually no more than six to twelve months after employment);
- soliciting clients (actual or prospective) of the company with whom the director personally dealt for a limited period (usually no more than twelve months after employment);
- dealing with clients (actual or prospective) of the company with whom the director personally dealt for a limited period (usually no more than twelve months after employment);
- poaching senior employees of the company for a limited period (usually no more than twelve months after employment); and
- doing anything to interfere with the company's relationship with a supplier for a limited period (usually no more than twelve months after employment).

33.29 Great care needs to be taken when drafting such provisions, to ensure they do no more than provide adequate protection to a legitimate business interest of the company. Examples of what is generally considered to be legitimate business interests are: (i) protecting trade secrets and other confidential information; (ii) maintaining a stable workforce; and (iii) protecting customer connections. Any provision that goes further than the protection of a legitimate business interest is likely to be struck down as unenforceable by the courts.

Other terms of a service agreement

33.30 There are, of course, other relevant terms in a service agreement which are not the main focus of this chapter. In particular, as with any other contract of employment, it is a legal requirement to ensure that certain main terms of employment are referred to, such as the hours of work, place of work, provision for holiday and sick pay, and commencement of employment. Other terms that are commonly seen in service agreements include restrictions on accepting gratuities, provisions to ensure compliance with codes of conduct and applicable statutory rules, and provisions dealing with the ownership of intellectual property (to name but a few).

NON-EXECUTIVE DIRECTORS' SERVICE AGREEMENTS (LETTERS OF APPOINTMENT)

33.31 As referred to above, non-executive directors are usually engaged by a company using a letter of appointment (which is a form of contract for services). The role of non-executives was subject to the scrutiny of the Higgs Review, which considered the role and effectiveness of non-executive directors. The recommendations of the Higgs Report have been incorporated into the *Combined Code*.

33.32 Non-executives are now seen as assuming the role of guardian of shareholders' interests and adviser to the company. In particular, their utility is seen to be in their experience, which is drawn on to provide impartial views and to augment the credibility of the company, particularly with outside investors.

33.33 Before drafting a letter of appointment, care should be taken to review the company's Articles of Association, as the letter will be subject to the articles and, in particular, the provisions dealing with appointment and re-election should be carefully examined.

33.34 Although ultimately a matter for determination by the Employment Tribunals or courts, the status of the non-executive director is generally considered to be that of a self-employed person. The letter of appointment should always state that this is the case.

33.35 A letter of appointment is usually a relatively short document (compared with the weightier executive director service agreement) and the key elements of the letter will comprise provisions dealing with the length of the appointment, required time commitment, role and duties, fees and the circumstances where the director is entitled to seek independent legal advice.

Length of the appointment

33.36 The letter of appointment should state the length and commencement date of the appointment. Following the recommendations in the Higgs Report, the initial term is usually fixed at three years, but the term is normally subject to notice, which should not exceed a year. Retirement and re-election provisions should be included, reflecting the company's Articles of Association and/or other agreed terms.

33.37 Notwithstanding the provision for notice within a fixed term, the letter should also stipulate the circumstances in which the company can seek the summary termination of the director, which will be similar to those applicable to executive directors (see Paragraph 33.22).

Time commitment

33.38 Normally, the time required from a non-executive will be limited and it is usually expressed in a letter of appointment in terms of the number of days work that will be expected of the director per month (including attending board meetings and the company's annual and general meetings).

33.39 The non-executive director, who is likely to hold a number of other director-ships, should be required to confirm that they will devote sufficient time to discharge their duties and disclose any other interests to the board of directors.

Role and duties

33.40 The duties of the non-executive director are similar to those applicable to the executive director (see Paragraph 33.6). However, in addition to the implied, statutory, common law and fiduciary duties, express provisions should be added to confirm that the director is expected to act as a guardian of the company, lending independent judgement and experience to the board of directors. Confirmation should also be provided of the committees of the company on which the director is expected to serve.

Fees

33.41 The letter should specify the fees payable to the director, the intervals at which fees will be paid and that the fee will be subject to PAYE and national insurance contributions.

33.42 Provision should also be made for the director to be reimbursed expenses incurred in the performance of their duties.

33.43 It is uncommon for a non-executive director to receive other benefits, such as healthcare insurance, bonus and pension. Additionally, the *Combined Code* recommends against the use of share options as a form of remuneration, as they may affect the director's ability to act impartially. If share options are contemplated being offered, the *Combined Code* recommends seeking prior shareholder approval. This will be an important area when considering the number of independent non-executive directors on the board and the board's ability to comply with corporate governance best practice (see Chapter 42, *Corporate governance for AIM companies*).

Independent legal advice

33.44   The *Combined Code* recommends that all directors should be able to take independent advice where they consider it necessary to discharge their duties. Accordingly, provision should be made in the letter to allow the director to take advice in appropriate circumstances, and the company may want to refer to any procedure it has adopted for this purpose.

Other provisions

33.45   In addition to the main terms set out above, the letter of appointment may refer to other requirements, including confidentiality provisions, provision for an appropriate induction for any new director, provision for review of the performance of the director, and confirmation that the company holds appropriate directors' and officers' insurance for the term of the appointment.

IN PRACTICE

As part of the AIM admission process, the service contracts and letters of appointment will come under scrutiny by the Nominated Adviser and also investors. Accordingly, it is important to make sure that the service contracts and letters of appointment of both executive and non-executive directors broadly comply with the standards that would be expected from a corporate governance perspective. In reality, it is often the length of notice period, or minimum fixed term, which is likely to be the most significant provision. In a private company it may be in the company's interest to make this as long as possible. However, from a corporate governance perspective these should be limited.

Acquisitions and disposals

Rule 12 of the *AIM Rules for Companies* imposes an obligation on an AIM company to make an announcement to a Regulatory Information Service of the details and effect on the AIM company of any substantial acquisition or disposal. Rule 12 of the *AIM Rules for Companies* provides that the analysis of whether a transaction is to be regarded as substantial is to be carried out by the application of tests known as the class tests. The class tests are set out in Schedule 3 to the *AIM Rules for Companies*. They involve a comparison of values involved in the transaction with corresponding values for the AIM company.

If an AIM company enters into an acquisition or a disposal with a related party, Rule 13 obliges the AIM company to make an announcement to a Regulatory Information Service of the details of the transaction and its effect on the AIM company if an analysis of the size of the transaction, using the class tests, produces a result in excess of 5 per cent.

Any acquisitions which exceed 100 per cent in any of the class tests, or any disposals which exceed 75 per cent in any of the class tests, are treated as reverse takeovers. The requirements relating to reverse takeovers are set out in Chapter 14, *Admission to trading on AIM by reverse takeover*.

SUBSTANTIAL TRANSACTIONS

34.1   Rule 12 of the *AIM Rules for Companies* requires notification by means of a Regulatory Information Service announcement of particulars of any acquisition or disposal which is substantial. The Rule relates to transactions both by the AIM company itself and by any of its subsidiaries. Whether a transaction is substantial or not is analysed by reference to the class tests which are set out in Schedule 3 to the *AIM Rules for Companies*. It should be noted, however, that the definition of "transaction" under Rule 12 of the *AIM Rules for Companies* is wide and specifically includes any non pre-emptive issues of securities. In addition, in applying the class tests to a transaction, Rule 16 of the *AIM Rules for Companies* requires that transactions completed during the 12 months prior to the date of the transaction must be aggregated with it if:

■ all transactions were entered into by the AIM company with the same person or persons or their families ("family" being defined in the *AIM Rules for*

Companies in relation to any person as his spouse, civil partner or child under age 18, any trust in which such individuals are trustees or beneficiaries and any company over which they have control or more than 20 per cent of its equity or voting rights in a general meeting); or

■ all transactions involved the acquisition or disposal of securities or an interest in one particular business; or

■ together all the transactions led to a principal involvement by the AIM company in any business activity or activities which did not previously form a part of the AIM company's principal activities. The Guidance Notes in Part 2 of the *AIM Rules for Companies* specify that the London Stock Exchange will only consider that an AIM company has "a principal involvement" in any such activity or activities where collectively a class test for any 12-month period produces a result in excess of 100 per cent.

34.2   The class tests are essentially the same as those which apply to listed companies under the *Listing Rules*, save that the *Listing Rules* do not include a turnover test. They require an analysis of the size of the transaction by reference to five criteria. If the result of the application of any of the tests shows that the transaction exceeds 10 per cent, the transaction is deemed to be substantial unless either:

■ the transaction is of a revenue nature in the ordinary course of business of the AIM company; or

■ the transaction is to raise finance which does not involve a change in the fixed assets of the AIM company.

34.3   The guidance in the *Listing Rules*, applicable to the similar exception for transactions of a revenue nature in the ordinary course of business, provides that in assessing whether a transaction is in the ordinary course of a company's business, the Financial Services Authority will have regard to the size and incidence of similar transactions which the company has entered into. The implication is that, even if the transaction is of a type which the company has entered into, it may not be treated as in the ordinary course of business if it is unusually large or the company only infrequently enters into transactions of that nature. Whilst not bound by this interpretation, it is binding on the London Stock Exchange when applying the equivalent test, and it would be a strong argument to use with AIM Regulation when discussing the application of the test.

34.4   Where, in the case of an acquisition, the class tests produce a result which is in excess of 100 per cent or, in the case of a disposal is in excess of 75 per cent, then the transaction is classified as a reverse takeover. The principal consequences of a reverse takeover are that the transaction must be subject to prior approval by the company's shareholders in general meeting. If the transaction is approved, the enlarged group must then reapply for admission to trading on AIM as if it were a new applicant. This includes the production of an AIM admission document as if it were a new applicant. Further information on the rules and procedures associated with reverse takeovers are set out in Chapter 14, *Admission to trading on AIM by reverse takeover*.

THE CLASS TESTS

34.5 There are five class tests. Each requires a comparison of the values involved in the transaction, with comparable values for the AIM company being:

- the gross assets test;
- the profits test;
- the turnover test;
- the consideration test; and
- the cross capital test.

The gross assets test

34.6 The gross assets which are the subject of the transaction must be expressed as a percentage of the gross assets of the AIM company. Gross assets means the total of fixed assets plus current assets. For this purpose, the gross assets of the AIM company are shown in its most recently notified (i.e. published by means of announcement released to a Regulatory Information Service) consolidated balance sheet unless:

- the AIM company has produced an AIM admission document following a reverse takeover that includes a pro forma assets statement, in which case the assets statement may be referred to, provided that the information in it was taken from the most recent audited consolidated accounts and adjustments to those figures are clearly shown and explained; or
- transactions which are the subject of the test are required to be aggregated, in which case the company's gross assets must be taken from the most recently notified balance sheet before the first of the transactions requiring to be aggregated.

34.7 For the purposes of the comparison, the "gross assets the subject of the transaction" are:

1 where the AIM company acquires an interest in an undertaking which will result in the consolidation of the undertaking's net assets in the accounts of the AIM company, 100 per cent of the undertaking's assets, irrespective of the interest acquired;
2 where the AIM company disposes of an interest in an undertaking, which will result in the undertaking's net assets no longer being consolidated in the accounts of the AIM company, 100 per cent of the undertaking's assets, irrespective of the interest disposed of;
3 where the AIM company acquires or disposes of an interest which does not fall within (1) or (2) above:
    - in the case of an acquisition, the consideration plus any liabilities assumed; and
    - in the case of a disposal, the book value of the assets attributed to that interest in the AIM company's last audited accounts;
4 where the AIM company acquires assets other than an interest in an undertaking, the book value of the assets.

The profits test

34.8 Profits attributable to the assets which are the subject of the transaction must be expressed as a percentage of the profits of the AIM company. For this purpose, the profits of the AIM company are profits before taxation and extra-ordinary items as stated either in the last published annual consolidated accounts or the last notified (i.e. published by means of announcement to a Regulatory Information Service) preliminary statement of annual results or, in a case where transactions are aggregated pursuant to Rule 16 of the *AIM Rules for Companies*, the last such accounts or statement prior to the earliest transaction.

34.9 In the case of an acquisition or disposal of an interest in an undertaking which will result in the consolidation of the undertaking's net assets in the accounts of the AIM company, or in the undertaking's net assets no longer being consolidated in the accounts of the AIM company, the "profits attributable to the assets which are the subject of the transaction" means 100 per cent of the profits of the undertaking, irrespective of what interest is acquired or disposed of.

The turnover test

34.10 Turnover attributable to the assets which are the subject of the transaction must be expressed as a percentage of the turnover of the AIM company. For this purpose, the turnover of the AIM company means the turnover figure which is stated in the last published annual consolidated accounts, or the last notified (i.e. published by means of announcement to a Regulatory Information Service) pre-liminary statement of annual results or, in a case where transactions are aggregated pursuant to Rule 16 of the *AIM Rules for Companies*, the last such accounts or statement prior to the earliest transaction. Similarly with the gross assets test and the profits test, if the AIM company is acquiring or disposing of an interest in an undertaking which will result in consolidation of the undertaking's net assets in the accounts of the AIM company, or in the undertaking's net assets no longer being consolidated in the accounts of the AIM company, the "turnover attribut-able to the assets which are the subject of the transaction" means 100 per cent of the turnover of the undertaking, irrespective of what interest is acquired or disposed of.

The consideration test

34.11 The consideration for the transaction must be expressed as a percentage of the aggregate market value of all the securities (excluding treasury shares) of the AIM company which have been admitted to trading on AIM. For this purpose, the consideration for the transaction means the amount paid to the vendors, but the London Stock Exchange may require the inclusion of further amounts. An example of circumstances in which the London Stock Exchange may make such a requirement is given in the guidance in the *Listing Rules* for class tests applicable to listed companies. In the *Listing Rules* it is specified that if the purchaser agrees to discharge any liabilities, including the repayment of inter-company or third party debt, whether actual or contingent, as part of the terms of the transaction, this may need to be added to the consideration. Again, although not binding on the London Stock Exchange, the London Stock Exchange is likely to follow the guidance.

34.12   Where all or part of the consideration is in the form of securities of the same class as are admitted to trading on AIM, the consideration attributable to those securities means the aggregate market value of those securities.

34.13   If deferred consideration is, or may be, payable or receivable by the AIM company in the future, the consideration means the maximum total consideration payable or receivable under the agreement.

34.14   The aggregate market value of all the securities of the AIM company (excluding treasury shares) means the value of its enfranchised securities of that class on the day prior to the notification of the transaction, by way of a Regulatory Information Service announcement, excluding treasury shares.

The gross capital test

34.15   The gross capital of the company or business being acquired must be expressed as a percentage of the gross capital of the AIM company. For this purpose, the gross capital of the company or business being acquired means the aggregate of: the consideration, of the company which is being acquired; any of its securities and debt securities which are not being acquired; all other liabilities (other than current liabilities) including for this purpose minority interests and deferred taxation; and any excess of current liabilities over current assets.

34.16   For the purposes of this test, "gross capital of the AIM company" means the aggregate of:

- the aggregate market value of its securities (excluding treasury shares);
- all its other liabilities (other than current liabilities), including minority interests and deferred taxation; and
- any excess of current liabilities over current assets.

In the case of the consideration test, the figures to be taken into account for the aggregate market value of the AIM company's securities must be the values on the day prior to the notification of the transaction by way of a Regulatory Information Service announcement, excluding treasury shares.

Substitute tests

34.17   In circumstances where the class tests produce anomalous results, or where the tests are inappropriate to the sphere of activity of the AIM company, the London Stock Exchange may (except in the case of a transaction with a related party) disregard the calculation and substitute other relevant indicators of size, including industry specific tests.

NOTIFICATION

34.18   If an acquisition or a disposal by an AIM company is found to be a substantial transaction, because the comparison of the relevant values involved in the transaction with comparable values in the AIM company expressed as a percentage results in a percentage greater than 10 per cent, a Regulatory Information Service announcement concerning the transaction is required. Rule 12 of the *AIM Rules for Companies* provides that a notification must be made without delay, as soon as the terms of any substantial transaction are agreed. The information which must be disclosed in the notification is set out in Schedule 4 to the *AIM Rules for Companies*.

34.19   The information required to be disclosed by Schedule 4 to the *AIM Rules for Companies* comprises not only factual information related to the transaction, but also information which is descriptive of the effect of the transaction on the AIM company. Factual information which must be disclosed is:

■ particulars of the transaction, including the name of any company or business;
■ a description of the business carried on by, or using, the assets which are the subject of the transaction;
■ the profits attributable to those assets;
■ the value of those assets;
■ the full consideration and how it is to be satisfied;
■ details of any service contracts of the AIM company's proposed directors;
■ in a case of a disposal, the application of the sale proceeds;
■ in the case of a disposal, if securities or other securities are to form part of the consideration received, a statement whether such securities are to be sold or retained.

34.20   Information which is descriptive is:

■ the effect of the transaction on the AIM company; and
■ any other information necessary to enable investors to evaluate the effect of the transaction upon the AIM company.

RELATED PARTY TRANSACTIONS

34.21   Rule 13 of the *AIM Rules for Companies* applies a more strict regime to transactions between an AIM company and a related party. The definition of a related party is set out in Figure 34.1. The regime is more strict in that:

1 notification by a Regulatory Information Service announcement is required if the application of any of the class tests to the transaction produces a percentage figure which exceeds 5 per cent, and
2 the notification must include a statement that, with the exception of any director who is involved in the transaction as a related party, the directors of the AIM company consider, having consulted with its Nominated Adviser, that the terms of the transaction are fair and reasonable in so far as its shareholders are concerned.

34.22   The requirement specified at (2) above results, in practice, in the AIM company being required to ensure that its Nominated Adviser is satisfied that a

FIGURE 34.1 Related parties for the purposes of Rule 13 of the *AIM Rules for Companies*

A related party is:

(a) any person who is a director of an AIM company or of any company which is its subsidiary or parent undertaking, other subsidiary undertaking of its parent company;

(b) a substantial shareholder;

(c) an associate of (a) or (b) being:

 (i) the family of such a person;

 (ii) the trustees (acting as such) of any trust of which the individual or any of the individual's family is a beneficiary or discretionary object (other than a trust which is either an occupational pension scheme as defined in regulation 3 of the *Financial Services and Markets Act 2000 (Regulated Activities) Order 2001*, or an employee share scheme which does not, in either case, have the effect of conferring benefits on persons all or most of whom are related parties);

 (iii) any company in whose equity securities such a person individually or taken together with his/her family (or if a director, individually or taken together with his/her family and any other director of that company) are directly or indirectly interested (or have a conditional or contingent entitlement to become interested) to the extent that they are or could be able:

 • to exercise or control the exercise of 30 per cent or more of the votes (excluding treasury shares) able to be cast at general meetings on all, or substantially all, matters; or

 • to appoint or remove directors holding a majority of voting rights at board meetings on all, or substantially all, matters;

 (iv) any other company which is its subsidiary undertaking, parent undertaking or subsidiary undertaking of its parent undertaking;

 (v) any company whose directors are accustomed to act in accordance with (a)'s directions or instructions;

 (vi) any company in the capital of which (a), either alone or together with any other company within (iv) or (v) or both taken together, is (or would on the fulfillment of a condition or the occurrence of a contingency be) interested in the manner described in (iii);

(d) for the purposes of Rule 13, any person who was a director of an AIM company or any of its subsidiaries, sister or parent undertakings or a substantial shareholder within the 12 months preceding the date of the transaction.

"Family" means a reference to a person's family and includes the following persons:

• his/her spouse or civil partner and any child where such child is under the age of 18;

• any trust in which such individuals are trustees or beneficiaries;

• any company of which they have control of more than 20 per cent of its equity or voting rights in a general meeting.

Note: Employee share or pension schemes are excluded from the definition of trust provided that such individuals are beneficiaries rather than trustees.

Source: extract from *AIM Rules for Companies*, February 2007. The full *AIM Rules for Companies* is available at www.londonstockexchange.com

proposed transaction with a related party is fair and reasonable, so far as the AIM company shareholders are concerned, before the transaction is entered into.

34.23   The definition of related party for an AIM company is more extensive than the corresponding definition of related party in the *Listing Rules* applicable to a listed company but does not include the concept, undefined in the *Listing Rules*, of a "person exercising significant influence" over the listed company, such a person being treated as a related party under the *Listing Rules*.

34.24   As is the case when analysing whether a transaction is substantial or not, when analysing whether a transaction with a related party produces a percentage result in excess of 5 per cent under any of the class tests, transactions with the same person or persons entered into during the 12 months prior to the date of the transaction in question must be aggregated with that transaction. As with the provisions in relation to substantial transactions under Rule 12 of the *AIM Rules for Companies*, related party transactions also includes non pre-emptive issues of securities.

COMPANIES ACT 2006

34.25   Notwithstanding that if a transaction by an AIM company is classified as a related party transaction, the *AIM Rules for Companies* require notification of the details of the transaction specified by Schedule 4. For companies incorporated in England and Wales, section 190 of the *Companies Act 2006* will require share-holder approval, either in advance or as a condition of the transaction, if the proposed transaction by the AIM company is with a director or a person con-nected with a director and is a transaction under which either the AIM company acquires, or is to acquire, a substantial non-cash asset (directly or indirectly) from him or he acquires, or is to acquire, a substantial non-cash asset (directly or indirectly) from the AIM company. A substantial non-cash asset is one the value of which exceeds 10 per cent of the company's asset value and is more than £5,000, or exceeds £100,000. The definition of "connected person" for the purposes of section 190 is set out in sections 252 to 254 of the *Companies Act 2006* and differs in ways which may easily be significant from the definition of "related party" for *AIM Rules for Companies* purposes. In particular, the measure of control of a company in the definition of "connected person" in section 254 of the *Companies Act 2006* is a 20 per cent shareholding, compared with the 30 per cent sharehold-ing references in the definition of "associate" in the related party definition in the *AIM Rules for Companies*.

SUBSTANTIAL DISPOSALS

34.26   Where, in the case of a disposal, any of the class tests produce a result which is in excess of 75 per cent, Rule 15 of the *AIM Rules for Companies* states that the transaction is automatically deemed to constitute a fundamental change in business. Such a test is subject to the usual requirement to aggregate the disposal in question with any other disposals over the previous 12 months, pursuant to Rule 16 of the *AIM Rules for Companies*.

34.27 The consequences of a transaction being classified as a fundamental change in business are that the transaction must be subject to prior approval by the AIM company's shareholders in a general meeting. In order to seek shareholders' approval, an AIM company must produce a shareholder circular convening the general meeting and containing the information required by Schedule 4 of the *AIM Rules for Companies*. In addition, where the proposal constitutes a related party transaction under Rule 13, the information required by that Rule (see Paragraph 21) must also be included. In addition, Rule 15 of the *AIM Rules for Companies* requires that the proposed disposal must be notified by way of an announcement distributed via a Regulatory Information Service without delay. The announcement has the same content requirements as the shareholder circular.

34.28 Rule 15 of the *AIM Rules for Companies* goes on to state that where the effect of the disposal is to divest an AIM company of all or substantially all of its trading business activities then, upon the date of approval of the disposal by shareholders, the AIM company is treated as an investing company. This means that it is a company which, in the opinion of AIM Regulation, is primarily involved with investing its funds in the securities of other companies or the acquisition of a particular business. In these circumstances, the shareholder circular and announcement which are published in relation to the disposal must also contain the AIM company's proposed investing strategy namely:

- information on the precise business sectors, geographical areas and type of company in which the AIM company can invest;
- how widely spread the investments will be;
- how long the AIM company can go without either making an investment or returning money to shareholders;
- whether it will be an active or passive investor; and
- information on the expertise the directors have in evaluating proposed investments.

Any investing strategy which is required to be produced however must always be approved by shareholders.

34.29 Where the disposal which constitutes a fundamental change in business arises as a result of insolvency proceedings, it will not always necessarily require shareholder approval. In such circumstances, AIM Regulation must always be consulted.

34.30 Within 12 months of the general meeting where shareholders approved the disposal by which the AIM company effectively divested itself of all or substantially all of its trading business activities, the AIM company is obliged to make an acquisition or acquisitions which constitutes a reverse takeover under Rule 14 of the *AIM Rules for Companies*. Alternatively, within the same timeframe the AIM company must implement the investing strategy which it outlined in the circular to shareholders, to the satisfaction of AIM Regulation. In the event that such acquisitions are not made or the investing strategy has not been implemented to the satisfaction of AIM Regulation it will be a breach of the AIM Rules, which may result in the company having to represent its investment strategy to shareholders or even a suspension.

IN PRACTICE

The obligations which the AIM Rules relating to acquisitions and disposals place upon AIM companies represent one of the most significant distinctions between the rules applicable to AIM companies and those applicable to companies whose securities have been admitted to the Official List and to trading on the Main Market of the London Stock Exchange. This is due to the absence of any requirement for AIM companies to seek prior shareholder consent to transactions, save where the transaction is classified as a reverse takeover or a disposal resulting in a fundamental change in business. The advantages that the more lenient regime under the *AIM Rules for Companies* confer upon AIM companies are aimed at encouraging growth, and not only does the absence of a requirement to seek prior shareholder approval remove an element of uncertainty from a proposed transaction, but also that the absence of the requirement to prepare and despatch a circular to shareholders represents a significant saving both in terms of expense and time.

Similarly, the obligation on an AIM company which proposes to enter into a transaction with a related party only to make an announcement of the terms and effect of the transaction is a significantly less onerous burden than the obligation on listed companies to seek prior shareholder consent. The apparent freedom which this might be thought to give to AIM companies is, however, in practice tempered to a considerable extent by the necessity for an AIM company to persuade its Nominated Adviser that the proposed transaction is fair and reasonable for shareholders.

Where an AIM company is subject to the provisions of the *City Code on Takeovers and Mergers* then this will add a layer of complexity when assessing potential transactions or offers which are to be made for the AIM company.

CHAPTER 35

Takeovers

AT A GLANCE

The conduct of takeovers and mergers of UK public companies in the United Kingdom is regulated principally by the *City Code on Takeovers and Mergers*. The Directive on Takeover Bids (2004/25/EC) (the *Takeovers Directive*) lays down minimum rules for the regulation of takeovers of companies whose securities are admitted to trading on a regulated market, which includes the London Stock Exchange but not AIM. The *Takeovers Directive* also required certain of the regulatory powers of the Panel on Takeovers and Mergers (the "Panel") and its rules (contained in the *City Code on Takeovers and Mergers* Rules) to be placed on a statutory footing. The *City Code on Takeovers and Mergers* is now on a statutory footing in relation to takeover offers to which the *Takeovers Directive* applies and in relation to the *City Code on Takeovers and Mergers* Rules that are subject to the requirements of the *Takeovers Directive*. The *City Code on Takeovers and Mergers* Rules is placed on a non-statutory footing for all other offers and transactions to which the *City Code on Takeovers and Mergers* applies. Therefore for takeovers of those AIM companies to which the *City Code on Takeovers and Mergers* applies, the Panel operates for such transactions on a non-statutory basis.

INTRODUCTION

35.1　As well as examining the application of the *City Code on Takeovers and Mergers* to certain companies and the Panel and the *City Code on Takeovers and Mergers* in general, this chapter identifies various areas of the *City Code on Takeovers and Mergers* which either should be considered during any potential takeover of an AIM company or which are often issues to be resolved before and during transactions to which the *City Code on Takeovers and Mergers* applies. This chapter cannot cover every aspect of the *City Code on Takeovers and Mergers* and does not attempt to.

35.2　There is no substitute for seeking specialist advice and consulting the Panel.

WHAT IS THE PANEL ON TAKEOVERS AND MERGERS?

35.3　The Panel was established in 1968. The Panel's main function is to direct and manage the application of the *City Code on Takeovers and Mergers*. The Panel is an independent body and its statutory function and role are set out in Chapter 1 of Part 28 of the *Companies Act 2006* (section 942).

35.4 The Panel has authority conferred on it, by virtue of these provisions, to do everything that it considers necessary or expedient for the purposes of, or in connection with, its functions.

35.5 Importantly, given the way the Panel administers the *City Code on Takeovers and Mergers* day-to-day through the Panel Executive, by way of a combination of permanent staff and secondees from City institutions (investment banks, accountancy firms and law firms), the Panel is by statute permitted to discharge its function through a committee, sub-committee, or a member of staff or a person acting as such (that is, a secondee).

35.6 Until recently the Panel had no statutory authority, however since the implementation of the *Takeovers Directive* this has changed (as reflected above) and the Panel may under section 955 of the *Companies Act 2006* seek enforcement of its decisions through the courts.

35.7 The Panel Executive is to be treated as the only reliable source and it expects to be consulted on the interpretation of the *City Code on Takeovers and Mergers*.

THE *CITY CODE ON TAKEOVERS AND MERGERS* – WHAT IS IT?

35.8 The *City Code on Takeovers and Mergers*, in its paper form, is contained in a blue A5 file (which is why it is sometimes referred to as the "blue book") and includes an introduction, the *City Code on Takeovers and Mergers*' six General Principles (derived from the *Takeovers Directive*), a series of Rules (with notes for interpretation) and various appendices. It is available on-line at www.thetakeoverpanel.org.uk.

35.9 The main content of the *City Code on Takeovers and Mergers* is based upon the six General Principles, which amount to a baseline of what are deemed to be acceptable standards of commercial behaviour for takeovers (and of course other matters to which the *City Code on Takeovers and Mergers* applies). The underlying spirit of the *City Code on Takeovers and Mergers* is to ensure that shareholders of companies which are subject to the *City Code on Takeovers and Mergers* are treated fairly, and not put into a position where they may not decide upon the merits of a takeover and, further, that shareholders (in the same class) are afforded equivalent treatment by a bidding entity.

35.10 Directors of AIM companies should be assured that neither the *City Code on Takeovers and Mergers* nor the Panel Executive are concerned with the financial merits of a proposed takeover, whether it is a "good deal" or not for shareholders. The *City Code on Takeovers and Mergers*' function is to ensure that a framework is in place within which proposed transactions can be played out with a certainty of process and clarity of regulation.

35.11 The Rules of the *City Code on Takeovers and Mergers* are set out in Section D onwards of the *City Code on Takeovers and Mergers*.

APPLICATION OF THE *CITY CODE ON TAKEOVERS AND MERGERS*

35.12   The *City Code on Takeovers and Mergers* applies to companies, transactions and a range of persons outlined in Part 3 of Section A of the *City Code on Takeovers and Mergers*.

35.13   It applies to all offers for companies which have registered offices in the United Kingdom, the Channel Islands or the Isle of Man, if any of their securities are admitted to trading on a regulated market in the United Kingdom (which includes the London Stock Exchange's Main Market but not AIM) or any stock exchange in the Channel Islands or the Isle of Man.

35.14   The *City Code on Takeovers and Mergers* also applies to all offers for other companies not falling into Paragraph 35.13, being public and certain private companies which have their registered offices in the United Kingdom, the Channel Islands or the Isle of Man, and which are considered to have their place of central management and control in one of those territories. This will cover a great many UK AIM listed companies.

35.15   There are specific provisions in the *City Code on Takeovers and Mergers* which set out when private companies may be subject to the *City Code on Takeovers and Mergers*. The most commonly applied are those provisions which relate to private companies that, broadly speaking, used to be listed, or in respect of whose securities dealings have taken place in the previous ten years.

35.16   Where the *City Code on Takeovers and Mergers* applies to a company, the Rules will regulate takeovers and merger transactions in respect of those relevant companies. This will include a court approved scheme of arrangement and other statutory merger arrangements. Further, the Rules will apply to transactions effected in securities of those relevant companies which have as their objective, or potential effect, (directly or indirectly) obtaining or consolidating control of such companies. This could, or can, be effected by share issues, acquisitions of securities, capital reorganisations and entry into put and call option arrangements. This is of course, not an exhaustive list.

35.17   The *City Code on Takeovers and Mergers* is very specific that the best (and only) way of obtaining a correct interpretation of the *City Code on Takeovers and Mergers* is to consult the Panel Executive. The *City Code on Takeovers and Mergers* is also specific that simply obtaining legal or all other professional advice should not be considered an appropriate alternative to seeking a view from the Panel Executive, in respect of interpretation of the *City Code on Takeovers and Mergers*.

35.18   Set out below are examples of companies and the locations of their management and assets and an indication of whether or not the *City Code on Takeovers and Mergers* will apply:

- A Canadian incorporated company, AIM listed, with assets in Africa and management in the UK – the *City Code on Takeovers and Mergers* would not apply.
- A Bermudian incorporated company, AIM listed, with assets in Canada and management in the United Kingdom – the *City Code on Takeovers and Mergers* would not apply.

- A UK incorporated company with no assets in the United Kingdom and no management in the United Kingdom, although listed on AIM and the Toronto Stock Exchange – the *City Code on Takeovers and Mergers* will probably not apply.
- A UK incorporated company, with no assets in the United Kingdom but with management in the United Kingdom and listed on AIM – the *City Code on Takeovers and Mergers* will apply.
- A public limited company not admitted to any exchange in the United Kingdom nor planning to be, although having its place of central management in the United Kingdom – the *City Code on Takeovers and Mergers* will apply, although waivers may be available from the Panel Executive in respect of the application of certain rules.

35.19 In recent years, there have been a great number of non-UK incorporated companies admitted to trading on AIM and raising money from the UK capital markets, and there have been attempts to transplant certain provisions of standard UK corporate practice onto the non-UK companies. For example, there have been attempts in the past to make a company not governed by the *City Code on Takeovers and Mergers* subject to the jurisdiction of the Panel Executive, simply by having such a deeming provision in its constitutional documentation. The Panel Executive will not seek to take jurisdiction over a company that would not otherwise be subject to the *City Code on Takeovers and Mergers*. An alternative approach sometimes adopted is that the directors are given such powers in place of the Panel. Neither solution is ideal, but disclosure of the provisions relating to takeovers is required in an AIM admission document.

THE *CITY CODE ON TAKEOVERS AND MERGERS* RULES

35.20 The *City Code on Takeovers and Mergers* Rules cover many aspects of conduct relevant to transactions that seek to obtain or consolidate control of the company to which the *City Code on Takeovers and Mergers* applies. The intention of this Chapter is not to cover all of these, but highlight several areas that, in practice, concern directors of AIM companies most consistently. These areas are as follows:

- What is Rule 9 and what is a concert party, and what are the implications of both?
- Issues to think about as a director of an AIM company that is subject to, or potentially is subject to, a takeover offer.
- Issues to consider as a director of a company that may or may not make an offer for an AIM listed company.

WHAT IS RULE 9 OF THE *CITY CODE ON TAKEOVERS AND MERGERS* AND WHAT IS A CONCERT PARTY, AND WHAT ARE THE IMPLICATIONS OF BOTH?

35.21 It is not unusual for many AIM companies to have several significant shareholders holding large percentages of the AIM company's securities. This is more commonplace than for other companies listed on regulated markets in the

United Kingdom, where thresholds for free float or securities held in "public hands" are strictly applied. Partly because of this, changes to shareholdings in AIM listed companies can have implications under the *City Code on Takeovers and Mergers* of which the directors of AIM companies should be aware.

35.22 Under Rule 9 of the *City Code on Takeovers and Mergers*, if a person acquires an interest in securities which carries 30 per cent or more of the voting rights of a company (to which the *City Code on Takeovers and Mergers* applies) then that person must extend an offer to acquire all of the securities of that company, and such offer must be an offer to pay cash for those securities (or have a cash alternative).

35.23 Additionally, also under Rule 9, where any person (together with any person acting in concert with him) is interested in securities which in aggregate carry not less than 30 per cent of the voting rights in a company, but does not hold securities carrying more than 50 per cent of such voting rights, and such person (or any person acting in concert with him) acquires an interest in any other securities which increases the percentage of securities carrying voting rights in which he is interested, then similar provisions apply in respect of making an offer and for it to be in cash or have a cash alternative. It is for these reasons that the question as to whether a concert party is in existence and levels of interest in securities is so crucial in relation to the *City Code on Takeovers and Mergers*. The offer to be made under Rule 9 is referred to as a mandatory cash offer.

35.24 For AIM companies, Rule 9 of the *City Code on Takeovers and Mergers* can be of particular importance, given shareholdings of AIM companies are often held in large percentage blocks and often with such shareholders represented on the board of directors of the AIM company. Therefore, where parties are perhaps acting in concert (even inadvertently), small purchases of securities by one member of that concert party could trigger the need to make a mandatory cash offer for all the other securities in the company not held in the concert party.

35.25 This chapter is not the place for a detailed account of the intricacies of the definitions of "concert parties". However, for all AIM company directors the following matters should be borne in mind.

- The co-operation of two or more parties is required for acting in concert to take place, and persons acting in concert are people who pursuant to an agreement or an understanding (whether formal or informal) co-operate to obtain or consolidate control of a company, or co-operate to frustrate the successful outcome of an offer for a company.
- A practical point for AIM company directors is that there are classes of persons who will be deemed by the *City Code on Takeovers and Mergers* to be acting in concert.
- Of the classes of persons who are deemed to be acting in concert, those of the greatest relevance to AIM company directors are:
  - a company and any of its directors (together with any of their close relatives and related trusts);
  - a company, its parent, subsidiaries and fellow subsidiaries and fellow associated companies and companies of which such companies are associated companies; and

- directors of a company which is subject to an offer or where directors have reason to believe a bona fide offer for their company might be imminent.
■ Any person and any affiliate of that person will be deemed to be acting in concert or with each other. Affiliates for these purposes means any undertaking in respect of which that person either controls, or is a majority shareholder, or has the power to exercise a dominant influence or control over. A question which arises for directors of AIM companies from time to time is whether the Panel needs to be consulted when the trustees of a company's Employee Benefit Trust (EBT) acquire or intend to acquire securities in the AIM company, and whether such acquisitions could make the trustees concert parties with others (perhaps the company's directors) and potentially trigger the need for a mandatory cash offer to be made.

35.26   Regarding the question relating to EBTs, advance consultation with the Panel is essential in order to obtain a ruling and avoid unnecessary costs and problems. However, the fact that an EBT is in existence and operating will not, by itself, give rise to a presumption that the trustees are acting in concert with others who are acting in concert. The Panel will consider all the relevant factors when determining whether there is a concert party, including the identities of the trustees, the nature of the funding arrangements for the EBT, the number of securities the EBT is interested in and the method by which securities will be purchased by the EBT. Importantly the *City Code on Takeovers and Mergers* in the notes to Rule 9 is specific that there will be no presumption of concertedness in respect of securities held within the EBT but controlled by the beneficiary of that EBT.

35.27   The directors of AIM companies to which the *City Code on Takeovers and Mergers* applies are not automatically considered to be acting in concert other than, as outlined above, during an offer period or when they believe an offer may be imminent. An offer period is any time when an offer or possible offer has been announced, until the first closing date of that offer (or until the offer lapses or is declared or becomes unconditional as to acceptances).

35.28   As a general overarching concept, the *City Code on Takeovers and Mergers* does not seek to prevent dealings by directors in a company's securities. At times other than those mentioned above, directors are not deemed to be acting in concert. Clearly, if directors of an AIM company are acting together to obtain, or consolidate control of, a company then this "deeming" provision will not be required and the Panel will consider them as concert parties. However, there are other constraints upon directors in terms of dealings arising under the *AIM Rules for Companies*, the market abuse regime and the *Criminal Justice Act 1993*, in which the *City Code on Takeovers and Mergers* does not seek to involve itself. Further information on these constraints is set out in Chapter 32, *Directors' dealings*.

35.29   In part, given the nature of shareholding structures and potential for the existence of concert parties, of crucial importance for AIM companies is that particular care and attention should be paid to Rule 37 of the *City Code on Takeovers and Mergers* when an AIM company proposes to undertake a share buy-back. Inadvertently, mandatory cash offers under Rule 9.1 of the *City Code on Takeovers and Mergers* can come about following a share buy-back. This is because Rule 37 stipulates that upon any redemption or buy-back of securities in a company, any resulting increase in percentage of securities carrying voting rights following the cancellation of any securities bought back in which a person or concert party is interested will be treated as an acquisition for the purposes of Rule 9 of the *City Code on Takeovers and Mergers*.

35.30 The Panel will waive the Rule 9 obligation that would arise if there is a vote of independent shareholders, which frequently arises on reverse takeovers. This is dealt with in greater detail in the Chapter 14, *Admission to trading on AIM by reverse takeover*.

35.31 The most frequent question arising on the application of Rule 9 of the *City Code on Takeovers and Mergers* revolves around whether or not a concert party is in existence. Therefore, AIM company directors should always have these particular Rules of (and the notes to) the *City Code on Takeovers and Mergers* in mind.

WHAT SHOULD A DIRECTOR BE CONSIDERING IF THEIR OWN COMPANY IS SUBJECT TO A POSSIBLE TAKEOVER?

35.32 There are of course many matters which require careful thought by the directors of a company which may be subject to a takeover. The following sections highlight the areas which are of particular importance for the directors of AIM companies. However, before examining those areas, it is important to explain what the Panel expects of directors, companies and their advisers in these situations regarding secrecy, confidentiality and knowledge of the *City Code on Takeovers and Mergers*.

35.33 The *City Code on Takeovers and Mergers* explicitly states that, as a matter of routine in these situations, directors should be warned of the importance of secrecy. The reasons for this are obvious given that securities of the company are traded publicly. Security is important, for example using appropriate code names in documentation, keeping certain matters out of email exchanges and by ensuring, at all times, that documentation is kept in an appropriate place. Also, directors must ensure that any documentation which is issued, or any statements made, during the course of an offer are prepared with the highest standards of care and accuracy and all information given must be fairly presented by them. Appendix 3 of the *City Code on Takeovers and Mergers* also sets out the general responsibilities expected of directors.

35.34 Confidential papers should not be taken out of secure locations unless absolutely necessary. There are many stories of confidential papers being left in taxis or briefcases being stolen from vehicles, and information has been known to leak out as a result. Any companies, and not just AIM companies, and their advisory teams should take the appropriate steps and approach the issues of security and confidentiality very seriously.

35.35 The Panel also expects the companies and the directors to know about and understand how the *City Code on Takeovers and Mergers* works. Ignorance of the application of the *City Code on Takeovers and Mergers*, or the implications of certain activities, are not excuses that mitigate any breach.

35.36 Rule 3.1 of the *City Code on Takeovers and Mergers* expressly sets out that a target company must retain "competent independent advice" on any offer. The target company is also required to make the substance of such advice known to its shareholders (whether by way of a statement in the offer document sent to shareholders or, as is sometimes the case, in a defence document where an offer is not recommended).

34.37 In certain situations only the independent directors of a company will be involved in assessing the offer, because of the identity of the offeror, for example if it is associated with a certain director or because there is a management buyout. In these circumstances, it will be the independent directors who appoint the adviser (under Rule 3) and receive the benefit of that advice. Great care will need to be taken to ensure that such adviser is in fact independent.

35.38 Directors of a potential takeover target need to bear in mind that information provided to a potential "friendly" bidder must also be made available equally and promptly to a third party bidder (perhaps less "friendly") if one emerges (Rule 20), although usually only during the course of a potential offer which the market has been made aware of, whether by way of a holding announcement or otherwise.

35.39 That less welcome bidder must ask specific questions, however, and is not permitted simply to request blanket access to the information already supplied to another bidder.

35.40 The existence of these provisions in Rule 20.2 of the *City Code on Takeovers and Mergers* need to be considered by target boards and their advisory teams and detailed lists of documents and information provided should be maintained, so that information requests can be met promptly and accurately.

35.41 Directors may simply suggest that another bidder signs up to a more restrictive undertaking in respect of the use of the information to be supplied. However, the *City Code on Takeovers and Mergers* stipulates that any restrictions placed on a third party bidder are to be no more onerous than those imposed on another bidder or potential bidder. In management buyout situations, the measure of what information should be provided to competing offerors is that information which has been provided by the target company buyout team to its provider or providers of finance for the proposed buyout.

Rule 21 – restrictions on frustrating action

35.42 When an offer is underway at any time, or when an offer is imminent (and the Panel should decide, after consultation with a company, whether an offer is imminent), the target company is restricted from undertaking certain matters without first obtaining its shareholders' consent. The *City Code on Takeovers and Mergers* provides for this to ensure that actions are not taken by the target company which may frustrate the offer or potential offer and deny its own shareholders an opportunity of deciding upon the merits of an offer.

35.43 The actions which are specified in the *City Code on Takeovers and Mergers* include issuing securities, the disposing of or the acquiring of assets (of a "material" amount), or entering into contracts which are not in the ordinary course of business.

35.44   The Panel should always be consulted on questions or queries in respect of this Rule. The Panel will usually consent to the granting of options and the issuance of securities in respect of exercise of options, if the timing or the level of the grants (or exercise) are in accordance with normal practice under an established share option scheme of the company.

35.45   There is guidance in the *City Code on Takeovers and Mergers* as to what the Panel considers when it is asked to establish what "material" means in the context of acquiring or disposing of assets.

35.46   Any change or improvement to a director's service agreement when an offer is underway, or considered to be imminent, will be considered by the Panel as a matter which is not in the ordinary course of business and will therefore require shareholder approval.

Inducement fees and break fees

35.47   A further practical point to mention is the question of fees, particularly inducement or break fees, perhaps payable to bidding companies; and also success fee arrangements payable to target company advisers.

35.48   Inducement fees (or break fees) are relatively common in the market and refer to a fee (a cash sum) that it is agreed will be paid by a target company to a bidder in certain circumstances. A common example of when a break fee may be payable is if the offer does not become unconditional in all respects, because the target board fails to recommend the offer or changes its recommendation or a third party offer is recommended by the target board. In this example, in recommending a competing offer the target directors would clearly need to weigh the cost of having to pay a break fee to the initial bidder. The *City Code on Takeovers and Mergers* provides that such fee arrangements must be of *de minimis* value (normally no more than 1 per cent of the value of the target), and that written confirmation is given to the Panel, not only by the target company but also by its Rule 3 adviser, that they consider that the fee arrangements are in the best interests of shareholders. Of course any such inducement or break fee must be fully disclosed in the offer documentation.

35.49   If a target company's Rule 3 adviser has a fee arrangement which, for example, has a success fee element, then this may raise questions as to whether such a Rule 3 adviser has a conflict of interest. The potential conflict of interest would disqualify that adviser from being regarded as an appropriate person to give the target company independent advice. An example of this might be when an adviser may be rewarded on the failure of a hostile offer (irrespective of the offer price).

ISSUES TO CONSIDER WHEN ACTING AS A DIRECTOR MAKING AN OFFER FOR AN AIM COMPANY WHICH IS SUBJECT TO THE *CITY CODE ON TAKEOVERS AND MERGERS*

35.50 The need for confidentiality and security have already been discussed. However, what has not are the circumstances when an announcement (via a Regulatory Information Service) is required, and who has the obligation to make such an announcement.

35.51 Before a target company is approached the obligation to make an announcement lies with the potential bidding company. The share price of a target company should be monitored, so that any untoward movements can be responded to appropriately by the advisory team. However, once an approach has been made to the potential target company the primary obligation to make an announcement about a potential offer will be with the target company. An announcement will be required for example:

- when a firm intention to make an offer is notified to the target board; or
- when, following an approach to a target company, that company is subject to rumour and speculation or there is an untoward movement in its share price; or
- when, before any approach by a bidder has been made to a target, the target is subject to rumour and speculation or there is an untoward movement in the target company's share price; *and* there are reasonable grounds for concluding that the potential bidder's actions have led to the situation.

35.52 Announcements can be made in the form of a simple "holding" announcement, from the offeree, which simply states that the target board "notes the recent movement in its share price . . . and that discussions are taking place that may or may not lead to an offer being made for the company". It may also go on to say that there is no certainty an offer will be made, or that if it is made it will be acceptable.

35.53 Announcements must use unambiguous language and, as previously noted, be prepared to the highest standards of care and accuracy. In spite of its general guidance on content, there are some forms of announcement on which the *City Code on Takeovers and Mergers* is very descriptive as to content, and as to implications arising from their release. The most prominent of these is a Rule 2.5 announcement, which declares a firm intention on behalf of a potential offeror to make an offer.

35.54 Whilst this chapter does not deal with the content requirements of a Rule 2.5 announcement, it is important to note that a bidder should not release such an announcement unless it has undertaken careful and very responsible consideration. A bidding entity must have every reason to believe that it can and will be able to implement the offer referred to in the announcement. An offer document (reflecting the terms set out in the Rule 2.5 announcement) must be posted to a shareholder or target within 28 days of such a Rule 2.5 announcement being released (Rule 30.1 of the *City Code on Takeovers and Mergers*). For all AIM companies, particular attention should be paid to the phrase "untoward movement in share price" as a reason for an announcement. This is because, as with all companies to which the *City Code on Takeovers and Mergers* applies, the Panel is the final arbiter of when a movement is untoward. However, AIM companies' share prices may be subject to the natural volatility of AIM, and for such securities, which may be priced in pennies not pounds, a few pence movement either upwards or downwards can be very significant and indeed untoward, in spite of the inherent volatility of AIM. AIM companies and their advisory teams need to be especially vigilant and aware of these factors in the early stages of potential bid discussions.

RULE 11 – WHEN A CASH OFFER IS REQUIRED

35.55   The provisions of Rule 11 provide that except with the consent of the Panel, a cash offer is a mandatory requirement where:

- the securities of any class under offer in the target company in which interests are acquired for cash by a bidder (and any person acting in concert with it) during the offer period and within 12 months prior to its commencement carry 10 per cent or more of the voting rights, the offer for that class of securities shall be in cash (or accompanied by a cash alternative (at not less than the highest price paid by the potential bidder) or any person acting in concert with it) for any interest acquired during the offer period and within 12 months prior to its commencement; or
- subject to the above Paragraph, any interest in securities of any class under offer in the target company is acquired for cash by a bidder or any person acting in concert with it during the offer period, in which case the offer for that class shall be in cash (or accompanied by a cash alternative (at not less than the highest price paid by the bidding company) or any person acting in concert with it) for any interest in securities for that class acquired during the offer period; or
- in the view of the Panel, the circumstances which render such a course necessary in order to give effect to General Principle 1 of the *City Code on Takeovers and Mergers*, which provides that all holders of securities in a target company of the same class must be afforded "equivalent treatment" and, moreover, where a person acquires control of the company, the other holders of securities in that company must be protected.

35.56   There are two further areas which a director of an AIM company ought to consider carefully prior to entering into a potential bid transaction and which such director should bear in mind during the course of the offer.

- Rule 16 of the *City Code on Takeovers and Mergers* prevents a bidding company or its concert parties from making arrangements with target shareholders where such arrangements have favourable conditions attached and which are not being extended to all shareholders of the target company. This is a Rule which is provided so that all shareholders are afforded equivalent treatment (General Principle 1) and it also should prevent shareholders who control larger stakes in a target company from seeking preferential treatment separately to smaller shareholders.
- When obtaining finance from a third party provider for the purpose of satisfying the cash element of any bid, it is common for the bank to provide that drawdown on the facilities will only be allowable when the compulsory purchase threshold of 90 per cent of the securities to which the offer relates has

been reached. It is not uncommon for active and aggressive investment firms to buy securities in the market of companies who they feel are undervalued at the time an offer is announced, with a view to obtaining 10.1 per cent of the issued share capital, and therefore blocking the ability of the bidding company to exercise its statutory compulsory purchase process, and in so doing seek advantage for themselves. This may cause problems for the threshold at which financing may become available to the bidding company. Attention should be paid by advisory teams and banks, in conjunction with companies, to ensure that the prospect of having a situation where the threshold of 90 per cent is not reached is at least discussed in principle, so that the ability to fund a takeover does not get called into question with the arrival of an investor seeking to take such a stake.

IN PRACTICE

The *City Code on Takeovers and Mergers* may apply to AIM companies. Directors of AIM companies should therefore first consider whether the *City Code on Takeovers and Mergers* applies and, thereafter, pay close attention to the Rules. Reliance on advisory teams is commonplace, but directors will need to take responsibility for matters themselves. This should ensure that the appropriate level of thought and application is given to the matters of takeovers.

Options and share incentives

Share options and share incentives remain popular with small and large companies alike as a way of remunerating employees and directors. Smaller companies with gross assets of less than £30 million can take advantage of the tax efficient Enterprise Management Incentives (EMI) scheme. Larger companies can utilise a range of products, but on the whole need to adopt a more sophisticated strategy for minimising tax costs and maximising the incentive effect of options and share incentives.

INTRODUCTION

36.1   Recent changes in tax law and accounting rules potentially threatened the continued widespread use of share options and incentives as a method of retaining employees and directors. However, the popularity of options and share incentives remains. The EMI scheme combines tax effectiveness and relative simplicity for smaller companies with gross assets of less than £30 million. Other companies can adopt tax approved company share option plans (CSOP), Save As You Earn (SAYE) schemes and tax approved Share Incentive Plans (SIP). Any scheme that does not have formal tax approval is unapproved. Unapproved schemes remain popular, either on their own or in a combination with other schemes.

36.2   Given the choices available, the differences between the schemes and their respective tax treatments are outlined in this chapter. The driver for the choice of schemes that a company adopts ought to be the strategic objectives of the company. The use of unissued shares for share incentive schemes dilutes shareholders' equity, which should be borne in mind. Recent changes in accounting rules can also mean that the AIM company suffers an accounting charge. Best practice and good corporate governance require companies to be clear about the objectives to be achieved from share options and share incentives. This chapter also outlines key considerations which remuneration committees should take into account.

CHOICE OF SCHEMES

36.3   The list of schemes an AIM company may select is as follows:

- EMI;
- HMRC approved CSOP;
- unapproved share option scheme;
- HMRC approved SAYE;
- HMRC approved SIP;
- long term incentive plan (LTIP);
- sale or free award of shares; and
- phantom share option scheme.

36.4   All of the above schemes can utilise issued or unissued shares. Phantom share option schemes, however, do not utilise any shares other than as a reference point for calculating the level of cash awards, normally by reference to the movement in the price of shares between two or more points in time. As mentioned above, the use of unissued shares dilutes shareholders' equity. Where a company wishes to avoid or limit dilution beyond a standard limit of 10 per cent of the company share capital, the company can utilise existing shares. However, when utilising existing shares, they need to be acquired for making awards. Until the advent of treasury shares in the United Kingdom, the prohibition on a company owning its own shares led to the widespread adoption of employee benefits trusts (EBTs) as a vehicle for acquiring and holding shares and making awards over them. The use of EBTs continues, in some cases alongside the utilisation of treasury shares, and in other cases in place of treasury shares. The company law requirement for companies incorporated in England and Wales, that shares cannot be issued at less than their nominal value, also encourages the use of EBTs, for example where a company wishes to adopt a scheme making awards over free shares or as part of an LTIP.

36.5   Share incentive schemes may be designed in any manner that the company wishes. LTIPs, for example, are normally designed to encourage longer term ownership of shares by directors and can take any form. They can incorporate features of other schemes and may involve a combination of share option awards and free share awards. Owing to their prospective complexity, remuneration committees should be clear about what the scheme is to achieve.

36.6   Share incentives can be divided into categories of discretionary awards and all employee awards. The only all employee awards are HMRC approved SAYE and SIP schemes. They are designed to encourage company wide participation and, provided employees satisfy minimum qualifying requirements, all qualifying employees must be offered awards on the same basis. All other types of share incentive schemes are discretionary in their nature; how widely they are offered to employees is at the discretion of the remuneration committee.

36.7   It is outside the scope of this chapter to look at various schemes in detail. However, as a guide Figure 36.1 compares discretionary awards of shares, unapproved share options schemes, CSOP awards and EMI awards. Figure 36.2 outlines the differences between the SAYE scheme and a SIP. The two Figures outline the key features of the respective schemes and specialist advice should be taken on more detailed points arising.

OPERATION OF THE SCHEMES

36.8 Best practice, dictated by the corporate governance rules considered in Chapter 42, *Corporate governance for AIM companies*, requires that all schemes should be operated by the remuneration committee. Smaller companies which either do not have a remuneration committee or have a remuneration committee in which the existing directors participate should avoid, where possible, the involvement of the executive directors. This is particularly important in relation to awards made to the executive directors concerned. A combination of seeking professional advice and consulting the Nominated Adviser often acts as a check on the company, to ensure that it is not operating contrary to current market best practice.

36.9 There are no specific guidelines on best practice for AIM companies. The guidelines of the Association of British Insurers (ABI) on remuneration and share based incentives for executives are principally aimed at companies listed on the Main Market of the London Stock Exchange. However, any company in which institutional shareholders have, or indeed may have, a stake should have regard to the ABI guidelines. The guidelines are available from the Institution Voting Information Service (IVIS) website and are updated from time to time. The most recent update of the guidelines was in December 2007. The key requirements under the guidelines are as follows:

■ New schemes and material amendments to schemes should be submitted to shareholders for advance approval.

■ The maximum dilution to shareholders' equity should be limited to 10 per cent of the issued ordinary share capital in any rolling ten-year period. The 10 per cent limit includes the re-issue of treasury shares.

■ The dilution to shareholder equity under executive discretionary schemes should not exceed 5 per cent of the issued ordinary share capital of the company in any rolling ten-year period. The 5 per cent limit may be relaxed where the vesting of awards is dependent on the achievement of significantly stretching performance criteria, and, in the case of smaller companies, the 5 per cent limited is disapplied where the total market value of shares used for the scheme at the time of grant does not exceed £1 million.

■ Awards under share options should be phased and generally should be over lower numbers of shares and perhaps more regular, rather than one-off awards. One object of this rule is to prevent options becoming "underwater" options, where their market value falls below their exercise price.

■ Awards of options should be conditional upon satisfaction of performance conditions (see Paragraphs 36.10 to 36.13).

■ Normally, options should not be allowed to vest within three years of grant and their exercise should be linked to measurement of performance over three years. Performance conditions should relate to overall corporate performance and they should be based on the "achievement of financial performance, which is demanding and stretching in the context of the prospects for the company, and the prevailing economic environment in which it operates".

■ Participation should be limited to bona fide employees and executive directors. Although payments to non-executive directors with shares acquired at market prices aligns the interest of the non-executive director with those of shareholders, incentive awards geared to the share price or corporate performance that would impair the impartiality of non-executive directors are inappropriate.

- The exercise price of awards should not be lower than the market value of the shares on the date of grant.
- Options should only be granted within 42 days following the announcement of full or interim results.
- Awards should not last longer than ten years and the scheme itself should not last more than ten years.
- All employee share schemes should also operate within the appropriate best practice framework.
- Where a company adopts an employee benefits trust it should be approved by shareholders in advance, and its term should prescribe that it should not hold more than 5 per cent of the company's share capital at any time.

Whilst for AIM companies it may be inappropriate to comply with the ABI guidelines, any action inconsistent with such guidelines should only be carried out following consultation with its advisers.

PERFORMANCE CONDITIONS

36.10 The principal object of performance conditions should be to align the interests of employees and shareholders. Although companies can use a range of criteria, AIM companies, especially smaller AIM companies, may base performance criteria on their own performance objectives. Where, for example, a company is developing product in the technology sector, performance conditions could be based on successful development of such products.

36.11 Performance criteria should generally be based on the underlying financial performance of the company, as well as relating to the overall corporate performance of the company. It is important that the performance criteria should be precise and measurable, so that it is clear to the employees what they have to achieve and so avoid disputes over the application of performance conditions.

36.12 Performance criteria can also be dictated by changes in market practice. Some companies still link vesting to growth in the value of shares, which may or may not be appropriate. The obvious risk is that the value of shares may be dictated by general market conditions rather than the performance of a particular company, although it goes without saying that it ought to be possible for many companies to buck market trends. Market based performance criteria mean that any accounting charge taken for the share incentives cannot be adjusted to take account of changes in the market value of shares.

36.13 Earnings per share, therefore, is perhaps a better financial measure of performance of company, although it should be defined carefully, in particular to exclude the effect of any distorting factors. In 2006, approximately 70 per cent of companies in the FTSE 250 index adopted performance conditions based on earnings per share, whereas 14 per cent adopted performance conditions based on total shareholder return. Performance conditions may also be based on the measurement of total shareholder return. It measures the growth in earnings and returns to shareholders in the form of dividends, as well as growth in the value of the shares. For example, the ABI guidelines recommend that the measurement of total shareholder return should be relative to a relevant index or peer group. However, it may not be easy to establish suitable comparators, which makes total shareholder return based performance conditions inappropriate for smaller companies.

PRE-ADMISSION SHARE AWARDS

36.14   Companies seeking admission of their securities to trading on AIM may already have share incentives in place or they may introduce a new scheme. It is not uncommon for awards to be made prior to an admission to trading on AIM. Where it is intended that awards should be made at the admission price, the timing of option grants and share awards can be critical.

36.15   Where a company is either adopting or using a tax approved scheme, such as an EMI scheme, CSOP or SAYE scheme, the market value on the date of grant means the market value at the close of business on that particular date of grant. If the awards under such tax approved schemes are to be made at the admission price, they must be made unconditionally before admission to trading on AIM. It is not possible for a company to grant options prior to admission to trading on AIM at the admission price, conditional upon admission to trading on AIM taking place, because the market value of the shares, for the purposes of those schemes, would be the market value at the close of dealing on the date of admission to trading on AIM. Companies which are concerned that they would not wish options to continue, should there be failure in achieving admission to trading on AIM, can provide in their relevant scheme rules that the options would lapse on a prescribed long-stop date if admission to trading on AIM has not taken place by that date.

36.16   Options that are outstanding on the date of admission to trading on AIM, as well as summaries of the scheme, would be disclosed in the AIM admission document, and if additional grants are to be made in the run up to admission to trading on AIM these should be discussed in advance with the Nominated Adviser.

DISCLOSURE

36.17   There are disclosure requirements in respect of share incentives under the tax code, company law, accounting standards and best practice guidelines issued by the ABI.

36.18   Employers and employees have disclosure requirements to the HMRC under self-assessment and, where applicable, PAYE. Employers must also notify the grant of options, in the case of unapproved options on Form 42, and in the case of approved options under specific returns under the code for each approved scheme. EMI options have to be notified within 92 days of grant in order to qualify for their attendant tax benefits. Other awards of shares and "chargeable events" also have to be reported to the HMRC, normally on Form 42. Where an employee benefits trust with offshore trustees is created, its creation must be reported within three months of the creation of the trust under the *Inheritance Tax Act*.

36.19   The *Companies Act 1985* or *2006* requires the directors' report or the notes to the annual accounts to contain details of the directors' interests in securities, including options. The *Companies Act 1985* or *2006* and the *Directors' Remuneration Report Regulations 2002* also require AIM companies to show in their annual accounts the aggregate amount of gains made by directors on the exercise of options, and the aggregate amounts of money paid or receivable by directors under LTIPs, as well as the net value of assets receivable or received by directors under such schemes.

36.20   Where accounting standards require the cost of share incentives to be recognised in the company's accounts, those costs will be disclosed in the annual report. The ABI guidelines also emphasise that the expected value of incentive awards should be disclosed at the outset. It is not clear whether the expected value is the same as the accounting charge for the awards. The ABI guidelines state that the expected value is essentially the estimate of the present value, or the sum of all the possible various outcomes at vesting or exercise of awards.

36.21   There are also disclosure requirements with respect to dealings in securities by directors, which are set out in Chapter 32, *Directors' dealings*.

IN PRACTICE

Share options and share incentives are very popular with AIM companies and are often fundamental in assisting an AIM company to attract and retain employees and executive directors. The attraction of such options and incentives are enhanced for smaller companies with gross assets of less than £30 million, which can take advantage of the tax efficient Enterprise Management Incentives scheme. Larger companies can utilise a range of products, but on the whole need to adopt a more sophisticated strategy for minimising tax costs and maximising the incentive effect of options and share incentives.

FIGURE 36.1 Overview of share options

	PARTICIPATION		
SHARES	UNAPPROVED OPTION	APPROVED CSOP OPTIONS	EMI OPTIONS
■ At the discretion of the company's remuneration committee.	■ At the discretion of the company's remuneration committee.	■ Only full-time directors and employees (regardless of hours of work) selected at the discretion of the company. ■ Individuals holding 25 per cent of the share capital directly or with associates cannot participate.	■ Only full-time employees working at least 25 hours per week or 75 per cent of their working time can participate. ■ Individuals owning 30 per cent directly or indirectly of equity capital with associates are disqualified. ■ Participation will be limited to 250 employees from the date Finance Act 2008 receives Royal Assent.

FURTHER RESTRICTIONS			
SHARES	UNAPPROVED OPTION	APPROVED CSOP OPTIONS	EMI OPTIONS
■ The company can set the terms of acquisition. – e.g: Securities can be sold on deferred payment terms through an EBT.	■ The company can set the terms subject to market best practice. ■ Companies normally set terms on: – when options can be granted; – exercise price; – individual and scheme limits; – first exercise of options; – good and bad leavers; and – effect of events, such as take-overs and variations of share capital.	■ Scheme shares must be fully paid ordinary shares. Certain restrictions on shares are not permitted, although for AIM companies such restrictions are rarely an issue. ■ Options cannot be exercised within three years of grant. ■ The exercise price cannot be lower than the market value of the shares on the date of grant. ■ Other terms similar to those for unapproved options, subject to HMRC approval.	■ Options can only be granted over fully paid ordinary shares. ■ There is no restriction on the exercise of options within 3 years under the EMI code. That is dictated by best market practice. ■ Options may be granted at an exercise price that is at a discount to the market value subject to market best practice. The discount is subject to income tax on the exercise of options whether or not the shares are sold.

Figure 36.1 continued

SHARES	UNAPPROVED OPTION	APPROVED CSOP OPTIONS	EMI OPTIONS
	■ Flexibility as to its operation. ■ No limit as such on benefits, subject to best practice.		■ Other terms similar to those for unapproved options. ■ Material changes to the EMI options, company's trade, share capital etc. may result in options being disqualified. ■ HMRC's EMI code is less rigid than the code of CSOP options so more flexible than CSOP options.

MECHANICS			
SHARES	**UNAPPROVED OPTION**	**APPROVED CSOP OPTIONS**	**EMI OPTIONS**
■ The mechanics of the scheme will be largely dictated by the objectives and the structuring of any plan. ■ AIM companies cannot add restrictions on shares in the Articles of Association. ■ Any restrictions must be in a contract or plan document.	■ Scheme rules can be combined with the rules for a CSOP and/or an EMI scheme. The statutory requirement of CSOP and EMI options are normally disapplied. ■ Options may be granted by agreement combined with EMI options or by a resolution of the company and evidenced by an option certificate.	■ Scheme rules require prior approval of HMRC. The discretion of the company is limited over, e.g., the timing of exercise, good and bad leaver provisions, etc. ■ Material changes to the scheme require prior HMRC approval.	■ EMI options must be granted by an agreement, which must contain features prescribed by the EMI code. ■ Prior HMRC approval of documents is not required. However, for an EMI option to qualify for tax benefits a notice of the EMI option must be given to HMRC within 92 days after the grant of the EMI option. ■ More flexibility than the CSOP scheme but need to comply with the EMI code.

Figure 36.1 continued

OUTLINE TAX TREATMENT

SHARES		OUTLINE TAX TREATMENT – GRANT		
UNRESTRICTED	**RESTRICTED (indefinite restriction <5 years)**	**UNAPPROVED OPTION**	**APPROVED CSOP OPTIONS**	**EMI OPTIONS**
■ Income tax (IT) on unrestricted market value (UMV) less price paid for the shares. ■ CGT taper relief/ entrepreneurs' relief period starts. ■ NIC on under value if the shares are readily convertible assets.	■ IT on restricted market value (RMV) less price paid. ■ CGT taper relief/ entrepreneurs' relief period starts and NIC as for unrestricted share. **Section 431 ITEPA election made within 14 days of acquisition:** ■ UMV – RMV = "discount" is subject to IT. ■ Future growth in value (GIV) within CGT, not IT; or ■ **If an election is made, treat as if unrestricted shares.** ■ **If no election is made, treat as restricted shares.**	■ No IT.	■ No IT provided the option cannot be exercised more than 10 years after grant. ■ The maximum benefit which can be conferred is limited to £30,000 per employee by reference to the market value of the shares at the date of grant.	■ No IT provided the options cannot be exercised more than 10 years after grant ■ CGT taper relief period starts ■ Maximum benefit per employee is limited to £120,000 (for option grants after 6 April 2008) by reference to the UMV of the shares at the date of grant. The limit for option grants before 6 April 2008 was £100,000. ■ HMRC has indicated that the 1-year period of ownership required for entrepreneurs' relief will not start on the grant of an option.

		OUTLINE TAX TREATMENT – EXERCISE		
SHARES		**UNAPPROVED OPTION**	**APPROVED CSOP OPTIONS**	**EMI OPTIONS**
UNRESTRICTED	**RESTRICTED (indefinite restriction <5 years)**			
N/A	N/A	■ IT on market value less price paid for the shares whether or not the shares are sold. ■ NIC if the shares are readily convertible assets. ■ CGT taper relief/entrepreneurs' relief period starts. ■ The amount subject to IT + price paid for the shares = base cost for CGT. NB: If option shares are restricted, see acquisition of restricted shares and consider section 431 ITEPA election.	■ No IT or NIC if the exercise is more than 3 years after grant. Deemed section 431 ITEPA election. ■ CGT taper relief/entrepreneurs' relief period starts. ■ The amount paid for the shares = base cost for CGT.	■ Any discount to market value on grant is subject to IT and NIC (if the shares are readily convertible assets). ■ Otherwise no charge to IT. Deemed section 431 ITEPA election. ■ The amount paid for shares + any amount subject to IT = base cost for CGT. NB: If option shares are restricted, and the exercise price was discounted consider section 431 ITEPA election.

Figure 36.1 continued

OUTLINE TAX TREATMENT – "CHARGEABLE EVENT" e.g. restriction removed or varied				
SHARES		UNAPPROVED OPTION	APPROVED CSOP OPTIONS	EMI OPTIONS
UNRESTRICTED	RESTRICTED (indefinite restriction <5 years)			
	UMV x per cent discount (for restriction removed) subject to IT.	**RESTRICTED SHARES – no section 431 ITEPA election** ■ UMV x per cent discount (for restriction removed) subject to IT.		**RESTRICTED SHARES – no section 431 ITEPA election** ■ UMV x per cent discount (for restriction removed) subject to IT.

OUTLINE TAX TREATMENT – DISPOSAL OF SHARES (another chargeable event)				
SHARES		UNAPPROVED OPTION	APPROVED CSOP OPTIONS	EMI OPTIONS
UNRESTRICTED	RESTRICTED (indefinite restriction <5 years)			
■ Tapered gain is subject to CGT after annual allowance (£9,200 for the tax year 2007/2008). ■ Entrepreneurs' relief will only be available if all of the following conditions are satisfied, namely throughout a period of 1 year:	■ UMV x per cent discount for any remaining restriction subject to IT. ■ Balance within CGT. ■ Entrepreneurs' relief will only be available if all of the following conditions are satisfied, namely	■ If shares restricted and no section 431 ITEPA election, consider IT. ■ Tapered gain (if any) is subject to CGT after annual allowance (£9,200 for the tax year 2007/2008). ■ Entrepreneurs' relief will only be available if all of the following	■ Gain is subject to CGT after any taper relief and annual allowance (£9,200 for the tax year 2007/2008).	■ If shares restricted and no section 431 ITEPA election, consider IT. ■ Tapered gain is subject to CGT after annual allowance (£9,200 for the tax year 2007/2008). ■ Entrepreneurs' relief will only be available if all of the following

– the employee held 5 per cent of the ordinary shares and 5 per cent of the voting rights; and – the company was a trading company or the holding company of a trading group.	throughout a period of 1 year: – the employee held 5 per cent of the ordinary shares and 5 per cent of the voting rights; and – the company was a trading company or the holding company of a trading group.	conditions are satisfied, namely throughout a period of 1 year: – the employee held shares after exercising the option; – the employee held 5 per cent of the ordinary shares and 5 per cent of the voting rights; and – the company was a trading company or the holding company of a trading group. ■ Entrepreneurs' relief is unlikely to be available, save in exceptional circumstances.	conditions are satisfied, namely throughout a period of 1 year: – the employee held shares as opposed to options; – the employee held 5 per cent of the ordinary shares and 5 per cent of the voting rights; and – the company was a trading company or the holding company of a trading group. ■ Entrepreneurs' relief is unlikely to be available, save in exceptional circumstances.

FIGURE 36.2 Overview of Share Incentives

	SAYE	SIP
ELIGIBILITY	■ The scheme must be open to all employees of the company. A qualifying period of employment of up to 5 years can be set.	■ The plan must be open to all employees of the company. A qualifying period of employment of up to 18 months can be set.

OVERVIEW	■ Each participating employee enters into an SAYE savings contract with a bank or building society (savings carrier) under which they agree to save a regular sum of money each month of between £5 and £250 for 3 or 5 years (as determined by the company). At the end of the savings contract a tax-free sum bonus is added to the savings. The bonus is fixed at the start of the contract. The current bonus rate is 2.4 × the monthly contribution for a 3-year contract and 7.2 × the monthly contribution for a 5-year contract, and 13.3 × the monthly contribution where the savings are retained for an additional 2 years.
	
	■ Savings are deducted from the participating employee's net pay and paid to the savings carrier by the employer.
	
	■ The employee is granted an option by the company to acquire a number of shares which have a total strike price equal to the projected proceeds of the savings contract. The strike price can be set at a discount of up to 20 per cent of the market value of a share at the time of grant.
	
	■ As a general rule if the option holder ceases to be an employee his option will lapse. The scheme rules can specify good and bad leaver provisions.
		Companies can award any one or more of the following:
		
		■ Free shares worth up to £3,000 per annum. The free shares must normally be allocated to employees on similar terms.
		  – Up to 80 per cent of the awards of free shares can be linked to performance (individual, team, divisional or corporate).
		  – The free shares must normally be held in the plan for at least 3 years, although the employer can specify a longer period of up to 5 years.
		
		■ Partnership shares:
		  – employees can buy shares (partnership shares) from their pre-tax pay subject to a limit of the lower of £1,500 or 10 per cent of pay per tax year;
		  – employees can withdraw their partnership shares from the plan at any time.
		
		■ Matching shares:
		  – up to two free shares can be given for each partnership share the employee buys.
		
		■ Dividend shares:
		  – tax-free dividends up to £1,500 per year can be reinvested in dividend shares.
		
		Free and matching shares may be subject to forfeiture if an employee leaves before the end of a qualifying period of up to 3 years (unless he is a good leaver).

	SAYE	SIP

TAX TREATMENT	■ No income tax charged on the grant of the option. At the end of the savings contract the employee has 6 months to exercise the option. The employee can then either:
	  – close the savings account and take the savings and tax-free bonus; or
	  – close the account and use all of the proceeds to exercise the option to purchase shares; or
	  – close the account and take up part of the option (any funds not used to buy shares are returned to the employee).
	
	■ There is no income tax or NIC when the option is exercised. Deemed section 431 ITEPA election.
	■ CGT liability will arise on a sale of the shares to the extent that the sale price exceeds the purchase price, subject to the annual allowance (£9,200 for the tax year 2007/2008).
		■ Shares held for less than 3 years:
		  – Free, matching and partnership shares: income tax and NICs on the market value of the shares when removed from the plan;
		  – Dividend shares: the original dividend is subject to income tax.
		■ Shares held for 3 to 5 years:
		  – Free and matching shares: income tax and NICs on the lower of the value of the shares at the time of the award and their value on removal;
		  – Partnership shares: income tax and NICs on the lower of the pay used to buy the shares and their value on removal;
		  – No charge to tax on dividend shares held in the plan for at least 3 years. Deemed section 431 election.
		■ Shares held for over 5 years can be removed free of income and NICs. Deemed section 431 election;
		■ No CGT is payable when the shares are taken out of the plan but CGT may arise on their subsequent disposal subject to the annual allowance (£9,200 in the tax year 2007/08). The base cost of the shares for CGT purposes is equal to the market value of the shares at the time when the shares are withdrawn from the plan. However, if the shares are retained in the plan until sale, there is no CGT on their disposal out of the plan.

SET-UP COSTS AND ADMINISTRATION	■ Scheme rules require prior HMRC approval. ■ To operate the scheme a savings carrier must be appointed. The savings carrier undertakes the administration of the scheme and may also help with the communication of the scheme to the employees.	■ Plan rules require HMRC approval. ■ Companies may outsource the administration of the plan.

Tax incentives

Smaller AIM companies qualify for a number of tax breaks granted to encourage investment in trading companies. AIM companies that qualify are those with gross assets of less than £7 million prior to the investment and £8 million after the investment. Until April 2006, those limits were £15 million and £16 million respectively. The tax reliefs are now less significant for AIM companies. However, where available, they can be valuable. Care should be taken to avoid the tax reliefs determining the AIM company's business and structure.

INTRODUCTION

37.1 The categories of tax breaks referred to above are as follows:

- Enterprise Investment Scheme (EIS);
- Venture Capital Trust (VCT); and
- Corporate Venturing Scheme (CVS).

37.2 The EIS and VCTs are designed to encourage investments by individuals. Structurally the two schemes are fundamentally different:

- EIS relief is available on direct investments in qualifying companies. An AIM company may be that qualifying company.
- VCTs are quoted investment companies that can invest in a range of unquoted qualifying companies, which may well be AIM companies. As direct investments may carry more risk, VCTs facilitate the spreading of risk among investments in a number of unquoted companies.

37.3 The CVS is designed to encourage investments by companies in other unquoted companies. An AIM company may be an investee company, or indeed an investor that qualifies for relief under the CVS. If the company is an investor, it should take care to ensure that adding the investment does not cause its trading status to be called into question, for example for the purposes of business asset taper relief, entrepreneurs' relief (being introduced with effect from 6 April 2008) or capital gain hold-over relief.

37.4 The three schemes offer tax breaks at the point of investment. They all involve a number of conditions that must be satisfied at the time of investments being made and afterwards. Ongoing requirements to satisfy conditions last for three years, and in some cases for five years. The requirements can create conflict between the business needs of the company and the need to ensure that tax breaks for investors are preserved.

KEY FEATURES OF EACH SCHEME

37.5   As there are a number of detailed conditions to be satisfied under each scheme, and given that the reliefs are only available for smaller AIM companies, it is outside the scope of this chapter to look at all the detailed conditions. However, Figure 37.1 compares the key features of each scheme. As can be seen from Figure 37.1, although there are a number of differences, where the AIM company is the investee company the trading requirements are the same under each scheme.

FUNDRAISING

37.6   Where an AIM company is raising funds and it is self evident that the company will be a small company, such that securities may be acquired by VCTs, other corporate investors or individual investors, it is well worth considering the availability of reliefs in advance. A priority is to consider whether the company would qualify for any such reliefs. As a key qualifying requirements is the gross assets test, that should be at the top of the list of things to be checked. Gross assets mean all of the assets of the company disregarding any liabilities. In the case of an AIM company, which is a single trading company, the test involves considering the balance sheet and testing whether the gross assets would satisfy the limits before and after the new funds have been raised. In the case of groups of companies the position is more complex. Each group company's accounts need to be examined. Although the consolidated accounts of the parent company may initially give an indication of whether or not the test is satisfied, the consolidated accounts are the incorrect set of accounts to look at. The gross assets of each group company need to be aggregated, but inter-company debts and liabilities (which would be assets in the debtor company) are disregarded.

37.7   Very often companies would seek professional advice on their qualifying status for the tax reliefs. However, as an AIM admission document for a new fundraising would need to give some indication as to whether or not the conditions are satisfied, HMRC can be approached for an advance assurance on whether or not the company would be a qualifying company. That exercise should be undertaken in good time. An advanced assurance from HMRC provides a measure of comfort that the company qualifies, but it is not conclusive. The position needs to be monitored, and the actual point at which an assessment needs to be made of whether the conditions have been satisfied is when the securities are issued. The securities are treated as issued on the date that the register of members is completed. Once the securities are issued, filings have to be made with HMRC confirming that the company is a qualifying company. The advanced assurance can be relied upon, provided there have not been any relevant changes in circumstances.

37.8   Great care needs to be taken over what is said in the AIM admission document about the company's qualifying status. In particular, care should be taken to ensure that representations are not made confirming that any one or more of the reliefs would be available. One reason why that would be dangerous is that, in any event, the availability of reliefs not only depends on the qualifying status of the company, but also on conditions being satisfied by the investor, which may be the individual, a VCT or another corporate investor. Therefore, the satisfaction of conditions for the reliefs will invariably be beyond the AIM company's control to a significant extent. The placing agreement to be entered into between the Nominated Adviser and the directors often contains warranties and representations about the availability of reliefs, where relevant statements have been included in the AIM admission document. Care needs to be taken over giving undertakings to ensure the continuing availability of the reliefs. As the future availability cannot be guaranteed, such undertakings may be framed in a manner to ensure that either the directors would use reasonable endeavours to avoid taking action that would cause the loss of reliefs, or the directors would perhaps notify the investors if they are about to do something that would cause the loss of reliefs.

37.9 As mentioned, it is outside the scope of this chapter to consider the matter in great depth, but the following points are worth considering at the time of a fundraising:

- EIS and VCT reliefs are only available on the issue of new securities. The gross assets test must not be breached at the time of the share issue.
- The EIS and CVS reliefs require that at least 80 per cent of the money raised from EIS and CVS investors must be employed for a qualifying purpose within 12 months, and all of the money must be utilised for qualifying purposes within 24 months. The 12-month and 24-month periods run from the issue of the securities or, if later, the date on which the company starts to trade, if it was not trading on the date of the issue of the securities. Trading must itself commence within 24 months of the issue of the securities. The filing requirements involve the company having to confirm that the relevant conditions have been satisfied. It is not necessary to place the funds raised from qualifying investors in a separate account, but the company needs to be able to satisfy HMRC that the money has been used for qualifying purposes only.
- As can be seen from Figure 37.1, various activities are disqualified. If the company is carrying on disqualified activities then it would not qualify if the disqualified activities are a substantial part of the company's trade. Two categories of activities that may unexpectedly cause difficulties are licensing activity and overseas trading activity. Where the company is due to receive licence fees or royalties, those fees and royalties must only accrue from intellectual property that has been created by the company. Where intellectual property that has been purchased generates significant levels of licence fees and royalties, relief may not be available. Overseas activities also need to be carefully monitored. The company must carry on substantially the whole of its trade in the United Kingdom. Overseas activity is permitted but it must not exceed broadly 20 per cent of the activities of the company or, where there is a group, of the group. Monitoring this can involve a detailed examination of the activities.
- Investors wishing to claim EIS reliefs must not be connected with the fundraising company. Existing directors and employees of the company are connected and normally do not qualify for EIS relief. However, existing directors can

qualify for EIS relief on a share issue, if they qualified for EIS relief on a previous subscription of securities when they were not directors at the time of the share issue. Investors, or business angels, as they are often known, may qualify for relief on the subscription of securities and then become directors. The directors who claim EIS relief on their investment may be remunerated, but the remuneration must not be excessive owing to anti-avoidance rules, which are designed to prevent investors from receiving post-acquisition benefits. Accordingly the remuneration and level of bonuses and any grants of options to such directors need to be carefully monitored, to ensure that the anti-avoidance rules are not breached.

ONGOING REQUIREMENTS

37.10 As mentioned, the conditions for the various reliefs have to be satisfied, not only at the time at which an investment in the company is made, but also for a period afterwards. Broadly, the position for EIS and CVS investments is that the relevant conditions must continue to be satisfied for three years after the share issue qualifying for the reliefs. It should be noted that where a second or further fundraising also qualifies for either relief, then a new three-year clock starts for the new investment. As the reliefs are designed for smaller businesses, with the view to encouraging investments to enable them to grow, the gross assets test only has to be satisfied at the point of each investment. Therefore, once an investment has been made, if within the restrictive period the assets of the company's gross assets become greater than £8 million, that does not disqualify the investments. In the case of VCT investments, where income tax relief is obtained on the issue of the securities, the securities must be held for five years.

37.11 The key categories of ongoing requirement that cause difficulties in practice are as follows:

- changes in the activities of the company, for example changes in the trade of the company or where a new trade is carried on (difficulties can also arise where either business or securities are acquired);
- value is received by EIS investors after the investment and during the restricted period;
- changes to the share capital of the company or on a reorganisation, although this should not be an issue for most AIM companies.

37.12 Share reorganisations in AIM companies should be relatively rare. A bonus issue would not cause the loss of reliefs. Where there is a rights issue, the new subscription may well qualify for a relief. Where, however, there is a buy-back of securities, that can cause a loss of relief. As AIM companies will rarely have different classes of share, the risks arising from changes to rights attaching to share should be rare.

37.13 Where the AIM company buys assets or securities of a company, or changes its activities, that can cause relief to be withdrawn. Money raised from an investment can only be used for qualifying activities. Qualifying activities do not include the purchase of securities, unless at the time the issue is made a clear intention is declared that funds would be used to buy securities of a trading company. The acquisition of securities would constitute an investment, which is not a permitted activity; very often the solution is to transfer the trade immediately up to the EIS company, but professional advice should be taken at the time.

37.14   Where an EIS investor receives value from the company, that can cause a loss of relief. Value can be received in a number of ways, which principally include repayment of any debt owed to the investor, the provision of benefits of facilities, and purchasing assets from the investor at more than their market value. A distribution made to the investor other than a dividend that does not exceed a normal return on the investment is also treated as a receipt of value. Furthermore, if the AIM company buys securities in a company which was controlled by the investor during the five-year period, that is also treated as the return of value.

37.15   In the case of EIS relief, relief is withdrawn in full if the individual ceases to be a qualifying individual, or the company ceases to be a qualifying company, or the securities cease to be eligible securities. Relief may be withdrawn or reduced, in whole or in part, where there is a receipt of value by the investor.

IN PRACTICE

Whilst a number of the tax incentives which are available for potential investors in AIM companies only apply to those companies which are relatively small, with gross assets of less than £7 million (before the investment), these incentives can be important when such companies are conducting a fundraising.

FIGURE 37.1 Overview of tax incentives

	EIS	VCT	CVS
ELIGIBILITY	■ Individual liable to UK tax. ■ Non-UK resident individuals may be eligible. Except for deferral relief the individual must be resident or ordinarily resident at the time of the original gain accruing. ■ Not connected with the qualifying company.	■ Individuals investing in the VCT within the UK tax net, but they do not have to be UK tax resident.	■ A company within the charge to corporation tax carrying on a non-financial trade, or a company that is a member of a group that carries on non-financial trade. ■ The investor company must not hold 30 per cent or more of the ordinary share capital of the investee company.

TAX RELIEFS IN OUTLINE	■ 20 per cent initial income tax relief on investment.
	■ CGT exemption on a disposal of the shares after 3 years.
	■ CGT deferral relief. Deferred gain crystallises on the disposal of EIS shares. Entrepreneurs' relief could be available in respect of the deferred gain if the deferred gain arose in respect of a business/securities that would have qualified had the entrepreneurs' relief been available when the deferred gain originally arose.
		■ Individual subscribing for VCT shares (after 6 April 2004) qualifies for income tax relief at 30 per cent.
		■ Individual subscribing for or acquiring VCT shares qualifies for:
		   – income tax exemption on dividends received from the VCT;
		   – CGT exemption on the disposal of the VCT shares after 3 years.
			■ Corporation tax relief at 20 per cent for investment in qualifying companies.
			■ Deferral relief on CVS gains on a reinvestment in other CVS qualifying companies.
			■ Losses on the disposal of investments can be set against taxable profits in year of disposal or carried back 1 year.

Figure 37.1 continued

	EIS	VCT	CVS

TAX RELIEFS IN OUTLINE (cont.)	■ 100 per cent IHT business property relief after 2 years.
	■ Loss relief on disposal, which can be set off against:
	  – capital gains in year of disposal or the losses can be carried forward; or
	  – income in year of loss or the previous year.
		■ VCT investment gains are free from corporation tax on their disposal.	

LIMITATIONS	■ £400,000 per spouse for initial income tax relief, which increased to £500,000 for shares issued after 6 April 2008 (such increase being subject to European Commission state aid approval). ■ Income tax relief limited to 20 per cent. ■ No limit on investment for deferral relief.	■ Individual investments in a VCT (per spouse) is limited to £200,000 per tax year. ■ 30 per cent relief available provided the shares are held for 5 years.	■ Corporation tax relief limited to 20 per cent. ■ No limits for deferral relief.

	EIS	VCT	CVS
QUALIFYING INVESTMENTS	■ Only new ordinary shares which must not be redeemable.	■ New non-redeemable ordinary shares in the VCT for the 30 per cent income tax relief. ■ Existing VCT shares for the dividend and CGT relief. ■ A VCT's investments in any investee company must not exceed 15 per cent of the company's ordinary share capital.	■ New ordinary shares of the qualifying company. ■ Investing company must not have any interest exceeding 30 per cent in the investee company during the qualifying period (normally 3 years).
QUALIFYING COMPANY	■ Must be unquoted: AIM companies qualify. ■ Maximum gross assets of £7 million before the investment and £8 million after the investment. EIS, VCT and CVS investments in the year ending with a qualifying share issue must not exceed £2 million for share issues after 6 April 2007. ■ Must exist for carrying on qualifying business activities. ■ Must be independent, i.e. not under the control of another company.	There are separate conditions for the VCT and the investee companies. **VCT** ■ The VCT must be listed on the Main Market. ■ Its income must be derived wholly from shares and securities. ■ After 3 years, 70 per cent of the VCT's investments must consist of investments in qualifying trading companies, which include AIM companies.	■ The investee company must be unquoted – AIM companies qualify. ■ Gross assets prior to the investment must not exceed £7 million and £8 million after the investment. ■ VCT, EIS, CVS investments in the investee company in the year ending with the qualifying share issue must not exceed £2 million for shares issued after 6 April 2007. ■ Must carry on a qualifying trade or be a company within a trading group.

Figure 37.1 continued

	EIS	VCT	CVS
QUALIFYING COMPANY (cont.)	■ The company or its qualifying 90 per cent subsidiary must carry on a trade; and it must not carry on disqualified activities.[1] ■ For post 17 March 2004 share issues, any subsidiary must be a 51 per cent subsidiary. – The EIS company (51 per cent) and qualifying subsidiaries must have less than 50 full-time employees (for shares issued after 19 July 2007).	■ VCT has up to 6 months to reinvest cash realised on the disposal of qualifying investments that were held for at least 6 months. ■ 30 per cent of the VCT's investments must be in new ordinary shares of unquoted qualifying companies. **Investee company** ■ Unquoted company: AIM companies qualify. ■ Gross assets must be less than £7 million before the investment and £8 million after the investment. ■ VCT, EIS, CVS investments in the investee company in the year ending with the qualifying share issue must not exceed £2 million for shares issued after 6 April 2007. ■ Must carry on a qualifying trade and not carry on disqualified activities.[1] The tests are the same as those for EIS relief. ■ The investee company and qualifying subsidiaries must have less than 50 full-time employees (for shares issued after 19 July 2007).	■ Must satisfy the independence requirement, i.e. not under the control of the investing company or another company or connected persons. ■ Must not be in partnership with any other person. ■ Any subsidiaries must be 51 per cent subsidiaries at the time of investment as for EIS. ■ Must carry on a qualifying trade and not carry on any disqualified activities.[1] The conditions are the same as those for EIS. ■ The investee company and qualifying subsidiaries must have less than 50 full time employees (for shares issued after 19 July 2007). ■ At least 20 per cent of its shares must be held by independent individuals.

	EIS	VCT	CVS
ONGOING REQUIREMENTS	■ Must use 80 per cent of funds raised within 12 months of the share issue or, if later, the commencement of the trade (which itself must start within 2 years of the share issue) ("the start date"). ■ Must use the balance of funds within 2 years of the start date. ■ Must use the money raised only for qualifying activities. ■ The qualifying conditions must be observed for 3 years after each issue of shares that qualify for EIS.	■ The investee company must continue to meet the qualifying conditions so long as the VCT holds the investment.	■ The investment must be held for at least 3 years. ■ The investee company must use 80 per cent of the funds raised within 12 months of the share issue (or, if later, the start of the trade) and the balance within the following 12 months.

1. Disqualified activities include the following:

    –   property development, dealing in land;

    –   dealing in shares, securities, commodities or futures;

    –   dealing in goods other than by normal wholesale or retail;

    –   banking, insurance, money lending, debt factoring, hire purchase or other financial activities.

    –   leasing or letting other assets on hire;

    –   legal or accountancy services;

Figure 37.1 continued

- market gardening, farming, forestry, woodlands or timber;
- operating or managing property backed establishments such as hotels, guest houses, nursing homes, residential care homes or managing property used for these activities;
- receiving licence fees or royalties except where the company created the intellectual property being exploited;
- providing services or facilities for business carried on by another person which consists of substantially non-qualifying activities, if person has controlling interest in both activities;
- shipbuilding and coal and steel production for shares issued or money raised after 6 April 2008.

Disclosure Rules and Transparency Rules

In the interests of transparency in the capital markets, obligations are put on UK and non-UK AIM companies to notify major movements in their shareholdings. Similar obligations are put on shareholders of UK companies to notify significant changes in their own shareholdings.

UK AIM companies and shareholders are subject to Chapter 5 of the *Disclosure Rules and Transparency Rules* (part of the *Financial Services Authority Handbook*), whilst both UK and non-UK AIM companies have to comply with Rule 17 of the *AIM Rules for Companies*.

INTRODUCTION

38.1   On 22 December 2006, the Financial Services Authority published the *Transparency Obligations Directive (Disclosure and Transparency Rules) Instrument 2006* (FSA 2006/70) containing the final rules which implemented certain provisions of the EU *Transparency Directive* (2004/109/EC). The new rules introduced three new chapters into the *Disclosure Rules* sourcebook, which was renamed the *Disclosure Rules and Transparency Rules* ("the DTRs"). All six of the chapters apply to Official List companies, but one of the chapters, DTR5, *Vote Holder and Issuer Notification Rules*, applies to some AIM companies also. As well as implementing certain aspects of the *Transparency Directive*, the transparency rules are also intended to ensure there is "adequate transparency of and access to information in the UK financial markets" (DTR 1A.1.3G). As its title suggests, DTR5 contains the notification requirements for major shareholdings in applicable AIM companies (see Paragraphs 38.10 to 38.16).

38.2   In addition to the requirements under DTR5, Rule 17 and Schedule 5 to the *AIM Rules for Companies* require AIM companies to deliver without delay an announcement to a Regulatory Information Service for distribution to the public of any "relevant changes" to any "significant shareholders" containing certain prescribed information. For this purpose, significant shareholders are those holding 3 per cent or more of the issued securities of the class which is admitted for trading on AIM.

DTRS

38.3 Because the DTRs are rather technical in nature, directors should seek advice from the company's financial and legal advisers, to ensure it complies with its obligations under DTR5. In the same way, relevant shareholders should take legal advice as to their obligations under DTR5.

UK issuers

38.4 UK issuers (i.e. UK incorporated AIM companies) and shareholders of UK issuers whose securities are listed on AIM must comply with DTR5.

Notification to the company

38.5 A shareholder must notify the company of the percentage of voting rights he holds as shareholder over issued securities or through his "direct or indirect holding of financial instruments" (see Paragraphs 38.8 and 38.9) if the percentage of his voting rights in the company reaches, exceeds or falls below 3 per cent and each subsequent 1 per cent threshold above that. This notification requirement applies if the voting rights are affected:

- as a result of an acquisition or disposal of securities or financial instruments; and/or
- as a result of a change in the total number of voting rights in issue (as disclosed by the issuer); and/or
- as a result of events changing the breakdown of voting rights in issue (as disclosed by the issuer).

In practice, this imposes an obligation on shareholders to notify any decrease or increase in the total number of securities in issue which may affect the percentage a shareholder owns. Accordingly, shareholders need to monitor changes in the company's share capital, as this may trigger a disclosure obligation even though the shareholder has not personally increased or decreased the level of his shareholding.

38.6 To calculate whether a percentage threshold has been reached or crossed, and whether a notification is therefore required, the proportion of voting rights held should be rounded down to the next whole number.

38.7 Voting rights attached to certain specified types of securities should be disregarded when determining whether a person has a notification obligation (e.g. securities held by a credit institution or investment firm, which fulfil certain requirements, should be disregarded); whilst other voting rights should be disregarded except at thresholds of 5 per cent and 10 per cent and above (for example, voting rights attaching to securities which may be exercisable by a person in his capacity as the operator of an authorised unit trust scheme). Because of the complicated nature of these provisions, a shareholder should take legal advice to establish whether or not he has a notification requirement.

Indirect voting rights

38.8 A shareholder must also notify certain voting rights which it holds indirectly. Indirect shareholders are broadly those that are entitled to acquire, dispose of, or exercise voting rights on behalf of a third party, and who may be able to control the manner in which voting rights are exercised (i.e. those with access to voting rights). This may be by way of securities or financial instruments. DTR 5.2.1R sets out a list of circumstances in which a person will be deemed to be an indirect holder of securities. The provisions of DTR 5.2.1R are not replicated here in full but they include:

■ where a person has agreed with a third party holding voting rights to adopt, by concerted exercise of the voting rights they hold, a "lasting common policy towards the management of the issuer in question" (i.e. a concert party arrangement); and

■ where a person has voting rights which the shareholder may exercise at its own discretion as a proxy in the absence of specific instructions from the shareholders. So, there will be a notification requirement on the chair of a meeting if the chair holds discretionary proxies representing more than 3 per cent of the voting rights. The Financial Services Authority has produced detailed guidance on the notification of proxy holdings in the United Kingdom Listing Authority publication *List!*, issue no. 14 (updated). Again, advice should be taken in this respect.

These indirect holdings must be aggregated with other notifiable interests to calculate the percentage of the holding, but also separately identified, in a notification to the issuer.

38.9 The same list of indirect holdings also applies in establishing whether a person is an indirect holder of qualifying financial instruments. Direct and indirect holdings of certain specified financial instruments are notifiable and must also be aggregated with other notifiable holdings. Qualifying financial instruments include options, futures and other derivative contracts relating to an unconditional entitlement on maturity to acquire issued securities to which voting rights are attached. Where a financial instrument relates to more than one underlying share, a separate notification should be made to each issuer of the underlying securities. Again, a holder of direct or indirect financial instruments should take legal advice if he is in any doubt as to his notification obligations.

Method of notification to the issuer

38.10 DTR 5.8R prescribes the information that must be included in the notification to the issuer. There are slightly different requirements for the notification of securities as opposed to financial instruments. The notification must be effected "as soon as possible", but no later than two trading days following the transaction in question. In calculating the two trading days, the first day is the day after the date on which the relevant person learns/should have learned of the acquisition or disposal or of the possibility of exercising voting rights (regardless of the date on which the acquisition or disposal or possibility of exercising voting rights actually took effect), or is informed about events changing the breakdown of voting rights. There is a concept of deemed knowledge, whereby a person is deemed to have knowledge of the acquisition, disposal or possibility to exercise voting rights no later than two trading days following the transaction if he has instructed a third party to act on his behalf in this regard. Where the transaction is subject to the fulfilment of particular conditions outside the control of the parties, the parties are deemed to have knowledge of the acquisition, disposal or possibility to exercise voting rights only when the appropriate conditions are met. The Financial Services Authority maintains a calendar indicating what are "trading days" in the United Kingdom for this purpose.

38.11   A person who is required to make a notification of voting rights is entitled to appoint another person to make the notification on their behalf. Equally, where two or more persons are required to make a notification, they may arrange for one single notification to be made. However, when the duty to make a notification lies with more than one person, although the notification may be made by a common notification, it does not release any of those persons from their responsibilities in relation to the notification.

38.12   There are also particular issues to consider when notifying proxy holdings – it may be necessary for the shareholder and proxy holder to make a notification – and it is advisable for the proxy holder (the chair, if appropriate) and shareholders to take advice in this regard.

38.13   An undertaking is not required to make a notification if it is made by its parent undertaking instead.

38.14   To calculate whether a threshold is reached, exceeded or fallen below, a shareholder should consider the number of voting rights in existence, according to the monthly disclosure made by the issuer (see Paragraph 38.17), disregarding voting rights attached to any treasury securities held by the issuer.

38.15   In determining whether a disclosure notification is required, a person's holding must be assessed by no later than midnight on the day of the acquisition or disposal (taking account of the net effect of acquisitions and disposals executed during that day).

38.16   There is a standard form (TR-1) available on the Financial Services Authority's website which should be used to make a voting rights notification to the company. Note that shareholders and holders of financial instruments in AIM companies do not need to fill in the Annex. The Financial Services Authority has also published notes on its website to assist in filling out the TR-1 form.

Disclosures by issuers

38.17   So that major shareholders can work out whether or not they have a notification requirement, an issuer must, at the end of each calendar month during which an increase or decrease has occurred, disclose to the public:

- the total number of voting rights and capital in respect of each class of share which it issues; and
- the total number of voting rights attaching to securities of the issuer which are held by it in treasury (DTR 5.6.1R).

38.18   Moreover, on receipt of a notification, the issuer must "as soon as possible", but no later than the end of the third trading day following receipt of the notification, make public the information contained within it. The Financial Services Authority has not set out in DTR5 the format that the notification should take. The Financial Services Authority has issued guidance in the United Kingdom

Listing Authority publication *List!*, issue no. 14 (updated), in which it has set out the options that are available to an issuer upon receipt of a major shareholding notification. These include:

- forwarding the TR-1 form to a Regulatory Information Service;
- forwarding an electronic version of the TR-1 form to a Regulatory Information Service;
- making the announcement in a "free-text format".

Notification obligation on a share buy-back

38.19   On a share buy-back, an issuer must make public the percentage of voting rights attributable to the securities not later than four trading days following the acquisition or disposal of securities where the percentage reaches, exceeds or falls below the thresholds of 5 per cent or 10 per cent of the voting rights. The Financial Services Authority provides further guidance on this area in the United Kingdom Listing Authority publication *List!*, issue no. 14 (updated). The Financial Services Authority has indicated that the following notifications may be required depending on the type of repurchase:

Type of repurchase	Notification required?
Securities held in treasury	If the repurchased securities are held in treasury and if this results in the percentage of voting rights held reaching, exceeding or falling below the thresholds of 5 per cent or 10 per cent of total voting rights.
	The 5 per cent and 10 per cent thresholds are related to the total number of treasury securities held and not whether the transaction itself is greater than 5 per cent or 10 per cent of total voting rights.
Securities which have been cancelled	No disclosure obligation unless the cancellation has the indirect effect of altering the proportion of securities held in treasury so that the proportion reaches, exceeds or falls below the 5 per cent or 10 per cent thresholds.

Non-UK issuers

38.20   Non-UK issuers do not have notification obligations under DTR5. However, both UK and Non-UK issuers have notification obligations under Rule 17 and Schedule 5 to the *AIM Rules for Companies* (see Chapter 28, *Announcements including price sensitive information*).

RULE 17

38.21   In addition to a UK AIM company's obligations under DTR5, all AIM companies remain under the obligation of Rule 17 of the *AIM Rules for Companies* to disclose to a Regulatory Information Service "without delay" any increases or decreases by a single percentage to the holding of a shareholder which has reached 3 per cent.

38.22   Schedule 5 sets out a list of the information that must be included in the notification. This includes:

■ the identity of the shareholder concerned;
■ the date on which the disclosure was made to the company;
■ the date on which the relevant change in shareholding was effected;
■ the price, amount and class of the AIM securities concerned;
■ the nature of the transaction; and
■ the nature and extent of the shareholder's interest in the transaction.

38.23   The AIM Rules do not include a definition of "without delay", however it is clear that this obligation requires a timely notification from the company.

Non-UK issuers

38.24   The Guidance Notes to Rule 17 of the *AIM Rules for Companies* make clear that non-UK issuers must use "all reasonable endeavours" to comply with Rule 17, even though the local law that applies to some AIM companies does not contain requirements similar to the DTRs (i.e. no requirements on shareholders to notify significant changes in their shareholdings).

38.25   Where there is no obligation on shareholders to make a notification to the issuer similar to the requirement on issuers under Rule 17 of the *AIM Rules for Companies*, the Guidance Notes advise the AIM company to amend its articles of association to add a requirement on shareholders with holdings of 3 per cent or more to notify changes above 3 per cent which increase or decrease the holding by a single percentage. These provisions should be similar to those in the DTRs, but noting the two differences between the DTRs and Rule 17 with regard to the time limits for notification and the notification method. However, such provisions may be of limited use in practice if the overseas company's securities are traded via depository interests as the depository may be the only registered shareholder. Non-UK issuer AIM companies are also encouraged to disclose that statutory disclosure of appropriate shareholdings is different, and may not always ensure compliance with, the requirements of Rule 17.

INTERACTION BETWEEN DTR5 AND AIM RULE 17

38.26   The Guidance Notes at the end of the *AIM Rules for Companies* consider the interaction between Rule 17 and DTR5. They indicate that compliance with the DTRs will usually mean that UK AIM companies are complying with the shareholder disclosure obligations in Rule 17 of the AIM Rules, save that:

■ Rule 17 requires a notification to be made "without delay" (i.e. this is a more onerous obligation); and
■ the information required to be released pursuant to Rule 17 must be delivered to a Regulatory Information Service for distribution to the public rather than being "made public" in accordance with the DTRs.

IN PRACTICE

UK issuers and shareholders of UK issuers must comply with both Rule 17 of the *AIM Rules for Companies* and DTR5, although in practice this means that the changes to the shareholdings need to be notified without delay, which is more onerous than would otherwise have been required under DTR5.

Clearly, the situation is also rather different for non-UK AIM companies, which have to notify major shareholdings and may not have appropriate procedures in place. Such companies should amend their Articles of Association to require major shareholders to notify relevant changes in their shareholdings (tracking the wording in DTR5 except where it diverges from Rule 17) and take legal advice on how to meet its obligations in practice.

CHAPTER 39

Mining, oil and gas companies

AT A GLANCE

The London Stock Exchange's specific guidelines relating to mining, oil and gas companies set out certain continuing obligations for these companies. They are the London Stock Exchange's minimum expectations of the content of and the review of notifications by mining, oil and gas companies, which include any notifications which contain results, reserves, estimates etc.

INTRODUCTION

39.1 The London Stock Exchange's guidance to mining, oil and gas companies is not only relevant to companies seeking admission of their securities to AIM, but also places additional ongoing obligations on mining, oil and gas companies when those securities are admitted to trading on AIM.

39.2 The London Stock Exchange's guidelines apply to mining, oil and gas companies, including exploration, prospecting and production companies, but not to consultancy or other companies providing advice or similar services to such companies.

39.3 The guidance sets out the minimum expectations of the London Stock Exchange in relation to companies in such sectors, and both AIM companies and their Nominated Advisers should note them when applying the *AIM Rules for Companies* to mining, oil and gas companies. Whilst the guidance is expressed to represent the minimum expectations of the London Stock Exchange, it must be followed, where applicable. If it is felt that the guidance for mining, oil and gas companies is not applicable or appropriate to a particular company which operates in these sectors, then the company's Nominated Adviser should consult with AIM Regulation, and should not simply disregard the guidance.

NOTIFICATIONS

39.4 The London Stock Exchange's guidance specifies that an internationally recognised standard should be used for all notifications which include results, reserves, estimates etc., and the relevant standard to which such notifications were prepared should be stated in the notification. For these purposes, the AIM team

FIGURE 39.1	Reporting standards for competent person's report

The standard to which a competent person's report should be prepared is an internationally recognised standard that is acceptable under the following codes and/or organisations:	
For mineral resources and reserves	Canadian Institute of Mining, Metallurgy and Petroleum (CIM) Institute of Materials, Minerals and Mining (IMMM) *The Australian Code for Reporting of Exploration Results, Mineral Reserves and Ore Reserves* as published by the Joint Ore Reserves Committee of the Australian Institute of Mining and Metallurgy, Australian Institute of Geoscientists and Mineral Councils of Australia (JORC) Gosstandart of Russia (GOST), the *National Russian Standard on Mining and Minerals* published by the National Certification Body of the Russian Federation *The South African Code for Reporting of Mineral Resources and Mineral Reserves*, as published by the South African Mineral Committee under the auspices of the South African Institute of Mining and Metallurgy (SAMREC) The Society for Mining, Metallurgy and Exploration (SME)
Oil and gas resources and reserves	Canadian Institute on Mining, Metallurgy and Petroleum (CIM) The Society for Petroleum Engineers (SPE).

recognises the standards set out in Figure 39.1, although submissions can be made to AIM Regulation to consider other codes that may be comparable.

39.5   Each notification to which the guidance applies must also contain a glossary of the key terms used in the notification. The glossary should be presented in a similar format to the reserve and/or resource disclosures which were made in the company's most recent AIM admission document (usually from the time it applied for admission to trading on AIM, unless it has undergone a reverse takeover).

39.6   Further, the London Stock Exchange emphasises that drilling updates should be issued and include information on the depth and zones tested, drilling intervals and average grade of mineralisation (in relation to ore and minerals) or the depth and zones tested, rock formation encountered and any liquids/gases recovered (in relation to oil and gas).

39.7   A qualified person from the mining or oil and gas company, or its advisers, should review each notification which includes results, reserves, estimates etc. The notification should include the name, position and qualifications of the qualified person who has reviewed it, together with a statement to the effect that they have reviewed such notification.

39.8 If a notification is required to be made urgently (e.g. if there has been a leak of price sensitive information) and there is insufficient time to review and present the notification of results, reserves, estimates etc., the AIM company must make this clear within the text of the notification and must make sure that any estimate as to reserves or resources is not false or misleading. The company must then present the information, according to an internationally recognised standard, as soon as practicable following the release of the original notification.

DUAL LISTED RESOURCE COMPANIES

39.9 For mining, oil and gas companies which are also listed on the Toronto Stock Exchange or the Australian Stock Exchange, compliance with the guidelines should be relatively straightforward, as the disclosure rules applicable to such exchanges already require verification of notifications of results, reserves, estimates etc. in accordance with applicable standards. In publishing the guidelines, the London Stock Exchange was effectively encouraging AIM mining, oil and gas companies to adopt international best practice. Nevertheless, AIM companies with multiple listings must ensure that they comply with both the *AIM Rules for Companies* and the rules of the other overseas exchange(s). In practice, companies with overseas listings should consider, with their advisers, adopting a protocol for ensuring compliance with both sets of rules and seeking advice on any specific problem regarding conflicts between such rules with AIM Regulation through their Nominated Adviser.

IN PRACTICE

In publishing the guidelines, the London Stock Exchange was encouraging AIM mining, oil and gas companies to comply with international best practice. In practice, many AIM companies will have a suitably qualified individual within their organisation who can review any notifications which include results, reserves, estimates etc. Given that each notification should, in any event, be verified, as the directors in the company are potentially liable for any false or misleading statements in such notification, the guidance should be viewed as a codification of best practice.

Overseas companies

Nearly 20 per cent of companies whose securities are admitted to trading on AIM are companies incorporated outside of the United Kingdom. For these overseas companies, post-admission, there are certain of the *AIM Rules for Companies* which will be particularly relevant and should be borne in mind. These are:

- Rule 10, relating to the timing of notifications;
- Rule 17, relating to the disclosure of relevant changes to significant shareholdings;
- Rules 18 and 19, relating to permissible accounting standards;
- Rule 26, relating to company information that must be provided on the website of the AIM company;
- Rule 30, relating to the language in which documentation required by the *AIM Rules for Companies* is to be presented; and
- Rules 32 and 36, dealing with transferability of securities and the settlement of trustees.

PRINCIPLES OF DISCLOSURE – RULE 10

40.1 Any information which is required by the *AIM Rules for Companies* to be announced by a company through a Regulatory Information Service must, pursuant to Rule 10, be notified in that manner no later than it is published elsewhere. A number of overseas companies whose securities are admitted to trading on AIM are also quoted on other exchanges, and it is important for the company to be aware of the timing of any announcements required by that exchange to ensure compliance with Rule 10. In practice, AIM companies should simultaneously make any announcement required by any market rules of all markets on which its securities are listed or traded.

DISCLOSURE OF CERTAIN INFORMATION – RULE 17

40.2 Among other things, Rule 17 requires companies to notify without delay any relevant changes to significant shareholdings disclosing, in so far as it has this information, the matters set out in Schedule 5 to the *AIM Rules for Companies*. This obligation will arise when the holding of a shareholder, which has already reached 3 per cent of any class of AIM security, increases or decreases by a single percentage. The information required by Schedule 5 to the *AIM Rules for Companies* in relation to those changes includes:

- the identity of the significant shareholder concerned;
- the date on which the disclosure was made to the company;
- the date on which the relevant change to the holding was effected;
- the price, amount and class of the AIM securities concerned;
- the nature of the transaction; and
- the nature and extent of the significant shareholder's interest in the transaction.

40.3 AIM companies incorporated in the United Kingdom will in effect comply with this aspect of Rule 17 when their shareholders and the company itself comply with their obligations pursuant to Chapter 5 of the *Disclosure Rules and Transparency Rules* ("the DTRs"), which is part of the *Financial Services Authority Handbook*. Such companies should, however, note the differences between the requirements of the DTRs and Rule 17: the information must be "notified" under Rule 17, rather than "made public" in accordance with the DTRs; and Rule 17 requires the notification to be issued "without delay", rather than at the end of each calendar month as required by the DTRs. Further details of an AIM company's obligations under Rule 17 are set out in Chapter 28, *Announcements including price sensitive information*, and in respect of the DTRs are set out in Chapter 38, *Disclosure Rules and Transparency Rules*.

40.4 In relation to companies which are not incorporated in the UK, the London Stock Exchange recognises that the shareholders of such companies may not have an obligation under the laws of the country of incorporation to disclose significant shareholdings to the company, or any changes to such shareholdings. However, the company is still under an obligation to use all reasonable endeavours to comply with Rule 17. In this regard, the London Stock Exchange's Guidance Note to Rule 17 of the *AIM Rules for Companies* advises companies to include provisions in their constitutional documents requiring significant shareholders to notify the company of any relevant changes to their shareholdings, in similar terms to the obligations under the DTRs which apply to UK incorporated companies. This is a point which companies may want to consider when planning the resolutions to be included at their next annual general meeting or equivalent meeting although it may be of little practical use where the shares are held through a depository.

40.5 The London Stock Exchange has indicated that it appreciates that it may not reasonably be practicable for an overseas company to change or amend its constitutional documents to account for Rule 17. However, in any event, overseas companies are recommended to include reference to the company's obligation pursuant to this rule in the investor relations section of their website, encouraging shareholders to notify the company of any relevant changes to their shareholding, so that the company will be able to comply with this aspect of Rule 17.

40.6 The Guidance Notes to the *AIM Rules for Companies* also recommend that the company makes appropriate disclosure of the fact that the statutory disclosure regime for significant shareholders in the company's country of incorporation is different to that required by the DTRs and may not always ensure compliance with the requirements of Rule 17. Again, such disclosure would be appropriately made on the investor relations section of the company's website.

INTERIM AND ANNUAL ACCOUNTS – RULES 18 AND 19

40.7   As discussed in Chapter 27, *Financial reporting*, an AIM company is required to prepare half-yearly accounts and annual audited accounts pursuant to Rules 18 and 19 of the *AIM Rules for Companies*. While AIM companies incorporated in a European Economic Area (EEA) country must prepare and present these accounts in accordance with international accounting standards, an AIM company which is incorporated in a non-EEA country is permitted to use either international accounting standards, US generally accepted accounting principles, Canadian generally accepted accounting principles, Australian International Financial Reporting Standards (as issued by the Australian Accounting Standards Board) or Japanese generally accepted accounting principles.

40.8   The London Stock Exchange has also indicated that, pending the finalisation of the European Commission's investigation into the equivalence of accounting standards used by third country issuers of securities to International Financial Reporting Standards, a wider range of generally accepted accounting principles may be permissible in future on AIM.

40.9   As at the date of publication, EEA countries are those countries which comprise the European Union member states, together with Norway, Iceland and Lichtenstein and, for the purposes of the *AIM Rules for Companies*, includes the Channel Islands and Isle of Man.

WEBSITES – RULE 26

40.10   In addition to the information that must be provided on the website of an AIM company incorporated in the UK, as discussed in Chapter 29, *Website disclosure*, an AIM company that is not incorporated in the UK must include a statement that the rights of shareholders may be different from the rights of shareholders in a UK incorporated company.

LANGUAGE – RULE 30

40.11   Companies whose securities are admitted to trading on AIM but who operate in jurisdictions other than the United Kingdom should also be aware that any documents sent to shareholders and any information required by the *AIM Rules for Companies* should be presented in English pursuant to Rule 30 of the *AIM Rules for Companies*. The Guidance Notes to the *AIM Rules for Companies* do provide, however, that where the original documents or information are not printed in English, an English translation may be provided.

TRANSFERABILITY OF SECURITIES – RULE 32

40.12 Pursuant to Rule 32 of the *AIM Rules for Companies*, an AIM company must ensure that any of its securities which are admitted to trading on AIM are freely transferable.

40.13 Rule 32 does provide a couple of specific exceptions to the requirement that securities are freely transferable, which include where the local law of a particular jurisdiction imposes restrictions on the transferability. This Rule may be of particular use to overseas companies who are applying for the admission of their securities to trading on AIM where their local law contains such restrictions. An example of this is commonly encountered in Jersey, where certain anti-money laundering requirements need to be completed before a person can be entered into the register of members as the holder of that security.

SETTLEMENT – RULE 36

40.14 A general principle of the *AIM Rules for Companies* is embodied in Rule 36, which provides that a company must ensure that appropriate settlement arrangements are in place and AIM securities must be eligible for electronic settlement, unless AIM Regulation agrees otherwise. Whilst such derogations are extremely rare, the situation where the London Stock Exchange envisages these derogations being useful is where a company's local law prohibits electronic settlement.

IN PRACTICE

The London Stock Exchange has indicated that it considers AIM to be a market designed to meet the needs of companies from around the world. In general, the *AIM Rules for Companies* are relatively relaxed in comparison with the rules of certain other exchanges, including the Main Market of the London Stock Exchange. The rules discussed in this chapter have particular relevance for overseas companies yet should not represent any great hardship for a company once it has undergone the due diligence involved in the admission to trading on AIM process. The Guidance Notes to the *AIM Rules for Companies* take into account certain differences in statutory regimes in a company's country of incorporation, and the London Stock Exchange has certainly indicated a desire to retain a flexible regulation regime and to encourage overseas companies to continue to join AIM.

CHAPTER 41

Disciplinary matters

AT A GLANCE

Breaches of the *AIM Rules for Companies* and the *AIM Rules for Nominated Advisers* ("the AIM Rules") are dealt with according to the disciplinary regime set down by the London Stock Exchange in the *AIM Disciplinary Procedures and Appeals Handbook*. The process is designed to be transparent, fair and to maintain the integrity of the London Stock Exchange.

After an investigation into a breach, the London Stock Exchange will decide what is the appropriate level of disciplinary proceedings to determine the allegation against the AIM company or Nominated Adviser that is the subject of the proceedings, by taking into account a number of factors set out in the *AIM Disciplinary Procedures and Appeals Handbook*. If the breach only merits a moderate sanction, this can be administered directly by the London Stock Exchange. More serious breaches will be referred to the AIM Executive Panel or the AIM Disciplinary Committee, depending on the appropriate range of potential sanctions.

The AIM company or Nominated Adviser that is the subject of the proceedings has the opportunity to put forward its case at any hearing that takes place. If either party believes that the outcome of the disciplinary proceedings is unfair, there is a process that allows for any decision of the London Stock Exchange to be appealed. The appeals process followed depends on the tribunal of first instance.

INTRODUCTION

41.1   The rules that govern the conduct of the AIM companies and Nominated Advisers are supported by a disciplinary process whose effective operation is a vital component of the regulatory regime. It gives the London Stock Exchange the capacity to take corrective and, where appropriate, punitive action against any parties who breach the AIM Rules.

41.2   The disciplinary process is set down in the *AIM Disciplinary Procedures and Appeals Handbook*. The *AIM Disciplinary Procedures and Appeals Handbook* is deemed to form part of the AIM Rules, so all AIM companies and Nominated Advisers are subject to the procedures that it sets down. However, neither the directors of AIM companies nor its Nominated Advisers can be held liable for a breach of the *AIM Rules for Companies*. The *AIM Disciplinary Procedures and*

Appeals Handbook is in two parts: the disciplinary process, and the non-disciplinary appeal procedure. There are three levels to the disciplinary process and the AIM company or Nominated Adviser that is the subject of the proceedings (the "Subject") will be referred to the most appropriate, depending on the range of sanctions likely to be imposed. These levels (on an escalating scale of the severity of potential penalty) are the London Stock Exchange itself, the AIM Executive Panel and the AIM Disciplinary Committee (the "Disciplinary Bodies", each a "Disciplinary Body"). The non-disciplinary appeal procedure enables the Subject to appeal any decision of the Disciplinary Bodies.

41.3 The *AIM Disciplinary Procedures and Appeals Handbook* was revised in February 2007, in order to make the disciplinary process more effective. This increased the range of disciplinary measures available to the London Stock Exchange and made the London Stock Exchange's approach to the disciplinary process more transparent.

41.4 This chapter will cover:

- the London Stock Exchange's approach to the disciplinary process;
- the investigation preceding the disciplinary process;
- the decision of the London Stock Exchange;
- the proceedings of the AIM Executive Panel;
- the proceedings of the AIM Disciplinary Committee; and
- the proceedings of the AIM Appeals Committee.

THE LONDON STOCK EXCHANGE'S APPROACH TO DISCIPLINARY MATTERS

41.5 The London Stock Exchange has recently clarified its objective and approach when dealing with disciplinary matters. The *AIM Disciplinary Procedures and Appeals Handbook* states that its approach is "aimed at maintaining the integrity, orderliness, transparency and good reputation" of AIM. These clear principles have been instituted as the standards by which both the disciplinary process and the conduct of market participants will be assessed. If a Subject or the London Stock Exchange does not believe that the disciplinary process has followed this approach, any of these principles may be used in support of an appeal.

41.6 The *AIM Disciplinary Procedures and Appeals Handbook* has also introduced the factors that the London Stock Exchange takes into account when considering the appropriate disciplinary action in relation to a rule breach. These factors establish a framework within which any Subject knows that its alleged breach will be assessed. This is designed to avoid potential misunderstandings between the parties and to make the process more efficient, by establishing common ground for the parties to discuss.

41.7 The factors that are considered are set out in the *AIM Disciplinary Procedures and Appeals Handbook*, and are as follows:

- the nature and seriousness of the breach;
- the duration and frequency of the misconduct which caused the breach;

- how the rule breach came to light;
- the actual or potential impact of the rule breach, and any other repercussions;
- the extent to which the rule breach was deliberate or reckless;
- the general compliance history of the Subject, and the specific history regarding the rule breach in question;
- consistent and fair application of the rules (with regard to any precedents of similar rule breaches); and
- the responsiveness and conduct of the Subject in relation to the matter under investigation.

It is not yet clear whether the Disciplinary Bodies will give more weight to some of these factors over others, so a Subject should be mindful of them all.

41.8 When addressing a disciplinary matter, the burden of proof is on the London Stock Exchange in keeping with the civil nature of the proceedings. The standard of proof used is the balance of probabilities: that is, the London Stock Exchange must prove that it is more likely than not that there has been a breach of the *AIM Rule(s)* in question.

41.9 It is also worth noting that the London Stock Exchange has a general duty to keep all disciplinary matters confidential while the procedure is ongoing, provided that no disclosure is permitted or required by law. Further, there are circumstances where the London Stock Exchange may make public certain aspects of proceedings, and these are dealt with in Paragraphs 41.34, 41.43 and 41.54. In connection with this, the London Stock Exchange reserves the right to publish details of the findings of any part of the disciplinary process (without identifying the relevant Subject) if it believes that doing so would be of assistance to the market. For example, if a specific AIM Rule is being breached on a regular basis, the London Stock Exchange may publish a bulletin to market participants highlighting the reasons that certain Subjects have found themselves breaching the rule and the sanctions imposed for such a breach.

THE INVESTIGATION PRECEDING THE DISCIPLINARY PROCESS

41.10 AIM Regulation is divided into several sub-units, one of which deals with investigations and enforcement. When a potential breach of the AIM Rules has come to the attention of AIM Regulation, it will be passed to the Investigations and Enforcement sub-unit, which will begin the investigation by liaising with the relevant Nominated Adviser.

41.11 The investigation can be a lengthy process, especially if a breach by an AIM company is being investigated because this involves both the relevant AIM company and its Nominated Adviser. Although the Nominated Adviser has an obligation under the *AIM Rules for Nominated Advisers* to provide the London Stock Exchange with any information that it requires, and to liaise with the London Stock Exchange when requested to do so, the Nominated Adviser balances this with its duty to its AIM company client under investigation. This does not mean that the Nominated Adviser acts in an untoward manner; simply that the Nominated Adviser makes sure that it is certain about the accuracy of the information provided to the London Stock Exchange, so as not to misrepresent the AIM company or breach its obligations under the AIM Rules.

41.12   The investigation will usually begin by correspondence, with requests from the London Stock Exchange for documents relevant to, and accounts of events from key personnel involved in, the breach. If this does not establish the full extent of the breach, members of the Investigations and Enforcement sub-unit will interview the key personnel involved and may also conduct full reviews of the relevant files. When this has been concluded, the Investigations and Enforcement sub-unit will make its recommendations to the management of AIM Regulation, who will then decide what should be the next step.

THE DECISION OF THE LONDON STOCK EXCHANGE

41.13   Where there is found to be a breach of the AIM Rules by a Subject, the options available to AIM Regulation are:

- to order the Subject to take action to remedy the breach;
- to issue a warning notice to the Subject;
- to refer the matter to the AIM Executive Panel; or
- to refer the matter to the AIM Disciplinary Committee.

It is worth noting that all of these form part of the disciplinary process, and a note of the London Stock Exchange's decision will be kept in the London Stock Exchange's records.

41.14   When the Subject is ordered to remedy the breach, it will also usually be required to implement sufficient measures to prevent the breach reoccurring. The London Stock Exchange will require the Nominated Adviser's confirmation that this has been done; usually in the form of a minute of the Subject's next board of directors meeting confirming action has been taken, or a copy of briefing notes reminding the Subject of its responsibilities under the *AIM Rules for Companies* or *AIM Rules for Nominated Advisers*, as appropriate. For example, this type of preventative action is not uncommon where an AIM company has failed to comply with its obligations under Rule 17 of the *AIM Rules for Companies* (Disclosure of Miscellaneous Information).

41.15   The concept of the warning notice was introduced by the revision of the disciplinary process in 2007. It is an intermediate measure, designed to be used where a breach is not so serious that it justifies a fine, censure or more serious action, but where simply remedying the cause of the breach is not sufficient. For example, this could be used where there has been a technical breach of a rule requiring an AIM company to notify a transaction as required by Rule 12 of the *AIM Rules for Companies* (Substantial Transactions).

41.16   If the alleged breach is more serious, the London Stock Exchange makes a decision whether to refer it to the Executive Panel or the Disciplinary Committee based on the facts that it has gathered so far. Although this may appear to be making a judgement of the likely outcome of the proceedings, the investigatory process is sufficiently thorough for the London Stock Exchange to be able to ascertain at this stage the range of likely sanctions if the Subject is found guilty of the alleged breach.

41.17   The two principal considerations for the London Stock Exchange are usually the likely amount of a potential fine – which will depend on the extent of financial benefit that the Subject has gained from the breach – or where there is a significant factor that justifies the case being put to the Disciplinary Committee, for example where the case is of such importance that the public needs to know about it.

41.18   If the London Stock Exchange has any doubt about which tribunal of first instance is more appropriate for the case, it is likely to refer it to the Executive Panel, as there will remain the option of referring it on to the Disciplinary Committee if the Executive Panel does not believe it has a sufficient sanction at its disposal.

41.19   The London Stock Exchange's decision to take further action gives the Subject a strong indication of the range of sanctions that may be imposed on it. At any stage thereafter, the London Stock Exchange and the Subject may decide to negotiate a settlement. The negotiation of the settlement may delay the disciplinary action, or halt it altogether if it has already begun.

41.20   If the parties agree a settlement, it will be submitted to the Executive Panel or Disciplinary Committee (depending on which body was to deal with the breach) ("the Relevant Tribunal") for approval. The Relevant Tribunal looks favourably upon the fact that the parties have worked together to reach a settlement and are jointly applying for the consent order. If the Relevant Tribunal approves the settlement, it will make a consent order without delay and this, as well as any penalties agreed, will have immediate effect.

41.21   If the Tribunal does not approve the consent order (usually it will only refuse approval if the sanction agreed by the parties is not appropriate to the scale of breach), the disciplinary process will re-commence from the stage that it was halted. In keeping with the principles of civil law, there will be no reference to the attempts to negotiate a settlement when the Subject's case comes before the Relevant Tribunal. If the request for approval of a consent order is being put before the Disciplinary Committee, the Subject may ask to remain anonymous, although the Disciplinary Committee may insist that its identity be disclosed to them.

41.22   The fact that both parties enter into the settlement process willingly, in order to avoid the more lengthy disciplinary process, obviates the possibility of the Subject appealing against it.

THE EXECUTIVE PANEL

41.23   The Executive Panel is charged with dealing with the less serious breaches of the AIM Rules. It has two discrete functions within the disciplinary process. Its first function is to act as a tribunal of first instance, hearing charges against a Subject and determining the appropriate action, if the allegation is proven.

Sanctions

41.24   The range of action available to the Executive Panel where it finds that a Subject has breached the AIM Rules is:

- censuring the Subject (in the form of a document setting out the relevant facts and the London Stock Exchange's findings, which will be part of the Subject's record but not made public);
- fining the Subject up to £50,000 (this was increased from a maximum of £25,000 when the disciplinary process was revised in 2007); or
- referring the case to the Disciplinary Committee (if the Executive Panel considers that it does not have the authority to impose a sufficient sanction; in this instance, no public announcement will be made until the Disciplinary Committee has reached a decision).

41.25   The Executive Panel's second function is to act as an appellate tribunal. It hears and determines appeals against decisions of the London Stock Exchange that have been made without reference to a tribunal. In this role, it can quash or vary a decision of the London Stock Exchange if it is satisfied that the decision was a misinterpretation or erroneous application of the AIM Rules, or that the decision was not justified on the basis of the evidence.

Composition of the Executive Panel

41.26   The Executive Panel is composed of experienced members of the London Stock Exchange's staff. In the interests of fairness, it may not include anybody who was involved in the investigation into the breach in question or, where acting as an appellate tribunal, anybody involved in the decision being appealed. There must be between three and five members, including a chairman who is appointed by the other members.

41.27   If the Subject objects to the involvement of a member of the Executive Panel on the grounds of conflict of interest or previous involvement, it must notify the Executive Panel promptly. The Subject may not appeal if the Executive Panel decides not to uphold this objection.

The opening process

41.28   When acting as a tribunal of first instance, the first step is for the London Stock Exchange to compose and send a statement of case to the Subject, setting out the charge(s) and all material facts, and attaching relevant documents. Within five business days of receiving this, the Subject should respond by issuing a statement setting out its defence and all material facts and attaching all material statements. The London Stock Exchange will then submit both statements, plus supporting documents, to the Executive Panel.

41.29   The process for the Executive Panel to act as an appellate tribunal is begun by the appellant serving a notice of appeal on the London Stock Exchange within ten business days of the London Stock Exchange's decision. Its contents should include the grounds of appeal and all material facts, and supporting documents should be attached. The Executive Panel will then be appointed and the London Stock Exchange will submit to it a statement in response, plus supporting documents, within a further ten business days.

Proceedings

41.30   Proceedings normally take place through the consideration of documents only. There will only be an oral hearing if either party notifies the chairman that it would be essential in order to establish all of the relevant facts. In this instance, the oral hearing would be held in private. Although both parties will be given five business days' notice, such a hearing may be held in the absence of either of the parties.

Decisions

41.31   The Executive Panel will deliberate at any time and may make its decisions on a majority basis. Once it has done so, the decision will be communicated to the parties in writing, along with the reasons for it, details of any penalty being imposed and a time limit for lodging an appeal (which must not be less than ten business days after the date that the decision was served on the parties). Fines must be paid within 30 days unless the Subject decides to appeal them.

Launching an appeal

41.32   Decisions of the Executive Panel can be appealed to the AIM Appeals Committee ("the Appeals Committee"). The notice to appeal must be served in line with the time limits imposed by the Executive Panel. The Appeals Committee will arrange a hearing as soon as reasonably practicable. However, if the appeal is on the grounds of new evidence having come to light, there will be a rehearing of the Executive Panel, which provides a further opportunity for the appellant, because the appellant will still have the right to appeal to the Appeals Committee afterwards, if required.

THE AIM DISCIPLINARY COMMITTEE

41.33   The Disciplinary Committee deals with more serious breaches of the AIM Rules than those dealt with by the Executive Committee. In particular, the integral role of the Nominated Adviser to the regulatory regime means that any allegation that a Nominated Adviser has acted in a way likely to impair the reputation or integrity of AIM will be referred to the Disciplinary Committee.

Sanctions

41.34   The range of action available to the Disciplinary Committee if it finds that a Subject has committed a breach of the AIM Rules is broader than that available to the Executive Committee, and consists of:

- censuring the Subject (this can be publicly relayed to the market);
- fining the Subject (there is no cap on the amount of the fine);
- publishing the action taken and the reasons behind it; and/or
- removing an AIM company's securities from AIM or a Nominated Adviser from the register (as appropriate).

Composition of the Disciplinary Committee

41.35 The membership of the Disciplinary Committee is not drawn from the London Stock Exchange but from a panel of external advisers. The panel consists of market practitioners, including lawyers, corporate finance advisers and sometimes investors, all of whom have been approved by the AIM Advisory Group as having sufficient levels of experience in dealing with the AIM marketplace. They are able to bring greater independence and a wider perspective to their role than members of the London Stock Exchange.

41.36 The Disciplinary Committee must have between three and seven members, including the chairman. This can include any person co-opted by the Disciplinary Committee because they have experience relevant to the proceedings, for example being an expert in a particular industry sector. The chairman may also appoint a legal adviser to advise the Disciplinary Committee, who will be independent.

41.37 The chairman will also deal with any instance of a potential conflict of interest that a member of the Disciplinary Committee or either party brings to his attention. If a new member of the Disciplinary Committee or a new legal adviser needs to be appointed (either as a replacement because of a conflict or illness, or because he is being co-opted) once proceedings have begun, each party must consent. If no consent is given, the Disciplinary Committee may decide not to, or may not have the quorum to, continue with the proceedings, so a new Disciplinary Committee will be appointed.

Opening process

41.38 Usually, the first notification that a Disciplinary Committee is required will come from the London Stock Exchange when it has concluded its investigation. However, it may also come from the Executive Panel if it refers a case that it does not believe it has suitable authority to administer. In both instances, this will be via a statement of case, setting out the charge and a summary of the main facts, which will then be served on the Subject (who may then serve a statement in response setting out the material facts and attaching relevant documents).

41.39 As a reflection of the more complex nature of matters heard by the Disciplinary Committee, either party can also inform the Disciplinary Committee whether or not it would like a pre-hearing review. The chairman may also decide that certain facts or issues need to be clarified and has a number of options, including holding one or more pre-hearing reviews, for this. The chairman also has the authority to give directions relating to the proceedings, such as the time and place for the hearing, the requirement for disclosure by any party, setting time limits and making any order for costs.

Proceedings

41.40 The Disciplinary Committee always resolves matters by way of a hearing, usually in private unless requested otherwise by the Subject. Either party may have legal representation at the hearing. The hearing closely follows the procedure of a civil court; after each allegation has been read, the Subject will state whether it is admitted. With the London Stock Exchange going first, each party will then present its evidence and/or call witnesses, who can be cross-examined by the other party and then re-examined, as well as be questioned by members of the Disciplinary Committee itself. The Disciplinary Committee is not subject to the same restrictions as a court of law on evidence; for example, it does not require evidence to be given under oath and may admit hearsay evidence.

Decisions

41.41 The Disciplinary Committee is not compelled to deliberate and make its decisions within a certain timeframe or in the presence of the parties. As with the Executive Panel, it may reach decisions on a majority basis, and need not reveal this fact. Where the members of the Disciplinary Committee have voted equally, the chairman has a second vote, which must be exercised in favour of the Subject, so the Subject will not be sanctioned unless the allegation is reasonably clear-cut in the eyes of the Disciplinary Committee.

41.42 Once the decision has been made, the parties will be notified in writing of it, together with any penalty being imposed, the reason for the decision, any order for costs to be paid and a time limit for lodging an appeal.

41.43 As with decisions of the Executive Panel, any fine must be paid within 30 days of receipt of the Disciplinary Committee's decision. However, the decision, penalty and costs order cannot take effect until the expiry of the time for lodging an appeal. Usually, this will be ten business days from the date that the decision has been deemed served on the parties, although the Disciplinary Committee may order a shorter period in exceptional circumstances. The decision may be published, in whole or in summary, but if the penalty is a private censure, the identity of the Subject must not be revealed.

Costs

41.44 As part of the proceedings, either party may make a submission on costs. The Disciplinary Committee can then make an order for costs and this can be made regardless of the outcome of the case. The costs that can be ordered include those of the Disciplinary Committee, the legal adviser or the other party. The provisions on this are drafted to protect the London Stock Exchange, which can only be ordered to pay costs if the Disciplinary Committee believes that it has acted in bad faith in bringing or conducting the proceedings.

Appeals

41.45 If a Subject wishes to appeal the decision, it must serve the relevant documents on the Secretary to the Disciplinary Committee (this should include any new evidence that it wishes to rely on). The Secretary will notify this to the Chairman of the Appeals Committee, who will arrange a hearing.

THE APPEALS COMMITTEE

41.46 The Appeals Committee hears and determines appeals that are brought against decisions of both the Executive Panel and the Disciplinary Committee, which can be brought by either the London Stock Exchange or the Subject. It has the authority to uphold, quash or vary any previous decisions, which includes increasing the level of any fines (to the maximum of £50,000 if a decision of the Executive Panel is being appealed, but with no limit if a decision of the Disciplinary Committee is being appealed).

Composition

41.47 In common with the Disciplinary Committee, the members of the Appeals Committee are drawn from the panel of market practitioners approved by the AIM Advisory Group, and there will be between three and seven members. However, this cannot include anyone who heard the same case while serving on the Disciplinary Committee, nor any member of the London Stock Exchange's staff.

41.48 Many of the same provisions shall apply to the Appeals Committee as apply to the Disciplinary Committee, in relation to:

■ the chairman's capacity to appoint a legal adviser, who will be independent of either party;
■ the requirement for a member of the Appeals Committee to notify the secretary of the Appeals Committee in the event of a possible conflict of interest; and
■ the appointment of a further person to the Appeals Committee once proceedings have begun.

Opening procedure

41.49 Once the party that wishes to appeal has served notice to appeal and the Appeals Committee has been selected, both the appellant and any other party may submit further statements plus supporting documents, especially if they would like fresh evidence to be considered.

Proceedings

41.50 If both parties consent in writing, the appeal may be by written submission only. Any hearing will be in private, although the appellant may request otherwise.

41.51 Unless there are exceptional circumstances and the Appeals Committee permits it, no party may present evidence (including calling new witnesses) that was not available to the tribunal of first instance. This is to ensure that parties are as thorough as possible when submitting their initial case and so that, as much as possible, the Appeals Committee is deliberating on no matters other than possible errors in fact or in law.

Decisions

41.52   Like the Disciplinary Committee, the Appeals Committee may:

- deliberate at any time;
- reach a decision in the absence of the parties; and
- reach a decision on a majority basis, without needing to state that publicly.

41.53   Although the chairman will have a second, casting vote, this shall always be in favour of the appellant (in contrast to the casting vote of the chairman of the Disciplinary Committee, which is always in favour of the Subject). However, in order to quash or vary a previous decision, the Appeals Committee must be satisfied that there has been a misinterpretation or erroneous application of the AIM Rules, or that the earlier decision was not justified on the evidence.

41.54   Once the decision has been made, the Appeals Committee will inform the parties of it in writing, including its reasons, any statement for publication and any order for costs to be made. Any order for costs will be on the same basis as any order made by the Disciplinary Committee.

41.55   Any appeal of a decision of the Appeals Committee will need to be through the civil courts, which will deal with the appeal under the principles of judicial review.

IN PRACTICE

The disciplinary regime is set out in order to provide a thorough means by which breaches of the AIM Rules can be both determined and, if necessary, punished. The changes set out by the London Stock Exchange in 2007, incorporating a greater range of sanctions and more transparency, were designed to increase the capacity of the London Stock Exchange to deal fairly with alleged breaches by market participants.

The regime strikes a balance between resolving disciplinary issues as expeditiously as possible and providing a full range of sanctions if required. The objective is to encourage as much co-operation from the relevant AIM companies and Nominated Advisers as possible, so that disciplinary matters are resolved without recourse to external proceedings. If the disciplinary regime enables this to be done efficiently, there is less likelihood of AIM being damaged by breaches of its rules.

Part V
Corporate Governance

INTRODUCTION

AIM companies do not have a formal requirement that they comply with the *Combined Code on Corporate Governance* or the *Quoted Companies Alliance Guidelines* and the *National Association of Pension Funds Guidelines*.

Practice as to which of these guidelines are followed by AIM companies is determined, in part, in consultation with a company's Nominated Adviser, and certain commitments will be given in an AIM admission document.

Chapter 42, *Corporate governance for AIM companies*, gives a brief overview of the principal framework for corporate governance in relation to AIM companies.

Chapters 43 to 45 deal with the proposed committees that an AIM company will set up to give effect to good corporate governance, namely:

- Chapter 43, *Remuneration committee*;
- Chapter 44, *Audit committee*; and
- Chapter 45, *Nomination committee*.

Chapter 46, *Share dealing code*, looks at codes for dealing in securities.

Chapter 47, *Relationship agreements*, looks at the agreement between the AIM company and any substantial shareholder which governs their relationship.

Chapter 48, *Health, safety, social and environment committee*, looks at the committee which is often set up by mining and oil and gas companies.

CHAPTER 42

Corporate governance for AIM companies

AT A GLANCE

Corporate governance is principally a means of safeguarding shareholders' interests. It centres around the way in which companies are managed and controlled, ensuring that those persons responsible for the management of the company (i.e. the directors) account to shareholders in relation to matters where transparency, fairness, independence, integrity and responsibility are required.

The *Combined Code* is the principal framework for corporate governance in the United Kingdom today. Whilst there is no formal requirement for AIM companies to comply with the *Combined Code*, the principal provisions and recommendations set out in the *Combined Code* should be followed by companies trading on AIM as a matter of good practice, given that both the *QCA Guidelines* and the *NAPF Guidelines*, which were specifically drafted for AIM companies, are derived from the *Combined Code*.

Practice as to which guidelines are followed by AIM companies is determined, in part, in consultation with a company's Nominated Adviser. Many AIM companies base their corporate governance regime on the full provisions of the *Combined Code*, ensuring, as a minimum, that they address the specific matters set out in these guidelines.

This chapter gives a brief overview of the principal framework for corporate governance in relation to AIM companies, looking at the provisions of the *Combined Code*, the *QCA Guidelines*, the *NAPF Guidelines* and reporting procedures.

INTRODUCTION

42.1 Corporate governance is principally a means of safeguarding shareholders' interests. It centres around the way in which companies are managed and controlled, ensuring that those persons responsible for the management of the company, i.e. the directors, account to shareholders in relation to matters where transparency, fairness, independence, integrity and responsibility are required. Over the past 15 years, a number of independent reports have been carried out in the United Kingdom in relation to corporate governance. The first report (the Cadbury Report) was published in 1992 and was followed, three years later, by the Greenbury Report. In 1998, the Hampel Report resulted in the publication of the *Combined Code*, which is the principal framework for corporate governance in the United Kingdom today. Following a number of high profile corporate failures, most notably the collapse of Enron and Worldcom, in April 2002, Derek Higgs was appointed by the then Department of Trade and Industry to review the role and effectiveness of non-executive directors in the United Kingdom. At the same time, a review of audit committees was carried out by a group led by Sir Robin Smith. As a result of the Higgs Review and the Smith Report, both completed in early 2003, a revised consolidated version of the *Combined Code* was published. In July 2006, the Financial Reporting Committee published an amended version of the *Combined Code* and this version applies to reporting years beginning on or after 1 November 2006.

42.2   Directors of AIM companies should be aware of the principles and detailed provisions of the *Combined Code*, being the code of desirable corporate governance practices and procedures for public companies trading on markets in the United Kingdom. The *Listing Rules* require companies whose securities are admitted to the Official List and admitted to trading on the Main Market of the London Stock Exchange to adhere to the *Combined Code* by way of a "comply or explain" approach, whereby the company must detail the extent to which it has complied with the *Combined Code* in its annual report and, where it has not complied with the *Combined Code*, explain why not. Whilst there is no formal requirement for AIM companies to comply with the *Combined Code*, the principal provisions and recommendations set out in the *Combined Code* should be followed by companies trading on AIM as a matter of good practice.

42.3   Given that AIM companies are not formally required to comply with the *Combined Code*, in July 2005, the Quoted Companies Alliance (QCA) published a set of corporate governance guidelines specifically for smaller companies entitled *Corporate Governance Guidelines for AIM Companies* (the "*QCA Guidelines*"). The QCA is an organisation which seeks to promote the interests of smaller quoted companies (being companies outside the FTSE 350). The *QCA Guidelines* are a simple set of guidelines which are largely based on standards set out in the *Combined Code*, and which are intended to provide a minimum standard for AIM companies to follow.

42.4   In March 2007, another organisation, the National Association of Pension Funds (NAPF) also published a set of guidelines, entitled *The Corporate Governance Policy and Voting Guidelines for AIM Companies*. Once again, the *NAPF Guidelines* are principally derived from the *Combined Code* and the introduction to the *NAPF Guidelines* states that "boards of directors of AIM companies should be familiar with the main principles of the [*Combined Code*] and should seek to apply them as appropriate to each company's circumstances".

42.5   Given that both the *QCA Guidelines* and the *NAPF Guidelines*, which were specifically drafted for AIM companies, are derived from the *Combined Code*, it is often recommended that AIM companies base their corporate governance regime on the full provisions of the *Combined Code*, ensuring, as a minimum, that they address the specific matters set out in these guidelines. The provisions of the *Combined Code* are considered further below, together with Figure 42.1, highlighting those matters covered by the *QCA Guidelines*.

42.6 In addition to the requirements of the *Combined Code* and *NAPF Guidelines* outlined above, AIM companies are required to comply with the continuing obligations contained in the *AIM Rules for Companies* (for further details of these see Part IV) as well as any specific corporate governance provisions contained within the company legislation of its country of incorporation.

THE *COMBINED CODE*

42.7 Many of the *Combined Code* provisions are reflected in the documents which will be adopted by the company at the time of its admission to trading on AIM, whilst others should be adopted as a matter of good practice. Each main principle of the *Combined Code* tends to be supported by a number of supporting principles and then a number of *Combined Code* provisions which are effectively guidelines on how a company can meet the objectives of the main principle. A summary of the principal areas of the *Combined Code* is set out below.

Directors

42.8 Every company should be headed by an effective board of directors which is collectively responsible for the success of the company (Principle A.1):

- The board of directors should meet sufficiently regularly to discharge its duties effectively (Provision A.1.1).

42.9 There should be a clear division of responsibilities at the head of the company between the running of the board of directors and executive responsibility for the running of the company's business. No single individual should have unfettered powers of decision (Principle A.2):

- The roles of chairman and chief executive should not be exercised by the same individual and the division of their responsibilities should be clearly established, set out in writing and agreed by the board of directors (Provision A.2.1).

42.10 The board of directors should include a balance of executive and non-executive directors (and, in particular, independent non-executive directors) such that no individual or small group of individuals can dominate the board of directors' decision taking (Principle A.3):

- Provision A.3.1 states examples of situations where a director may not be considered to be independent.

The question of independent directors for AIM companies is considered in more detail in Paragraph 42.29.

42.11 There should be a formal, rigorous and transparent procedure for the appointment of new directors to the board of directors (Principle A.4):

- There should be a nomination committee which should lead the process of the board of directors' appointments and make recommendations to the board of directors (Provision A.4.1).

Further information on nomination committees is set out in Chapter 45, *Nomination committee*.

42.12   The board of directors should be supplied, in a timely manner, with information in a form and of a quality appropriate to enable it to discharge its duties. All directors should receive induction on joining the board of directors and should regularly update and refresh their skills and knowledge (Principle A.5).

42.13   The board of directors should undertake a formal and rigorous annual evaluation of its own performance and that of its committees and individual directors (Principle A.6).

42.14   All directors should be submitted for re-election at regular intervals, subject to continued satisfactory performance. The board of directors should ensure planned and progressive refreshing of the board of directors (Principle A.7).

Remuneration

42.15   Levels of remuneration should be sufficient to attract, retain and motivate directors of the quality required to run the company successfully, but a company should avoid paying more than is necessary for this purpose. A significant proportion of executive directors' remuneration should be structured so as to link rewards to corporate and individual performance (Principle B.1).

42.16   There should be a formal and transparent procedure for developing policy on executive remuneration and for fixing the remuneration packages of individual directors. No director should be involved in deciding his or her own remuneration (Principle B.2):

- The board of directors should establish a remuneration committee of at least three (two in the case of smaller companies) independent non-executive directors (Provision B.2.1).
- Further information on remuneration committees is set out in Chapter 43, *Remuneration committee*.

Financial reporting

42.17   The board of directors should present a balanced and understandable assessment of the company's position and prospects (Principle C.1);

42.18   The board of directors should maintain a sound system of internal control to safeguard shareholders' investment and the company's assets (Principle C.2);

42.19   The board of directors should establish formal and transparent arrangements for considering how they should apply the financial reporting and internal control principles and for maintaining an appropriate relationship with the company's auditors (Principle C.3):

- The board of directors should establish an audit committee of at least three (two in the case of smaller companies) non-executive directors with written terms of reference which deal clearly with authority and duties (Provisions C.3.1/C.3.2).
- The audit committee should review arrangements by which staff of the company may, in confidence, raise concerns about possible improprieties in matters of financial reporting or other matters (Provision C.3.4).

- The audit committee should monitor and review the effectiveness of the internal audit activities (Provision C.3.5).
- The audit committee should have primary responsibility for making a recommendation on the appointment, reappointment and removal of the external auditors (Provision C.3.6).
- The annual report should explain to shareholders how, if the auditor provides non-audit services, auditor objectivity and independence is safeguarded (Provision C.3.7).

Further information on audit committees is set on in Chapter 44, *Audit committee*.

Relations with shareholders

42.20 There should be a dialogue with shareholders based on the mutual understanding of objectives. The board of directors as a whole has responsibility for ensuring that a satisfactory dialogue with shareholders takes place (Principle D.1).

42.21 The board of directors should use the AGM to communicate with investors and to encourage their participation (Principle D.2).

THE *QCA* GUIDELINES

42.22 The *QCA Guidelines* set out the minimum standard of corporate governance which should be followed by AIM companies. Figure 42.1 details the relevant *QCA Guideline* and its nearest equivalent principle/provision of the *Combined Code*.

42.23 The *QCA Guidelines* also set out the minimum requirements regarding reporting on corporate governance matters and these are considered further in Paragraphs 42.35 to 42.38.

THE *NAPF* GUIDELINES

42.24 The *NAPF Guidelines* for AIM companies are based on the *NAPF Corporate Governance Policy and Voting Guidelines* (the "*NAPF Policy*") which is largely derived from the *Combined Code*. As a starting point, the *NAPF Guidelines* state that "the boards of directors of AIM companies should be familiar with the Main Principles of the *Combined Code* and should seek to apply them as appropriate to each company's circumstances". The *NAPF Guidelines* then consider certain of the key matters covered by the requirements of the *Combined Code* and the *QCA Guidelines* and addresses how smaller AIM companies in particular should apply these. Matters covered include those detailed below.

Combined roles of the chairman and chief executive

42.25 In relation to the combined roles of the chairman and chief executive, the *NAPF Guidelines* follow the *NAPF Policy*. The *NAPF Policy* reiterates the *Combined Code* and *QCA Guidelines* provision that the functions of chairman and

FIGURE 42.1	Comparison of *QCA Guidelines* and *Combined Code* corporate governance provisions

QCA Guideline	*Combined Code* Reference
There should be a formal schedule of matters specifically reserved for the board's decision.	Provision A.1.1 – see Paragraph 42.8
The board should be supplied in a timely manner with information (including regular management financial information) . . . to enable it to discharge its duties.	Main principle A.5 – see Paragraph 42.12
The board should review the effectiveness of the group's system of internal controls (including financial, operational and compliance controls and risk management systems) at least annually and report to shareholders that they have done so.	Provision C.2.1 – see Paragraph 42.18
The roles of chairman and chief executive should not be exercised by the same individual. If they are, there should be a clear explanation of how other board procedures provide protection against the risk of concentration of power within the company.	Provisions A.2.1/A.2.2 – see Paragraph 42.9
A company should have at least two independent non-executive directors (one of whom may be the chairman) and the board should not be dominated by one person or group of people.	Principle A.3 – Provision A.3.2 – see Paragraph 42.10
All directors should be submitted for re-election at regular intervals, subject to continued satisfactory performance, and the board should ensure planned and progressive refreshing of the board.	Principle A.7 – see Paragraph 42.14
The board should establish an audit committee of at least two members who should be independent non-executive directors. There should be formal terms of reference for the committee.	Provision C.3.1 – see Paragraph 42.19
The board should establish a remuneration committee of at least two members who should be independent non-executive directors.	Provision B.2.1 – see Paragraph 42.16
Recommendations for appointments to the board should be made by a nomination committee after due evaluation.	Provision A.4.1 – see Paragraph 42.11
There should be a dialogue with shareholders based on the mutual understanding of objectives. The board as a whole has responsibility for ensuring that a satisfactory dialogue with shareholders takes place.	Principle D.1 – see Paragraph 42.20

chief executive are different and should be clearly distinguished and not confused or compromised by being combined. If these roles of chairman and chief executive are combined, the company should provide details of the exceptional circumstances which caused the roles to become combined and make a forward looking statement explaining the company's intentions to separate the roles.

Chief executive becoming chairman

42.26 In relation to the chief executive becoming chairman, *NAPF Policy* states that the chief executive should not become chairman of the same company. Should this happen, the company must disclose in its annual report the reasons for the appointment and describe the selection process.

Appointment of a senior independent director

42.27 Whilst it is a *Combined Code* requirement that a senior independent director be appointed, the *QCA Guidelines* do not specifically consider this requirement. However, *NAPF Policy* suggests a senior independent director should be appointed where the role of chairman and chief executive has been combined, primarily to ensure that there is an independent voice on the board of directors who can provide a communication channel for shareholders if needed. Where the roles of chairman and chief executive have not been combined, a senior independent director is encouraged but not required.

Balance of the board of directors

42.28 The *NAPF Guidelines* on the balance of the board of directors is that larger boards of directors should follow the *NAPF Policy*, which requires at least two independent directors, excluding the chairman. Smaller boards of directors should have at least two independent non-executive directors, to comprise not less than one-third of the board of directors, one of whom may be the chairman. See Figure 42.2 for more information regarding the test of independence for NAPF purposes. This less stringent requirement is appropriate for AIM companies who have boards of directors comprising no more than four directors. *NAPF Policy* suggests that such a board of directors might consist of the chairman, chief executive and, at the most, two non-executive directors, of which one should be independent. Most Nominated Advisers will apply this guidance to smaller AIM companies and seek to ensure that an AIM company has at least one independent non-executive director, and for larger AIM companies the Nominated Adviser may require it to have two independent non-executive directors who should comprise not less than one-third of the board of directors. This position should be contrasted with the *QCA Guidelines* set out in Figure 42.1 which recommends that there be at least two non-executive directors.

Composition of the audit, remuneration and nomination committees

42.29 Where possible, the *NAPF Policy* supports the *Combined Code* provisions in relation to the composition of the audit, remuneration and nomination committees. However, it recognises that in some AIM companies the lack of independent membership and insufficient numbers of non-executive directors on the board of directors make compliance with the *Combined Code* provisions unachievable. Where this is the case, *NAPF Policy* recommends that each of the three committees should ideally comprise only independent non-executive directors, with a majority of independent directors on board of directors committees, at the very least. The chairman may be a member of the audit, remuneration or nomination committee, provided that they fulfil the independence test and provided that they do not sit as chairman on the committee. Again, this should be contrasted with the *QCA Guidelines* set out in Figure 42.1, which recommend that for the audit and remuneration committees there should be at least two members, each member being independent. For smaller AIM companies it is not unusual for Nominated Advisers to accept the NAPF position of a majority of the committee being independent. Notwithstanding the *NAPF Guidelines* and *QCA Guidelines*, some AIM companies do not have nomination committees (see Chapter 45, *Nomination committee*).

Remuneration arrangements

42.30 The *NAPF Guidelines* here suggest that AIM companies adhere to current best practice guidelines (*ABI & NAPF Remuneration Guidelines*) and states that a significant component of senior management's remuneration should be linked to performance and that there should be disclosure of the performance conditions attaching to any bonuses or long-term incentive plans. AIM companies are also strongly encouraged to put remuneration reports to a vote at the annual general meeting.

Director independence

42.31 The NAPF believes that some of the independence criteria specified in the *Combined Code* may need to be applied more flexibly to directors of AIM companies, given that they may be significant shareholders, have received option grants and may have a guaranteed term of office. Figure 42.2 shows the factors which could compromise a director's independence, according to each of the *Combined Code*, the *QCA Guidelines* and the *NAPF Guidelines*.

Pre-emption rights

42.32 The NAPF recommends that AIM companies seek annual approval from shareholders to issue securities on a non pre-emptive basis, following the *Pre-emption Group's Statement of Principles*. It goes on to state that there may be good reasons for smaller AIM companies wanting to waive pre-emption rights, for example, reasons of cost, shareholder structure or speed. Where this is the case, companies should consult with their leading shareholders in advance and give them a full justification for a decision to seek authority to issue more than 5 per cent as the annual limit, as well as accounting for usage in the company's annual report. However, in practice it is not unusual for an AIM company to exceed this limit, following consultation with its Nominated Adviser, but in any event the increase should be justified to shareholders either in the AIM admission document or shareholder circular accompanying the notice of general meeting at which such approval is to be sought. Even when increases are agreed, unless it is being obtained for a specific purpose it is unusual for such an increase to be beyond 10 per cent of the issued share capital.

42.33   Given the minimum standards set out in the *QCA Guidelines*, the *NAPF Guidelines* are only likely to have any bearing on a particularly small AIM company.

REPORTING PROCEDURES

42.34   The recommended minimum reporting procedures in relation to corporate governance for AIM companies are set out in the *QCA Guidelines*. It should be noted that AIM Rule 26 also requires an AIM company to disclose the composition of the remuneration, audit and nomination committees on its website and the *QCA AIM Website Guide* suggests that their terms of reference and broader corporate governance information is also included on the website. First, the *QCA Guidance* states that an AIM company should have a corporate governance statement on its website. The statement should be updated annually and describe how the company has achieved good governance. As an alternative to publication on the company's website, the statement could be included in the company's annual report and accounts, but where such a report is published on the company's website, the directors' report should identify where the corporate governance statement can be found and confirm the date at which it was reviewed and updated. The corporate governance statement should, at a minimum, describe how each of the *QCA Guidelines* is put into practice by the company, together with a description of any additional corporate governance standards and procedures that the company applies beyond this basic level. Where a company is not able to apply all of the *QCA Guidelines* (there is an expectation that each company should be able to), the statement should describe how the features of good governance are being achieved. This is effectively applying the "comply or explain" approach to corporate governance taken by the *Listing Rules* in relation to companies whose securities are traded on the Official List. Where an AIM company complies with the *Combined Code* as opposed to the *QCA Guidelines*, similar statements should be included in respect of the *Combined Code*.

42.35   The *QCA Guidelines* also recommend that each AIM company's annual report includes the following basic disclosures:

■ a statement of how the board of directors operates, including a high-level statement of which types of decisions are to be taken by the board of directors and which are to be delegated to management;

- the identity of the chairman, the deputy chairman (where there is one), the chief executive, the senior independent director and the chairman and members of the nomination, audit and remuneration committees. It should be noted that this is required in any event under Rule 26 of the *AIM Rules for Companies*;
- the identity of those directors the board of directors considers to be independent and the reasons why it has determined a director to be independent notwithstanding factors which may appear to impair that status;
- the board of directors should describe any performance evaluation procedures it applies;
- the names of directors, accompanied by sufficient biographical details (and any other relevant information) to enable shareholders to take an informed decision on the balance of the board of directors and the re-election of certain of them;
- the number of meetings of the board of directors and of the committees and individual directors' attendance at them;
- an explanation of the directors' responsibility for preparing the accounts and a statement by the auditors about their reporting responsibilities;
- a statement by the directors that the business is a going concern, with supporting assumptions or qualifications as necessary; and
- an explanation to shareholders of how, if the auditor provides significant non-audit services, auditor objectivity and independence is safeguarded.

42.36 Again, many of these disclosure requirements are derived from the provisions of the *Combined Code*, which should ideally be the first point of reference for corporate governance requirements.

42.37 Finally, the *QCA Guidelines* recommend that the following items are available for inspection on the company's website (and this is now embodied in the *QCA AIM Website Guide*, Rule 26) or made available to shareholders on request:

- the terms and conditions of appointment of non-executive directors;
- the terms of reference for each of the audit, remuneration and nomination committees, together with an explanation of each committee's role and the authority delegated to it by the board of directors. Where an AIM company has not appointed a nomination committee, the board of directors should explain its processes in relation to matters normally dealt with by such a committee.

Directors' independence

42.38 The question of whether or not a non-executive director is independent is largely for the board of directors to determine, taking into account the various tests of directors' independence set out in the *Combined Code*, the *QCA Guidelines for AIM Companies* and the *NAPF Corporate Governance Policy and Voting Guidelines for AIM Companies*. It is a recommendation of the *Combined Code* and is best practice for the board of directors to identify in the annual report each non-executive director it considers to be independent.

42.39 When determining whether a board member is independent, the board of directors should determine whether the director is independent in character and judgement and whether there are any relationships or circumstances which are likely to affect or could appear to affect the director's judgement. Figure 42.2 sets

FIGURE 42.2 Relationships or circumstances which should be taken into account when determining independence of directors

	Combined Code	QCA Corporate Governance Guidelines for AIM Companies	NAPF Corporate Governance Policy and Voting Guidelines for AIM Companies
Non-executive director should not have been an employee in the group within past five years	X	X	
Non-executive director should not have had a material business relationship with the company in the past three years (whether directly or as a partner, shareholder, director, senior employee)	X	X	
Non-executive director should not receive or have received additional remuneration (other than a non-executive director's fee)	X	X **If fee paid in securities this does impair independence**	
Non-executive director should not participate in the company's share option or a performance-related pay scheme, or be a member of the company's pension scheme	X	X	X **Previously issued options to non-executive directors in the form of a one-off grant acceptable, provided the quantum is not considered to be material**
Non-executive director should not have close family ties with any of the company's advisers, non-executive directors or senior employees	X	X	

	Combined Code	QCA Corporate Governance Guidelines for AIM Companies	NAPF Corporate Governance Policy and Voting Guidelines for AIM Companies
Non-executive director should not hold cross-non-executive directorships or have significant links with other non-executive directors through involvement in other companies	X	X	
Non-executive director should not be or represent a significant shareholder	X	X	X **Independence may be compromised if a director has a beneficial or non-beneficial shareholding of more than 3 per cent of the company's issued share capital**
Non-executive director should not have served on the board for more than nine years	X	X	X **But nine to twelve years acceptable if this is the only factor affecting independence**

out the factors which the board of directors should take into account when determining whether a director is independent in character and judgement under the respective guidelines.

42.40 Where the board of directors determines that a director is independent, notwithstanding the existence of relationships or circumstances which may appear relevant to the determination then, again, it is best practice for this to be stated in the annual report and accounts.

IN PRACTICE

Every AIM company should have some corporate governance procedures in place. The bigger the company, the more stringent these should be. As a minimum, all AIM companies should meet the requirements of the QCA Guidelines or NAPF

Guidelines, as appropriate following discussions with its Nominated Adviser but, ideally, the board of directors of an AIM company should be looking to apply the provisions of the full *Combined Code*, so far as reasonably practicable.

Market practice is to include a statement in the AIM admission document of an AIM company that the company intends to comply with the provisions of the *Combined Code* (as opposed to the *QCA Guidelines* or *NAPF Guidelines*) so far as is practicable and appropriate for a company of its size and constitution. By adopting relatively high standards of corporate governance and consistently applying the principles, or explaining non-compliance with the principles, in a manner appropriate to the size and development of the company in question, AIM companies are likely to attract more institutional investors, thereby enabling them to raise capital more readily as and when required. In the current economic environment, stringent corporate governance obligations have become a necessity and public companies will find themselves facing criticism if they do not apply the recommended procedures in practice.

CHAPTER 43

Remuneration committee

AT A GLANCE

Whilst AIM companies are not required to comply with the *Combined Code*, in accordance with the *Combined Code* provisions and the *QCA Guidelines*, it is best practice for AIM companies to establish a remuneration committee to set and check the remuneration of individual directors and senior executives.

The remuneration committee should set the level and structure of remuneration for all executive directors and the chairman, including pension rights and compensation payments. The committee should also recommend and monitor the level and structure of remuneration for senior management.

This chapter looks at considerations to be borne in mind when establishing a remuneration committee and details the specific duties which should be included in the terms of reference for the remuneration committee.

INTRODUCTION

43.1   As part of corporate governance best practice and in accordance with the recommendations of the *Combined Code* and the *QCA Guidelines*, the board of directors should establish committees of non-executive directors to deal with executive remuneration, audit matters and nominations to the board of directors. The remuneration of executive directors is a chief concern of the *Combined Code* and there are a number of provisions relating to the level and make up of remuneration, remuneration policy, service contracts and compensation. One of the main principles of the *Combined Code* states that there must be a formal and transparent procedure for developing policy on executive remuneration and for fixing the remuneration packages of individual directors. Furthermore, no director should be involved in deciding their own remuneration. Whilst AIM companies are not required to comply with the *Combined Code*, it is best practice for AIM companies to establish a remuneration committee to check the remuneration of individual directors and senior executives. Many Nominated Advisers will also require applicant companies to establish such a committee and summarise the constitution of the committee and their role in any AIM admission document. In addition, following the introduction of Rule 26 of the *AIM Rules for Companies* and Rule 26 of the *QCA AIM Website Guide* it is best practice to set out the terms of reference and details of the remuneration committee on the AIM company's website. Under

Rule 26 of the *AIM Rules for Companies*, composition of the relevant committees must be set out on the website.

APPOINTMENT OF REMUNERATION COMMITTEE AND CONDUCT OF MEETINGS

43.2 The remuneration committee should comprise at least three independent non-executive directors, although two will suffice in the case of smaller companies. AIM companies and small companies whose securities are attached to the Main Market of the London Stock Exchange (those listed below the FTSE 350), therefore only require two members on the committee. In June 2006, there was a relaxation of the *Combined Code* to permit a chairman to sit on the remuneration committee if he is considered independent on appointment (although he should not also chair the committee). The chairman should be in addition to the minimum number of independent directors outlined above. As to factors determining the independence of directors, see Chapter 42, *Corporate governance for AIM companies*.

43.3 Appointments to the committee should be for a period of three years. These can be extended for two further three-year periods, provided that the majority of the committee members remain independent.

43.4 The remuneration committee should set the level and structure of remuneration for all executive directors and the chairman, including pension rights and compensation payments. The committee should also recommend and monitor the level and structure of remuneration for senior management.

43.5 In accordance with the *Supporting Principles and Provisions of the Combined Code*, the board of directors or, where required by the Articles of Association of the company, the shareholders, should determine the remuneration of the non-executive directors, including members of the remuneration committee. In practice, a maximum amount payable to all non-executive directors is set out in the Articles of Association of an applicant company and the Nominated Adviser is involved in setting this amount at an appropriate level. If permitted by the Articles, the task of setting the individual non-executive directors' remuneration may be delegated to a sub-committee, which might include the chief executive officer. It is important that the remuneration committee also looks at pay packages of executives below board level, for compensation purposes, to maintain the differential and to take account of the fact that new board members will probably be promoted from the sub-board ranks.

43.6 Whilst there is no fixed requirement as to the number of committee meetings which must be held each year, the *ICSA Guidance on Terms of Reference – Remuneration Committee* recommends that the committee meets at least twice a year in order to discharge its responsibilities properly. In practice, particularly in larger companies, the remuneration committee may have to meet more frequently to discharge its duties. It is thought that, on average, remuneration committees normally meet three times a year and, to ensure that attendance is maximised, these meetings will usually take place before a full meeting of the board of directors.

43.7 As provided in the *Combined Code*, the remuneration committee will need to work closely with the nomination committee (see Chapter 45, *Nomination committee*) to ensure that incentives are appropriately structured for directors and senior executives and any termination terms are carefully considered, the broad aim being to avoid rewarding poor performance.

DUTIES OF THE REMUNERATION COMMITTEE

43.8 There are two principal sources in relation to the duties and remit of the remuneration committee. These are:

- the *Combined Code* (together with the *Related Guidance and Good Practice Suggestions of the Combined Code*); and
- *ICSA Guidance on Terms of Reference – Remuneration Committee* published by the Institute of Chartered Secretaries and Administrators dated October 2007 (the "*ICSA Guidance*").

43.9 The duties and remit of the remuneration committee should be set out in formal terms of reference, which should be approved by the board of directors and made available on the company's website. Although this is not mandatory for AIM companies it is best practice to include this on the company's website together with an explanation of the remuneration committee's role and the authority delegated to it by the board of directors.

43.10 In accordance with the *Related Guidance and Good Practice Suggestions of the Combined Code*, the duties of the remuneration committee usually include the following:

- to determine and agree with the board of directors the framework or broad policy for the remuneration of the company's chief executive, chairman, the executive directors, the company secretary and such other members of the executive management as it is designated to consider. The remuneration of non-executive directors should be a matter for the chairman and the executive members of the board of directors, ensuring no director or manager is involved in any decisions as to their own remuneration;
- to take into account all factors which it deems necessary (in determining such a policy). The objective of such policy is to ensure that members of the executive management of the company are provided with appropriate incentives to encourage enhanced performance and are, in a fair and responsible manner, rewarded for their individual contributions to the success of the company;
- to review the ongoing appropriateness and relevance of the remuneration policy;
- to approve the design of and determine targets for, any performance-related pay schemes operated by the company and to approve the total annual payments made under such schemes;
- to review the design of all share incentive plans for approval by the board of directors and shareholders and, in relation to such plans, determine each year whether awards will be made and, if so, the overall amount of such awards and the performance targets to be used;

- to determine the policy for, and scope of, pension arrangements for each executive director and other senior executives;
- to ensure that contractual terms on termination, and any payments made, are fair to the individual and the company, that failure is not rewarded and that the duty to mitigate loss is fully recognised;
- within the terms of the agreed policy and in consultation with the chairman and/or chief executive, to determine the total individual remuneration package of each executive director and other senior executives including bonuses, incentive payments and share options or other share awards;
- in determining such packages and arrangements, to give due regard to any relevant legal requirements, the provisions and recommendations in the *Combined Code* and the *AIM Rules for Companies* and associated guidance;
- to review and note annually the remuneration trends across the company or group;
- to oversee any major changes in employee benefit structures throughout the company/group;
- to agree the policy for authorising claims for expenses from the chief executive and chairman;
- to ensure that all provisions regarding disclosure of remuneration, including pensions, are fulfilled;
- to be exclusively responsible for establishing the selection criteria, selecting, appointing and setting the terms of reference for any remuneration consultants who advise the committee; and
- to obtain reliable, up-to-date information about remuneration in other companies.

43.11 To assist the remuneration committee in meeting its obligations, it should be given full authority to commission any reports, surveys or information which it deems necessary (within any budgetary restraints imposed by the board). Furthermore, the committee should be authorised by the board of directors to seek any information it requires from any employee of the company and to obtain, at the company's expense, any outside legal or other professional advice it deems necessary to help fulfil its obligations.

43.12 The chairman of the remuneration committee should report formally to the board of directors on its proceedings after each committee meeting and the committee shall make any recommendations to the board of directors that it deems appropriate on any area within its remit where action or improvement is needed.

43.13 The committee will usually be required to produce an annual report of the company's remuneration policy and practices, which will form part of the company's annual report and, whilst it is not a requirement for an AIM company to put the separate remuneration report to shareholders for approval at the AGM, it is best practice to do so.

IN PRACTICE

Whilst it is not a requirement for an AIM company to establish a remuneration committee, virtually all AIM companies do so to ensure that they have a formal process for considering the remuneration of executive directors and senior management. There would be concern among shareholders, in particular any institutional shareholders, if a company were not to have a properly constituted remuneration committee with clear pre-determined terms of reference. In addition, AIM companies should, as a matter of best practice, include the terms of reference on their websites.

CHAPTER 44

Audit committee

The 2003 Smith Report recommended certain changes to the *Combined Code* and provided principle based guidance regarding the establishment of audit committees and the manner in which members of an audit committee should carry out their role. The importance of having an independent audit committee is such that there are three main principles of the *Combined Code* which deal with accountability and audit issues. Whilst AIM companies are not required to comply with the *Combined Code*, in accordance with the *Combined Code* provisions and the *QCA Guidelines* it is best practice for AIM companies to establish an audit committee to deal with financial reporting, audit and internal control issues and virtually all Nominated Advisers will require AIM companies to establish an audit committee.

This chapter looks at the considerations to be borne in mind when establishing an audit committee and details the specific duties which should be included in the terms of reference for an audit committee.

INTRODUCTION

44.1   In the summer of 2002, the Financial Reporting Committee (FRC) set up an independent group, chaired by Sir Robert Smith, to clarify the roles and responsibilities of audit committees. The resultant Smith Report was published in early 2003. It recommended certain changes to the *Combined Code* and provided principle based guidance regarding the establishment of audit committees and the manner in which members of an audit committee should carry out their role (the "*Smith Guidance*").

44.2   The importance of having an independent audit committee is such that there are three main principles of the *Combined Code* which deal with accountability and audit issues. Principle C.1 regarding financial reporting states that the board of directors should present a balanced and understandable assessment of the company's position and prospects. There are two provisions which support this principle in the *Combined Code*. These state, first, that the directors should explain in the annual report their responsibility for preparing the accounts and there should be a statement by the auditors about their reporting responsibilities and, second, that directors should report that the business is a going concern with supporting assumptions or qualifications as necessary.

44.3 Principle C.2 states that the board of directors should maintain a sound system of internal control to safeguard shareholders' investment and the company's assets. The relevant *Combined Code* provision goes on to say that the board of directors should, at least annually, conduct a review of the effectiveness of the group's system of internal controls and should report to shareholders that they have done so. The review should cover all material controls, including financial, operational and compliance controls and risk management systems.

44.4 Finally, Principle C.3 of the *Combined Code* states that the board of directors should establish formal and transparent arrangements for considering how they should apply the financial reporting and internal control principles and for maintaining an appropriate relationship with the company's auditors. It is the *Combined Code* provision related to this principle which states that the board of directors should establish an audit committee of at least three or, in the case of smaller companies, two members who should all be independent non-executive directors. The board of directors should furthermore satisfy itself that at least one member of the audit committee has recent and relevant financial experience. The *Combined Code* provisions go on to set out certain roles and responsibilities of the audit committee which should be included in the committee's terms of reference. These will be considered further below. Once again, whilst AIM companies are not required to comply with the *Combined Code*, in accordance with the *Combined Code* provisions and the *QCA AIM Website Guidance*, it is best practice for AIM companies to establish an audit committee to deal with financial reporting, audit and internal control issues. Virtually all AIM companies establish an audit committee either voluntarily or at the request of their Nominated Adviser. Following the introduction of Rule 26 of the *AIM Rules for Companies* and the *QCA AIM Website Guidance* on best practice regarding Rule 26, it is best practice to set out the terms of reference of the audit committee on the AIM company's website. Under Rule 26 of the *AIM Rules for Companies*, composition of the relevant committees must be set out on the website.

APPOINTMENT OF AUDIT COMMITTEE AND CONDUCT OF MEETINGS

44.5 In accordance with the *Combined Code*, the audit committee should comprise at least three independent non-executive directors, although two will suffice in the case of AIM companies as it does in the case of smaller companies whose securities are traded on the Main Market of the London Stock Exchange (being those below the FTSE 350). As to the factors determining the independence of directors, see Chapter 42, *Corporate governance for AIM companies*. At least one member of the audit committee must have recent and relevant financial experience. The *Smith Guidance* adds a further recommendation that the chairman should not be a member of the audit committee.

44.6 As with the remuneration committee, it is recommended that appointments to the audit committee should be for a period of three years. Again, these can be extended for two further three-year periods, provided the directors on the audit committee remain independent.

44.7 Whilst there is no fixed requirement as to the number of committee meetings which must be held each year, it is recommended that the audit committee meets at least three times a year at appropriate times in the financial reporting and audit cycle and otherwise as required.

DUTIES OF THE AUDIT COMMITTEE

44.8 The principal sources in relation to the duties and remit of the audit committee are as follows:

- the *Combined Code*;
- the *Smith Guidance* contained in the *Related Guidance and Good Practice Suggestions* of the *Combined Code*; and
- *ICSA Guidance on Terms of Reference – Audit Committee* published by the Institute of Chartered Secretaries and Administrators dated October 2007.

44.9 The duties and remit of the audit committee, together with an explanation of the role of the audit committee and the authority delegated to it by the board of directors, should be set out in formal terms of reference which should be approved by the board of directors and made available on request, as well as by publication on the company's website. It has not always been the practice of AIM companies to set out the terms of reference of the audit committee on their websites; however, following the introduction of Rule 26 of the *AIM Rules for Companies* and the *QCA AIM Website Guide* on best practice regarding Rule 26, it is best practice for an AIM company to set out the terms of reference on the AIM company's website.

44.10 The duties to be carried out by the audit committee fall under the headings of "financial reporting", "internal controls and risk management systems", "whistle-blowing and fraud", "internal audit" and "external audit".

Financial reporting

44.11 With regard to financial reporting, the duties and responsibilities of the audit committee should include:

- to monitor the integrity of the financial statements of the company, including its annual and half-yearly reports, interim management statements, preliminary results' announcements (where applicable) and any other formal announcement in relation to its financial performance, reviewing significant financial reporting issues and judgments which they contain. The committee shall also review summary financial statements, significant financial returns to regulators and any financial information contained in certain other documents, such as announcements of a price sensitive nature;
- to review and challenge where necessary:
  - the consistency of, and changes to, accounting policies both on a year-on-year basis and across the company/group;

- the methods used to account for significant or unusual transactions where different approaches are possible;
- whether the company has followed appropriate accounting standards and made appropriate estimates and judgments, taking into account the views of the external auditor;
- the clarity of disclosure in the company's financial reports and the context in which statements are made; and
- all material information presented with the financial statements, such as the operating and financial review and the corporate governance statement (insofar as it relates to the audit and risk management); and
■ to review the annual financial statements of the pension funds where not reviewed by the board of directors as a whole.

Internal controls and risk management systems

44.12 In relation to internal controls and risk management systems, the audit committee should:

■ keep under review the effectiveness of the company's internal controls and risk management systems; and
■ review and approve the statements to be included in the annual report concerning internal controls and risk management.

Whistle-blowing and fraud

44.13 The committee should:

■ review the company's arrangements for its employees to raise concerns, in confidence, about possible wrongdoing in financial reporting or other matters;
■ ensure that these arrangements allow proportionate and independent investigation of such matters and appropriate follow-up action; and
■ review the company's procedures for detecting fraud.

Internal audit

44.14 In relation to internal audits, the audit committee should:

■ monitor and review the effectiveness of the company's internal audit function in the context of the company's overall risk management system;
■ approve the appointment and removal of the head of the internal audit function;
■ consider and approve the remit of the internal audit function and ensure it has adequate resources and appropriate access to information to enable it to perform its function effectively and in accordance with the relevant professional standards. The committee should also ensure the function has adequate standing and is free from management or other restrictions;
■ review and assess the annual internal audit plan;
■ review promptly all reports on the company from the internal auditor;

- review and monitor management responsiveness to the findings and recommendations of the internal auditor; and
- meet the head of internal audit at least once a year, without management being present, to discuss their remit and any issues arising from the internal audits carried out. In addition, the head of internal audit should be given the right of direct access to the chairman of the board of directors and to the audit committee.

44.15 Due to the size and stage of their development, some AIM companies might agree with their Nominated Adviser that it is not appropriate for them to carry out the internal audit functions. Where the Nominated Adviser agrees, this should be set out in any AIM admission document and the terms of reference of the audit committee amended accordingly.

External audit

44.16 With regard to external audit, the committee should:

- consider and make recommendations to the board of directors, to be put to shareholders for approval at the AGM, in relation to the appointment, re-appointment and removal of the company's external auditor. The committee should also oversee the selection process for new auditors and, if an auditor resigns, the committee should investigate the issues leading to this and decide whether any action is required;
- oversee the relationship with the external auditor including (but not limited to):
  - approval of their remuneration, whether fees for audit or non-audit services and that the level of fees is appropriate to enable an adequate audit to be conducted;
  - approval of their terms of engagement, including any engagement letter issued at the start of each audit and scope of the audit;
  - assessing annually their independence and objectivity taking into account relevant UK professional and regulatory requirements and the relationship with the auditor as a whole, including the provision of any non-audit services;
  - satisfying itself that there are no relationships (such as family, employment, investment, financial or business) between the auditor and the company (other than in the ordinary course of business);
  - agreeing, with the board of directors, a policy on the employment of former employees of the company's auditor, then monitoring the implementation of this policy;
  - monitoring the auditor's compliance with relevant ethical and professional guidance on the rotation of audit partners, the level of fees paid by the company compared to the overall fee income of the firm, office and partner and other related requirements;
  - assessing annually their qualifications, expertise and resources and the effectiveness of the audit process, which shall include a report from the external auditor on their own internal quality procedures; and

- seeking to ensure co-ordination with the activities of the internal audit function;
- meet regularly with the external auditor, including once at the planning stage before the audit and once after the audit at the reporting stage. The committee should also meet the external auditor at least once a year, without management being present, to discuss their remit and any issues arising from the audit;
- review and approve the annual audit plan and ensure that it is consistent with the scope of the audit engagement;
- review the findings of the audit with the external auditor. This shall include but not be limited to, the following:
  - discussion of any major issues which arose during the audit;
  - any accounting and audit judgments; and
  - levels of errors identified during the audit;
- review the effectiveness of the audit;
- review any representation letters requested by the external auditor before they are signed by management;
- review the management letter and management's response to the auditor's findings and recommendations; and
- develop and implement a policy on the supply of non-audit services by the external auditor, taking into account any relevant ethical guidance on the matter.

44.17 The audit committee should also be responsible for co-ordination of the internal and external auditors, oversee any investigation of activities which are within its terms of reference and act for internal purposes as a court of last resort.

44.18 In accordance with the *Smith Guidance*, to assist the audit committee in meeting its obligations, the management of the company should ensure that the audit committee is kept properly informed and is regularly supplied with information. It should also be made clear to all directors and staff that they must co-operate with the audit committee and provide it with any information it requires. Furthermore, the committee should have sufficient resources to undertake its duties, including access to the company secretary for assistance on audit committee matters as required. Finally, the committee should be authorised to obtain, at the company's expense, outside legal or other professional advice on any matter within its terms of reference, as and when the audit committee reasonably considers it necessary to do so. All of these details are usually set out in the audit committee's terms of reference.

44.19 Given the nature of the responsibilities falling to members of the audit committee, the *Smith Guidance* recommends that audit committee members be given appropriate and timely training, both in the form of an induction programme for new members and on an ongoing basis for all members. Such training may include attendance at formal courses and conferences, internal company talks and seminars and briefings by external advisers. The *Smith Guidance* recommends that induction training should cover the role of the audit committee, its terms of reference, the expected time commitment by members and an overview of the company's business, identifying the main business and financial dynamics and risks. With regard to ongoing training, the *Smith Guidance* recommends that this should include an understanding of the principles of, and developments in, financial reporting and related company law. It may also include, for example, understanding financial statements, applicable accounting standards and recommended practice, the regulatory framework for the company's business, the role of internal and external auditing and risk management.

44.20 The audit committee chairman should report formally to the board of directors on its proceedings after each meeting on all matters within the remit of its duties and responsibilities. Furthermore, the committee should make recommendations to the board of directors as and when it deems appropriate on any area within its remit where action or improvement is needed.

44.21 The committee will usually be required to compile a report to shareholders on its activities, to be included in the company's annual report in accordance with the *Combined Code*. The *Combined Code* contains specific provisions which cover additional disclosures that a company should make in relation to the audit committee; for example, where there is no internal audit function, the *Combined Code* states that the reasons for the absence of such a function should be explained in the relevant section of the annual report. One of the duties of the audit committee is responsibility for the appointment, re-appointment and removal of the external auditors. The *Combined Code* provides that if the board of directors does not accept the audit committee's recommendation, it should include in the annual report a statement from the audit committee explaining the recommendation and then set out the reasons why the board of directors has taken a different approach. Finally, the *Combined Code* provides that the annual report should explain to shareholders how, if the auditor provides non-audit services, auditor objectivity and independence is safeguarded.

IN PRACTICE

As with remuneration committees, whilst it is not a requirement for an AIM company to establish an audit committee, virtually all AIM companies do so, as an independent body monitoring financial reporting procedures ensures investor confidence. However, not all AIM companies have an internal audit function. Alongside the remuneration committee, an audit committee is regarded by shareholders, in particular institutional shareholders, as an integral part of the management of an AIM company.

CHAPTER 45

Nomination committee

AT A GLANCE

Whilst AIM companies are not required to comply with the *Combined Code*, in accordance with the *Combined Code* provisions and the *QCA Guidelines* it is best practice for AIM companies to establish a nomination committee which will be responsible for the appointment and re-appointment of both directors and senior executive officers. This Chapter looks at considerations when establishing a nomination committee and details the specific duties which should be included in the terms of reference for the nomination committee.

INTRODUCTION

45.1 One of the main principles of the *Combined Code* states that there should be a formal, rigorous and transparent procedure for the appointment of new directors to the board of directors. Again, whilst AIM companies are not required to comply with the *Combined Code*, it is best practice for AIM companies to establish a nomination committee which will be responsible for the appointment and re-appointment of both directors and senior executive officers. However, due to the size and stage of development, it might not be appropriate for all AIM companies to have a nomination committee, although this is a matter to be discussed with the Nominated Adviser. Where there is a formal nomination committee, the Nominated Adviser will require the constitution of the nomination committee to be set out in any AIM admission document and on the website pursuant to Rule 26 of the *AIM Rules for Companies*. In addition, following the introduction of Rule 26 of the *AIM Rules for Companies* and the *QCA Website Guide*, on best practice regarding Rule 26, it is best practice to set out the terms of reference of the nomination committee on the AIM company's website. Where it is felt that it is not appropriate to have a nomination committee, the reasons for this should be set out in any AIM admission document.

APPOINTMENT OF THE NOMINATION COMMITTEE AND CONDUCT OF MEETINGS

45.2 The members of the nomination committee will be appointed by the board of directors. As with all corporate governance board committees, a majority of the members of the nomination committee should be independent non-executive directors. As to factors determining the independence of directors, see Paragraph 45.3. The *Combined Code* recommends that the chairman or an independent non-executive director chairs the committee. However, the chairman should not preside as chair when dealing with the appointment of a successor to the chairmanship.

45.3 There are a number of factors which determine whether a non-executive director is to be regarded as being independent. For example, a non-executive director will not be regarded as being independent if the director:

- has been an employee of the company or the company's group within the past five years;
- has or has had in the past three years, a material business relationship with the company either directly, or as a partner, shareholder, director or senior employee of a body which has had such a relationship with the company;
- has received or receives additional remuneration or benefits from the company apart from their fee;
- has any close family ties with any of the company's advisers, directors or senior employees;
- holds cross-directorships or has significant links with other directors of the company;
- is or represents a significant shareholder; or
- has served on the board of directors for more than nine years.

45.4 Generally, as a matter of best practice there will be three members on the nomination committee, although two members will suffice for an AIM company, as it does for small companies whose securities are traded on the Main Market of the London Stock Exchange (below the FTSE 350). Ideally, the chairman of the board of directors will not also be the chairman of the committee. However, many smaller companies have the same person acting as chair of both. This is fine, provided that the chairman does not act as chair on the committee when it is dealing with the appointment of the chairman's successor.

45.5 Appointments to the committee should be for a period of three years. These can be extended for two further three-year periods provided that the majority of the committee members remain independent.

45.6 To meet with best practice recommendations, the nomination committee should meet at least twice a year, although the frequency of meetings is likely to depend on the size of the company and the remit of the committee. In practice, it is likely to meet on an ad hoc basis, as and when appointments need to be made, rather than at fixed times.

DUTIES OF THE NOMINATION COMMITTEE

45.7 With regard to the duties and remit of the nomination committee, there are two principal sources to be considered:

- the provisions of the *Combined Code* (together with the *Related Guidance and Good Practice Suggestions* of the *Combined Code*); and
- *ICSA Guidance on the Terms of Reference – Nomination Committees* published by the Institute of Chartered Secretaries and Administrators dated October 2007 (the "*ICSA Guidance*").

45.8   The duties and remit of the nomination committee should be set out in formal terms of reference which are approved by the board of directors. Again, the terms of reference should be made available by publication on the company's website, together with an explanation of the nomination committee's role and the authority delegated to it by the board of directors.

45.9   An annex to the Higgs Review contained a summary of the principal duties of nomination committees. This summary now forms part of the *Related Guidance and Good Practice Suggestions* of the *Combined Code*, the provisions of which are usually incorporated into the nomination committee's terms of reference.

45.10   Usually, the nomination committee will be required to do the following:

- regularly review the structure, size and composition of the board of directors (having regard to the balance of skills, knowledge and experience of the directors) and make recommendations to the board of directors with regard to any changes;
- give full consideration to succession planning for directors and senior executives, taking into account the challenges and opportunities facing the company and evaluating the skills and expertise that will be needed on the board of directors in the future;
- be responsible for identifying and nominating, for the approval of the board of directors, candidates to fill board vacancies as and when they arise;
- before any appointment to the board of directors is made, evaluate the balance of skills, knowledge and expertise on the board of directors and, in the light of such evaluation, prepare a description of the role and capabilities required for a particular appointment (in identifying suitable candidates the committee must use open advertising or the services of external advisers; consider candidates from a wide range of backgrounds; and consider candidates on merit and against objective criteria, ensuring that appointees have enough time to devote to the position being considered);
- keep under review the leadership needs of the organisation, both executive and non-executive, with a view to ensuring the continued ability of the organisation to compete effectively in the marketplace;
- keep up to date and fully informed about strategic issues and commercial changes affecting the company and the market in which it operates;
- review annually the time required from non-executive directors. Performance evaluation should be used to assess whether the non-executive directors are spending enough time to fulfil their duties; and
- ensure that, on appointment to the board of directors, non-executive directors receive a formal letter of appointment setting out clearly what is expected of them in terms of time commitment, committee service and involvement outside board of directors meetings.

45.11   In addition, the nomination committee should make recommendations to the board of directors concerning:

- formulating succession plans for both executive and non-executive directors and, in particular, for the key roles of chairman and chief executive;
- suitable candidates for the role of senior independent director;

- membership of the audit and remuneration committees, in consultation with the chairmen of those committees;
- the re-appointment of any non-executive director at the conclusion of their specific term of office, having given due regard to their performance and ability to continue to contribute to the board of directors in the light of the knowledge, skills and experience required;
- the continuation (or not) in service of any director who has reached the age of 70 (if required by the Articles of Association);
- the re-election by shareholders of any director under "retirement by rotation" provisions in the company's Articles of Association, having due regard to their performance and ability to continue to contribute to the board of directors in the light of the knowledge, skills and experience required;
- any matters relating to the continuation in office of any director at any time including the suspension or termination of service of an executive director as an employee of the company (subject to the provisions of the law and their service contract); and
- the appointment of any director to executive or other office.

45.12 It is the responsibility of the committee chairman to report formally to the full board of directors on the proceedings of the committee after each committee meeting. The committee shall make whatever recommendations to the board of directors it deems appropriate on any area within its remit where action or improvement is required. Where a company has a nomination committee, it is best practice to include a statement in the company's annual report about the committee's activities, the process used to make appointments and, if external advice or open advertising has not been used, an explanation why not.

45.13 Finally, the nomination committee shall, at least once a year, review its own performance, constitution and terms of reference to ensure it is operating at maximum effectiveness and recommend any changes it considers necessary to the board of directors for approval.

45.14 The *ICSA Guidance* provides that the nomination committee should be authorised to seek any information it requires from any employee of the company in order to perform its duties. Furthermore, the committee should be authorised to obtain, at the company's expense, outside legal or other professional advice on any matters within its terms of reference.

IN PRACTICE

At the time the Higgs Review was carried out in 2002, it was noted that almost all FTSE 100 companies had nomination committees, whereas only 30 per cent of companies outside the FTSE 350 had nomination committees. In recent years, there has been an improvement in this regard and, even though it is not a formal requirement, many large AIM companies now establish a nomination committee alongside the remuneration and audit committees, resulting in the procedure for selection and recruitment of directors and senior executives being streamlined in a formal and systematic manner. That said, following discussion with their Nominated Adviser, many smaller AIM companies elect not to establish a nomination committee on the basis it is not appropriate, given the size of the company, setting out the reasons for this in any AIM admission document.

Share dealing code

As part of its corporate governance compliance, companies whose securities are admitted to trading on AIM will adopt a share dealing code. This code covers the circumstances in which the directors and certain employees and their families, related companies and related trusts can deal in the company's securities. It also sets out a notification procedure so that the company is aware of any such transactions and can comply with its requirements to notify these transactions to the market pursuant to Rule 17 of the *AIM Rules for Companies*.

SHARE DEALING CODE

46.1 In order to address corporate governance requirements and best practice in respect of dealings by directors and employees and their families, related companies and related trusts as well as seeking to ensure compliance with Rule 21 of the *AIM Rules for Companies*, the board of directors of the company will adopt a code on dealings in securities. Rule 21 of the *AIM Rules for Companies* states that an AIM company must ensure that its directors and applicable employees and their families, related companies and related trusts do not deal in any of its AIM securities during a close period. In addition, the purchase or early redemption by an AIM company of its AIM securities or sale of any AIM securities held as treasury shares must not be made during a close period. This rule will not apply, however, where such persons have entered into a binding commitment prior to the AIM company being in such a close period where it was not reasonably foreseeable at the time such commitment was made that a close period was likely and provided that the commitment was notified at the time it was made.

46.2 The company's code for dealing in securities incorporates and builds on the restrictions set out in the *AIM Rules for Companies* and its purpose is to ensure that the directors, applicable employees and their families, related companies and related trusts do not abuse, or place themselves under suspicion of abusing, price sensitive information that they may, or may be thought to have, especially in periods leading up to the announcements of results.

46.3 A company's code on dealings in securities applies to any person who acts as a director of the company, whether or not officially appointed, and as such would catch shareholder directors. The company's code on dealing in securities also applies to applicable employees, being any employee who is likely to be in possession of unpublished price sensitive information in relation to the company because of their employment in the company and/or any of its subsidiaries.

46.4 The company's code on dealing in securities will also apply to the family of the directors and employees likely to be in possession of price sensitive information and, for the purposes of the *AIM Rules for Companies*, family means any of the people set out in Figure 46.1, which includes certain related companies and related trusts.

FIGURE 46.1   Definition of family

A reference to a person's family includes the following persons:

- his or her spouse or civil partner and any child where such child is under the age of 18;
- any trust in which such individuals are trustees or beneficiaries;
- any company of which they have control of more than 20 per cent of its equity or voting rights in a general meeting.

It should be noted that employee share or pension schemes are excluded from the definition of trust provided that such individuals are beneficiaries rather than trustees.

46.5 It should be remembered that, generally, a person's freedom to deal in the company's securities is restricted in a number of ways as a matter of law and regulation under the *AIM Rules for Companies, Criminal Justice Act 1993* and *Financial Services and Markets Act 2000* (see Chapter 2, *Regulation of AIM*) and also by the provisions of the code for dealing in securities. Compliance with the code for dealing in securities may not constitute a defence to any charge under applicable law.

PRICE SENSITIVE INFORMATION

46.6 A code for dealing in securities will restrict directors and employees and their families, related companies and related trusts dealing when they are in possession of price sensitive information. Price sensitive information is information of a precise nature which:

- is not generally available;
- relates, directly or indirectly to the company or to its securities; and
- would, if generally available, be likely to have a significant effect on the price of the company's securities.

Generally speaking, information is precise if it:

- indicates circumstances that exist or may reasonably be expected to come into existence or an event that has occurred or may reasonably be expected to occur; and
- is specific enough to enable a conclusion to be drawn as to the possible effect of those circumstances or that event on the price of the company's securities.

46.7 Information would be likely to have a significant effect on price if and only if it is information of a kind which a reasonable investor would be likely to use as part of the basis of an investment decision. Information which can be obtained by research or analysis conducted by, or on behalf of, users of a market is to be regarded for the purposes of market abuse, as being generally available to them.

WHAT IS A DEALING?

46.8 Subject to the specific exceptions listed in the guidance to Rule 21 of the *AIM Rules for Companies* and the London Stock Exchange's guidance to Rule 21 discussed at Paragraph 46.1, dealing means any change whatsoever to the holding of securities of which the holder is a director or an applicable employee or their families including:

- any sale or purchase of, or agreement to sell or purchase, any securities of the company;
- the grant to, or acceptance by such a person, of any option relating to such securities or of any other right or obligation, present or future, conditional or unconditional, to acquire or dispose of any such securities;
- the acquisition, disposal, exercise or discharge of, or any dealing with, any such option, right or obligation in respect of such securities;
- dealings between directors and/or applicable employees of the company;
- off-market dealings;
- transfers for no consideration;
- any securities taken into or out of treasury; and
- the acquisition, disposal or discharge (whether in whole or in part) of a related financial product referenced to AIM securities of the company in which the holder is a director or an applicable employee or their families.

This is a very wide definition which means that if a transaction concerns the AIM securities held by the directors, the employees and their families, related companies and related trusts it is likely to be caught by the company's code for dealing in securities and Rule 21 of the *AIM Rules for Companies*.

DEALINGS BY DIRECTORS, APPLICABLE EMPLOYEES AND THEIR FAMILIES

46.9 One of the principal purposes of the code for dealing in securities is to dissuade directors, applicable employees and their families, related companies and related trusts from dealing in any AIM securities on considerations of a short term nature.

46.10 In addition, the code for dealing in securities will usually set out when the directors, applicable employees, their families and related companies and related trusts should not deal in the lead up to the announcement of the financial results and, in particular, during the following periods which are referred to as "close periods":

- the period of two months immediately preceding the preliminary announcement of the company's annual results or, if shorter, the period from the relevant financial year end up to and including the time of announcement; and
- if the company reports on a half-yearly basis, the period of two months immediately preceding the notification of its half-yearly report or, if shorter, the period from the relevant financial period end up to and including the time of the notification; or
- if the company reports on a quarterly basis, the period of one month immediately preceding the notification of the quarterly results or, if shorter, the period from the relevant financial period end up to and including the time of the notification (save for the final quarter where the rule regarding annual results applies).

Whilst this is clear, it should be noted that in respect of the publication of financial information in order to work out what period will be covered it requires a certain amount of forward planning. The period in which any such dealings will be prohibited is determined by a date in the future and a company cannot delay the announcement of the results as it is required to notify these without delay pursuant to Rule 17 of the *AIM Rules for Companies*. As a result, the timetable for the announcement of results will need to be carefully considered before any person covered by the company's code for dealing in securities undertakes any transaction in securities following the end of the relevant financial period.

CLEARANCE TO DEAL

46.11   In order to enforce the code for dealing in securities, it sets out a procedure for notification and seeking clearance to deal by persons to whom it applies. Accordingly, it is usual for the code for dealing in securities to include a provision restricting any dealing in the securities of the company without first ensuring that the chairman (or one or more other directors designated for this purpose) is advised in advance and gives clearance.

46.12   In the case of the chairman or other designated director they must advise the board of directors in advance at a board meeting or, where there is more than one designated director, advise another designated director and receive clearance from them prior to dealing.

46.13   The code for dealing in securities will usually also contain forms for application for clearance to deal and a form of response from the company. Best practice is for the company to maintain a written record of any advice received from a director or applicable employee or their family, related companies and related trusts pursuant to the code for dealing in securities and any clearance given.

CIRCUMSTANCES OF REFUSAL

46.14   A director or applicable employee and their families, related companies and related trusts must not be given clearance to deal in any AIM securities of the company during a prohibited period. A prohibited period means:

1 any close period (see Paragraph 46.10); or
2 any period when there exists any matter which constitutes unpublished price sensitive information in relation to the company's AIM securities or the company (whether or not the director or applicable employee has knowledge of such matter) (see Paragraph 46.6); or
3 any time where it has become reasonably probable that an announcement under the *AIM Rules for Companies* of a matter under (2) above will be required; or
4 any period when the person responsible for the clearance otherwise has reason to believe that the proposed dealing is in breach of the company's code for dealing in securities.

When is dealing permitted

46.15   Notwithstanding the restrictions set out in the company's code for dealing in securities, provided there is no other reason why the director cannot deal, for example because he had agreed to a lock-in (see Chapter 17, *Lock-ins for new businesses*), dealing will be allowed in certain limited circumstances. These include where the director or applicable employee or the member of their family, related company or related trust has entered into a binding commitment prior to the company being in a close period, provided it was not reasonably foreseeable at the time the commitment was made that a dealing would be required to be made in a close period. In order to benefit from this exception, the commitment must also have been notified to a Regulatory Information Service at the time it was made. An example of such a situation may be where a director holds an option and the option will lapse if it is not exercised but the latest date for its exercise falls within a period which is a close period. Such an example may fall within this exception provided that it is notified at the time of grant but such status should be discussed with the company's advisers and, if it is felt appropriate, with AIM Regulation, particularly if the latest date for exercise falls in a close period due to the publication of financial information and this could have been predicted.

46.16   In addition, the London Stock Exchange may, in exceptional circumstances, permit a director or applicable employee or their families, related companies and related trusts to sell his AIM securities in the company during a close period to alleviate severe personal hardship. However, it should be noted that in the cases of severe personal hardship this relaxation can only be given by the London Stock Exchange and not by the Nominated Adviser or the company.

THE MODEL CODE – A WORD OF CAUTION

46.17   For companies whose securities are admitted to trading on the Main Market of the London Stock Exchange, the Model Code on Directors Dealings, as set out in the Appendix to Chapter 9 of the *Listing Rules*, is usually incorporated in any code for dealing in securities. It should be noted that, whilst it is usual best practice for AIM companies to follow guidance and procedures for companies whose securities are admitted to trading on the Main Market, dealings in AIM securities in circumstances permitted under the Model Code is one exception to this rule. The *AIM Rules for Companies* are very narrowly drafted in order to protect investor confidence and the circumstances in which dealings are permitted under the *AIM Rules for Companies* are more restrictive than those permitted under the Model Code. Accordingly, the dealings which are not prohibited by the AIM company's code for dealing in securities are usually limited to the following:

- undertakings or elections to take up entitlements under a rights issue or other pre-emptive offer (including an offer of securities in lieu of a cash dividend);
- the take up of entitlements under a rights issue or other pre-emptive offer (including an offer of securities in lieu of a cash dividend);
- allowing entitlements to lapse under a rights issue or other pre-emptive offer (including an offer of securities in lieu of a cash dividend);
- the sale of sufficient entitlements nil-paid to allow take up of the balance of the entitlements under a rights issue;
- undertakings to accept, or the acceptance of, a takeover offer.

IN PRACTICE

Whilst it is not a requirement for an AIM company to establish a code on dealing in securities (as Rule 21 of the *AIM Rules for Companies* applies in any event), virtually all companies do so as a matter of good corporate governance in order to monitor and control dealings by directors, senior employees and their related persons and to assist the company with its disclosure requirements related thereto. AIM companies need to be careful that the codes adopted by them do not follow the Model Code but comply with Rule 21 of the *AIM Rules for Companies*.

CHAPTER 47

Relationship agreements

AT A GLANCE

Where AIM companies have one or more major shareholders with a holding of
more than 25 per cent of the issued share capital of the AIM company, there has
been a growing trend of putting in place a "relationship agreement", as a matter of
best practice or at the instigation of the Nominated Adviser. A relationship
agreement is designed to ensure that the AIM company is capable of carrying on
its business independently of any controlling shareholder, managing its cash and
assets independently. It is also designed to ensure that all transactions and
relationships in the future between the AIM company and any such controlling
shareholder are at arm's length and on normal commercial terms.

INTRODUCTION

47.1 A significant number of AIM companies have one or more major shareholders with a holding of more than 25 per cent in their issued share capital
(major shareholders) often referred to as "cornerstone" investors. For these
companies it is best practice for them to put in place an agreement with such major
shareholders, the principal purpose of which is to ensure that the AIM company
and its subsidiaries are capable of carrying on business independently of the major
shareholders and of any of their associates. These relationship agreements are
also aimed at ensuring that any transactions and relationships with the major
shareholders and their associates are at arm's length and on normal commercial
terms. Whether or not the AIM company and the major shareholder decide to
enter into such an agreement, it may be that the Nominated Adviser requires
such an agreement as part of its review of the suitability of the company and its
securities for admission to AIM.

PARTIES TO THE RELATIONSHIP AGREEMENT

47.2 A relationship agreement will usually be entered into between the major
shareholder and the company. Other parties may include any related parties of the
major shareholder, such as its subsidiaries or related trusts, where these can be
identified. The Nominated Adviser may also want to be a party to this agreement
to be able to police the relationship on behalf of the investors, although this is the

subject of negotiation and may not be necessary, for example where following a reverse takeover there is an independent committee of directors established to take decisions on any matter between the vendors (who become major shareholders) and the AIM company. In addition, many of the items usually covered by a relationship agreement are enshrined in UK company law and so the Nominated Adviser may not feel it is necessary to be a party (although this may not be the case for companies incorporated outside the United Kingdom).

CONTENTS OF RELATIONSHIP AGREEMENTS

47.3 A relationship agreement normally contains undertakings from the major shareholder not to exercise its voting rights and other powers of control available to it in relation to the AIM company, regardless of whether such rights or powers arise through representation on the board or through its holding of shares in the AIM company, including:

- to alter the composition of the board in such a way that the majority of directors thereon would not be regarded as being independent of the major shareholder;
- not to enter into any contract or relationship with the AIM company whether legally binding or otherwise save where such contract or relationship is entered into in the ordinary and proper course of business and on an arm's length and commercial basis. All such agreements may also be required to be conditional upon shareholders' or independent directors' approval;
- not to vary the company's Articles of Association which would be contrary to the maintenance of the company's independence; and
- other than bona fide in the interest of the AIM company as a whole.

47.4 The relationship agreement will also usually contain undertakings by the major shareholder to observe the provisions of the relationship agreement. In order to back up these undertakings, in the relationship agreement there is often an undertaking that none of the major shareholders or its related parties will exercise its voting rights as a holder of shares and no director connected to the major shareholder will vote at any meeting of the directors, in relation to any transaction or agreement whether proposed, existing or completed between any member of the AIM company's group and the major shareholder or any of its related parties or relating to the enforcement, implementation or amendment thereof.

47.5 Other undertakings in a relationship agreement often include an undertaking to notify the AIM company if a business approach is made to it in relation to the AIM company.

47.6 In many cases the relationship agreement will also contain an undertaking from the major shareholder that it and its related parties will not compete with the AIM company in any business operated by the AIM company or operated by any subsidiary of it.

47.7 Generally, relationship agreements are drafted to automatically expire upon the major shareholder's shareholding falling below a certain percentage level. The appropriate shareholding level is a matter for negotiation between the parties.

DISCLOSURE

47.8 The terms of any relationship agreements are required to be disclosed in the AIM admission document as being agreements entered into by the AIM company outside of the ordinary course of its business.

IN PRACTICE

The use of relationship agreements is fairly common where there is a potential dominant shareholder, and Nominated Advisers are increasingly insisting that such agreements are put in place as a matter of good governance where they have not been volunteered by the major shareholder.

CHAPTER 48

Health, safety, social and environment committee

There is no requirement in the *Combined Code* for an applicant company to form a health, safety, social and environment committee (HSSE). However, in certain situations a company applying for admission to trading on AIM may want to voluntarily observe best practice in social and environmental matters or will find that its Nominated Adviser will ask for one to be put in place. Such a committee is primarily of relevance to mining and oil and gas companies because of the direct impact their corporate decisions may have on the environment and community local to their assets, although they are not limited to these companies. The *ABI Guidelines on Responsible Investment Disclosure* (January 2007) are guidelines regarding the level of public disclosure an institutional shareholder should expect to see concerning social and environmental issues generally. The ABI guidelines a useful source of reference for an AIM company which is establishing an HSSE committee.

INTRODUCTION

48.1 Public debate on the role of companies in the wider social setting and their responsibility towards society has increased dramatically over recent years. It is a frequent occurrence to see listed companies attracting adverse publicity where they do not take adequate steps to mitigate the impact their business may have on the surrounding environment or community. When an applicant company is listing on AIM, it is taking a step which means that its actions and corporate strategy will be subject to far greater public scrutiny than it would as a private company. As a result, many companies may wish to voluntarily establish an HSSE committee. In addition, many institutional shareholders will require evidence of minimum standards of corporate social responsibility for a company before they consider making an investment.

48.2 In the case of mining and oil and gas companies who have a much greater exposure in this area, a Nominated Adviser may request that an HSSE committee is established in order to ensure that the AIM company has appropriate procedures in place to deal with the management of health, safety, environment and community relations risks, although the application of HSSE committees is not limited to mining and oil and gas companies.

HEALTH, SAFETY, SOCIAL AND ENVIRONMENT COMMITTEE

48.3   The principal role of an HSSE committee will be to provide an administrative framework under which the AIM company can identify and manage the environmental and social risks to the long and short-term value of the company. It has responsibility for formulating and recommending to the board the company's policy for HSSE issues as they affect the company's operations. The HSSE committee will also be responsible for reviewing management investigations of incidents or accidents that occur in order to assess whether policy improvements are required.

48.4   The ABI guidelines set out recommendations regarding the disclosures in connection with HSSE matters which institutional shareholders should expect to see in the annual report of the company in which they are invested. The guidelines recommend that the annual report should make disclosures stating whether the board takes HSSE matters into account in its regular risk assessment procedures, whether the board has identified and assessed the significant HSSE risks to the company's long and short-term value and the corresponding opportunities to enhance value, whether the board receives adequate information to make these assessments, whether directors receive training in HSSE matters and whether the board has effective systems for managing and mitigating significant HSSE risks which are arise.

48.5   In addition to the statements concerning the board's level of involvement in HSSE matters, the ABI guidelines recommend that the annual report should contain disclosure of the following items:

- the HSSE risks and opportunities that may significantly affect the company's short and long-term value, and how they might impact on the future of the business;
- in the description of the company's policies and procedures for managing risks, the possible impact on short and long-term value arising from HSSE matters;
- the extent to which the company has complied with its policies and procedures for managing material risks arising from HSSE matters, using key performance indicators where appropriate, and about the role of the board in providing oversight;
- where performance falls short of the objectives, the measures the board has taken to put it back on track; and
- the procedures for verification of HSSE disclosures.

The guidelines state that if the annual report states that the company has no such policies and procedures, the board should provide reasons for their absence.

48.6   The ABI guidelines envisage that in aiming to meet these disclosure requirements, a company will develop its internal procedures and policies on corporate responsibility. By setting up an HSSE committee, the company creates a forum through which these issues can be managed and decisions recorded.

48.7   The principal duties of an HSSE committee should usually include the following:

- formulating the company's policies and systems for identifying and managing HSSE risks within the company's operations;
- evaluating the effectiveness of the company's policies and systems;
- assessing the policies and systems within the company for ensuring compliance with HSSE regulatory requirements;
- assessing the performance of the company with regard to the impact of HSSE decisions and actions upon employees, communities and other third parties and the impact of such decisions and actions on the reputation of the company;
- receiving reports from management concerning all fatalities and serious accidents within the company and any ensuing action to be taken; and
- reviewing the results of independent audits of the company's performance in regard to HSSE matters, reviewing any strategies and action plans developed by management in response to issues raised and, where appropriate, making recommendations to the board.

HSSE COMMITTEE COMPOSITION, APPOINTMENT AND CONDUCT OF MEETINGS

48.8   There are no recommended guidelines for the practicalities of implementing an HSSE committee, so in terms of practical detail of the terms of reference, those of the HSSE committee are likely to track the terms of reference of the company's other committees (See Chapter 43, *Remuneration committee*, Chapter 44, *Audit committee* and Chapter, 45 *Nomination committee*). It is common for such a committee to meet four times a year, however this will depend on the size of the company in question and the extent of its operations. The composition requirements vary according to the size of the company and the size of the board, but it is not uncommon to require that of the minimum number of individuals on the committee, only one needs to be a board director.

IN PRACTICE

The HSSE committee is going to be most relevant to mining and oil and gas companies but will be applicable to all companies whose operations are likely to have a social or environmental impact. Due to the nature of their business, many of these companies will already have in place some form of internal procedure for considering their impact on the safety of their employees, the local community and the environment. However, it will not be uncommon for the Nominated Adviser to request that this is put on a more formal footing prior to admission to trading on AIM.

Part VI
De-Listing

INTRODUCTION

The AIM Market will not be suitable for all companies, others may outgrow AIM and seek to move to another market, and some may be taken over.

This Part looks at the cancellation process in Chapter 49, *Cancellation of trading on AIM*, and at some of the issues which arise on a move to the Main Market of the London Stock Exchange in Chapter 50, *Moving from AIM to the Main Market*.

Cancellation of trading on AIM

AT A GLANCE

AIM will not be suitable for all companies and a number of companies may choose to have the trading of their securities on AIM cancelled for a variety of reasons including following a takeover, a move to another market or discovering that the disclosure requirements and processes and procedures that are part of being a public company are not suited to them or their business. Cancellation of the trading facility is a relatively straightforward process requiring notification to the market and, unless comparable dealing facilities are put in place, shareholder approval.

WHY SEEK A CANCELLATION

49.1   Even if a company was suited to being a public company whose securities are traded on AIM at the time of its admission to trading on AIM, companies develop and change, which may mean that it is no longer suitable or some of the perceived advantages have failed to materialise. This may occur for a variety of reasons. Some companies find that they outgrow AIM and move up to the Main Market of the London Stock Exchange. This is considered further in Chapter 50, *Moving from AIM to the Main Market.* Another common reason why a company may seek the cancellation of the trading of its securities on AIM is where it becomes a subsidiary of another company or has only one shareholder, for example pursuant to a successful takeover offer. Other reasons why companies may seek cancellation of the trading of their securities on AIM are as a result of some of the disadvantages of being a public company with its securities traded on a public market including:

- volatility – the price of the company's securities may be adversely affected by considerations outside the control of the company and affecting the market as a whole;
- illiquidity – the company may find that even minor events trigger a significant move in the share price if the market for those securities is relatively illiquid;
- transparency – the requirement for the company to announce news, whether positive or negative, without delay can put additional pressures on the share price; and

- scrutiny – the actions and decisions and results of the company are subject to increased scrutiny as a public company.

CANCELLATION PROCESS

49.2 Pursuant to Rule 41 of the *AIM Rules for Companies*, the first step in the cancellation process is for the company to issue a notification to AIM of its intention to seek a cancellation of its admission to AIM. This notification must set out the preferred date of the cancellation and the reasons why the company is seeking a cancellation. The notification must also include a description of how shareholders will be able to effect transactions in the securities once they have been cancelled, as well as any other information which will be relevant to shareholders in reaching an informed decision on the issue of the proposed cancellation.

49.3 At the same time that the notification is released, the company must separately inform the London Stock Exchange of its preferred cancellation date.

49.4 Following notification of the preferred cancellation date to the London Stock Exchange, it is a requirement of Rule 41 of the *AIM Rules for Companies* that the cancellation shall be conditional upon the consent of shareholders, unless the London Stock Exchange otherwise agrees. Shareholder consent requires 75 per cent of the votes cast in person, or by proxy, at a general meeting of the company to be in favour of the proposed cancellation.

49.5 The London Stock Exchange has discretion as to whether or not shareholder approval of the proposed cancellation will be required, but generally it will not be required if the cancellation is being sought following a takeover offer which has become unconditional and valid acceptances have been received from people holding in excess of 75 per cent of the security which is traded on AIM. Similarly, the London Stock Exchange will generally not require shareholder approval of a proposed cancellation where comparable dealing facilities are put in place to enable shareholders to trade in their securities in the future. Whilst the AIM team retain discretion as to whether comparable dealing facilities have been put in place, in its guidance the London Stock Exchange states that such comparable dealing facilities include those on an EU regulated market or certain AIM Designated Markets, which currently include those markets set out in Figure 49.1.

49.6 Where shareholder approval is required, cancellation will not take effect until at least five business days have passed following that approval.

49.7 Whether or not shareholder approval is required, cancellation then becomes effective when a dealing notice to that effect has been issued by the London Stock Exchange.

49.8 Examples of timelines for seeking cancellation of trading of securities on AIM, with and without shareholder authority, are set out in Figures 49.2 and 49.3.

FIGURE 49.1   AIM Designated Markets

The AIM Designated Markets are as follows:

- Australian Stock Exchange
- Euronext
- Deutsche Börse
- Johannesburg Stock Exchange
- Nasdaq
- NYSE
- Stockholmsbörsen
- Swiss Exchange
- Toronto Stock Exchange
- United Kingdom Listing Authority Official List

The London Stock Exchange may, at any time, remove a market from its list of AIM Designated Markets where that market no longer satisfies the relevant criteria and add additional markets which do, so the London Stock Exchange's website (www.londonstockexchange.com) should be checked when considering utilising the "fast-track" exemption.

Source: extract from *AIM Designated Markets*

FIGURE 49.2   Example timeline for cancellation of AIM listing where shareholder approval is needed

Date	Action
−20 business days	Notification issued to a Regulatory Information Service of intention to seek cancellation, specifying the proposed date of cancellation.
	Nominated Adviser to inform the London Stock Exchange of proposed cancellation.
−19 business days[1]	Latest date for despatch of Circular to Shareholders convening a General Meeting to approve the cancellation.
−7 business days	Shareholder meeting to approve cancellation.
Impact day	Dealing Notice issued by the London Stock Exchange.
	Trading in the AIM securities cancelled.[2]

1 This date is subject to change depending on the notice provisions of the company's Articles of Association.
2 Provided that the impact day is the date specified in the notification as being the proposed date of cancellation.

FIGURE 49.3	Example timeline for cancellation of AIM listing where shareholder approval is not needed

Date	Action
–20 business days	Notification issued to a Regulatory Information Service of intention to seek cancellation, specifying the proposed date of cancellation. Nominated Adviser to inform the London Stock Exchange of proposed cancellation.
Impact day	Dealing Notice issued by the London Stock Exchange. Trading in the AIM securities cancelled.[1]

1 Provided that the impact day is the date specified in the notification as being the proposed date of cancellation.

IN PRACTICE

The cancellation of an AIM trading facility is fairly straightforward provided that the simple procedures are followed.

CHAPTER 50

Moving from AIM to the Main Market

AT A GLANCE

Companies who are successful on AIM and reach a certain size and stage of development, may seek to move their securities from trading on AIM to having them admitted to trading on the Main Market of the London Stock Exchange, provided that they meet the eligibility criteria. While a move to the Main Market may subject the company to increased regulation, and therefore increased costs, it may bring benefits in terms of attracting investors.

WHY CONSIDER A MOVE TO THE MAIN MARKET?

50.1 Once a company reaches a certain size and stage of development, it may find that its shareholders and other potential investors request that the company has its securities admitted to trading on the Main Market of the London Stock Exchange. The board of directors and its advisers may also perceive advantages to the company in attracting investors if the company moves to the Main Market.

50.2 In order to consider a move to the Main Market a company will need to meet the basic eligibility thresholds, which generally include a requirement that the company has a minimum 25 per cent free float (i.e. at least 25 per cent of the relevant class of securities are held by people other than the board of directors and shareholders who hold more than five per cent each) and a three-year trading record (although there are exceptions to the trading record set out in the *Listing Rules* for some companies such as mineral companies). There are some other requirements which should be less problematic, such as having a minimum market capitalisation of at least £700,000. While there may be exceptions to some of these requirements for certain companies (e.g. mineral companies), the first step in the process for any company considering a move to the Main Market is to ensure that it meets the eligibility criteria.

50.3 The main advantages of a move to the Main Market of the London Stock Exchange predominantly centre around the company's ability to attract investors and access to capital.

50.4 Due to the increased regulation on the Main Market of the London Stock Exchange, investors, both private and institutional, tend to have more confidence in companies with securities admitted to the Official List of the United Kingdom Listing Authority and to trading on the Main Market of the London Stock

Exchange. As a result, companies can often find that they have a wider pool of investors who are willing to invest in the company.

50.5   Many companies also find that they have increased passive investment from FTSE trackers which can increase liquidity, in particular when a company would be eligible for inclusion in either the FSTE 100 or FSTE 250 indices.

50.6   As the company increases in size and profile, it will also find that by moving to the Main Market of the London Stock Exchange there will usually be an increase in research analyst's coverage, which again can help lead to a demand in the company's securities.

50.7   Having highlighted some of the possible advantages, any move to the Main Market of the London Stock Exchange is not without its own disadvantages or drawbacks.

50.8   Even if a company can meet the eligibility criteria, an application for admission to the Official List and to trading on the Main Market of the London Stock Exchange requires the production of a prospectus, which has to be pre-vetted by the United Kingdom Listing Authority. This can be time consuming and a significant expense, particularly where a company is not seeking to raise additional funds at the time of its listing.

50.9   In addition, once a company has been admitted to the Official List of the United Kingdom Listing Authority and to trading on the Main Market of the London Stock Exchange it is required to comply with the *Listing Rules*, which are significantly longer and more detailed than the *AIM Rules for Companies*. Of particular note are the class tests and rules surrounding acquisitions and disposals. The most significant change for an AIM company is that the threshold at which shareholder approval is needed for a transaction is reduced from 100 per cent to 25 per cent.

50.10   Another significant change for an AIM company when it moves to the Main Market of the London Stock Exchange is in connection with corporate governance. As part of the investor confidence, a company which is admitted to the Official List of the United Kingdom Listing Authority, and whose securities are admitted to trading on the Main Market, is expected to adhere to the *Combined Code* on corporate governance. In practice, the approach is still largely comply or explain; however, a company whose securities are admitted to trading on the Main Market of the London Stock Exchange would be expected to comply with the main principles.

50.11   Another significant change for the shareholders is that, whilst AIM securities are treated as unquoted for certain tax purposes, this is not the case once securities are admitted to trading on the Main Market of the London Stock Exchange.

50.12   AIM companies that move to the Main Market cease to be treated as "unquoted" for tax purposes. As a general rule, although the tax advantages afforded on AIM securities for the future cease to be available, the advantages granted in the period when the securities were traded on AIM are preserved, subject to detailed conditions in the respective parts of the tax code for each relief. In particular:

- prior to April 2008, although the securities ceased to be business assets for taper relief purposes, they were subject to tax at a blended effective rate for business and non-business assets. There was a gradual increase in the effective rate of tax the longer the stock was held after the move to the Main Market;
- with the introduction of flat rate capital gains tax at 18 per cent, broadly the move from AIM to the Main Market will become tax neutral for capital gains tax purposes;
- business property relief for inheritance tax purposes ceases to be available, except for controlling holdings (i.e. exceeding 50 per cent) of the Main Market company. However, gifts and transfers made when the stock was traded on AIM maintain the benefits of inheritance tax relief;
- capital gains tax holdover relief is not crystallised on the move from AIM to the Main Market but only on the subsequent disposal of securities in the normal way. Gifts of quoted securities, however, do not qualify for holdover relief unless the individual owner of the securities broadly owns 5 per cent or more of the voting rights in the Main Market company;
- Enterprise Investment Scheme (EIS), Venture Capital Tax (VCT) and the Corporate Venturing Scheme reliefs are broadly preserved on the move from AIM to the Main Market and reliefs previously granted are not withdrawn, provided that at the time that the original AIM securities were issued there were no arrangements in place for the move to the Main Market. A number of conditions apply, so specialist advice should be taken; and
- share loss relief will still be available, provided that when the AIM securities were issued, there were no arrangements in existence for a move to the Main Market.

50.13 Specialist advice should be sought on how the move will affect shareholders, particularly private shareholders, and this should be summarised in the prospectus.

50.14 An example of the timeline when moving from AIM to the Main Market is set out in Figure 50.1.

FIGURE 50.1 Example timeline for cancellation of AIM listing when moving to the Main Market of the London Stock Exchange

Date	Action
−20 business days	Notification issued to a Regulatory Information Service specifying the proposed date of cancellation. Nominated Adviser to inform the London Stock Exchange of proposed cancellation.
Impact day	Dealing Notice issued, trading and securities cancelled.[1]

1 Provided that the impact day is the date specified in the notification as being the proposed date of cancellation.

IN PRACTICE

For larger or established companies, the process of moving from AIM to the Main Market of the London Stock Exchange is not an unusual development, but the advantages of increasing the shareholder base and pool of investors should be carefully weighed up against the one-off costs involved and the increased regulatory burden to which the company would be subject.

Appendix 1

Useful Sources of Information

GENERAL SOURCES

AIM Rules for Companies, February 2007: London Stock Exchange
www.londonstockexchange.com/NR/rdonlyres/91B19E7D-550C-440A-BCCA-
52A32F1913DB/0/AIMRULESFORCOMPANIES_2007.pdf

AIM Rules for Nominated Advisers, February 2007: London Stock Exchange
www.londonstockexchange.com/NR/rdonlyres/8104E31B-946D-49F1-A82B-
CC14499B435A/0/AIMNominatedAdviser.pdf

AIM Disciplinary Procedures and Appeals Handbook, February 2007: London Stock
Exchange
www.londonstockexchange.com/NR/rdonlyres/7A81FE1C-5920-43AB-AB01-
6B83306F8FED/0/AIM03.pdf

Guidance Note for Mining, Oil and Gas Companies, March 2006: London Stock Exchange
www.londonstockexchange.com/NR/rdonlyres/01B3C887-9559-458C-B19B-
B41A6E641F9B/0/FinalGuidanceMOG.pdf

The Combined Code on Corporate Governance
www.frc.org.uk/corporate/combinedcode.cfm

Prospectus Rules (part of the *FSA Handbook*)
http://fsahandbook.info/FSA/html/handbook/PR

The FSA Handbook
http://www.fsa.gov.uk

The London Stock Exchange website
www.londonstockexchange.co.uk

SPECIFIC SOURCES

Introduction

Chapter 1 – What is AIM and why seek admission to AIM?

AIM Brochure
www.fsa.gov.uk/Pages/Library/Other_publications/UKLA/index.shtml

Chapter 3 – AIM and tax

A Guide to AIM Tax Benefits: London Stock Exchange
www.londonstockexchange.com/NR/rdonlyres/1C0B640F-787A-44A7-B82C-
E6D19316E03B/0/AIMtaxguideupdatedMay2007.pdf

Simon's Direct Tax Service: LexisNexis Butterworths

Tolley's Yellow Tax Handbook 2007–08: LexisNexis Butterworths

HMRC Manuals: LexisNexis Butterworths

Part I: Key Team

Chapter 4 – Role of AIM Regulation

Listing Rules (part of the *FSA Handbook*)
http://fsahandbook.info/FSA/html/handbook/LR

Chapter 5 – Role of the Nominated Adviser

A Professional Handbook – Joining AIM: London Stock Exchange
www.londonstockexchange.com/NR/rdonlyres/8AA27C31-D68F-4275-A140-
EF2FCD81F191/0/LSEAIMGuidenographicsFINAL.pdf

Chapter 6 – Role of the broker

A Professional Handbook – Joining AIM: London Stock Exchange
www.londonstockexchange.com/NR/rdonlyres/8AA27C31-D68F-4275-A140-
EF2FCD81F191/0/LSEAIMGuidenographicsFINAL.pdf

Chapter 7 – Role of the reporting accountant

A Professional Handbook – Joining AIM: London Stock Exchange
www.londonstockexchange.com/NR/rdonlyres/8AA27C31-D68F-4275-A140-
EF2FCD81F191/0/LSEAIMGuidenographicsFINAL.pdf

Chapter 8 – Role of the other advisers

A Professional Handbook – Joining AIM: London Stock Exchange
www.londonstockexchange.com/NR/rdonlyres/8AA27C31-D68F-4275-A140-
EF2FCD81F191/0/LSEAIMGuidenographicsFINAL.pdf

Part II: Admissions to AIM

Chapter 9 – Suitability and preparation for admission

Listing Rules (part of the *FSA Handbook*)
http://fsahandbook.info/FSA/html/handbook/LR

NOMAD Declaration
www.londonstockexchange.co.uk/NR/rdonlyres/EA808AC5-54A2-4CBC-9CC8-
8DB13CA6E322/0/Nomaddeclaration2002073.doc

Chapter 14 – Admission to trading on AIM by reverse takeover

The City Code on Takeovers and Mergers
www.thetakeoverpanel.org.uk/new/codesars/DATA/code.pdf

Chapter 16 – CREST, settlement and depository interests

The CREST Rules: issued 04.01.08
www.euroclear.co.uk/publications/reference/manual/rules.pdf

The CREST Reference Manual: issued 05.11.07
www.euroclear.co.uk/publications/reference/manual/ref-manual.pdf

The Domestic Legal Framework, March 2002: issued by CRESTCo Limited
www.euroclear.co.uk/publications

The International Legal Framework, July 2001: issued by CRESTCo Limited
www.euroclear.co.uk/publications

Joining CREST, 2005: issued by CRESTCo Limited
www.euroclear.co.uk/publications

Tolley's Company Law, Issue 91, February 2007

Part III: Fundraisings
Chapter 19 – Offers to the public

Frequently asked questions regarding Prospectus: Common positions agreed by CESR members: updated versions February and September 2007
www.cesr-eu.org

List!, Issue 16, July 2007: UKLA Publications
www.fsa.gov.uk/Pages/Library/Other_publications/UKLA/index.shtml

Chapter 23 – Price stabilisation, over-allotment, greenshoes and when-issued trading

Precedent Global Lending Agreement: London Stock Exchange

Disclosure Rules and Transparency Rules (part of *FSA Handbook*)
http://fsahandbook.info/FSA/html/handbook/DTR

Chapter 24 – Analyst research

Conduct of Business Sourcebook (part of the *FSA Handbook*)
http://fsahandbook.info/FSA/html/handbook/COBS

Part IV: Continuing Obligations
Chapter 28 – Announcements including price sensitive information

Disclosure Rules and Transparency Rules (part of *FSA Handbook*)
http://fsahandbook.info/FSA/html/handbook/DTR

AIM Website Guide – Rule 26: QCA
www.quotedcompaniesalliance.co.uk/guidance_booklets.asp

Chapter 29 – Website disclosure

AIM Website Guide – Rule 26: QCA
www.quotedcompaniesalliance.co.uk/guidance_booklets.asp

Chapter 31 – Directors' responsibility

Code of Market Conduct
www.fsa.gov.uk/Pages/Library/Policy/Policy/2001/PS59_76.shtml
DTI Ministerial Statements on duties of company directors under the Companies Act 2006: issued June 2007
www.berr.gov.uk/files/file40139.pdf

Chapter 33 – Directors' service agreements

Keen v. *Commerzbank AG* [EWCA Civ 1536]
Micklefield v. *SAC Technology Ltd* [1990] IRLR 218
National Association of Pension Funds Guidelines

Chapter 34 – Acquisitions and disposals

Listing Rules
http://fsahandbook.info/FSA/html/handbook/LR

Chapter 36 – Options and share incentives

Tolley's Yellow Tax Handbook 2007–08: LexisNexis Butterworths
HMRC Manuals: LexisNexis Butterworths
Executive Remuneration – ABI Guidelines on Policies and Practices, December 2007: Association of British Insurers
Employee Share Schemes, edited by David Pett of Pinsent Curtis: Sweet & Maxwell

Chapter 37 – Tax incentives

A Guide to AIM Tax Benefits: London Stock Exchange
www.londonstockexchange.com/NR/rdonlyres/1C0B640F-787A-44A7-B82C-E6D19316E03B/0/AIMtaxguideupdatedMay2007.pdf
Simon's Direct Tax Service: LexisNexis Butterworths
Tolley's Yellow Tax Handbook 2007–08: LexisNexis Butterworths
HMRC Manuals: LexisNexis Butterworths

Chapter 38 – Disclosure Rules and Transparency Rules

Disclosure Rules and Transparency Rules (part of *FSA Handbook*)
http://fsahandbook.info/FSA/html/handbook/DTR
List!, Issue 14 Updated, April 2007: UKLA Publications
www.fsa.gov.uk/pubs/ukla/list14_apr07.pdf
FAQs for Shareholders: FSA website (accessed 21 August 2007)
www.fsa.gov.uk
Form TR-1. FSA version 2.1 updated April 2007; and Notes to form TR-1. FSA version 1.1 updated March 2007
www.fsa.gov.uk

Chapter 40 – Overseas companies

Disclosure Rules and Transparency Rules (part of *FSA Handbook*)
http://fsahandbook.info/FSA/html/handbook/DTR

2006/891/EC: Commission Decision of 4 December 2006 on the use by third country issuers of securities of information prepared under internationally accepted accounting standards (notified under document number C(2006) 5804)

Part V: Corporate Governance
Chapter 42 – Corporate governance for AIM companies

AIM Website Guide – Rule 26: QCA
www.quotedcompaniesalliance.co.uk/guidance_booklets.asp

The NAPF Guidelines
www.napf.co.uk

Corporate Governance Guidelines: QCA
www.quotedcompaniesalliance.co.uk/guidance_booklets.asp

Chapter 43 – Remuneration committee

AIM Website Guide – Rule 26: QCA
www.quotedcompaniesalliance.co.uk/guidance_booklets.asp

ICSA Guidance Note: Terms of Reference – Remuneration Committee
www.icsa.org.uk

Chapter 44 – Audit committee

'The Smith Guidance' in the Related Guidance and Good Practice Suggestions of the *Combined Code*

AIM Website Guide – Rule 26: QCA
www.quotedcompaniesalliance.uk/guidance_booklets.asp

ICSA Guidance Note: Terms of Reference – Audit Committee
www.icsa.org.uk

Chapter 45 – Nomination committee

AIM Website Guide – Rule 26: QCA
www.quotedcompaniesalliance.co.uk/guidance_booklets.asp

ICSA Guidance on Terms of Reference – Nomination Committee
www.icsa.org.uk

Chapter 48 – Health, safety, social and environment committee

Association of British Insurers – Guidelines on Responsible Investment Disclosure
www.ivis.co.uk

Part VI: De-Listing
Chapter 50 – Moving from AIM to the Main Market

Listing Rules (part of *FSA Handbook*)
http://fsahandbook.info/FSA/html/handbook/LR

Appendix 2

Charles Russell LLP

Charles Russell LLP is a top 50 full service City legal practice with offices in London, Guildford, Cheltenham, Cambridge, Oxford, Geneva and Bahrain. Charles Russell has the expertise and size to advise on complex, cross-border transactions and to project manage the input of our international networks of major law firms. Charles Russell's clients range from international, FTSE and AIM-listed businesses to governments, not-for-profit bodies, private individuals, trustees and intermediaries.

Charles Russell has a simple strategy – to help clients achieve their goals through excellent service.

Charles Russell is a member of two international non-exclusive associations: The Association of European Lawyers and ALFA International (American Law Firm Association). It also has a dedicated British Virgin Islands service.

Charles Russell's Capital Markets Team comprises an experienced team of more than 15 partners and 30 solicitors who work on a broad range of high-profile UK-based and cross-border mergers, acquisitions and disposals (both public and private) as well as IPOs and offerings of securities on the Official List, and AIM and private placements, acting for issuers, financial advisers and brokers.

Charles Russell also has considerable expertise in venture capital and in management buy-outs and buy-ins, advising investors as well as companies seeking venture capital investment and management teams.

Charles Russell provides a full service for each transaction, with experts in tax (corporate and personal), financial services, EU and competition law, employment, employee benefits and pensions, property and environmental law, intellectual property and IT law, and commercial dispute resolution.

Any enquiries should be directed to Alexander Keepin, a partner at the London office, by telephone or on his email: alexander.keepin@charlesrussell.co.uk

Website: www.charlesrussell.co.uk

CHARLES RUSSELL LLP OFFICES:

Charles Russell LLP
London
8–10 New Fetter Lane
London EC4A 1RS

Tel: 020 7203 5000
Tel: 020 7203 5000

Charles Russell LLP
Cheltenham
Compass House
Lypiatt Road
Cheltenham
Gloucestershire GL50 2QJ

Tel: 01242 221 122
Fax: 01242 584 700

Charles Russell LLP
Guildford
Buryfields House
Bury Fields
Guildford
Surrey GU2 4AZ

Tel: 01483 252 525
Fax: 01483 252 550

Charles Russell LLP
Oxford
7600 The Quorum
Oxford Business Park North
Oxford OX4 2JZ

Tel: 0845 3559 0090
Fax: 0845 359 0099

Charles Russell LLP
Cambridge
Ground Floor
Clarendon House
Clarendon Road
Cambridge CB2 8FH

Tel: 01223 465 465
Fax: 01223 465 400

Charles Russell LLP
St James's (London)
Kinsgbury House
15–17 King Street
London SW1Y 6QU

Tel: 020 7203 5000

Charles Russell LLP
Geneva
14 Rue du Rhone
1204 Geneva
Switzerland

Tel: 00 41 22 819 1768
Fax: 00 41 22 819 1970

Charles Russell LLP
Bahrain
PO Box 20705
Level 22
Bahrain Financial Harbour
West Tower
Manama Kingdom of
Bahrain

Tel: +973 17 50 28 20
Tel: +973 17 50 28 21
Fax: +973 17 50 28 22

Glossary

ABI Association of British Insurers.

admission/admitted Admission of any class of securities to trading on AIM effected by a dealing notice under Rule 6 of the *AIM Rules for Companies*.

AIM The AIM Market operated by the London Stock Exchange.

AIM admission document The document produced by a company that is applying to have its securities admitted to trading on AIM. Such an admission document must be produced in accordance with the *AIM Rules for Companies*.

AIM company A company with a class of security admitted to trading on AIM.

AIM Designated Market A market whose name appears on the latest publication by the London Stock Exchange of the document entitled *AIM Designated Markets*.

AIM guidance The Guidance Notes for companies set out in Part Two of the *AIM Rules for Companies*.

AIM guidance for mining, oil and gas companies The booklet entitled *AIM Guidance for Mining, Oil and Gas companies* published by the London Stock Exchange.

AIM Regulation The AIM Regulation team at the London Stock Exchange.

AIM Rules for Companies The booklet entitled *AIM Rules for Companies* published by the London Stock Exchange.

AIM Rules for Nominated Advisers The booklet entitled *AIM Rules for Nominated Advisers* published by the London Stock Exchange.

AIM securities Securities of an AIM company which have been admitted to trading on AIM.

allotment The issue of shares by a company.

allottee A person to whom shares have been allotted by a company.

Annex I/Annex II/Annex III Annex I, Annex II and Annex III of Regulation 809/2004 of the European Commission (referred to as the PD Regulation in the Financial Services Authority Handbook), as reprinted in the *Prospectus Rules*.

applicable employee Any employee of an AIM company, its subsidiary or parent undertaking who:
- for the purposes of Rule 7 of the *AIM Rules for Companies*, together with that employee's family, has a holding or interest, directly or indirectly, in 0.5 per cent or more of a class of AIM securities (excluding treasury shares); or
- for the purposes of Rule 21 of the *AIM Rules for Companies*, is likely to be in possession of unpublished price sensitive information in relation to the AIM company because of his employment in the AIM company, its subsidiary or parent undertaking, irrespective of his holding or interest.

applicant An issuer that is applying to have a class of its securities admitted to AIM and which is seeking to have a notification issued pursuant to Rule 2 of the *AIM Rules for Companies*.

application form The latest publication of the standard form which must be completed by an applicant or a quoted applicant under Rule 5 of the *AIM Rules for Companies*.

Articles/Articles of Association The internal regulations of a company.

authorised or nominal capital The face value of the securities of a company which the company is permitted to issue under its constitution.

authorised person A person who, under EU directive or UK domestic legislation, is authorised to conduct investment business in the United Kingdom.

bankruptcy The formal state in personal insolvency where a person's assets move by operation of law to his trustee in bankruptcy for the benefit of his creditors.

block admission The admission of a specified number of securities of a class which have been admitted to trading on AIM, which are to be issued by an AIM company on a regular basis.

broker A member firm which is appointed by an AIM company pursuant to Rule 35 of the *AIM Rules for Companies*.

BTR Business asset taper relief

business day Any day upon which the London Stock Exchange is open for business. It should be noted that references to business days in the *AIM Rules for Companies* is to clear business days.

cancel/cancelled/cancellation The cancellation of any class of securities admitted to trading on AIM effected by a dealing notice.

capital The money or money's worth through which a company finances its business.

certificate of incorporation The document that brings a company into existence.

CESR The Committee of European Securities Regulators.

CGT Capital gains tax.

class right A right attaching to a class of share, usually in regard to a right to receive a dividend, the right to receive a return of capital on a winding up or the right to vote in general meeting.

class tests The tests set out in Schedule 3 to the *AIM Rules for Companies* which are used to determine whether certain of the *AIM Rules for Companies* apply.

close period
- The period of two months preceding the publication of an AIM company's annual results (or, if shorter, the period from its financial year end to the time of publication); and
    - if it reports only half-yearly, the period of two months immediately preceding the notification of its half-yearly report or, if shorter, the period from the relevant financial period end up to and including the time of the notification; or
    - if it reports on a quarterly basis, the period of one month immediately preceding the notification of its quarterly results or, if shorter, the period from the relevant financial period end up to and including the time of the notification.
- Any other period when the AIM company is in possession of unpublished price sensitive information.
- Any time it has become reasonably probable that such information will be required by the *AIM Rules for Companies* to be notified to a Regulatory Information Service.

CVS Corporate Venturing Scheme, a form of tax relief.

deal
- Any change whatsoever to the holding of AIM securities of an AIM company in which the holder is a director of the AIM company or part of a director's family (and for the purpose of Rule 21 of the *AIM Rules for Companies* an applicable employee) including:
  - any sale or purchase, or any agreement for the sale or purchase of such securities;
  - the grant to, or acceptance by such a person of any option relating to such securities or of any other right or obligation, present or future, conditional or unconditional, to acquire or dispose of any such securities;
  - the acquisition, disposal, exercise or discharge of, or any dealing with, any such option, right or obligation in respect of such securities;
  - deals between directors and/or applicable employees of the AIM company;
  - off-market deals;
  - transfers for no consideration; and
  - any shares taken into or out of treasury.
- The acquisition, disposal or discharge (whether in whole or in part) of a related financial product referenced to AIM securities of an AIM company in which the holder is a director or part of a director's family (and for the purpose of Rule 21 of the *AIM Rules for Companies* an applicable employee).
- However, for the purposes of Rule 21 of the *AIM Rules for Companies*, the following are not included:
  - undertakings or elections to take up entitlements under a rights issue or other pre-emptive offer (including an offer of shares in lieu of a cash dividend);
  - the take up of entitlements under a rights issue or other pre-emptive offer (including an offer of shares in lieu of a cash dividend);
  - allowing entitlements to lapse under a rights issue or other pre-emptive offer (including an offer of shares in lieu of a cash dividend);
  - the sale of sufficient entitlements nil-paid to allow take up of the balance of the entitlements under a rights issue; nor
  - undertakings to accept, or the acceptance of, a take-over offer.

dealing notice A notification by the London Stock Exchange disseminated through a Regulatory Information Service which either admits securities to AIM or cancels or suspends them from trading on AIM or restores them to trading on AIM.

director A person who acts as a director whether or not officially appointed to such position.

Disciplinary Procedures and Appeals Handbook The most recent publication by the London Stock Exchange of the document so entitled for AIM.

dividend That part of the profits made by a company that is paid to the members.

DTR The *Disclosure Rules and Transparency Rules* published by the Financial Services Authority from time to time.

DTR company An AIM company that is required to make disclosures in accordance with the DTR. A non-DTR company is an AIM company that is not required to make disclosures in accordance with the DTR.

EEA country A European Economic Area (EEA) country. The EEA comprises all European Union member stated together with Norway, Iceland and Lichtenstein. For the purposes of the *AIM Rules for Companies* only, an EEA country shall also be deemed to include the Channel Islands and the Isle of Man. A non-EEA country is any country that is not an EEA country.

EIS Enterprise Investment Scheme, a form of tax relief.

employee share scheme An arrangement whereby employees can acquire shares in the company for which they work.

family In relation to any person his or her spouse or civil partner and any child where such child is under the age of 18 years. It includes any trust in which such individuals are trustees or beneficiaries and any company over which they have control or more than 20 per cent of its equity or voting rights (excluding treasury shares) in a general meeting. It excludes any employee share or pension scheme where such individuals are beneficiaries rather than trustees.

fiduciary duty The duty owed by a director to his company that requires him to act in good faith and not to allow any conflict to arise between his interest in himself and his duty to his company.

financial promotion A communication of an invitation or inducement to engage in investment activity.

flotation The process of making securities available to be traded on a market such as AIM.

FSMA The *Financial Services and Markets Act 2000*.

general meeting A meeting of the members of a company.

generally accepted accounting principles There is no formal definition of the term "generally accepted accounting principles", but in simple terms it has been understood to mean compliance with relevant company law, accounting standards and best practice.

holding Any legal or beneficial interest, whether direct or indirect, in the AIM securities of a person who is a director or, where relevant, an applicable employee or significant shareholder. It should be noted that for the purposes of the *AIM Rules for Companies* it includes holdings by the family of such a person.

holding company A company having subsidiary companies.

instrument of transfer Stock transfer form.

interim dividend A dividend paid by the directors of a company of their own initiative between annual general meetings.

international accounting standards Standards adopted for use in the European Union in accordance with Article 3 of the *International Accounting Standards Regulation* (EC) No. 1606/2002.

investing company Any AIM company which, in the opinion of the London Stock Exchange, has as a primary business the investing of its funds in the securities of other companies or the acquisition of a particular business. An investing company must have an investing strategy.

investing strategy The investing strategy of an investing company containing the information required by Schedule Two to the *AIM Rules for Companies*, paragraph (j), published in an AIM admission document, a circular produced pursuant to Rule 15 of the *AIM Rules for Companies* or, in the case of a quoted applicant, in its pre-admission announcement.

ISIN/International Stock Identification Number A unique number used to identify a class of security.

IPO Initial public offering.

listed Admitted to the Official List of the United Kingdom by the Competent Authority or any corresponding list maintained by a competent authority in an EEA state (but not the Channel Islands and the Isle of Man) for the United Kingdom.

listed company A company whose securities are listed.

Markets in Financial Instruments Directive The European Parliament and Council Directive on markets in financial instruments (No. 2004/39/EC).

member A holder of securities in a company.

member firm A partnership, corporation, legal entity or sole practitioner admitted currently to London Stock Exchange membership.

Memorandum/Memorandum of Association The key constitutional document of a company setting out, among other things, its name, objects and capital.

Nominated Adviser An adviser whose name appears on the London Stock Exchange's most recent register of Nominated Advisers.

Nominated Adviser's declaration The latest form of declaration contained in the *AIM Rules for Nominated Advisers*.

not in public hands AIM securities held, directly or indirectly (including via a related financial product) by:
- a related party;
- the trustees of any employee share scheme or pension fund establishment for the benefit of any directors/employees of the applicant/AIM company (or its subsidiaries);
- any person who under any agreement has a right to nominate a person to the board of directors to the applicant/AIM company;
- any person who is the subject of a lock-in agreement pursuant to Rule 7 or otherwise; or
- the AIM company as treasury shares.

notify/notified/notification The delivery of an announcement to a Regulatory Information Service for distribution to the public.

off-market purchase The purchase back by a company of its securities when such securities are not dealt with on a market.

ordinary resolution A resolution passed by a simple majority of the members in a general meeting.

paid-up capital That amount of a company's issued share capital that has been paid by its members.

pathfinder A draft admission document or prospectus used to market the offering to qualified investors. A pathfinder usually contains no information as to the price or number of securities to be issued. A pathfinder is usually accompanied by additional disclosures and warranties.

person An individual, corporation, partnership, association, trust or other entity.

personal representative An executor or administrator who administers a deceased person's estate.

placing letter A contractual document pursuant to which a placee agrees to purchase or subscribe for securities as part of an offer of the securities.

placee A person who agrees to purchase or subscribe for securities.

placing proof/p-proof A draft admission document or prospectus which is complete other than it has not been dated. A placing proof is usually marked with a "p" in the top right-hand corner. A placing proof is sent to potential placees with the placing letter.

premium The amount paid for a share by an allottee over and above the nominal value of that share.

private company Any company that is not a public company.

pro rata Rateably; in proportion.

promoter A person who undertakes to form a company and who takes the necessary steps to achieve that end.

prospectus A prospectus prepared and published in accordance with the *Prospectus Rules*.

Prospectus Directive The Directive of the European Parliament and of the Council of 4 November 2003 on the prospectus to be published when securities are offered to the public or admitted to trading (No. 2003/71/EC).

Prospectus Regulation Commission Regulation (EC) No. 809/2004 implementing the *Prospectus Directive*. The *Prospectus Regulation* specifies details of the form and content of a prospectus as required by the *Prospectus Directive*.

Prospectus Rules The *Prospectus Rules* published by the Financial Services Authority from time to time as defined in section 73A(4) of the FSMA.

public limited company A company the name of which ends with the letters plc (or the names represented by those letters in full), the Memorandum of which states that it is a public company, the share capital of which has a nominal value of at least £50,000 and which is registered as a public company.

QCA Quoted Companies Alliance.

quoted applicant An issuer which has had its securities traded upon an AIM Designated Market for at least 18 months prior to applying to have those securities admitted to AIM and which seeks to take advantage of that status in applying for the admission of its securities.

record date The last date upon which investors must appear on the register of securities of the AIM company in order to receive a benefit from the company.

register The latest publication of the register of nominated advisers held by the London Stock Exchange. The definitive register is kept by the London Stock Exchange.

register of members The record that a company must keep of its members.

registered office The address of the office of a company to which formal notices and legal documents should be addressed and sent.

registration The process whereby a company comes into existence.

Regulatory Information Service A service approved by the London Stock Exchange for the distribution to the public of AIM announcements and included within the list maintained on the London Stock Exchange's website: www.londonstockexchange.com

related financial product Any financial product whose value in whole or in part is determined directly or indirectly by reference to the price of AIM securities or securities being admitted, including a contract for difference or a fixed odds bet.

related party
  (a) any person who is a director of an AIM company or of any company which is its subsidiary or parent undertaking, or other subsidiary undertaking of its parent company;
  (b) a substantial shareholder;

(c) an associate of (a) or (b) being;

   (i)   the family of such a person;

   (ii)   the trustees (acting as such) of any trust of which the individual or any of the individual's family is a beneficiary or discretionary object (other than a trust which is either an occupational pension scheme as defined in regulation 3 of the *Financial Services and Markets Act 2000 (Regulated Activities) Order 2001*, or an employee share scheme which does not, in either case, have the effect of conferring benefits on persons all or most of whom are related parties);

   (iii) any company in whose equity shares such a person individually or taken together with his or her family (or if a director, individually or taken together with his family and any other director of that company) are directly or indirectly interested (or have a conditional or contingent entitlement to become interested) to the extent that they are or could be able:

      • to exercise or control the exercise of 30 per cent or more of the votes (excluding treasury shares) able to be cast at general meetings on all, or substantially all, matters; or

      • to appoint or remove directors holding a majority of voting rights at board meetings on all, or substantially all, matters;

   (iv) any other company which is its subsidiary undertaking, parent undertaking or subsidiary undertaking of its parent undertaking;

   (v)   any company whose directors are accustomed to act in accordance with (a)'s directions or instructions;

   (vi) any company in the capital of which (a), either alone or together with any other company within (iv) or (v) or both taken together, is (or would on the fulfillment of a condition or the occurrence of a contingency be) interested in the manner described in (iii).

For the purposes of Rule 13 of the *AIM Rules for Companies*, a related party includes any person who was a director of an AIM company or any of its subsidiaries, sister or parent undertakings or a substantial shareholder within the twelve months preceding the date of the transaction.

relevant changes Changes to the holding of a significant shareholder above 3 per cent (excluding treasury shares) which increase or decrease such holding through any single percentage.

retirement by rotation The process whereby one-third of the directors of a company retire and present themselves for re-election.

RNS The Regulatory Information Service operated by the London Stock Exchange.

shadow director Any person in accordance with whose directions or instructions the directors are accustomed to act.

share certificate The documentary evidence issued by a company and held by a shareholder to indicate the ownership of securities.

shareholder A holder of any legal or beneficial interest, whether direct or indirect, in an AIM security.

significant shareholder A shareholder of 3 per cent or more of any class of AIM security (excluding treasury shares).

special resolution A resolution passed by a three-quarters vote of those members present and voting or voting by proxy.

stock transfer form Instrument of transfer; the form completed by the transferor of shares to transfer title to the shares to the transferee.

subsidiary company A company which is controlled by another company, known as its parent or subsidiary company, which usually holds the majority of its voting shares.

substantial shareholder In relation to a transaction any person who holds any legal or beneficial interest directly or indirectly in 10 per cent or more of any class of AIM security (excluding treasury shares) or 10 per cent or more of the voting rights (excluding treasury shares) of an AIM company. This includes, for the purpose of Rule 13 of the *AIM Rules for Companies*, such holding in any subsidiary, sister or parent undertaking and excluding, for the purposes of Rule 7 of the *AIM Rules for Companies*, any authorised person and any company with securities quoted upon the exchange's markets, unless the company is an investing company.

take-over The process whereby one company acquires another company.

transfer The process whereby a share passes from one person to another either on sale or by way of a gift.

Transparency Directive The European Parliament and Council Directive on the harmonisation of transparency requirements in relation to information about issuers whose securities are admitted to trading on a regulated market or through a comparable mechanism for the disclosure of information under national requirements of a member state concerning the dissemination of information (No. 2004/109/EC).

transmission The process whereby a share passes from one person to another by operation of law; following death, shares pass to the deceased's personal representative; following bankruptcy, shares pass to the trustee in bankruptcy.

treasury shares Shares bought by certain quoted or listed companies and held either for onward sale or transfer into an employee share scheme.

UK United Kingdom.

ultra vires Literally "beyond its powers". The expression is usually used to refer to a transaction entered into by a company that is beyond its powers. Sometimes it is also used to refer to a transaction beyond the powers of the directors.

underwriter A person who agrees to take up a flotation if they are not applied for by the public.

United Kingdom Listing Authority The Financial Services Authority, acting as the competent authority for listing, is referred to as the United Kingdom Listing Authority (UKLA).

unpublished price sensitive information Information which:
- relates to particular AIM securities or to a particular AIM company rather than securities or issuers in general;
- is specific or precise;
- has not been made public; and
- if it were made public would be likely to have a significant effect on the price or value of any AIM security.

VCT Venture Capital Trusts

warning notice A private letter issued by the London Stock Exchange pursuant to the *Disciplinary Procedures and Appeals Handbook* to an AIM company or nominated adviser outlining a breach of these rules or of the *AIM Rules for Nominated Advisers*.

Index